Angular 2 Development with TypeScript

Angular 2 Development with TypeScript

YAKOV FAIN
ANTON MOISEEV

MANNING
Shelter Island

Manning Publications Co.
20 Baldwin Road
PO Box 761
Shelter Island, NY 11964

Development editor: Cynthia Kane
Review editor: Donna Clements
Technical development editor: Alain M. Couniot
Project editor: Kevin Sullivan
Copyeditor: Andy Carroll
Proofreader: Tiffany Taylor
Technical proofreader: Cody Sand
Typesetter: Gordan Salinovic
Cover designer: Marija Tudor

ISBN 9781617293122
Printed in the United States of America
1 2 3 4 5 6 7 8 9 10 – EBM – 21 20 19 18 17 16

brief contents

contents

preface

Our quest for a good JavaScript framework started about four years ago. We were working on a platform for the insurance industry, and most of the UI for the system was written using the Apache Flex framework (formerly Adobe Flex). Flex is an excellent framework for developing web UIs, but it requires Flash Player, which wasn't in favor anymore.

After trying several pilot JavaScript projects, we noticed a substantial drop in our developers' productivity. A task that required one day in Flex would need three days in other JavaScript frameworks, including AngularJS. The main reasons were the lack of types in JavaScript, poor IDE support, and the absence of compiler support.

When we learned that Google had started development on the Angular 2 framework, with TypeScript as a recommended language for development, we became early adopters in the summer of 2015. At that time, there was very little information about Angular 2 other than several blogs and videos from the conference where the Angular team introduced the new framework. Our main source of knowledge was the framework's source code. But because we recognized great potential in Angular, we decided to start writing courseware for our company's training department. At the same time, Mike Stephens, Manning's associate publisher, was looking for authors who were interested in writing a book about Angular 2. That's how this book was born.

After a year of working with the Angular 2 / TypeScript duo, we can confirm that it offers the most productive way of developing mid- to large-size web applications that can run in any modern browser as well as on mobile platforms. These are the main reasons we believe that Angular 2 and TypeScript are the right tools for developing web applications:

- *Clean separation of UI and app logic*—There's a clean separation between the code that renders the UI and the code that implements application logic. The UI doesn't have to be rendered in HTML, and there are already products that support native UI rendering for iOS and Android.
- *Modularization*—There's a simple mechanism for modularizing applications with support for the lazy loading of modules.
- *Navigation support*—The router supports complex navigation scenarios in single-page applications.
- *Loose coupling*—Dependency injection gives you a clean way to implement loose coupling between components and services. Binding and events allow you to create reusable and loosely coupled components.
- *Component lifecycle*—Each component goes through a well-defined lifecycle, and hooks for intercepting important component events are available for application developers.
- *Change detection*—An automatic (and fast) change-detection mechanism spares you from having to manually force UI updates while also providing a way to fine-tune this process.
- *No callback hell*—Angular 2 comes with the RxJS library, which allows you to arrange subscription-based processing of asynchronous data, eliminating the callback hell.
- *Forms and validation*—Support for forms and custom validation is well designed. You can create forms either by adding directives to form elements in the template or programmatically.
- *Testing*—Unit and end-to-end testing are well supported, and you can integrate tests into your automated build process.
- *Webpack bundling and optimization*—Bundling and optimizing the code with Webpack (and its various plugins) keeps deployed applications small.
- *Tooling*—The tooling support is as good as on the Java and .NET platforms. The TypeScript code analyzer warns you about errors as you type, and a scaffolding and deployment tool (Angular CLI) spares you from writing boilerplate code and configuration scripts.
- *Concise code*—Using TypeScript classes and interfaces makes your code more concise and easy to read and write.
- *Compilers*—The TypeScript compiler generates JavaScript that a human can read. The TypeScript code can be compiled into the ES3, ES5, or ES6 version of JavaScript. Ahead-of-time (AoT) compilation of Angular-specific code (not to be confused with the TypeScript compiler) eliminates the need to package the Angular compiler with your app, which further minimizes the overhead of the framework.

- *Server-side rendering*—Angular Universal turns your app into HTML in an offline build step that can be used for server-side rendering, which in turn greatly improves indexing by search engines and SEO.
- *Modern UI components*—A library of modern-looking UI components (Angular Material 2) is in the works.

As you can see from this list, Angular 2 comes with the batteries included.

From a management perspective, Angular 2 is appealing because there are already more than a million AngularJS developers, and most of them will switch to Angular 2. Angular 2.0 was released in September of 2016, and new major releases will be published semiannually. The Angular team spent two years developing Angular 2.0, and on its release date about half a million developers were already using it. We expect this number to double within the year. Having a large pool of workers with specific skills is an important consideration when you're selecting a technology for new projects. Besides, there are more than 15 million Java and .NET developers combined, and many of them will find the syntax of TypeScript a lot more appealing than JavaScript because of its support for classes, interfaces, generics, annotations, class member variables, and private and public variables, not to mention its helpful compiler and solid support from familiar IDEs.

Creating a book about Angular 2 was difficult, because we started with early alpha versions of the framework, which changed through the beta and release candidate versions. But we like the final result, and we've already started developing real-world projects in Angular 2.

acknowledgments

Both authors would like to thank Manning Publications, as well as Alain M. Couniot for his suggestions on the technical content, and Cody Sand for giving the chapters a full technical proofread. Several reviewers also contributed valuable feedback on the manuscript: Chris Coppenbarger, David Barkol, David DiMaria, Fredrik Engberg, Irach Ilish Ramos Hernandez, Jeremy Bryan, Kamal Raj, Lori Wilkins, Mauro Quercioli, Sébastien Nichèle, Polina Keselman, Subir Rastogi, Sven Lösekann, and Wisam Zaghal.

Yakov would like to thank his best friend Sammy for creating a warm and cozy environment while Yakov was working on this book. Unfortunately, Sammy can't talk, but he loves Yakov unconditionally. Sammy's breed is mini golden retriever.

Anton would like to thank Yakov Fain and Manning Publications for giving him the opportunity to coauthor this book and obtain invaluable writing experience. He's also grateful to his family for being patient while he spent numerous hours working on the book.

about this book

Angular 2 applications can be developed in two flavors of JavaScript (ES5 and ES6), in Dart, or in TypeScript. The framework itself was developed in TypeScript, and in this book we use TypeScript for all the code examples. Appendix B has a section titled "Why write Angular apps in TypeScript?" where we explain our reasons for selecting this language.

Both of us are practitioners, and we wrote this book for practitioners. Not only do we explain the features of the framework using basic code samples, but we also gradually show you how to build a single-page online auction application over the course of the book.

While we were still writing and revising, we ran several training workshops using the code samples. This allowed us to get early (and overwhelmingly positive) feedback about the book's content. We really hope that you'll enjoy the process of learning Angular 2.

This book covers Angular 2.0.0 Final.

How to read this book

Our early drafts of this book started with chapters on ECMAScript 6 and TypeScript. Several reviewers suggested we move this material to the appendixes, so readers could start learning about Angular sooner. We made this change, but if you aren't already familiar with the syntax of ECMAScript 6 and TypeScript, looking through the appendices first will make it easier to follow the code samples in the chapters.

Roadmap

This book consists of 10 chapters and 2 appendixes.

Chapter 1 provides a high-level overview of the Angular 2 architecture, gives a brief summary of popular JavaScript frameworks and libraries, and introduces the sample online auction application that you'll start to develop in chapter 2.

You'll be developing this sample application in TypeScript. Appendix B can get you up to speed with this excellent language, which is a superset of JavaScript. Not only will you learn how to write classes, interfaces, and generics, but you'll also learn how to compile TypeScript code into today's JavaScript (ECMAScript 5), which can be deployed in all web browsers. TypeScript implements most of the syntax of the latest ECMAScript 6 specification (covered in appendix A) and some syntax that should be included in the future releases of ECMAScript.

In chapter 2, you'll start developing simple Angular 2 applications, and you'll create your first Angular components. You'll learn how to work with the SystemJS module loader, and we'll offer you our version of the Angular seed project that will be used as a starting point for all the sample applications in the book. At the end of this chapter, you'll create the first version of the home page for the online auction.

Chapter 3 is about the Angular router, which offers a flexible way of arranging navigation in single-page applications. You'll learn how to configure routes in parent and child components, how to pass data from one route to another, and how to lazy-load modules. At the end of this chapter, you'll refactor the online auction into several components and add routing capabilities to it.

In chapter 4, you'll learn about the Dependency Injection design pattern and how Angular implements it. You'll get familiar with the concept of providers, which allow you to specify how injectable objects should be instantiated. In the new version of the online auction, you'll apply dependency injection to populate the Product Details view with data.

In chapter 5, we'll discuss different flavors of data binding, introduce reactive programming with observable data streams, and show you how to work with pipes. The chapter ends with a new version of the online auction that adds an observable event stream to filter featured products on the home page.

Chapter 6 is about developing components that can communicate with each other in a loosely coupled manner. We'll discuss components' input and output parameters, the Mediator design pattern, and a component's lifecycle. This chapter also includes a high-level overview of Angular's change-detection mechanism. The online auction gets a product-rating feature.

Chapter 7 is about handling forms in Angular. After covering the basics of the Forms API, we'll discuss form validation and implement it in the search component, in yet another version of the online auction.

Chapter 8 explains how an Angular client app can communicate with servers using the HTTP and WebSocket protocols, including examples. You'll create a server app using the Node.js and Express frameworks. Then you'll deploy Angular's portion of the online auction in the Node server. The front end of the online auction starts communicating with the Node.js server via the HTTP and WebSocket protocols.

Chapter 9 is about unit testing. We'll cover the basics of Jasmine and the Angular testing library. You'll learn how to test services, components, and the router. You'll also learn how to configure and use Karma for running tests, and you'll implement several unit tests in the online auction.

Chapter 10 is about automating the build and deployment processes. You'll see how to use the Webpack bundler to minimize and package your code for deployment. You'll also see how to use Angular CLI for project generation and deployment. The size of the deployed version of the online auction will be decreased from 5.5 MB (in development) to 350 KB (in production).

Appendix A will get you familiar with the new syntax introduced in ECMAScript 2015 (a.k.a. ES6). Appendix B is an introduction to the TypeScript language.

Code conventions and downloads

This book contains many examples of source code, both in numbered listings and in line with normal text. In both cases, source code is formatted in a `fixed-width font like this` to separate it from ordinary text. In many cases, the original source code has been reformatted; line breaks have been added and indentation reworked as necessary to accommodate the available page space in the book. In some cases, where this was not enough, the listings include line-continuation markers (➥). Additionally, comments in the source code have often been removed from the listings when the code is described in the text. Code annotations accompany many of the listings, highlighting important concepts.

Source code for the examples in this book is available for download from the publisher's website at https://www.manning.com/books/angular-2-development-with-typescript.

The authors have also created a GitHub repository with the source code examples at https://github.com/Farata/angular2typescript. If future releases of Angular break any of the code examples from the book, you can open an issue there, and authors will address it.

Author Online

Purchase of *Angular 2 Development with TypeScript* includes free access to a private web forum run by Manning Publications where you can make comments about the book, ask technical questions, and receive help from the authors and from other users. To access the forum and subscribe to it, point your web browser to https://www.manning.com/books/angular-2-development-with-typescript. This page provides information on how to get on the forum once you're registered, what kind of help is available, and the rules of conduct on the forum.

Manning's commitment to our readers is to provide a venue where a meaningful dialog between individual readers and between readers and the authors can take place. It is not a commitment to any specific amount of participation on the part of the authors, whose contributions to the AO forum remain voluntary (and unpaid). We suggest you ask the authors challenging questions, lest their interest stray!

About the authors

 **Yakov Fain** is a cofounder of two companies: Farata Systems and SuranceBay. Farata Systems is an IT consulting boutique. Yakov runs the training department there and teaches Angular and Java workshops around the globe. SuranceBay is a product company that automates various workflows in the insurance industry in the United States, offering applications that use the software as a service (SaaS). Yakov manages various projects there.

Yakov is a Java Champion. He has authored multiple books on software development and written more than a thousand blog entries at yakovfain.com. Although most of his books are printed, his *Java Programming for Kids, Parents and Grandparents* is available as a free download in several languages at http://myflex.org/books/java4kids/java4kids.htm. His Twitter handle is @yfain.

 **Anton Moiseev** is a lead software developer at SuranceBay. He's been developing enterprise applications for 10 years with Java and .NET technologies. He has a solid background in developing rich internet applications using various platforms. Anton has a strong focus on web technologies, implementing best practices to make the front end work seamlessly with the back end. He has taught a number of training sessions on the AngularJS and Angular 2 frameworks.

Anton occasionally blogs at antonmoiseev.com. His Twitter handle is @antonmoiseev.

about the cover illustration

The illustration on the cover of *Angular 2 Development with TypeScript* is taken from the 1805 edition of Sylvain Maréchal's four-volume compendium of regional dress customs. This book was first published in Paris in 1788, one year before the French Revolution. Each illustration is colored by hand. This figure, captioned "Le Tuteur" or "The Tutor," is just one of many figures in Maréchal's collection. Their diversity speaks vividly of the uniqueness and individuality of the world's towns and regions just 200 years ago. This was a time when the dress codes of two regions separated by a few dozen miles identified people uniquely as belonging to one or the other. The collection brings to life a sense of the isolation and distance of that period and of every other historic period—except our own hyperkinetic present.

Dress codes have changed since then and the diversity by region, so rich at the time, has faded away. It is now often hard to tell the inhabitant of one continent from another. Perhaps we have traded cultural diversity for a more varied personal life—certainly for a more varied and fast-paced technological life.

We at Manning celebrate the inventiveness, the initiative, and the fun of the computer business with book covers based on the rich diversity of regional life two centuries ago, brought back to life by Maréchal's pictures.

Introducing Angular 2

This chapter covers

- A brief overview of JavaScript frameworks and libraries
- A high-level overview of Angular 1 and 2
- A toolbox for the Angular developer
- Introducing the sample application

Angular 2 is an open source JavaScript framework maintained by Google. It's a complete rewrite of its popular predecessor, AngularJS. Angular applications can be developed in JavaScript (using the syntax of ECMAScript 5 or 6), Dart, or TypeScript. In this book we'll use TypeScript; our reasons for this are explained in appendix B.

> **PREREQUISITES** In this book, we don't expect you to have any experience with AngularJS. We do expect you to know the syntax of JavaScript and HTML and to understand what web applications consist of. We also assume that you know what CSS is and that you're familiar with the role of the DOM object in a browser.

1

We'll start this chapter with a very brief overview of some popular JavaScript frameworks. Then we'll review the architecture of the older AngularJS and the newer Angular 2, highlighting the improvements that the new version of this framework brings to the table. We'll also quickly run through the tools that Angular developers use. Finally, we'll introduce the sample application that we're going to build in this book.

> **NOTE**   This book is about the Angular 2 framework, and for brevity we'll call it Angular throughout. If we mention AngularJS, we're talking about the 1.x versions of this framework.

1.1   A sampler of JavaScript frameworks and libraries

Do you have to use frameworks? No, you can program the front end of web applications in pure JavaScript. In this case, there's nothing new to learn, because you already know JavaScript. The cons of not using a framework are the difficulties in maintaining cross-browser compatibility and longer development cycles. In contrast, frameworks can give you full control over the architecture, design patterns, and code styles in your application. Most modern web applications are written using some combination of frameworks and libraries.

Angular is one of many frameworks used for developing web apps, and this section will briefly cover some popular JavaScript frameworks and libraries. What's the difference between frameworks and libraries? *Frameworks* provide a structure for your code and force you to write the code in a certain way. *Libraries* usually offer a number of components and APIs that can be used à la carte in any code. In other words, frameworks are more opinionated than libraries about the design of your application.

1.1.1   Feature-complete frameworks

Feature-complete frameworks include everything you need to develop a web application. They impose a certain structure on your code and come with a library of UI components and tools for building and deploying the application.

For example, *Ext JS* is a mature, full-featured framework created and maintained by Sencha. It comes with an excellent set of rich UI components, including an advanced data grid and charts, which are crucial for developing back-office enterprise applications. Ext JS adds a substantial amount of code to your application, and you won't find an application built with Ext JS that's less than 1 MB in size. Ext JS is also intrusive—it's not easy to switch to a different framework if need be.

Sencha also has the Sencha Touch framework, which is used for creating web applications for mobile devices.

1.1.2   Lightweight frameworks

Lightweight frameworks add structure to your web application, offer a way to arrange navigation between different views, and typically split the application into layers implementing the Model-View-Controller (MVC) design pattern. There is also a group of lightweight frameworks specialized for testing applications written in JavaScript.

Angular is an open source framework for developing web applications. The framework makes it simpler to create custom components that can be added to HTML documents and to implement application logic. Angular uses data binding extensively, includes a dependency injection module, supports modularization, and offers a routing mechanism. Whereas AngularJS was MVC-based, Angular is not. This framework doesn't include UI components.

Ember.js is an open source MVC-based framework for developing web applications. It includes a routing mechanism and supports two-way data binding. This framework uses a lot of code conventions, which increases the productivity of software developers.

Jasmine is an open source framework for testing JavaScript code. Jasmine doesn't require a DOM object. It includes a set of functions that test whether certain parts of your application behave as expected. Jasmine is often used with Karma, which is a test runner that allows you to run tests in different browsers.

1.1.3 Libraries

The libraries discussed in this section serve different purposes and can be used in web applications with or without other frameworks.

jQuery is a popular JavaScript library. It's simple to use and doesn't require you to dramatically change the way you program for the web. jQuery helps in finding and manipulating DOM elements, processing browser events, and dealing with browser incompatibilities. jQuery is an extensible library, and thousands of plugins have been created by developers from around the world. If you can't find a plugin that fits your needs, you can create one yourself.

Bootstrap is an open source library of UI components developed by Twitter. The components are built using the responsive web design principles, which makes this library extremely valuable if your web application needs to automatically adjust its layout depending on the screen size of the user's device. In this book we'll use Bootstrap while developing a sample online auction application.

> **NOTE** Google developed a library of UI components based on the set of guidelines called Material Design, which may become an alternative to Bootstrap. Material Design is optimized for cross-device use and comes with a set of nice-looking UI components. At the time of writing, only the AngularJS version of Material Design is ready. The Angular version of this library is called Angular Material, and it should be released shortly after this book is published.

React is an open source library by Facebook for building user interfaces. React represents the *V* in MVC. It's nonintrusive and can be used with any other library or a framework. React creates its own virtual DOM object, minimizing access to the browser's DOM, which results in better performance. For content rendering, React introduces the JSX format, which is a JavaScript syntax extension that looks like XML. Using JSX is recommended but optional.

Polymer is a library created by Google for building custom components based on the Web Components standard. It comes with a set of nice-looking customizable UI components that can be included in HTML markup as tags. Polymer also includes components for applications that need to work offline, as well as components that use various Google APIs (such as calendar, maps, and others).

RxJS is a set of libraries for composing asynchronous and event-based programs using observable collections. It allows applications to work with asynchronous data streams, such as a server-side stream of stock price quotes or mouse move events. With RxJS, the data streams are represented as observable sequences. This library can be used with or without any other JavaScript framework. In chapters 5 and 8, you'll see examples of using observables in Angular.

To see statistics on which top websites use a particular JavaScript framework or library, you can visit the BuiltWith JavaScript Usage Statistics page: http://trends .builtwith.com/javascript.

Moving from Flex to Angular

We work for a company, Farata Systems, that over the years developed pretty complex software using the Adobe Flex framework. Flex is a very productive framework built on top of the strongly typed, compiled ActionScript language, and the applications are deployed in the Flash Player browser plugin (a VM). When the web community started moving away from using plugins, we spent two years trying to find a replacement for Flex. We experimented with different JavaScript-based frameworks, but the productivity of our developers seriously suffered. Finally we saw a light at the end of the tunnel with a combination of the TypeScript language, the Angular 2 framework, and a UI library such as Angular Material.

1.1.4   What is Node.js?

Node.js (or *Node*) isn't just a framework or a library, but a runtime environment as well. In most of this book, we'll use the Node runtime for running various utilities like Node Package Manager (npm). For example, to install TypeScript, you can use npm from a command line:

```
npm install typescript
```

The Node.js framework can be used to develop JavaScript programs that run outside the browser. You can develop the server-side layer of a web application in JavaScript or Typescript; you'll write a web server using Node in chapter 8. Google developed a high-performance V8 JavaScript engine for the Chrome browser, and it can be used to run code written using the Node.js API. The Node.js framework includes an API to work with the filesystem, access databases, listen to HTTP requests, and more.

Members of the JavaScript community have built lots of utilities that are useful for developing web applications, and with the help of Node's JavaScript engine, you can run them from a command line.

1.2   *High-level overview of AngularJS*

Let's now return to the main topic of this book: the Angular framework. This is the only section dedicated to AngularJS, the previous version of Angular.

Misko Hevery and Adam Abronsa started work on the AngularJS framework in 2009 as an effort to help web designers customize web pages, and AngularJS 1.0 was officially released in 2012. By 2015, several minor versions had been released, and at the time of writing the stable version of AngularJS is 1.5. Google continues to improve the functionality of AngularJS 1.x and address its issues while developing Angular 2 in parallel. Let's see what made AngularJS so popular:

- AngularJS has a mechanism for creating custom HTML tags and attributes using the concept of *directives*, which allow you to extend the set of HTML tags according to your application's needs.
- AngularJS is not too intrusive. You can add an ng-app attribute to any <div> tag, and only the content of this <div> will be controlled by AngularJS. The rest of the web page can be pure HTML and JavaScript.
- AngularJS allows you to bind data to views easily. Changing data results in automated updates of the corresponding view element and vice versa.
- AngularJS comes with a configurable router that allows you to map URL patterns to corresponding application components that change the view on the web page according to the mapping.
- The application data flow is defined in *controllers*, which are JavaScript objects containing properties and functions.
- AngularJS applications use a hierarchy of *scopes*, which are objects for storing data shared by controllers and views.
- AngularJS includes a dependency injection module that allows you to develop applications in a loosely coupled manner.

Whereas jQuery simplified DOM manipulations, AngularJS allowed developers to decouple the application logic from the UI by structuring the application according to the MVC design pattern. Figure 1.1 depicts a sample workflow of an AngularJS application that deals with products.

If you want AngularJS to control the entire web application, include the ng-app directive in the <body> HTML tag:

```
<body ng-app="ProductApp">
```

In figure 1.1, to get the product data, the user loads the application ❶ and enters the product ID ❷. The view informs the controller ❸, which updates the model ❹ and makes an HTTP request ❺ to a remote server via the $http service. AngularJS populates the properties of the model with the retrieved data ❺, and the changes in the model are automatically reflected in the UI via a *binding expression* ❻. The user then sees the data about the requested product ❼.

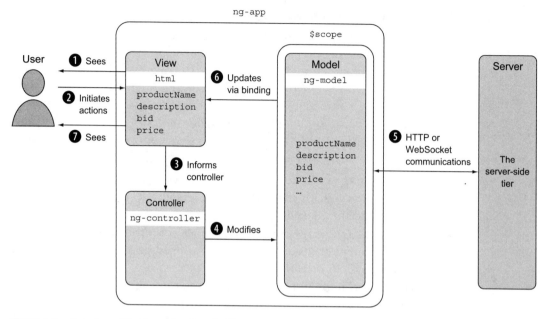

Figure 1.1   Sample architecture of an AngularJS app

AngularJS automatically updates the view when the data in the model changes. The changes in the UI are propagated to the model if the user modifies the data in the input controls in the view. This two-directional update mechanism is called *two-way data binding*, and it's illustrated in figure 1.2.

In AngularJS, the model and the view are tightly bound because the two-way binding means each automatically updates the other. It's nice to have these automatic view updates without writing much code, but it doesn't come for free.

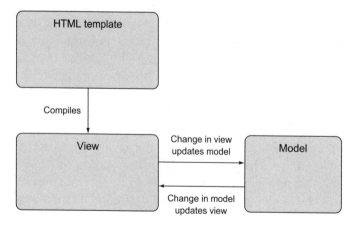

Figure 1.2   Two-way binding

Every time the model is updated, AngularJS runs a special $digest loop that goes through the entire application, applying the data bindings and updating the DOM when needed. Cascading updates result in multiple runs of the $digest cycle, which can affect performance in large applications that use multiple two-way bindings. Manipulating the browser's DOM object is the slowest operation—the less your application updates the DOM, the better it performs.

The model data exists in the context of a particular $scope object, and AngularJS scopes form a hierarchy of objects. The $rootScope is created for the entire application. Controllers and directives (custom components) have their own $scope objects, and understanding how AngularJS scopes work can be challenging.

You can implement modularization by creating and loading module objects. When a particular module depends on other objects (such as controllers, modules, or services), the instances of these objects are created and *injected* by AngularJS's Dependency Injection mechanism. The following code snippet illustrates one of the ways AngularJS injects one object into another:

```
var SearchController = function ($scope) {     ⟵  Defines SearchController as a
    //..                                            constructor function with the
};                                                  $scope argument

SearchController['$inject'] = ['$scope'];      ⟵  Adds the $inject property on the
                                                    controller, asking to inject the $scope
                                                    object into the constructor function

angular.module('auction').controller('SearchController', SearchController);   ⟵
                                               Assigns the SearchController object to
                                               be a controller on the auction module
```

In the preceding code snippet, the square brackets represent an array, and AngularJS can inject multiple objects as follows: ['$scope', 'myCustomService'].

AngularJS is often used for creating single-page applications, where only certain portions of the page (sub-views) are updated as a result of the user's actions or data being sent from the server. A good example of these sub-views is a web application showing stock quotes: only the price element on the view is updated as the stock is traded.

Navigation between views in AngularJS is arranged by configuring the ng-route router component. You can specify a number of .when options to route the application to the appropriate view based on the URL pattern. The next code fragment instructs the router to use the markup from home.html and the controller HomeController unless the URL contains /search, in which case the view will render search.html and the SearchController object will be used as a controller:

```
angular.module('auction', ['ngRoute'])
    .config(['$routeProvider', function ($routeProvider) {
        $routeProvider
          .when('/', {
            templateUrl: 'views/home.html',
            controller: 'HomeController' })
```

```
      .when('/search', {
          templateUrl: 'views/search.html',
          controller: 'SearchController' })
      .otherwise({
          redirectTo: '/'
  });
}]);
```

The AngularJS router supports *deep linking*, which is the ability to bookmark not just an entire web page, but a certain state within the page.

Now that you've had a very high-level overview of AngularJS, let's see what Angular 2 brings to the table.

1.3   *High-level overview of Angular*

The Angular framework is better performing than AngularJS. It's easier to learn, the application architecture has been simplified, and the code is simpler to write and read. This section contains a high-level overview of Angular, highlighting the improvements made since AngularJS. For a more detailed architectural overview of Angular, see the product documentation at https://angular.io/docs/ts/latest/guide/architecture.html.

1.3.1   *Code simplification*

First of all, an Angular application consists of standard modules in ECMAScript 6 (ES6), Asynchronous Module Definition (AMD), and CommonJS formats. Typically, one module is one file. There's no need to use a framework-specific syntax for loading and using modules. Use the universal module loader SystemJS (covered in chapter 2), and add import statements to use functionality implemented in the loaded modules. You don't need to worry about the proper order of the <script> tags in your HTML files. If module A needs the functionality from module B, just import module B into module A.

The HTML file for your application's landing page includes Angular modules and their dependencies. Your application code is bootstrapped by loading the root module of your application. All required components and services will be loaded based on the declarations in the module and import statements.

The following snippet shows typical content for the index.html file of an Angular application, where you include the required framework modules. The script systemjs.config.js contains the configuration of the SystemJS loader. System .import('app') loads the top-level app component configured in systemjs.config.js (shown in chapter 2). The custom tag <app> is a value defined in the selector property of the root component:

```
<!DOCTYPE html>
<html>
<head>
  <title>Angular seed project</title>
  <meta charset="UTF-8">
  <meta name="viewport" content="width=device-width, initial-scale=1">
```

```
<script src="node_modules/core-js/client/shim.min.js"></script>
<script src="node_modules/zone.js/dist/zone.js"></script>

<script src="node_modules/typescript/lib/typescript.js"></script>
<script src="node_modules/systemjs/dist/system.src.js"></script>
<script src="node_modules/rxjs/bundles/Rx.js"></script>
<script src="systemjs.config.js"></script>
<script>
  System.import('app').catch(function(err){ console.error(err); });
</script>
</head>

<body>
<app>Loading...</app>
</body>
</html>
```

The HTML fragment of each application component is inlined either inside the component (the `template` property) or in the file referenced from the component using the `templateURL` property. The latter option allows designers to work on the UI of your application without the need to learn Angular.

The Angular component is the centerpiece of the new architecture. Figure 1.3 shows a high-level diagram of a sample Angular application that consists of four components and two services; all of them are packaged inside a module. Angular's Dependency Injection (DI) module injects the `Http` service into `Service1`, which in turn is injected into the `GrandChild2` component. This diagram is quite different from figure 1.1, which illustrated AngularJS.

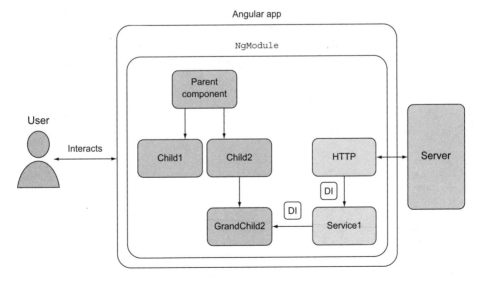

Figure 1.3 Sample architecture of an Angular app

The simplest way of declaring a component is to write a class in TypeScript (you can use ES5, ES6, or Dart as well). In appendix B, we'll give you a brief introduction to how to write Angular components in TypeScript, followed by the sample code. See if you can understand the code with minimum explanation.

A TypeScript class prepended with a @NgModule metadata annotation represents a module. A TypeScript class prepended with a @Component metadata annotation represents a component. The @Component annotation (a.k.a. decorator) contains the template property that declares an HTML fragment to be rendered by the browser. Metadata annotations allow you to modify the properties of the component during design time. The HTML template may include the data-binding expressions, which are surrounded by double curly braces. References to event handlers are placed in the template property of the @Component annotation and are implemented as methods of the class. Another example of a metadata annotation is @Injectable, which allows you to mark a component to be handled by the DI module.

The @Component annotation also contains a selector declaring the name of the custom tag to be used in the HTML document. When Angular sees an HTML element whose name matches the selector, it knows which component implements it. The following HTML fragment illustrates the <auction-application> parent component with one child component, <search-product>:

```
<body>
  <auction-application>
    <search-product [productID]= "123"></search-product>
  </auction-application>
</body>
```

A parent component sends data to its child components using bindings to the input properties of the child (note the square brackets in the preceding code), and children communicate with their parents by emitting events via their output properties. At the end of the chapter, figure 1.7 shows the main page (the parent component) with its child components surrounded with thick borders.

The following code snippet shows a SearchComponent. You can include it in an HTML document as <search-product> because its declaration includes the selector property with the same name:

```
@Component({
  selector: 'search-product',
  template:
    `<form>
      <div>
        <input id="prodToFind" #prod>
        <button (click)="findProduct(prod.value)">Find Product</button>
        Product name: {{product.name}}
      </div>
    </form>`
})
```

```
class SearchComponent {
   @Input() productID: number;

   product: Product; // code of the Product class is omitted

   findProduct(prodName: string){
    // Implementation of the click handler goes here
   }
   // Other code can go here
}
```

If you're familiar with any object-oriented language that has classes, you should understand most of the preceding code. The annotated class SearchComponent declares a product variable, which may represent an object with multiple properties, one of which (name) is bound to the view ({{product.name}}). The template local variable #prod will have a reference to the hosting <input> element, so you don't need to query the DOM to get the entered value.

The (click) notation represents a click event. The event handler function gets the argument value from the productID input parameter that will be populated by the parent component via binding.

This was just a quick look at the sample component. We'll provide a detailed description of what components are made up of starting in the next chapter. If you've never worked with classes before, no worries. They're covered in appendixes A and B. Figure 1.4 illustrates the inner working of a sample component that searches for some products.

Component instance

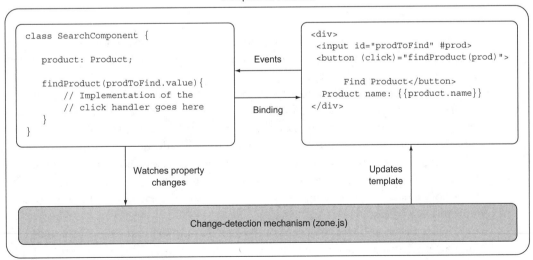

Figure 1.4 Component internals

A component renders the product data from the service represented by a class. In TypeScript, the Product class could look like this:

```
class Product{
    id: number,
    name: string;
    description: string;
    bid: number;
    price: number;

    // constructor and other methods go here
}
```

Note that TypeScript allows you to declare class variables with types. To let the UI component SearchComponent know about its data, you can declare a class variable, such as product:

```
@Component({ /* code omitted for brevity */ })
class SearchComponent {
    product: Product;

    findProduct(productID){
        // The implementation of the click handler
        // for the Find Components button goes here
    }
}
```

If the search component may return multiple products, you can declare an array to store them:

```
products: Array<Product>;
```

The *generics* notation is explained in appendix B. In the preceding code snippet, <Product> tells the TypeScript compiler that only objects of the type Product are allowed to be stored in this array.

Angular is not an MVC-based framework, and your app won't have separate controllers (the *C* in the MVC pattern). The component and injected services (if need be) include all required code. In our example, the SearchProduct class would contain the code that performs the controller's responsibilities in addition to the code required for a UI component on the HTML view. For a cleaner separation of TypeScript and HTML, the content of the template section of the @Component annotation can be stored in a separate file by using templateUrl instead of template, but that's a matter of preference.

Now let's look at how the design of Angular is simpler than that of AngularJS. In AngularJS, all directives were loaded to the global scope, whereas in Angular you specify the required directives on the module level, providing better encapsulation.

You don't have to deal with the hierarchy of scope objects as in AngularJS. Angular is component-based, and the properties are created on the `this` object, which becomes the component's scope.

One way of creating object instances is by using the `new` operator. If object A depends on object B, in the code of object A you can write `let myB = new B();`. Dependency Injection is a design pattern that inverts the way of creating objects your code depends on. Instead of explicitly creating object instances (such as with `new`), the framework will create and inject them into your code. Angular comes with a DI module, and we'll cover that topic in chapter 4.

In AngularJS there were several ways of registering dependencies, which could be confusing at times. In Angular, you can only inject dependencies into the component via its constructor. The following TypeScript code fragment shows how you'd inject the `ProductService` component into `SearchComponent`. You just need to specify a provider and declare the constructor argument with the type that matches provider's type:

```
@Component({
  selector: 'search-product',
  providers: [ProductService],
  template:`<div>...<div>`
})
class SearchComponent {
  products: Array<Product> = [];

  constructor(productService: ProductService) {
    this.products = productService.getProducts();
  }
}
```

This code doesn't use the `new` operator—Angular will instantiate the `ProductService` and provide its reference to the `SearchComponent`.

To summarize, Angular is simpler than AngularJS for several reasons:

- Each building block of your app is a component with the well-encapsulated functionality of a view, controller, and auto-generated change detector.
- Components can be programmed as annotated classes.
- You don't have to deal with scope hierarchies.
- Dependent components are injected via the component's constructor.
- Two-way binding is turned off by default.
- The change-detection mechanism was rewritten and works faster.

The concepts of Angular are easy to understand for Java, C#, and C++ programmers, which represent the majority of enterprise software developers. Like it or not, a framework becomes popular when it's adopted by enterprises. AngularJS has been widely adopted by enterprises, and AngularJS skills are in demand. Because developing applications with Angular is easier than with AngularJS, this trend should continue.

1.3.2 *Performance improvements*

The Repaint Rate Challenge website (http://mathieuancelin.github.io/js-repaint-perfs) compares the rendering performance of various frameworks. You can compare the performance of AngularJS with Angular 2—Angular shows serious performance improvements.

The rendering improvements mainly result from the internal redesign of the Angular framework. The UI rendering and application API were separated into two layers, which allows you to run the non-UI related code in a separate web worker thread. In addition to being able to run the code of these layers concurrently, web browsers allocate different CPU cores to these threads when possible. You can find a detailed description of the new rendering architecture in the document on Google Docs titled "Angular 2 Rendering Architecture" available at http://mng.bz/K403.

Creating a separate layer for rendering has an additional important benefit: you can use different renderers for different devices. Every component includes the `@Component` annotation that contains an HTML template defining the look of the component. If you want to create a `<stock-price>` component to display stock prices in the web browser, its UI portion might look like this:

```
@Component({
  selector: 'stock-price',
  template: '<div>The price of an IBM share is $165.50</div>'
})
class StockPriceComponent {
...
}
```

Angular's rendering engine is a separate module, which allows third-party vendors to replace the default DOM renderer with one that targets non-browser-based platforms. For example, this allows you to reuse the TypeScript code across devices with third-party UI renderers for mobile devices that render native components. The TypeScript portion of the components remains the same, but the content of the `template` property of the `@Component` decorator may contain XML or another language for rendering native components.

One such custom Angular 2 renderer is already implemented in the NativeScript framework, which serves as a bridge between JavaScript and native iOS and Android UI components. With NativeScript you can reuse the component's code by just replacing the HTML in the template with XML. Another custom UI renderer allows you to use Angular 2 with React Native, which is an alternative way of creating native (not hybrid) UIs for iOS and Android.

A new and improved change-detection mechanism is another contributor to Angular's better performance. Angular doesn't use two-way binding unless you manually program it. One-way binding simplifies the detection of changes in an application that may have lots of interdependent bindings. You can now mark a component to be excluded from the change-detection workflow, so it won't be checked when a change is detected in another component.

NOTE Although Angular is a complete redesign of AngularJS, if you use AngularJS you can start writing code in Angular style by using `ng-forward` (see https://github.com/ngUpgraders/ng-forward). The other approach (`ng-upgrade`) is to gradually switch to a newer version of this framework by running Angular and AngularJS in the same application (see https://angular.io/docs/ts/latest/guide/upgrade.html), but this will increase the size of the application.

1.4 An Angular developer's toolbox

Say you need to hire a web developer experienced with Angular. What would you expect the developer to know? They'd need to understand the architecture, components, and concepts of Angular applications mentioned in the previous sections, but that's not enough. The following rather long list identifies languages and tools that professional Angular developers use. Not all of them are needed for developing and deploying any given application. We'll use only half of them in this book:

- JavaScript is a de facto standard programming language for the front end of web applications. ES6 is the latest standardized specification for scripting languages, and JavaScript is its most popular implementation.

- TypeScript is a superset of JavaScript that makes developers more productive. TypeScript supports most of the features of ES6 and adds optional types, interfaces, metadata annotations, and more.

- The TypeScript code analyzer uses type-definition files for code that's not originally written in TypeScript. DefinitelyTyped is a popular collection of such files describing the APIs of hundreds of JavaScript libraries and frameworks. Using type-definition files allows the IDEs to provide context-sensitive help and highlight errors. You'll be installing type-definition files from the @types organization of npmjs.org (see appendix B).

- Because most web browsers support only ECMAScript 5 (ES5) syntax, you'll need to *transpile* (convert from one language to another) the code written in TypeScript or ES6 to ES5 for deployment. Angular developers may use Babel, Traceur, and the TypeScript compiler for code transpiling (see appendixes A and B for details).

- SystemJS is a universal module loader that loads modules created in ES6, AMD, and CommonJS standards.

- Angular CLI is a code generator that allows you to generate new Angular projects, components, services, and routes, as well as build the application for deployment.

- Node.js is a platform built on Chrome's JavaScript engine. Node includes both a framework and a runtime environment for running JavaScript code outside of the browser. You won't be using the Node.js framework in this book, but you'll use its runtime to install the required tools for developing Angular applications.

- npm is a package manager that allows you to download tools as well as JavaScript libraries and frameworks. This package manager has a repository of thousands of items, and you'll use it for installing pretty much everything from developer tools (such as the TypeScript compiler) to application dependencies (such as Angular 2, jQuery, and others). npm can also be used for running scripts, and you'll use this feature to start HTTP servers as well as for build automation.

- Bower used to be a popular package manager for resolving application dependencies (such as for Angular 2 and jQuery). We don't use Bower any longer because everything we need can be downloaded using npm.

- jspm is yet another package manager. Why do we need another one if npm can take care of all dependencies? Modern web applications consist of loadable modules, and jspm integrates SystemJS, which makes loading modules a breeze. In chapter 2, we'll give you a brief comparison of npm and jspm.

- Grunt is a task runner. Lots of steps need to be performed between developing and deploying the code, and all these steps must be automated. You may need to transpile code written in TypeScript or ES6 into widely supported ES5 syntax, and the code, images, and CSS files need to be minimized. You may also want to include the tasks that will check the code quality and unit-test your application. With Grunt, you can configure all the tasks and their dependencies in a JSON file so the process is 100% automated.

- Gulp is yet another task runner. It can automate tasks just as Grunt does, but instead of configuring the process in JSON, you program it in JavaScript. This allows you to debug it if need be.

- JSLint and ESLint are code analyzers that look for problematic patterns in JavaScript programs or JSON-formatted documents. These are code-quality tools. Running a JavaScript program through JSLint or ESLint results in a number of warning messages suggesting how you can improve the code quality of the program.

- TSLint is a code-quality tool for TypeScript. It has a collection of extendable rules to enforce the recommended coding style and patterns.

- Minifiers, like UglifyJS, make files smaller. In JavaScript they remove code comments and line breaks, and they make variable names shorter. Minification can also be applied to HTML, CSS, and image files.

- Bundlers, such as Webpack, combine multiple files and their dependencies into a single file.

- Because JavaScript syntax is very forgiving, the application code requires testing, so you'll need to pick one of the testing frameworks. In this book, you'll use the Jasmine framework and the test runner called Karma.

- Both JavaScript and TypeScript are well supported by modern IDEs and text editors such as WebStorm, Visual Studio, Visual Studio Code, Sublime Text, Atom, and others.
- All major web browsers come with developer tools that allow you to debug your programs right inside the browser. Even if the program was written in TypeScript and deployed in JavaScript, you can debug the original source code using source maps. We use Chrome Developer Tools.
- Web applications should be usable on mobile devices. You should use UI components that internally support a responsive web design approach to ensure that the UI layout automatically changes depending on the screen size of the user's device.[1]

This list may look intimidating, but you don't have to use each and every tool mentioned. In this book, you'll use the following tools:

- npm for configuring applications, installing utilities, and dependencies. You'll use npm scripts for starting web servers and as task runners in build automation.
- Node.js as a runtime environment for running utilities and as a framework for writing a web server (chapter 8).
- SystemJS for loading the application code and transpiling TypeScript on the fly in the browser.
- The command-line TypeScript compiler tsc for running examples from appendix B and programming a Node application in chapter 8.
- Jasmine for programming unit tests, and Karma for running them (chapter 9).
- Webpack for minimizing and bundling applications for deployment (chapter 10).

NOTE Programming in Angular is much simpler than in AngularJS, but the initial setup of the application is more involved because you'll be using transpilers and module loaders, which were not required for developing with JavaScript and AngularJS. In general, the introduction of ES6 modules changes the way applications will be loaded to the browser in the future, and we'll use the new approach in this book.

Figure 1.5 illustrates how tools can be applied at different stages of the development and deployment processes. The tools you'll use in this book are shown in bold.

Programming in Angular is easier than in AngularJS, but the initial environment setup must be done right so you can really enjoy the development process. In the next chapter, we'll discuss the initial project setup and tooling in greater detail.

---

[1] See Wikipedia for an explanation of responsive web design: https://en.wikipedia.org/wiki/Responsive_web_design.

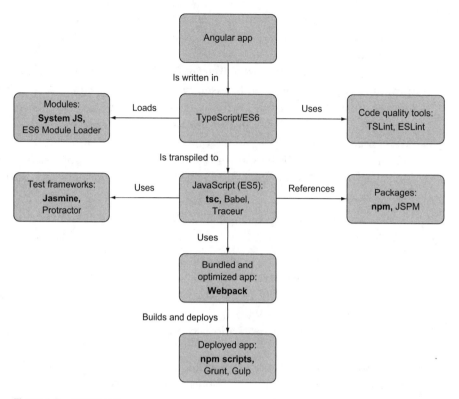

Figure 1.5   Using tools

1.5   *How things are done in Angular*

To give you a taste of how things are done in Angular, we came up with table 1.1, which lists the tasks that you may want to do (the left column) and what the Angular/TypeScript combo offers to accomplish each task (the right column). This is not a complete list of tasks that you can do, and we show you just fragments of the syntax, but it gives you the general idea. All these features will be explained in the book.

Table 1.1   How things are done in Angular

Task	How
Implement business logic.	Create a class, and Angular will instantiate and inject it into your component. You can also use the `new` operator.
Implement a component with UI.	Create a class annotated with `@Component`.
Specify the HTML template to be rendered by a component.	Either inline the HTML code in the `@Component` annotation using its `template` property, or specify the name of the HTML file in `templateUrl`.

Table 1.1   How things are done in Angular *(continued)*

Task	How
Manipulate HTML.	Use one of the structural directives (*ngIf, *ngFor), or create a custom class annotated with @Directive.
Refer to the class variable on the current object.	Use the this keyword: this.userName="Mary";.
Arrange navigation on a single-page app.	Configure the component-based router, mapping components to URL segments, and add the <router-outlet> tag to the template where you want the component to be rendered.
Display a value of a component's property on the UI.	Place the variables inside double curly brackets on the template: {{customerName}}.
Bind a component property to the UI.	Use property binding with square brackets: <input [value]= "greeting" >.
Handle UI events.	Surround the event name with parentheses, and specify the handler: <button (click)="onClickEvent()">Get Products </button>.
Use two-way binding.	Use the [()] notation: <input [(ngModel)] = "myComponentProperty">.
Pass data to a component.	Annotate component properties as @Input, and bind the values to it .
Pass data from a component.	Annotate component properties as @Output, and use EventEmitter to emit events.
Make an HTTP request.	Inject the Http object into a component, and invoke one of the HTTP methods: this.http.get('/products').
Handle HTTP responses.	Use the subscribe() method on the result that arrives as an observable stream: this.http.get('/products') .subscribe(...);.
Pass an HTML fragment to a child component.	Use <ng-content> in the child's template.
Intercept modifications of components.	Use the component's lifecycle hooks.
Deploy.	Use third-party bundlers like Webpack to package the application files and frameworks into JavaScript bundles.

1.6   *Introducing the online auction example*

To make this book more practical, we'll start every chapter by showing you small applications that illustrate Angular syntax or techniques. At the end of each chapter, you'll use the new concepts and see how components and services are combined into a working application.

Imagine an online auction where people can browse and search products. When the results are displayed, the user can select a product and bid on it. Each new bid will be validated on the server and will be either accepted or rejected. The information on the latest bids will be pushed by the server to all users subscribed to such notifications.

The functionality of browsing, searching, and placing bids will be implemented by making requests to the server's RESTful endpoints, implemented in the server developed with Node.js. The server will use WebSockets to push notifications about the user's bid acceptance or rejection and about bids placed by other users. Figure 1.6 depicts sample workflows for the online auction.

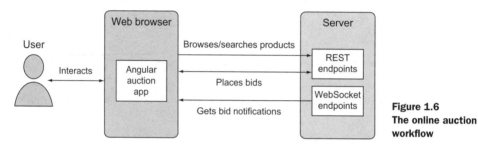

Figure 1.6
The online auction workflow

Figure 1.7 shows how the auction home page will be rendered on desktop computers. Initially you'll use gray placeholders instead of product images.

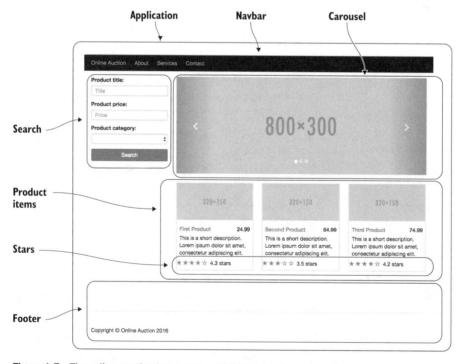

Figure 1.7   The online auction home page with highlighted components

You'll use responsive UI components, so on smartphones the home page will be rendered as in figure 1.8.

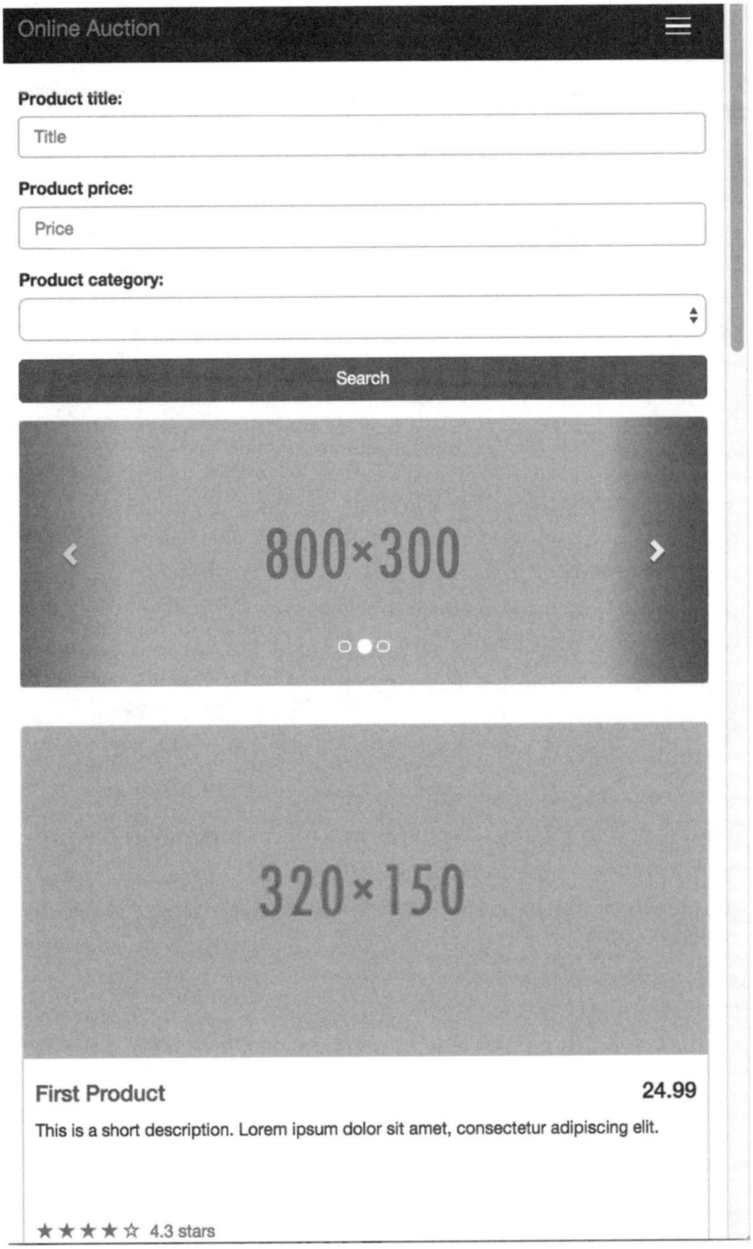

Figure 1.8 The online auction home page on a smartphone

The development of an Angular application comes down to creating and composing components. The code of the online auction will be written in TypeScript, and the view portion of the components will be developed as HTML templates with data binding. Figure 1.9 shows the initial project structure for the online auction app.

The index.html file will just load the main application component represented by two files: application.html and application.ts. The application component will include other components like product, search, and so on. All dependencies of the application component will be loaded automatically.

1.7   *Summary*

In this chapter we took a high-level look at the Angular 2 framework in comparison with its previous version, AngularJS. We also introduced a sample online auction application that you'll be developing throughout this book.

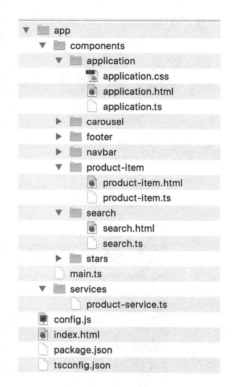

Figure 1.9   The initial project structure for the online auction app

- The architecture of Angular is simpler than that of AngularJS.
- Angular applications can be developed in TypeScript or JavaScript.
- The source code has to be transpiled into JavaScript before deployment.
- The Angular developer has to be familiar with multiple tools.
- Angular is a component-based framework.
- Good frameworks allow application developers to write less code, and Angular is a good one.

Getting started with Angular

This chapter covers

- Writing your first Angular application
- Getting familiar with the SystemJS universal module loader
- The role of package managers
- The first version of the online auction application

In this chapter, we'll start discussing how you develop Angular applications using modern tools and web technologies like annotations, ES6 modules, and module loaders. Angular changes the way you'll develop JavaScript applications. You'll write three versions of a Hello World application, and we'll briefly discuss package managers and the SystemJS universal module loader.

After that, we'll create a small project that can serve as boilerplate for creating your own Angular projects. Then we'll discuss the main building blocks of Angular applications, such as components and views, and we'll briefly cover dependency injection and data binding. At the end of the chapter, we'll go over the online auction application that you'll be developing throughout the book.

> **NOTE** All code samples in this book are based on the Angular 2.0.0 Final version. If the API of future releases of Angular changes, we'll update the code samples at https://github.com/Farata/angular2typescript accordingly.

> **TIP** If you're not familiar with the syntax of TypeScript and ECMAScript 6, we suggest you read appendixes A and B first, and then start reading from this chapter on.

2.1 *A first Angular application*

In this section we'll show you three versions of the Hello World application written in TypeScript, ES5, and ES6. This will be the only section where you'll see Angular applications written in ES5 and ES6—all other code samples will be written in TypeScript.

2.1.1 *Hello World in TypeScript*

This first application will be quite minimalistic to get you quickly started programming with Angular. This application will consist of two files:

```
├──  index.html
└──  main.ts
```

Both files are located in the hello-world-ts directory in the downloadable code for the book. The index.html file is the entry point for the application. It will contain references to the Angular framework, its dependencies, and the main.ts file, which contains the code to bootstrap your application. Some of these references can be located in the configuration file of the module loader (you'll use the SystemJS and Webpack loaders in this book).

LOADING ANGULAR IN THE HTML FILE

The code of the Angular framework consists of modules (one file per module), which are combined into libraries, which are logically grouped into packages, such as `@angular/core`, `@angular/common`, and so on. Your application has to load required packages before the application code.

Let's create an index.html file, which will start by loading the required Angular scripts, the TypeScript compiler, and the SystemJS module loader. The following code loads these scripts from the unpkg.com content delivery network (CDN).

Listing 2.1 TypeScript index.html

```html
<!DOCTYPE html>
<html>
<head>
  <script src="//unpkg.com/zone.js@0.6.12"></script>
  <script src="//unpkg.com/typescript@2.0.0"></script>
```

Zone.js is a library that powers the change-detection mechanism.

The TypeScript compiler transpiles your source code into JavaScript right in the browser.

Configures SystemJS loader for loading and transpiling TypeScript code

The SystemJS library dynamically loads the application code into the browser. We'll discuss SystemJS later in this chapter.

```
<script src="//unpkg.com/systemjs@0.19.37/dist/system.src.js"></script>
<script src="//unpkg.com/core-js/client/shim.min.js"></script>
<script>
  System.config({
    transpiler: 'typescript',
    typescriptOptions: {emitDecoratorMetadata: true},
    map: {
      'rxjs': 'https://unpkg.com/rxjs@5.0.0-beta.12',
      '@angular/core'                    : 'https://unpkg.com/@angular/
        ➥ core@2.0.0',
      '@angular/common'                  : 'https://unpkg.com/@angular/
        ➥ common@2.0.0',
      '@angular/compiler'                : 'https://unpkg.com/@angular/
        ➥ compiler@2.0.0',
      '@angular/platform-browser'        : 'https://unpkg.com/@angular/
        ➥ platform-browser@2.0.0',
      '@angular/platform-browser-dynamic': 'https://unpkg.com/@angular/
        ➥ platform-browser-dynamic@2.0.0'
    },
    packages: {
      '@angular/core'                    : {main: 'index.js'},
      '@angular/common'                  : {main: 'index.js'},
      '@angular/compiler'                : {main: 'index.js'},
      '@angular/platform-browser'        : {main: 'index.js'},
      '@angular/platform-browser-dynamic': {main: 'index.js'}
    }
  });
  System.import('main.ts');
</script>
</head>
<body>
  <hello-world></hello-world>
</body>
</html>
```

Maps the names of the Angular modules to their CDN locations

Specifies the main script for each Angular module

Instructs SystemJS to load the main module from the main.ts file

The <hello-world></hello-world> custom HTML element represents the component that's implemented in main.ts.

When the application is launched, the <hello-world> tag will be replaced with the content of the template from the @Component annotation shown in listing 2.2.

TIP If you use Internet Explorer, you may need to add the additional script system-polyfills.js.

Content delivery networks (CDNs)

unpkg (https://unpkg.com) is a CDN for packages published to the npm (https://www.npmjs.com/) package manager's registry. Check npmjs.com to find the latest version of a particular package. If you want to see which other versions of the package are available, run the npm info packagename command.

> **(continued)**
> Generated files aren't committed into a version control system, and Angular 2 doesn't include ready-to-use bundles in its Git repository. They're generated on the fly and published along with the npm package (https://www.npmjs.com/~angular), so you can use unpkg to directly reference production-ready bundles in HTML files. Instead, we prefer using a local install of Angular and its dependencies, so you'll install them using npm in section 2.4.2. Everything that's installed by npm will be stored in the node_modules directory in each project.

THE TYPESCRIPT FILE

Now let's create a main.ts file, which has the TypeScript/Angular code and three parts:

1 Declare the Hello World component.
2 Wrap it into a module.
3 Load the module.

Later in this chapter, you'll implement these parts in three separate files, but here, for simplicity, you'll keep all the code of this tiny app in one file.

Listing 2.2   TypeScript main.ts

Imports the bootstrap method and the @Component annotation from the corresponding Angular packages, making them available for the application's code

```
import {Component} from '@angular/core';
import { NgModule }       from '@angular/core';
import { BrowserModule } from '@angular/platform-browser';
import { platformBrowserDynamic } from '@angular/platform-
browser-dynamic';

// Component
@Component({
  selector: 'hello-world',
  template: '<h1>Hello {{ name }}!</h1>'
})
class HelloWorldComponent {
  name: string;

  constructor() {
    this.name = 'Angular';
  }
}

// Module
@NgModule({
  imports:        [ BrowserModule ],
  declarations: [ HelloWorldComponent ],
  bootstrap:      [ HelloWorldComponent ]
})
```

The template property defines the HTML markup for rendering this component.

The @Component annotation placed above the HelloWorldComponent class turns it into an Angular component.

The name property is used in the data-binding expression on the component's template.

The annotated HelloWorldComponent class represents the component.

Inside the constructor, you initialize the name property with the value Angular 2 bound to the template.

Declares the content of the module

```
                export class AppModule { }        ◁──── Declares the class representing the module
Loads the  │   // App bootstrap
   module  └─▷ platformBrowserDynamic().bootstrapModule(AppModule);
```

We'll introduce the annotations @Component and @NgModule in section 2.2.

> ### What's metadata?
> In general, metadata is additional information about data. For example, in an MP3 file, the audio is the data, but the name of the artist, the song title, and the album cover are metadata. The MP3 player includes a metadata processor that reads the metadata and displays some of it while playing the song.
>
> In the case of classes, metadata is additional information about the class. For example, the @Component decorator (a.k.a annotation) tells Angular (the metadata processor) that this is not a regular class, but a component. Angular generates additional JavaScript code based on the information provided in the properties of the @Component decorator.
>
> In the case of class properties, the @Input decorator tells Angular that this class property should support binding and be able to receive data from the parent component.
>
> You can also think of a decorator as a function that attaches some data to the decorated element. The @Component decorator doesn't change the decorated class but adds some data describing the class so the Angular compiler can properly generate the final code of the component, either in the browser's memory (dynamic compilation) or in the file on disk (static compilation).

Any app component can be included in an HTML file (or a template of another component) by using the tag that matches the component's name in the selector property of the @Component annotation. Component selectors are similar to CSS selectors, so given the 'hello-world' selector, you'd render this component in an HTML page with an element named <hello-world>. Angular will convert this line into document .querySelectorAll(selector).

Notice how in listing 2.2 the entire template is wrapped in backticks to turn the template into a string. That way, you can use single and double quotes inside the template and break it into multiple lines for better formatting. The template contains the data-binding expression {{ name }}, and at runtime Angular will find the name property on your component and replace the data-binding expression in curly braces with a concrete value.

You'll use TypeScript for all the code examples in this book except for the two versions of Hello World shown next. One example will show an ES5 version, and the other is written in ES6.

2.1.2   *Hello World in ES5*

To create applications with ES5, you should use a special Angular bundle distributed in Universal Module Definition (UMD) format (note the *umd* in the URLs). It publishes all Angular APIs on the global ng object. The HTML file of the ES5 Angular Hello World application might look like the following (see the hello-world-es5 folder).

Listing 2.3   ES5 index.html

```html
<!DOCTYPE html>
<html>
<head>
  <script src="//unpkg.com/zone.js@0.6.12/dist/zone.js"></script>
  <script src="//unpkg.com/rxjs@5.0.0-beta.11/bundles/Rx.umd.js"></script>
  <script src="//unpkg.com/core-js/client/shim.min.js"></script>
  <script src="//unpkg.com/@angular/core@2.0.0/bundles/core.umd.js"></script>
  <script src="//unpkg.com/@angular/common@2.0.0/bundles/common.umd.js">
  </script>
  <script src="//unpkg.com/@angular/compiler@2.0.0/bundles/
      compiler.umd.js"></script>
  <script src="//unpkg.com/@angular/platform-browser@2.0.0/bundles/
      platform-browser.umd.js"></script>
  <script src="//unpkg.com/@angular/platform-browser-dynamic@2.0.0/
bundles/platform-browser-dynamic.umd.js"></script>
</head>
<body>
<hello-world></hello-world>
<script src="main.js"></script>
</body>
</html>
```

Because ES5 doesn't support the annotations syntax and has no native module system, the main.js file should be written differently from its TypeScript version.

Listing 2.4   ES5 main.js

```js
// Component
(function(app) {
  app.HelloWorldComponent =
      ng.core.Component({
        selector: 'hello-world',
        template: '<h1>Hello {{name}}!</h1>'
      })
      .Class({
        constructor: function() {
          this.name = 'Angular 2';
        }
      });
}) (window.app || (window.app = {}));
```

```
// Module
(function(app) {
  app.AppModule =
      ng.core.NgModule({
        imports: [ ng.platformBrowser.BrowserModule ],
        declarations: [ app.HelloWorldComponent ],
        bootstrap: [ app.HelloWorldComponent ]
      })
          .Class({
            constructor: function() {}
          });
})(window.app || (window.app = {}));

// App bootstrap
(function(app) {
  document.addEventListener('DOMContentLoaded', function() {
    ng.platformBrowserDynamic
        .platformBrowserDynamic()
        .bootstrapModule(app.AppModule);
  });
})(window.app || (window.app = {}));
```

The first immediately invoked function expression (IIFE) invokes the `Component()` and `Class` methods on the global Angular core namespace `ng.core`. You define the `HelloWorldComponent` object, and the `Component` method attaches the metadata defining its selector and template. By doing this, you turn the JavaScript object into a visual component.

The business logic of the component is coded inside the `Class` method. In this case, you declare and initialize the `name` property that's bound to the component's template.

The second IIFE invokes the `NgModule` method to create a module that declares `HelloWorldComponent` and specifies it as a root component by assigning its name to the `bootstrap` property. Finally, the third IIFE launches the app by invoking `bootstrapModule()`, which loads the module, instantiates `HelloWorldComponent`, and attaches it to the browser's DOM.

2.1.3 Hello World in ES6

The ES6 version of the Hello World application looks very similar to the TypeScript version, but it uses Traceur as the transpiler for SystemJS. The index.html file looks like this.

Listing 2.5   ES6 index.html

```
<!DOCTYPE html>
<html>
<head>
  <script src="//unpkg.com/zone.js@0.6.21"></script>
  <script src="//unpkg.com/reflect-metadata@0.1.3"></script>
```

```
<script src="//unpkg.com/traceur@0.0.111/bin/traceur.js"></script>
<script src="//unpkg.com/systemjs@0.19.37/dist/system.src.js"></script>
<script>
  System.config({
    transpiler: 'traceur',
    traceurOptions: {annotations: true},
    map: {
      'rxjs': 'https://unpkg.com/rxjs@5.0.0-beta.12',

      '@angular/core'                    : 'https://unpkg.com/@angular/
        ➥ core@2.0.0',
      '@angular/common'                  : 'https://unpkg.com/@angular/
        ➥ common@2.0.0',
      '@angular/compiler'                : 'https://unpkg.com/@angular/
        ➥ compiler@2.0.0',
      '@angular/platform-browser'        : 'https://unpkg.com/@angular/
        ➥ platform-browser@2.0.0',
      '@angular/platform-browser-dynamic': 'https://unpkg.com/@angular/
        ➥ platform-browser-dynamic@2.0.0'
    },
    packages: {
      '@angular/core'                    : {main: 'index.js'},
      '@angular/common'                  : {main: 'index.js'},
      '@angular/compiler'                : {main: 'index.js'},
      '@angular/platform-browser'        : {main: 'index.js'},
      '@angular/platform-browser-dynamic': {main: 'index.js'}
    }
  });
  System.import('main.js');
</script>
</head>
<body>
  <hello-world></hello-world>
</body>
</html>
```

> **ES6 isn't fully supported across browsers, and you use Traceur to transpile (in the browser) ES6 code into an ES5 version.**

> **The extension of the script file is .js now.**

The only difference between the ES6 main.js file compared to the TypeScript main.ts file is that now you don't have the predeclared name class member:

Listing 2.6 ES6 main.js

```
import {Component} from '@angular/core';
import { NgModule }      from '@angular/core';
import { BrowserModule } from '@angular/platform-browser';
import { platformBrowserDynamic } from '@angular/platform-browser-dynamic';

// Component
@Component({
  selector: 'hello-world',
  template: '<h1>Hello {{ name }}!</h1>'
})
```

```
class HelloWorldComponent {

  constructor() {
    this.name = 'Angular 2';
  }
}

// Module
@NgModule({
  imports:      [ BrowserModule ],
  declarations: [ HelloWorldComponent ],
  bootstrap:    [ HelloWorldComponent ]
})
export class AppModule { }

// App bootstrap
platformBrowserDynamic().bootstrapModule(AppModule);
```

2.1.4 Launching applications

To run any web application, you'll need a basic HTTP server, such as http-server or live-server. The latter performs live reloads of the web page as soon as you modify the code and save the file of the running application.

To install http-server, use the following npm command:

```
npm install http-server -g
```

To start the server from the command line in the project root directory, use this command:

```
http-server
```

We prefer to see live reloads in the browser, so install and start live-server using a similar routine:

```
npm install live-server -g
```

```
live-server
```

If you use http-server, you'll need to manually open the web browser and enter the URL http://localhost:8080, whereas live-server will open the browser for you.

To run the Hello World application, launch live-server in the root directory of the project; it will load index.html in your web browser. You should see "Hello Angular 2!" rendered on the page (see figure 2.1). In the browser's Developer Tools panel, you can see that the template you specified for `HelloWorldComponent` becomes the content of the <hello-world> element, and the data-binding expression is replaced with the actual value you used to initialize the `name` property in the constructor of the component.

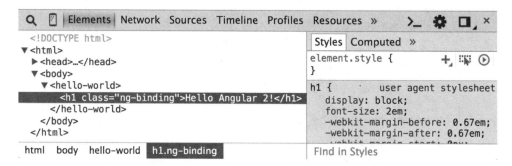

Figure 2.1   Running Hello World

2.2   *The building blocks of an Angular application*

In this section, we'll give you a high-level overview of the main building blocks of an Angular application so that you can read and understand Angular code. We'll discuss each of these topics in detail in future chapters.

2.2.1   *Modules*

An Angular module is a container for a group of related components, services, directives, and so on. You can think of a module as a library of components and services that implements certain functionality from the business domain of your application, such as a shipping module or a billing module. All elements of a small application can be located in one module (the root module), whereas larger apps may have more than one module (feature modules). All apps must have at least a root module that is bootstrapped during the app launch.

> **NOTE** ES6 modules just offer you a way to hide and protect functions or variables and create loadable scripts. Angular modules, in contrast, are used for packaging related application functionality.

From the syntax perspective, a module is a class annotated with the NgModule decorator and that can include other resources. In section 2.1 you already used a module, which looked like this:

Declares that
HelloWorldComponent
belongs to the
AppModule. Each
module member must
be listed here.

Every browser app must import
BrowserModule and can import
other modules (such as
FormsModule) if need be.

During app launch, the
module renders the root
component that's assigned
to the bootstrap property
of @NgModule.

```
@NgModule({
  imports:      [ BrowserModule ],
  declarations: [ HelloWorldComponent ],
  bootstrap:    [ HelloWorldComponent ]
})
export class AppModule { }
```

Importing `BrowserModule` is a must in the root module, but if your app will consist of the root and feature modules, the latter will need to import `CommonModule` instead. Members of all imported modules (such as `FormsModule` and `RouterModule`) are available to all components of the module.

To load and compile a module on application startup, you need to invoke the `bootstrapModule` module:

```
platformBrowserDynamic().bootstrapModule(AppModule);
```

Your app modules can be loaded either immediately (eagerly), as in the preceding code snippet, or lazily (as needed) by the router (see chapter 3). You'll use `@NgModule` in every chapter of this book, so you'll have a chance to see how to declare modules with multiple members. For a detailed description of Angular modules, read the documentation at https://angular.io/docs/ts/latest/guide/ngmodule.html.

2.2.2 Components

The main building block of an Angular application is the *component*. Each component consists of two parts: a view that defines the user interface (UI) and a class that implements the logic behind the view.

Any Angular application represents a hierarchy of components packaged in modules. An app must have at least one module and one component, which is called the *root component*. There's nothing special about the root component compared to other components. Any component assigned to the `bootstrap` property of the module becomes the root component.

To create a component, declare a class and attach the `@Component` annotation to it:

```
@Component({
  selector: 'app-component',
  template: '<h1>Hello !</h1>'
})
class HelloComponent {}
```

Each `@Component` annotation must define `selector` and `template` (or `templateUrl`) properties, which determine how the component should be discovered and rendered on the page.

The `selector` property is similar to a CSS selector. Each HTML element that matches the selector is rendered as an Angular component. You can think of the `@Component` decorator as a configuration function that complements the class. If you look at the transpiled code of the main.ts file from listing 2.2, you'll see what the Angular compiler did with the `@Component` decorator:

```
var core_1;
var HelloWorldComponent;

HelloWorldComponent = (function () {
    function HelloWorldComponent() {
        this.name = 'Angular 2';
    }
    HelloWorldComponent = __decorate([
        core_1.Component({
            selector: 'hello-world',
            template: '<h1>Hello {{ name }}!</h1>'
        }),
        __metadata('design:paramtypes', [])
    ], HelloWorldComponent);
    return HelloWorldComponent;
})
```

Each component must define a view, which is specified in either a `template` or a `templateUrl` property of the `@Component` decorator:

```
@Component({
  selector: 'app-component',
  template: '<h1>App Component</h1>' })
class AppComponent {}
```

For web applications, a `template` contains HTML markup. You can also use another markup language for rendering native mobile applications provided by third-party frameworks. If the markup consists of a couple of dozen lines or less, we keep it inline using the `template` property. We didn't use backticks in the preceding example because it's a single line of markup and doesn't contain single or double quotes. Larger HTML markup should be located in a separate HTML file referred to in `templateUrl`.

Components are styled with regular CSS. You can use the `styles` property for inline CSS and `styleUrls` for an external file with styles. External files allow web designers to work on the styles without modifying the application code. Ultimately, the decision of where to keep the HTML or CSS is yours.

You can think of a view as the result of merging UI layout with data. The code snippet for `AppComponent` has no data to merge, but the TypeScript version of Hello World (see the main.ts file in listing 2.2) would merge the HTML markup with the value of the `name` variable to produce the view.

> **NOTE** In Angular, the view rendering is decoupled from components, so the template can represent a platform-specific native UI, such as NativeScript (https://www.nativescript.org) or React Native (https://facebook.github.io/react-native).

2.2.3   *Directives*

The @Directive decorator allows you to attach custom behavior to an HTML element (for example, you can add an autocomplete feature to an <input> element). Each component is basically a directive with an associated view, but unlike a component, a directive doesn't have its own view.

The following example shows a directive that can be attached to an input element in order to log the input's value to the browser's console as soon as the value is changed:

```
@Directive({
  selector: 'input[log-directive]',
  host: {
    '(input)': 'onInput($event)'
  }
})
class LogDirective {
  onInput(event) {
    console.log(event.target.value);
  }
}
```

This selector requires the target HTML element to have an input element and the log-directive attribute.

The host element is the one you attach your directive to.

The handler for the <input> element logs its value to the console.

To bind events to event handlers, enclose the event name in parentheses. When the input event occurs on the host element, the onInput() event handler is invoked and the event object is passed to this method as an argument.

Here's an example of how you can attach the directive to an HTML element:

```
<input type="text" log-directive/>
```

The next example shows a directive that changes the background of the attached element to blue:

```
import { Directive, ElementRef, Renderer } from '@angular/core';

@Directive({ selector: '[highlight]' })

export class HighlightDirective {
  constructor(renderer: Renderer, el: ElementRef) {
    renderer.setElementStyle(el.nativeElement, 'backgroundColor', 'blue');
  }
}
```

This directive can be attached to various HTML elements, and the constructor of this directive gets the references to the renderer and the UI element injected by Angular. Here's how this directive can be attached to the <h1> HTML element:

```
<h1 highlight>Hello World</h1>
```

All directives that are used in the module need to be added to the declaration property of the @NgModule decorator, as in this example:

```
@NgModule({
   imports:        [ BrowserModule ],
   declarations:   [ HelloWorldComponent,
                     HighlightDirective ],
   bootstrap:      [ HelloWorldComponent ]
})
```

2.2.4   *A brief introduction to data binding*

Angular has a mechanism called *data binding* that allows you to keep a component's properties in sync with the view. This mechanism is quite sophisticated, and we'll cover data binding in detail in chapter 5. In this section we'll just cover the most common forms of data-binding syntax.

To display a value as a string in the template, use double curly braces:

```
<h1>Hello {{ name }}!</h1>
```

Use square brackets to bind an HTML element's property to a value:

```
<span [hidden]="isValid">The field is required</span>
```

To bind an event handler for an element's event, use parentheses:

```
<button (click)="placeBid()">Place Bid</button>
```

If you want to reference a DOM object's property within the template, add a local template variable (its name must start with #) that will automatically store a reference to the corresponding DOM object, and use dot notation:

```
<input #title type="text" />
<span>{{ title.value }}</span>
```

Now that you know how to write a simple Angular application, let's see how the code can be loaded into the browser with the SystemJS library.

2.3   *The SystemJS universal module loader*

Most existing web applications load JavaScript files into an HTML page using <script> tags. Although it's possible to add Angular code to a page the same way, the recommended way is to load code using the SystemJS library. Angular also uses SystemJS internally.

In this section, we'll give you a brief overview of SystemJS so you can get started developing Angular applications. For a detailed tutorial on SystemJS, see the SystemJS page on GitHub: https://github.com/systemjs/systemjs.

2.3.1   *An overview of module loaders*

The final ES6 specification introduces modules and covers their syntax and semantics (http://mng.bz/ri01). The early specification drafts included a definition of the global System object responsible for loading modules into the execution environment, whether that's a web browser or a standalone process. But the definition of the System object was removed from the final version of the ES6 spec and is currently tracked by the Web Hypertext Application Technology Working Group (see http://whatwg.github.io/loader). The System object may become a part of the ES8 specification.

The ES6 Module Loader polyfill (https://github.com/ModuleLoader/es6-module-loader) offers one way to use the System object today (without waiting for future EcmaScript specifications). It strives to match the future standard, but this polyfill supports only ES6 modules.

Because ES6 is fairly new, most third-party packages hosted on the NPM registry don't use ES6 modules yet. The first nine chapters of this book use SystemJS, which not only includes the ES6 Module Loader but also allows you to load modules written in AMD, CommonJS, UMD, and global module formats. The support for these formats is completely transparent for the SystemJS user, because it automatically figures out what module format the target script uses. In chapter 10, you'll use another module loader called Webpack.

2.3.2 Module loaders vs. <script> tags

Why even use module loaders as opposed to loading JavaScript with a <script> tag? The <script> tags have several issues:

- A developer is responsible for maintaining <script> tags in the HTML file. Some of them can become redundant over time, but if you forget to clean them up, they will still be loaded by the browser, increasing the load time and wasting network bandwidth.
- Often the order in which scripts are loaded matters. Browsers can only guarantee the execution order of scripts if you place the <script> tags in the <head> section of the HTML document. But it's considered bad practice to put all your scripts in <head>, because it prevents the page from being rendered until all the scripts are downloaded.

Let's consider the benefits of using module loaders both during development and while preparing a production version of your application:

- In development environments, the code is usually split into multiple files, and each file represents a module. Whenever you import a module in your code, the loader will match the module name to a corresponding file, download it into the browser, and then execute the rest of the code. Modules allow you to keep projects well organized; the module loader automatically assembles everything together in the browser when you launch the application. If a module has dependencies on other modules, all of them will be loaded.
- When you're preparing a production version of an application, a module loader takes the main file, traverses the tree of all modules reachable from it, and combines all of them into a single bundle. This way, the bundle contains only the code that's actually used by the application. It also solves the problem with script loading order and cyclic references.

These benefits apply not only to your application's code but also to third-party packages (such as Angular).

> **NOTE**   In this book, we use the terms *module* and *file* interchangeably. A module can't span multiple files. A bundle is usually represented by a single file and contains multiple modules registered in it. When the difference between *module* and *file* is important, we'll explicitly mention it.

2.3.3   Getting started with SystemJS

When you use SystemJS in an HTML page, this library becomes available as a global `System` object that has a number of static methods. The two primary methods you'll use are `System.import()` and `System.config()`.

To load a module, use `System.import()`, which accepts the module name as an argument. A module name can be either a path to the file or a logical name mapped to the file path:

```
                                                        A path to the file
System.import('./my-module.js');      ⟵⎯⎵
System.import('@angular2/core');      ⟵⎯⎯⎯ A logical name
```

If the module name starts with `./` it's a path to the file even when the name extension is omitted. SystemJS first tries to match the module name against the configured mapping provided either as an argument to the method `System.config()` or in a file (such as systemjs.config.js). If the mapping for the name isn't found, it's considered to be a path to a file.

> **NOTE**   In this book, we'll use both the prefix `./` as well as the mapping configuration to find out which file will be loaded. If you see `System.import('app')` and can't find the file named app.ts, check the mapping configuration of your project.

The `System.import()` method immediately returns a `Promise` object(see appendix A). When the promise is resolved with a module object, the `then()` callback is invoked when the module is loaded. If the promise is rejected, the errors are handled in the `catch()` method.

An ES6 module object contains a property for each exported value in the loaded module. The following code snippet from two files shows how you can export a variable in the module and use it in another script:

```
// lib.js
export let foo = 'foo';

// main.js
System.import('./lib.js').then(libModule => {
  libModule.foo === 'foo'; // true
});
```

Here you use the `then()` method to specify the callback function to be invoked when lib.js is loaded. The loaded object is passed as an argument to the fat arrow expression.

In ES5 scripts, you use the `System.import()` method to load the code either eagerly or lazily (dynamically). For example, if an anonymous user browses your website, you may not need a module that implements the user profile functionality. But as soon as the user logs in, you can dynamically load the profile module. This way, you decrease initial page load size and time.

But what about the ES6 `import` statements? In your first Angular application, you used `System.import()` in the index.html file to load the root application module, main.ts. In turn, the main.ts script imports Angular's modules using its own `import` statement.

When SystemJS loads main.ts, it automatically transpiles it into ES5-compatible code, so there are no `import` statements in the code that browsers execute. In the future, when ES6 modules are natively supported by major browsers, this step won't be required and `import` statements will work similarly to `System.import()`, except they won't control the moment when the module is loaded.

NOTE When SystemJS transpiles files, it automatically generates the source map for each .js file, which allows you to debug the TypeScript code in the browser.

A DEMO APPLICATION

Let's consider an application that needs to load both ES5 and ES6 scripts. This application will consist of three files (see the systemjs-demo folder):

```
├── index.html
├── es6module.js
└── es5module.js
```

In a typical web application, the index.html file would contain the `<script>` tags referencing both es6module.js and es5module.js. Each of these files would be automatically loaded and executed by the browser. But this approach has several issues that we discussed in section 2.3.2. Let's see how you can address these issues with SystemJS in the demo application.

You use the ES6 `export` statement to make the es6module.js module's name available from outside of the script. The presence of the `export` statement automatically turns the file into an ES6 module:

```
export let name = 'ES6';

console.log('ES6 module is loaded');
```

The es5module.js file doesn't include any ES6 syntax and uses the CommonJS module format to export the name of the module. Basically, you attach to the `exports` object the variables you want to be visible outside of the module:

```
exports.name = 'ES5';

console.log('ES5 module is loaded');
```

The following index.html file seamlessly imports both CommonJS and ES6 modules with the help of SystemJS.

Listing 2.7   index.html with SystemJS

The ES6 Promise.all() method returns a Promise object that resolves (or rejects) when all iterable arguments are complete.

You don't use the ES6 arrow function here because the index.html file itself isn't processed by SystemJS, so the code wouldn't be transpiled and wouldn't work in all browsers.

After the arguments of Promise.all() are loaded, they're given to the then() method as the modules array.

Here you use the relative path to the file es6module.js that uses the ES6 module syntax.

Load es5module.js similar to the previous one, but this time SystemJS uses the CommonJS format.

This map() method invokes the function that transforms the result by extracting the name property exported from each module.

The method join() combines all module names into a comma-separated string.

```
<!DOCTYPE html>
<html>
<head>
  <script src="//unpkg.com/es6-promise@3.0.2/dist/es6-promise.js">
  </script>
  <script src="//unpkg.com/traceur@0.0.111/bin/traceur.js">
  </script>
  <script src="//unpkg.com/systemjs@0.19.37/dist/system.src.js">
  </script>
  <script>

    Promise.all([
      System.import('./es6module.js'),
      System.import('./es5module.js')
    ]).then(function (modules) {
      var moduleNames = modules
        .map(function (m) { return m.name; })
        .join(', ');

      console.log('The following modules are loaded: ' + moduleNames);
    });
  </script>
</head>
<body></body>
</html>
```

Because `System.import()` returns a `Promise` object, you can start loading multiple modules at once and execute some other code when all modules are loaded.

When the application is launched, the following result is printed to the browser's console (keep the Developer Tools panel open to see it):

```
Live reload enabled.
ES6 module is loaded
ES5 module is loaded
The following modules are loaded: ES6, ES5
```

The first line comes from the live-server, not from the app. As soon as one of the modules is loaded, it immediately prints its log message. When all modules are loaded, the callback function is executed and the last log message is printed.

CONFIGURING SYSTEMJS

You've used a default SystemJS configuration so far, but you can configure almost any aspect of its work using the `System.config()` method, which accepts a configuration object as an argument. `System.config()` can be invoked multiple times with different configuration objects. If the same option is set more than once, the latest value is applied. You can either inline the script with `System.config()` in the HTML file using the `<script>` tag (see section 2.1) or store the code for `System.config()` in a separate file (such as systemjs.config.js) and include it into the HTML file using the `<script>` tag.

The complete list of configuration options for SystemJS is available on GitHub (http://mng.bz/8N60). We'll just briefly discuss some of the configuration options used in this book.

BASEURL

All modules are loaded relative to this URL unless the module name represents an absolute or a relative URL:

```
System.config({ baseURL: '/app' });
System.import('es6module.js');    // GET /app/es6module.js
System.import('./es6module.js'); // GET /es6module.js
System.import('http://example.com/es6module.js'); // GET http://example.com/
➥ es6module.js
```

DEFAULTJSEXTENSIONS

If `defaultJSExtensions` is `true`, the .js extension will be automatically added to all file paths. If a module name already has an extension other than .js, the .js will be appended anyway:

```
System.config({ defaultJSExtensions: true });
System.import('./es6module');    // GET /es6module.js
System.import('./es6module.js'); // GET /es6module.js
System.import('./es6module.ts'); // GET /es6module.ts
```

> **WARNING** The `defaultJSExtensions` property exist
> bility and will be deprecated in future versions of Syst

MAP

The `map` option allows you to create an alias for a module
module, the module name is replaced with an associated

module name represents any kind of path (absolute or relative). The map parameter is applied before baseURL:

```
System.config({ map: { 'es6module.js': 'esSixModule.js' } });
System.import('es6module.js');   // GET /esSixModule.js
System.import('./es6module.js'); // GET /es6Module.js
```

Here's another map example:

```
System.config({
  baseURL: '/app',
  map: { 'es6module': 'esSixModule.js' }
});
System.import('es6module'); // GET /app/esSixModule.js
```

PACKAGES

Packages provide a convenient way to set metadata and a map configuration that's specific to a common path. For example, the following fragment instructs SystemJS that System.import('app') should load the module located in the main_router _sample.ts file by providing just the name of the file and the default extension ts for TypeScript:

```
System.config({
  packages: {
    app: {
      defaultExtension: "ts",
      main: "main_router_sample"
    }
  }
});
System.import('app');
```

PATHS

The paths option is similar to map, but it supports wildcards. It's applied after map but before baseURL (see listing 2.6). You can use both map and paths, but remember that paths is part of the Loader specification (see http://whatwg.github.io/loader) and the ES6 Module Loader implementation (see https://github.com/ModuleLoader/es-module-loader), but map is only recognizable by SystemJS:

```
System.config({
  baseURL: '/app',
  map: { 'es6module': 'esSixModule.js' },
  paths: { '*': 'lib/*' }
});

System.import('es6module'); // GET /app/lib/esSixModule.js
```

In many code examples in this book, you'll find System.import('app'), which opens file with a different name (that is, not app) because the map or packages property was configured. When you see something like `import {Component} from '@angular/core';`, the `@angular` refers to the name mapped to the actual directory where the Angular framework is located. `core` is a subdirectory, and the main file in that subdirectory is specified in the SystemJS configuration, as in this example:

```
packages: {
        '@angular/core' : {main: 'index.js'}
}
```

TRANSPILER

The `transpiler` option allows you to specify the name of the transpiler module that should be used while loading application modules. If a file doesn't contain at least one `import` or `export` statement, it won't be transpiled. The `transpiler` option can contain one of the following values: `typescript`, `traceur`, and `babel`:

```
System.config({
  transpiler: 'traceur',
  map: {
    traceur: '//unpkg.com/traceur@0.0.108/bin/traceur.js'
  }
});
```

TYPESCRIPTOPTIONS

The `typescriptOptions` option allows you to set the TypeScript compiler options. The list of all available options can be found in the TypeScript documentation: http://mng.bz/rf14.

2.4 *Selecting a package manager*

It's very unlikely that you'll be writing a web application without using any libraries. This book uses several in the code samples. You'll use the Angular framework for most of the code samples, and for the online auction app you'll also use Twitter's library called Bootstrap, which has jQuery as a dependency. Your application may require specific versions of these dependencies.

The loading of libraries, frameworks, and their dependencies is managed by a package manager, and you need to decide which of several popular ones to choose. JavaScript developers may be overwhelmed by the variety of package managers available: npm, Bower, jspm, Jam, and Duo, to name a few.

A typical project includes a configuration file that lists the names and versions of the required libraries and frameworks. Here's a fragment from the package.json npm configuration, which you'll use for the online auction application:

```
"scripts": {
    "start": "live-server"
  },
  "dependencies": {
    "@angular/common": "2.0.0",
    "@angular/compiler": "2.0.0",
```

```
  "@angular/core": "2.0.0",
  "@angular/forms": "2.0.0",
  "@angular/http": "2.0.0",
  "@angular/platform-browser": "2.0.0",
  "@angular/platform-browser-dynamic": "2.0.0",
  "@angular/router": "3.0.0",

  "core-js": "^2.4.0",
  "rxjs": "5.0.0-beta.12",
  "systemjs": "0.19.37",
  "zone.js": "0.6.21",

  "bootstrap": "^3.3.6",
  "jquery": "^2.2.2"
},
"devDependencies": {
  "live-server": "0.8.2",
  "typescript": "^2.0.0"
}
```

The scripts section specifies the command to run if you enter npm start on the command line. In this case, you'll want to start the live-server. The dependencies section lists all the third-party libraries and tools required for the runtime environment where the application is deployed.

The devDependencies section adds the tools that must be present on your computer. For example, you won't be using live-server in production as it's a pretty simple server that suffices for development only. The preceding configuration also states that the TypeScript compiler is needed only during development, and you can guess that during deployment all TypeScript code will be transpiled into JavaScript.

The preceding configuration includes version numbers as well. If you see a ^ sign in front of the version number, it indicates that the project requires either the specified or any newer minor version of this library or package. When we used the beta version of Angular, and we wanted to specify the exact package version because newer ones might have some breaking changes.

When we started working with Angular, we knew that we'd use the SystemJS module loader. Then we learned that the author of SystemJS (Guy Bedford) has also created a jspm package manager that uses SystemJS internally, so we decided to use jspm. For some time we've been using npm for installing tools and jspm for application dependencies. This setup worked, but with jspm a web browser was making 400+ requests to the server to show the first page of a rather simple application. Waiting for 3.5 seconds just to start the app on a local machine is a little too long.

We decided to try using npm for dependency management during development. The results were much better: only 30 server requests and 1.5 seconds to start the same app.

We'll still give you a brief overview of both package managers and will show you how to start a new project with each of them. jspm is pretty young and may improve over time, but we decided to use npm for our Angular projects.

2.4.1 Comparing npm and jspm

npm is a package manager for Node.js. It was originally created to manage Node.js modules, which are written in the CommonJS format. CommonJS wasn't designed for web applications, because modules were supposed to be loaded synchronously. Consider the following code snippet:

```
var x = require('module1');
var y = require('module2');
var z = require('module3');
```

The loading of `module2` won't start until `module1` is loaded, and the loading of `module3` will wait for `module2`. This is OK for desktop applications written in Node.js because the loading is done from the local computer, but such a synchronous loading process would slow the downloading of applications.

Another weak point of npm was that it historically used *nested* dependencies. If packages A and B depended on package C, each of them would keep a copy of C in its directory because A and B might depend on different versions of C. Although this was OK for Node.js applications, it didn't work well for applications loaded into a web browser. Even loading the same version of a library twice in a browser can cause issues. If two different versions are loaded, the chances of breaking the app are even higher.

The nested dependencies issue was addressed in npm 3, but the problem is only partially solved. By default, npm attempts to install package C in the same directory as A and B, so a single copy of C is shared between A and B. But if A and B require conflicting versions of C, npm falls back to the nested dependencies approach. Libraries created for client-side applications usually include built versions (single-file bundles) in their npm packages. The bundles don't contain third-party dependencies, so you should manually load them on the page. This helps avoid the nested dependencies issue.

jspm is a package manager created with ES6 modules and module loaders in mind. jspm doesn't host packages itself. It has a concept of registries, which allow you to create custom source locations for packages. Out of the box, jspm lets you install packages either from the npm registry or directly from the GitHub repositories.

It's designed to work together with SystemJS. When you initialize a new project or install a package with jspm, it automatically creates a configuration for SystemJS to load modules. Unlike npm, it uses the *flat* dependencies approach, so there's always only one copy of a library in a project. This allows you to use `import` statements to load even third-party code. It solves the issue with the loading order of scripts and makes sure the application loads only those modules that it actually uses.

jspm packages usually don't include bundles. Instead they preserve the original project structure and files, so each module can be loaded individually. Although having the original version of a file might improve the debugging experience, it doesn't pay off in practice. Importing each module individually leads to loading hundreds of files into the browser before starting the app. This slows down development and doesn't suit production deployment.

Another weak point of jspm is that you can't necessarily use any npm package or GitHub repository as a jspm package right away. They may require additional configuration so jspm can properly set up SystemJS to load the modules from the package. At the time of writing, there are fewer than 500 packages in the jspm registry that are SystemJS-ready, compared with 250,000 packages hosted by npm.

2.4.2 *Starting an Angular project with npm*

To start a new project managed by npm, create a new directory (such as angular-seed) and open it in the command window. Then run the `npm init -y` command, which will create the initial version of the package.json configuration file. Normally `npm init` asks several questions while creating the file, but the `-y` flag makes it accept the default values for all options. The following example shows this command running in the empty angular-seed directory.

```
$ npm init -y
Wrote to /Users/username/angular-seed/package.json:

{
  "name": "angular-seed",
  "version": "1.0.0",
  "description": "",
  "main": "index.js",
  "scripts": {
    "test": "echo \"Error: no test specified\" && exit 1"
  },
  "keywords": [],
  "author": "",
  "license": "ISC"
}
```

Most of the generated configuration is needed either for publishing the project into the npm registry or while installing the package as a dependency for another project. You'll use npm only for managing project dependencies and automating development and build processes.

Because you're not going to publish it into the npm registry, you should remove all of the properties except name, `description`, and `scripts`. Also, add a `"private": true` property because it's not created by default. It will prevent the package from being accidentally published to the npm registry. The package.json file should look like this.

Listing 2.8 package.json

```
{
  "name": "angular-seed",
  "description": "An initial npm-managed project for Chapter 2",
  "private": true,
  "scripts": {
    "test": "echo \"Error: no test specified\" && exit 1"
  }
}
```

The `scripts` configuration allows you to specify commands that you can run in the command window. By default, `npm init` creates the `test` command, which can be run like this: `npm test`. Let's replace it with the `start` command that you'll use to launch the live-server that you installed in section 2.4.1. Here's the configuration of the `scripts` property:

```
{
  ...
  "scripts": {
    "start": "live-server"
  }
}
```

You can run any npm command from the `scripts` section using the `npm run mycommand` syntax, such as `npm run start`. You can also use the shorthand `npm start` command instead of `npm run start`. The shorthand syntax is available only for predefined npm scripts (see the npm documentation at https://docs.npmjs.com/misc/scripts).

Now you want npm to download Angular to this project as a dependency. In the TypeScript version of the Hello World application, you used the Angular code located at unpkg CDN server, but here you want it to be downloaded to your project directory. You also want local versions of SystemJS, live-server, and the TypeScript compiler.

npm packages often consist of bundles optimized for production use that don't include the source code of the libraries. Let's add the section to the package.json file that uses the source code (not the optimized bundles) of specific packages. Add this section right after the license line (update the versions of the dependencies so you're current).

> **Listing 2.9 Using package source code in package.json**

```
"dependencies": {
    "@angular/common": "2.0.0",
    "@angular/compiler": "2.0.0",
    "@angular/core": "2.0.0",
    "@angular/forms": "2.0.0",
    "@angular/http": "2.0.0",
    "@angular/platform-browser": "2.0.0",
    "@angular/platform-browser-dynamic": "2.0.0",
    "@angular/router": "3.0.0",

    "core-js": "^2.4.0",
    "rxjs": "5.0.0-beta.12",
    "systemjs": "0.19.37",
    "zone.js": "0.6.21"
},
"devDependencies": {
  "live-server": "0.8.2",
  "typescript": "^2.0.0"
}
```

Now run the npm install command on the command line from the directory where your package.json is located, and npm will start downloading the preceding packages and their dependencies into the node_modules folder. After this process is complete, you'll see dozens of subdirectories in node_modules, including @angular, systemjs, live-server, and typescript:

```
angular-seed
├── index.html
├── package.json
└── app
│     └── app.ts
├── node_modules
│     ├── @angular
│     ├── systemjs
│     ├── typescript
│     ├── live-server
│     └── ...
```

In the angular-seed folder, let's create a slightly modified version of index.html with the following content.

Listing 2.10   index.html

```html
<!DOCTYPE html>
<html>
<head>
  <title>Angular seed project</title>
  <meta charset="UTF-8">
  <meta name="viewport" content="width=device-width, initial-scale=1">

  <script src="node_modules/typescript/lib/typescript.js"></script>
  <script src="node_modules/core-js/client/shim.min.js"></script>
  <script src="node_modules/zone.js/dist/zone.js"></script>
  <script src="node_modules/systemjs/dist/system.src.js"></script>
  <script src="systemjs.config.js"></script>
  <script>
    System.import('app').catch(function(err){ console.error(err); });
  </script>
</head>

<body>
<app>Loading...</app>
</body>
</html>
```

Note that the script tags now load the required dependencies from the local directory node_modules. The same applies to the SystemJS configuration file systemjs.config.js shown here.

Listing 2.11 systemjs.config.js

```
System.config({
    transpiler: 'typescript',
    typescriptOptions: {emitDecoratorMetadata: true},
    map: {
      '@angular': 'node_modules/@angular',
      'rxjs'    : 'node_modules/rxjs'
    },
    paths: {
      'node_modules/@angular/*': 'node_modules/@angular/*/bundles'
    },
    meta: {
      '@angular/*': {'format': 'cjs'}
    },
    packages: {
      'app'                              : {main: 'main', defaultExtension:
      ➥ 'ts'},
      'rxjs'                             : {main: 'Rx'},
      '@angular/core'                    : {main: 'core.umd.min.js'},
      '@angular/common'                  : {main: 'common.umd.min.js'},
      '@angular/compiler'                : {main: 'compiler.umd.min.js'},
      '@angular/platform-browser'        : {main: 'platform-
      ➥ browser.umd.min.js'},
      '@angular/platform-browser-dynamic': {main: 'platform-browser-
      ➥ dynamic.umd.min.js'}
    }
});
```

The preceding SystemJS configuration is a little different than the one shown in listing 2.1. This time you don't use the source code of Angular packages; you use their bundled and minimized versions instead. This will minimize the number of network requests required to load the Angular framework, and this version of the framework is smaller. Each Angular package comes with a directory called bundles that contains the minimized code. In the packages section of the SystemJS config file, you map the name app to the main script located in main.ts, so when you write System.import(app) in index.html, it'll load main.ts.

Add one more config file in the root of the project, where you'll specify the tsc compiler's options.

Listing 2.12 tsconfig.json

```
{
  "compilerOptions": {
    "target": "ES5",
    "module": "commonjs",
    "experimentalDecorators": true,
    "noImplicitAny": true
  }
}
```

If you're new to TypeScript, read appendix B, which explains that in order to run TypeScript code it must first be transpiled to JavaScript with the TypeScript compiler `tsc`. The code samples in chapters 1–7 work without explicitly running `tsc` because SystemJS uses `tsc` internally to transpile TypeScript to JavaScript on the fly as it loads a script file. But you'll still keep the tsconfig.json file in the project root because some IDEs rely on it.

> **NOTE**   If the Angular code is dynamically compiled in the browser (not to be confused with transpiling), this is called *just-in-time* (JIT) compilation. If the code is precompiled with a special ngc compiler, it's called *ahead-of-time* (AoT) compilation. In this chapter, we'll describe the app with JIT compilation.

The app code will consist of three files:

- *app.component.ts*—The one and only component of your app
- *app.module.ts*—The declaration of the module that will include your component
- *main.ts*—The bootstrap of the module

In section 2.3.3, you mapped the name app to main.ts, so let's create a directory called app containing an app.component.ts file with the following content.

Listing 2.13   app.component.ts

```
import {Component} from '@angular/core';

@Component({
    selector: 'app',
    template: `<h1>Hello {{ name }}!</h1>`
})
export class AppComponent {
    name: string;

    constructor() {
        this.name = 'Angular 2';
    }
}
```

Now you need to create a module that will contain `AppComponent`. Place this code in the app.module.ts file.

Listing 2.14   app.module.ts

```
import { NgModule }      from '@angular/core';
import { BrowserModule } from '@angular/platform-browser';
import { AppComponent }  from './app.component';

@NgModule({
    imports:      [ BrowserModule ],
    declarations: [ AppComponent ],
    bootstrap:    [ AppComponent ]
})
export class AppModule { }
```

This file just contains the definition of the Angular module. The class is annotated with @NgModule, which includes the BrowserModule that every browser must import. Because the module contains only one class, you need to list it in the declarations property and list it as the bootstrap class:

```
import { platformBrowserDynamic } from '@angular/platform-browser-dynamic';
import { AppModule }  from './app.module';

platformBrowserDynamic().bootstrapModule(AppModule);
```

Start the application by executing the npm start command from the angular-seed directory, and it'll open your browser and show the message "Loading…" for a split second, followed by "Hello Angular 2!" Figure 2.2 shows what this application looks like in the Chrome browser. The figure shows the browser with its Developer Tools panel opened in the Network tab, so you can see a fragment of what's been downloaded by the browser and how long it took.

Don't be scared by the size of the download; you'll optimize it in chapter 10. Because you're using live-server, as soon as you modify and save the code of this application, it'll reload the page in the browser with the latest code version. Now let's apply what you've learned to an application that's more complex than Hello World.

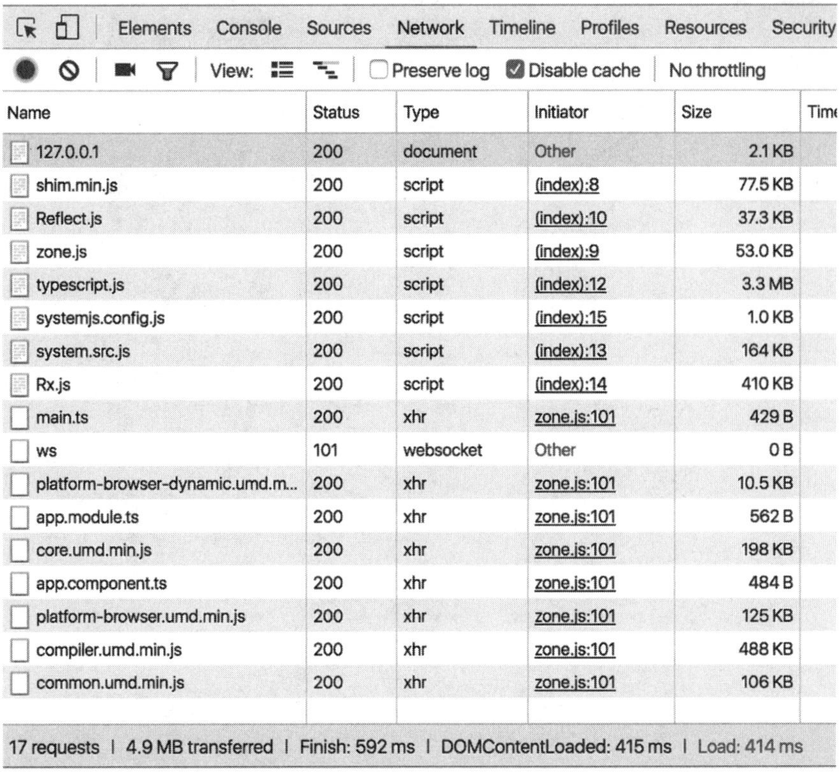

Name	Status	Type	Initiator	Size	Time
127.0.0.1	200	document	Other	2.1 KB	
shim.min.js	200	script	(index):8	77.5 KB	
Reflect.js	200	script	(index):10	37.3 KB	
zone.js	200	script	(index):9	53.0 KB	
typescript.js	200	script	(index):12	3.3 MB	
systemjs.config.js	200	script	(index):15	1.0 KB	
system.src.js	200	script	(index):13	164 KB	
Rx.js	200	script	(index):14	410 KB	
main.ts	200	xhr	zone.js:101	429 B	
ws	101	websocket	Other	0 B	
platform-browser-dynamic.umd.m...	200	xhr	zone.js:101	10.5 KB	
app.module.ts	200	xhr	zone.js:101	562 B	
core.umd.min.js	200	xhr	zone.js:101	198 KB	
app.component.ts	200	xhr	zone.js:101	484 B	
platform-browser.umd.min.js	200	xhr	zone.js:101	125 KB	
compiler.umd.min.js	200	xhr	zone.js:101	488 KB	
common.umd.min.js	200	xhr	zone.js:101	106 KB	

Elements   Console   Sources   Network   Timeline   Profiles   Resources   Security

View: ☰ ▚   ☐ Preserve log   ☑ Disable cache | No throttling

17 requests | 4.9 MB transferred | Finish: 592 ms | DOMContentLoaded: 415 ms | Load: 414 ms

Figure 2.2   Running the app from the npm-managed project

2.5   *Hands-on: getting started with the online auction*

Every chapter from here on will end with a hands-on section containing instructions for developing a certain aspect of the online auction, where people can see a list of featured products, view details for a specific product, perform a product search, and monitor bidding by other users. You'll gradually add code to this application to practice what you'll learn in each chapter. The source code that comes with this book includes the completed version of each chapter's hands-on section in the auction folder, but we encourage you to try these exercises on your own.

In this exercise, you'll set up the development environment and create the initial auction project layout. You'll create the home page, split it into Angular components, and create a service to fetch products. If you follow all the instructions in this section, the auction's home page should look like what you see in figure 2.3.

You'll use gray rectangles provided by the convenient Placehold.it service (http://placehold.it), which generates placeholders of specified sizes. To see these generated images, you'll have to be connected to the internet while running this application. The following sections contain the instructions that you should follow to complete this hands-on exercise.

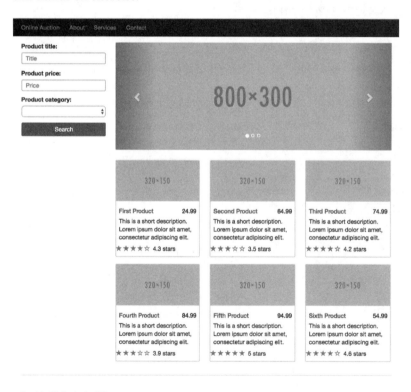

Figure 2.3   The online auction home page

NOTE If you prefer to just read the code of the working version of the online auction, use the code for the auction directory that comes with this chapter. To run the provided code, switch to the auction directory, run `npm install` to install all the required dependencies in the node_modules directory, and start the application by running the `npm start` command.

2.5.1 Initial project setup

To set up the project, first copy the contents of the angular-seed directory into a separate location and rename it "auction". Next, modify the name and description fields in the package.json file. Open a command window, and switch to the newly created auction directory. Run the command `npm install`, which will create the node_modules directory with dependencies specified in package_json.

In this project, you'll use Twitter Bootstrap as a CSS framework, and the UI library of responsive components. Responsive web design is an approach that allows you to create sites that change layout based on the width of the user's device viewport. The term *responsive components* means that the components' layout can adapt to the screen size.

Because the Bootstrap library is built on top of jQuery, you need to run the following commands to install them:

```
npm install bootstrap --save
npm install jquery --save
```

> **Install Bootstrap. The --save option will add this dependency to the package.json file.**

> **The Bootstrap package doesn't specify jQuery as a dependency, so you have to install it separately. Such dependencies are also known as peer dependencies.**

TIP We recommend you use an IDE like WebStorm or Visual Studio Code. Most of the steps required to complete this hands-on project can be performed inside the IDE. WebStorm even allows you to open the Terminal window inside the IDE.

Now create a systemjs.config.js file to store the SystemJS configuration. You'll include this file in the `<script>` tag in index.html.

Listing 2.15 systemjs.config.js file

> **Instructs the TypeScript compiler of SystemJS to preserve decorators metadata in the transpiled code, because Angular relies on annotations to discover and register components**

```
System.config({
    transpiler: 'typescript',
    typescriptOptions: {emitDecoratorMetadata: true,
        target: "ES5",
        module: "commonjs"},
    map: {
        '@angular': 'node_modules/@angular',
        'rxjs'    : 'node_modules/rxjs'
    },
    paths: {
        'node_modules/@angular/*': 'node_modules/@angular/*/bundles'
```

> **Transpiles the code into the ES5 syntax**

> **Uses CommonJS module format**

```
        },
        meta: {
            '@angular/*': {'format': 'cjs'}
        },
        packages: {
            'app'                                    : {main: 'main',
            ➥ defaultExtension: 'ts'},
            'rxjs'                                   : {main: 'Rx'},
            '@angular/core'                          : {main: 'core.umd.min.js'},
            '@angular/common'                        : {main: 'common.umd.min.js'},
            '@angular/compiler'                      : {main: 'compiler.umd.min.js'},
            '@angular/platform-browser'              : {main: 'platform-
            ➥ browser.umd.min.js'},
            '@angular/platform-browser-dynamic': {main: 'platform-browser-
            ➥ dynamic.umd.min.js'}
        }
    });
```

> **You'll keep your application code in the app directory, and the code to launch the auction application will be located in the main.ts file.**

The systemjs.config.js file has to be included in index.html as shown in the next section in listing 2.9. This configuration of the package app allows you to use the line `<script>System.import ('app')</script>` in index.html, which will load the content of app/main.ts.

This completes the configuration of the development environment for the auction project. You're now ready to start writing the application code.

> **NOTE** At the time of writing, the Angular team is developing Angular Material components for Angular (see https://material.angular.io), which you may want to use instead of Twitter Bootstrap when it's ready.

2.5.2   *Developing the home page*

In this exercise, you'll create a home page that will be split into several Angular components. This makes the code easier to maintain and allows you to reuse components in other views. In figure 2.4, you can see the home page with all the components highlighted.

You'll need to create directories for storing all the components and services of the application, as follows:

```
app
└── components
    ├── application
    ├── carousel
    ├── footer
    ├── navbar
    ├── product-item
    ├── search
    └── stars
└── services
```

Each directory inside the components directory has code for the corresponding component. This allows you to keep all files related to a single component together. Most

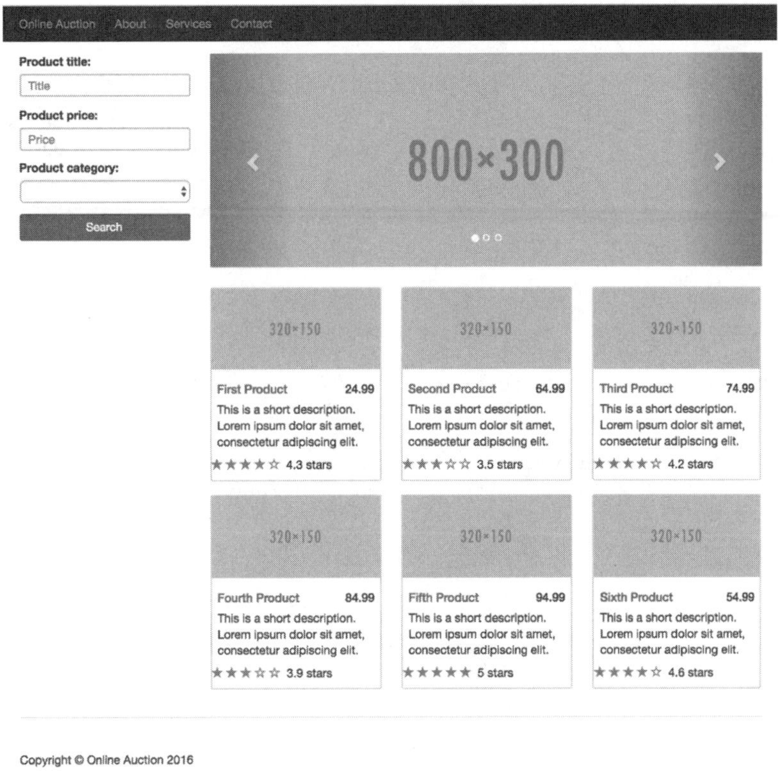

Figure 2.4   The online auction home page with highlighted components

of the components consist of two files—an HTML file and a TypeScript file. But sometimes you may want to add a CSS file with component-specific styling. The services directory will contain the file with classes that serve data to the application.

The first version of the home page consists of seven components. In this exercise, we'll discuss and you'll create the three the most interesting components, located in the application, product-item, and stars directories. This will give you a chance to write some code, and at the end of this exercise you can copy the rest of the components into your project directory.

> **NOTE**   In the hands-on section in chapter 3, you'll refactor the code to integrate the carousel and products into `HomeComponent`.

The entry point of the application is index.html. You've copied this file from the angular-seed directory, and now you'll need to modify it. The index.html file is rather small, and it won't grow much because most of your dependencies will be loaded by SystemJS, and the entire UI is represented by a single Angular root (top level) component that will internally use child components.

Listing 2.16   index.html

Adds the Bootstrap CSS

```html
<!DOCTYPE html>
<html>
<head>
  <title>CH2: Online Auction</title>
  <link rel="stylesheet" href="node_modules/bootstrap/dist/css/
  ➥ bootstrap.css">

  <script src="node_modules/jquery/dist/jquery.min.js"></script>
  <script src="node_modules/bootstrap/dist/js/bootstrap.min.js"></script>

  <script src="node_modules/core-js/client/shim.min.js"></script>
  <script src="node_modules/zone.js/dist/zone.js"></script>

  <script src="node_modules/typescript/lib/typescript.js"></script>
  <script src="node_modules/systemjs/dist/system.src.js"></script>
  <script src="systemjs.config.js"></script>

  <script>
    System.import('app').catch(function (err) {console.error(err);});
  </script>
</head>
<body>
<auction-application></auction-application>
</body>
</html>
```

Adds Bootstrap and jQuery to support the carousel component

Loads main.ts according to the configuration in systemjs.config.js

The content of the main.ts file in the app directory remains the same as it was in the angular-seed project:

```typescript
import { platformBrowserDynamic } from '@angular/platform-browser-dynamic';
import { AppModule }  from './app.module';
platformBrowserDynamic().bootstrapModule(AppModule);
```

Let's update the app.module.ts file to declare all the components and services that you'll use in the auction app.

Listing 2.17   Updated app.module.ts

```typescript
import { NgModule } from '@angular/core';
import { BrowserModule } from '@angular/platform-browser';
import ApplicationComponent from '. /components/application/application';
import CarouselComponent from "./components/carousel/carousel";
import FooterComponent from "./components/footer/footer";
import NavbarComponent from "./components/navbar/navbar";
import ProductItemComponent from "./components/product-item/product-item";
import SearchComponent from "./components/search/search";
import StarsComponent from "./components/stars/stars";
import {ProductService} from "./services/product-service";
```

```
@NgModule({
    imports:       [ BrowserModule ],
    declarations:  [ ApplicationComponent,
                     CarouselComponent,
                     FooterComponent,
                     NavbarComponent,
                     ProductItemComponent,
                     SearchComponent,
                     StarsComponent],
    providers:     [ProductService],
    bootstrap:     [ ApplicationComponent ]
})
export class AppModule { }
```

Declares all components that your module will use

Declares the provider for the ProductService that you'll inject into the ApplicationComponent a bit later

In this module, you declare all the components and the provider for one service that you're about to create. Declaring a provider for a service is required by the dependency injection mechanism. We'll talk about providers and injection in chapter 4.

THE APPLICATION COMPONENT

The application component is the root component of the auction and is declared as such in the AppModule. It serves as a host for all the other components. The component's source code consists of three files: application.ts, application.html, and application.css. We'll assume you know the basics of CSS, so we won't be going into that file here. We'll go through the first two files.

Let's create ApplicationComponent and save it in the application.ts file located in the app/components/application directory. The content of this file is shown here.

Listing 2.18   application.ts

Turns the Application-Component class into an Angular component by annotating it with the @Component decorator

Imports the classes that implement the product service. These classes will serve you data.

The HTML template will be located in the application.html file.

Uses generics (see appendix B) to ensure that the products array contains only objects of type Product

```
import {Component, ViewEncapsulation} from '@angular/core';
import {Product, ProductService} from '../../services/
    product-service';

@Component({
    selector: 'auction-application',
    templateUrl: 'app/components/application/application.html',
    styleUrls: ['app/components/application/application.css'],
    encapsulation:ViewEncapsulation.None
})

export default class ApplicationComponent {

    products: Array<Product> = [];
```

Selector defines the name of the custom HTML tag used in index.html.

CSS is located in the application.css file.

Exports the ApplicationComponent because it's used in another class: AppModule

```
constructor(private productService: ProductService) {     ◁─┐
    this.products = this.productService.getProducts();         │
}                                                               │
}                                                               │
```

Gets a list of products and assigns them to the products property. All of a component's properties become available in the view template via data binding.

In TypeScript you can ask Angular to inject required objects (such as ProductService) via constructor arguments.

Just declaring the constructor's arguments with a type will instruct Angular to instantiate and inject this object (`ProductService`). Injectable objects need to be configured with providers, and you declared one in the `AppModule` earlier. The `private` qualifier will turn `productService` into a member variable of the class, so you'll access it as `this.productService`.

> **NOTE** Listing 2.18 uses the view encapsulation strategy `ViewEncapsulation` `.None` to apply the styles from application .css not only to the `Application-Component`, but to the entire application. We'll discuss different view encapsulation strategies in chapter 6.

Create the application.html file with the following content.

Listing 2.19   application.html

```html
<auction-navbar></auction-navbar>

<div class="container">
  <div class="row">

    <div class="col-md-3">
      <auction-search></auction-search>
    </div>

    <div class="col-md-9">
      <div class="row carousel-holder">
        <div class="col-md-12">
          <auction-carousel></auction-carousel>
        </div>
      </div>
      <div class="row">
        <div *ngFor="let prod of products" class="col-sm-4 col-lg-4 col-md-4">
          <auction-product-item [product]="prod"></auction-product-item>
        </div>
      </div>
    </div>
  </div>
</div>

<auction-footer></auction-footer>
```

You'll be using multiple custom HTML elements that represent your components: `<auction-navbar>`, `<auction-search>`, `<auction-carousel>`, `<auction-product-item>`, and `<auction-footer>`. You'll add them the same way as `<auction-application>` in index.html.

The most interesting part in this file is how you can display the list of products. Each product will be represented by the same HTML fragment on the web page. Because there are multiple products, you need to render the same HTML multiple times. The `NgFor` directive is used inside a component's `template` to loop through the list of items in the data collection and render HTML markup for each item. You can use the shorthand syntax `*ngFor` to represent the `NgFor` directive.

```
<div *ngFor="let prod of products" class="col-sm-4 col-lg-4 col-md-4">
  <auction-product-item [product]="prod"></auction-product-item>
</div>
```

Because `*ngFor` is in `<div>`, each loop iteration will render a `<div>` with the content of the corresponding `<auction-product-item>` inside. To pass an instance of a product to `ProductComponent`, you use the square brackets for property binding: `[product]="prod"`, where `[product]` refers to the property-named product inside the component represented by `<auction-product-item>`, and prod is a local template variable declared on the fly in the `*ngFor` directive as `let prod`. We'll discuss property bindings in detail in chapter 5.

The `col-sm-4 col-lg-4 col-md-4` styles come from Twitter's Bootstrap library, where the window's width is divided into 12 invisible columns. In this example, you want to allocate 4 columns (one third of the `<div>`'s width) if a device has small (sm means 768 pixels or more), large (lg is for 1200 px or more), and medium (md is for 992 px or more) screen sizes.

Because this doesn't specify any columns for extra-small devices (xs is for screens under 768 px), the entire width of a `<div>` will be allocated for a single `<auction-product>`. To see how the page layout changes for different screen sizes, narrow your browser's window to make it less than 768 pixels wide. You can read more about the Bootstrap grid system in the Bootstrap documentation at http://getbootstrap.com/css/#grid.

> **NOTE** `ApplicationComponent` relies on the existence of other components (such as `ProductItemComponent`) that you'll create in the subsequent steps. If you try to run the auction now, you'll see errors in the Developer Console of your browser.

THE PRODUCT ITEM COMPONENT

In the product-item directory, create a product-item.ts file that declares a `ProductItemComponent` representing a single product item from the auction. The source code of product-item.ts is structured much like the code of application.ts: the `import` statements go on top, and then comes the component class declaration annotated with `@Component`.

Listing 2.20   product-item.ts

```
import {Component, Input} from '@angular/core';
import StarsComponent from 'app/components/stars/stars';
import {Product} from 'app/services/product-service';

@Component({
  selector: 'auction-product-item',
  templateUrl: 'app/components/product-item/product-item.html'
})
export default class ProductItemComponent {
  @Input() product: Product;
}
```

The component's product property is annotated with @Input(). This means the value for this property will be exposed to the parent component, which can bind a value to it. We'll discuss input properties in detail in chapter 6.

Create a product-item.html file to contain the following template of the product component (which will be represented by its price, title, and description).

Listing 2.21   product-item.html

```
<div class="thumbnail">
  <img src="http://placehold.it/320x150">
  <div class="caption">
    <h4 class="pull-right">{{ product.price }}</h4>
    <h4><a>{{ product.title }}</a></h4>
    <p>{{ product.description }}</p>
  </div>
  <div>
    <auction-stars [rating]="product.rating"></auction-stars>
  </div>
</div>
```

Here you use another type of data binding: an expression within double curly braces. Angular evaluates the value of the expression within the braces, turns the result into a string, and replaces this expression in the template with the resulting string. Internally this process is implemented using string interpolation.

Note the <auction-stars> tag that represents the StarsComponent and was declared in AppModule. You bind the value of product.rating to the rating property of the StarsComponent. For this to work, rating must be declared as an input property in the StarsComponent that you'll create next.

THE STARS COMPONENT

The stars component will display the rating of a product. In figure 2.5, you can see that it displays an average rating number of 4.3 as well as star icons representing the rating.

★ ★ ★ ★ ☆ 4.3 stars

Figure 2.5   Stars component

Angular provides component lifecycle hooks (see chapter 6) that allow you to define the callback methods that will be invoked at certain moments of the component's lifecycle. In this component, you'll use the ngOnInit() callback, which will be invoked as soon as an instance of the component is created and its properties are initialized. Create the stars.ts file in the stars directory with the following content.

Listing 2.22 stars.ts

```
import {Component, Input, OnInit} from '@angular/core';
```
Imports the interface OnInit, where ngOnInit() is declared

Marks rating and count as inputs so that other components can assign values to them via data-binding expressions
```
@Component({
    templateUrl: 'app/components/stars/stars.html',
    styles: [` .starrating { color: #d17581; }`],
    selector: 'auction-stars'
})
export default class StarsComponent implements OnInit {
    @Input() count: number = 5;
    @Input() rating: number = 0;
    stars: boolean[] = [];
```
Each element of the array represents a single star to be rendered.

Initializes stars based on the value provided by the parent component
```
    ngOnInit() {
        for (let i = 1; i <= this.count; i++) {
            this.stars.push(i > this.rating);
        }
    }
}
```

The count property specifies the total number of stars to be rendered. If this property isn't initialized by the parent, the component renders five stars by default.

The rating property stores the average rating that determines how many stars should be filled with the color and how many should remain empty. In the stars array, the elements with the false value represent empty stars, and those with true represent stars filled with color.

You initialize the stars array in the ngOnInit() lifecycle callback, which will be used in the template to render stars. ngOnInit() is called only once, right after the component's data-bound properties have been checked for the first time, and before any of its children have been checked. When ngOnInit() is invoked, all properties passed from the parent view are already initialized, so you can use the rating value to compute the values in the stars array.

Alternatively, you could turn stars into a getter to compute it on the fly, but the getter would be invoked each time Angular synchronizes the model with the view. Exactly the same array would be computed multiple times.

Create the template of the StarsComponent in the stars.html file, as shown next.

Listing 2.23   stars.html

```
<p>
  <span *ngFor="let star of stars"
        class="starrating glyphicon glyphicon-star"
        [class.glyphicon-star-empty]="star">
  </span>
  <span>{{ rating }} stars</span>
</p>
```

You already used the NgFor directive and curly braces data-binding expression in ApplicationComponent. Here you bind a CSS class name to an expression: [class .glyphicon-star-empty]="star". If an expression within the double quotes on the right evaluates to true, the glyphicon-star-empty CSS class will be added to the class attribute of the <span> element.

COPYING THE REST OF THE CODE

To finish this project, copy the missing components from the chapter2/auction directory to the corresponding directories of your project:

- The services directory contains the product-service.ts file that declares two classes: Product and ProductService. This is where the data for the auction comes from. We'll provide more details about the content of this file in the hands-on section of chapter 3.
- The navbar directory contains the code for the top navigation bar.
- The footer directory contains the code for the footer of the page.
- The search directory contains the initial code for the SearchComponent, which is a form that you'll develop in chapter 7.
- The carousel directory contains the code that implements a Bootstrap slider in the top portion of the home page.

2.5.3   *Launching the online auction application*

To launch the auction application, open a command window and start live-server in your project directory. You can do it by running the npm start command, which is configured in the package.json file to start the live-server. It'll open the browser, and you should be able to see the home page as shown in figure 2.4. The product details page isn't implemented yet, so the product title links won't work.

We recommend that you use the Chrome browser for development, because it has the best tools for debugging your code. Keep the Developer Tools panel open while running all code samples. If you see unexpected results, check the Console tab for error messages.

Also, there's a great Chrome browser extension called Augury, which is a convenient debugging tool for Angular apps. After installing this extension, you'll see an additional Augury tab in the Chrome development tools panel (see figure 2.6), which allows you to see and modify the values of your app components at runtime.

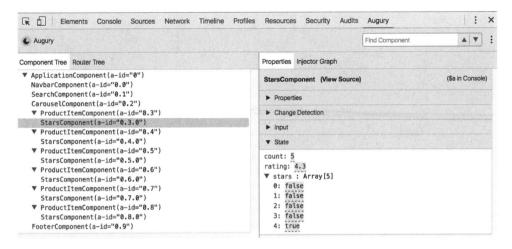

Figure 2.6   The Augury panel

2.6   *Summary*

In this chapter, you've had your first experience writing an Angular application. We briefly covered the main principles and most important building blocks of an Angular application. In future chapters, we'll discuss them in detail. You've also created an initial version of the online auction application. This has shown you how to set up a development environment and structure an Angular project.

- An Angular application is represented by a hierarchy of components that are packaged into modules.
- Each Angular component contains a template for the UI rendering and an annotated class implementing this component's functionality.
- Templates and styles can be either inlined or stored in separate files.
- The SystemJS module loader allows you to split the application into ES6 modules and dynamically assembles everything together at runtime.
- Configuration parameters for SystemJS can be specified in a separate configuration file.
- Using npm for managing dependencies is the simplest way of configuring a new Angular project.

Navigation with
the Angular router

This chapter covers

- Configuring routes
- Passing data while navigating from one route to another
- Having more than one area for navigation (a.k.a. outlet) on the same page using auxiliary routes
- Lazy-loading modules with the router

In chapter 2, you built the home page of the online auction with the intent to create a single-page application (SPA): the main page won't be reloaded, but its parts may change. You now want to add navigation to this application so it'll change the content area of the page (we'll define that a bit later) based on the user's actions. Imagine that the user needs to be able to see product details, bid on products, and chat with sellers. The Angular router allows you to configure and implement such navigation without performing a page reload.

Not only do you want to be able to change the view inside the page, but you may also want to bookmark its URL so you can get to specific product details faster. To do this, you need to assign a unique URL for each view.

In general, you can think of a router as an object responsible for the view state of the application. Every application has one router, and you need to configure the router to make it work.

We'll first cover the main features of the router, and then you'll add a second view (Product Details) to the online auction so that if the user clicks a particular product on the home page, the page's content will change to display the details of the selected product.

3.1 Routing basics

You can think of a SPA as a collection of states, such as Home state, Product Details state, and Shipping state. Each state represents a different view of the same SPA. So far, the online auction has only one view state: the home page.

The online auction (see figure 2.4) has a navigation bar (a component) on top, a search form (another component) on the left, and a footer (yet another component) at the bottom, and you want these components to remain visible all the time. The rest of the page consists of a content area that displays the `<auction-carousel>` and several `<auction-product>` components. You'll reuse this content area (the *outlet*) for displaying different views based on the user's actions.

To do this, you'll need to configure the router so it can display different views in the outlet, *replacing one view with another.* This content area is represented by the tag `<router-outlet>`. Figure 3.1 shows the area you'll use for displaying different views.

> **NOTE** There can be more than one outlet on the page. We'll cover that in section 3.5.

You'll be assigning a component for each view that you want to display in this area. In chapter 2, you didn't create a parent component that would encapsulate the carousel and auction products, but by the end of this chapter you'll refactor the code to create a `HomeComponent` to serve as a parent for the carousel and products. You'll also create `ProductDetailComponent` to represent each product's details. At any given time, the user will see either `HomeComponent` or `ProductDetailComponent` in the `<router-outlet>` area.

The router is responsible for managing client-side navigation, and in section 3.1.2 we'll provide a high-level overview of what the router is made up of. In the non-SPA world, site navigation is implemented as a series of requests to a server, which refreshes the entire page by sending the appropriate HTML documents to the browser. With SPA, the code for rendering components is already on the client (except for the lazy-loading scenarios), and you just need to replace one view with another.

As the user navigates the application, it can still make requests to the server to retrieve or send data. Sometimes a view (the combination of the UI code and the

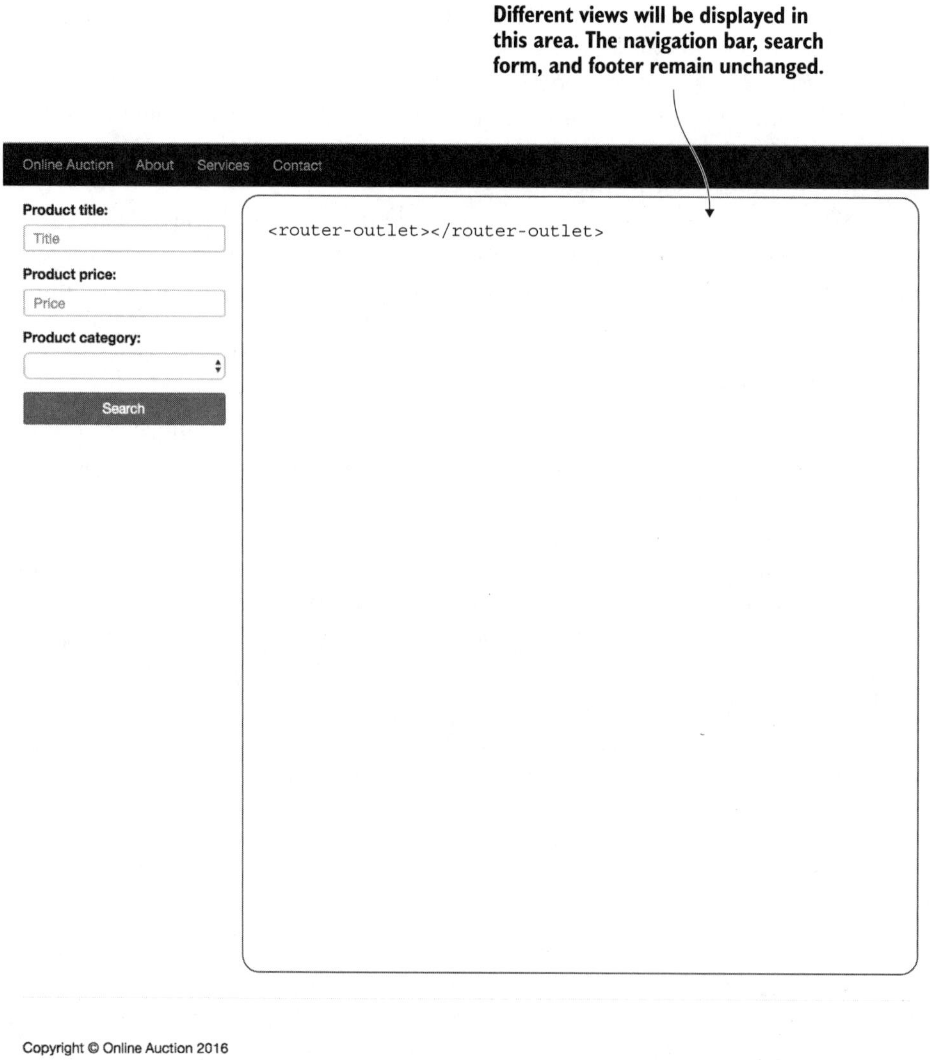
Different views will be displayed in this area. The navigation bar, search form, and footer remain unchanged.
Online Auction
About
Services
Contact
Product title:
Title
Product price:
Price
Product category:
Search
<router-outlet></router-outlet>
Copyright © Online Auction 2016

Figure 3.1 Allocating the area for changing views

data) has everything it needs already downloaded to the browser, but other times a view will communicate with the server by issuing AJAX requests or via WebSockets. Each view will have a unique URL shown in the location bar of the browser, and we'll discuss that next.

3.1.1 Location strategies

At any given time, the browser's location bar displays the URL of the current view. A URL can contain different parts (segments). It starts with a protocol followed by a domain name, and it may include a port number. Parameters that need to be passed to the server may follow a question mark (this is true for HTTP GET requests), like this:

http://mysite.com:8080/auction?someParam=123

Changing any character in the preceding URL results in a new request to the server.

In SPAs, you need the ability to modify the URL without making a server-side request so the application can locate the proper view on the client. Angular offers two location strategies for implementing client-side navigation:

- `HashLocationStrategy`—A hash sign (#) is added to the URL, and the URL segment after the hash uniquely identifies the route to be used as a web page fragment. This strategy works with all browsers, including the old ones.
- `PathLocationStrategy`—This History API–based strategy is supported only in browsers that support HTML5. This is the default location strategy in Angular.

HASH-BASED NAVIGATION

A sample URL that uses hash-based navigation is shown in figure 3.2. Changing any character to the right of the hash sign doesn't cause a direct server-side request, but navigates to the view represented by the path (with or without parameters) after the hash. The hash sign serves as a separator between the base URL and the client-side locations of the required content.

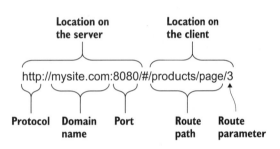

Figure 3.2 Dissecting the URL

Try to navigate a SPA like Gmail, and watch the URL. For the Inbox, it looks like this: https://mail.google.com/mail/u/0/#inbox. Now go to the Sent folder, and the hash portion of the URL will change from *inbox* to *sent*. The client-side JavaScript code invokes the necessary functions to display the Sent view.

But why does the Gmail app still shows you the "Loading…" message when you switch to the Sent box? The JavaScript code of the Sent view can still make AJAX requests to the server to get the new data, but it doesn't load any additional code, markup, or CSS from the server.

In this book, we'll use hash-based navigation, and `@NgModule` will include the following `providers` value (providers are explained in chapter 4):

```
providers:[{provide: LocationStrategy, useClass: HashLocationStrategy}]
```

HISTORY API-BASED NAVIGATION

The browser's History API allows you to move back and forth through the user's navigation history as well as programmatically manipulate the history stack (see "Manipulating the browser history" in the Mozilla Developer Network, http://mng.bz/i64G).

In particular, the pushState() method is used to attach a segment to the base URL as the user navigates your SPA.

Consider the following URL: http://mysite.com:8080/products/page/3. The products/page/3 URL segment can be pushed (attached) to the base URL programmatically without using the hash tag. If the user navigates from page 3 to 4, the application's code will push products/page/4, saving the previous products/page/3 state in the browser history.

Angular spares you from invoking pushState() explicitly—you just need to configure the URL segments and map them to the corresponding components. With the History API–based location strategy, you need to tell Angular what to use as a base URL in your application so it can properly append the client-side URL segments. You can do it in one of two ways:

- Add the <base> tag to the header of index.html, such as <base href="/">.
- Assign a value for the APP_BASE_HREF Angular constant in the root module, and use it as the providers value. The following code snippet uses / as a base URL, but it can be any URL segment that denotes the end of the base URL:

```
import { APP_BASE_HREF } from '@angular/common';
...
@NgModule({
...
  providers:[{provide: APP_BASE_HREF, useValue: '/'}]
})
class AppModule { }
```

3.1.2 The building blocks of client-side navigation

Let's get familiar with the main concepts of implementing client-side navigation using the Angular router. In the Angular framework, the implementation of routing functionality is implemented in a separate RouterModule module. If your application needs routing, make sure your package.json file includes the dependency @angular/router. Our package.json includes the following line: "@angular/router": "3.0.0".

Remember, the goal of this chapter is to explain how to navigate between the different views of a SPA, so the first thing we need to focus on is how to configure the router and add it to the module declaration.

Angular offers the following main players for implementing routing in your application:

- Router—An object that represents the router in the runtime. You can use its navigate() and navigateByUrl() methods to navigate to a route either by the configured route path or by the URL segment, respectively.
- RouterOutlet—A directive that serves as a placeholder within your web page (<router-outlet>) where the router should render the component.
- Routes—An array of routes that map URLs to components to be rendered inside the <router-outlet>.

- RouterLink—A directive for declaring a link to a route if the navigation is done using HTML anchor tags. RouterLink may contain parameters to be passed to the route's component.
- ActivatedRoute—An object that represents the route or routes that are currently active.

You configure routes in a separate array of objects of type Route. Here's an example:

```
const routes: Routes = [
    {path: '',        component: HomeComponent},
    {path: 'product', component: ProductDetailComponent}
];
```

Because route configuration is done on the module level, you need to import routes in the @NgModule decorator. If you declare routes for the root modules, you should use the forRoot() method, like this:

```
import { BrowserModule } from '@angular/platform-browser';
import { RouterModule } from '@angular/router';
...
@NgModule({
  imports: [ BrowserModule, RouterModule.forRoot(routes)],
    ...
})
```

If you're configuring routes for a feature module (not for the root one), use the forChild() method:

```
import { CommonModule } from '@angular/common';
import { RouterModule } from '@angular/router';
...
@NgModule({
  imports: [ CommonModule, RouterModule.forChild(routes)],
    ...
})
```

Note that in feature modules you import CommonModule instead of BrowserModule.

In a typical scenario, you'll be implementing navigation by performing the following steps:

1 Configure your app routes to map the URL segments to the corresponding components, and pass the configuration object to either RouterModule.forRoot() or RouterModule.forChild() as an argument. If some of the components expect to receive input values, you can use route parameters.
2 Import the returned value of forRoot() or forChild() in the @NgModule decorator.
3 Define the outlet where the router will render components by using the <router-outlet> tag.

4 Add HTML anchor tags with bounded [routerLink] properties (square brackets denote property binding), so that when the user clicks the link, the router will render the corresponding component. Think of a [routerLink] as a client-side replacement for the href attribute of the HTML anchor tag.

Invoking the router's navigate() method is an alternative to using [routerLink] for navigating to a route. In either case, the router will find a match to the provided path, will create (or find) the instance of the specified component, and will update the URL accordingly.

Let's illustrate these steps in a sample application (see the router_samples folder in the code samples). Say you want to create a root component that has two links, Home and Product Details, at the top of the page. The application should render either HomeComponent or ProductDetailComponent, depending on which link the user clicks. HomeComponent will render the text "Home Component" on a red background, and ProductDetailComponent will render "Product Details Component" on cyan. Initially the web page should display HomeComponent, as shown in figure 3.3. After the user clicks the Product Details link, the router should display Product-DetailComponent, as shown in figure 3.4.

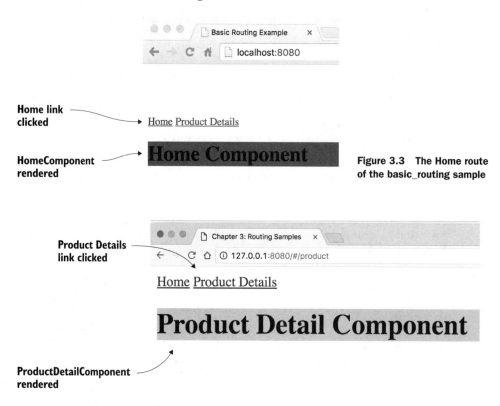

Figure 3.3   The Home route of the basic_routing sample

Figure 3.4   The Product Details route of the basic_routing sample

The main goal of this exercise is to get familiar with the router, so the components will be very simple. Here is the code of HomeComponent.

Listing 3.1 `HomeComponent`

```
import {Component} from '@angular/core';

@Component({
    selector: 'home',
    template: '<h1 class="home">Home Component</h1>',
    styles: ['.home {background: red}']})
export class HomeComponent {}
```

The code of ProductDetailComponent looks similar, but instead of red it uses a cyan background.

Listing 3.2 `ProductDetailComponent`

```
import {Component} from '@angular/core';

@Component({
    selector: 'product',
    template: '<h1 class="product">Product Details Component</h1>',
    styles: ['.product {background: cyan}']})
export class ProductDetailComponent {}
```

Configure the routes in a separate file called app.routing.ts.

Listing 3.3 app.routing.ts

Imports Routes and RouterModule

If there are no URL segments after the base URL, renders the HomeComponent in the router outlet

```
import { Routes, RouterModule } from '@angular/router';
import {HomeComponent} from "./home";
import {ProductDetailComponent} from "./product";

const routes: Routes = [
    {path: '',        component: HomeComponent},
    {path: 'product', component: ProductDetailComponent}
];

export const routing = RouterModule.forRoot(routes);
```

Exports the router configuration so it can be imported by the root module

If the URL has the "product" segment after the base URL, renders ProductDetailComponent in the router outlet

HomeComponent is mapped to a path containing an empty string, which implicitly makes it a default route.

The `Routes` type is just a collection of the objects with properties declared in the `Route` interface, as shown here:

```
export interface Route {
    path?: string;
    pathMatch?: string;
    component?: Type | string;
    redirectTo?: string;
    outlet?: string;
    canActivate?: any[];
    canActivateChild?: any[];
    canDeactivate?: any[];
    canLoad?: any[];
    data?: Data;
    resolve?: ResolveData;
    children?: Route[];
    loadChildren?: string;
}
```

TypeScript interfaces are described in appendix B, but we'd like to remind you that the question mark after the property name means that this property is optional. You can pass to the function `forRoot()` or `forChild()` a configuration object that only has a couple of properties filled in. In the basic app, you use just two properties of `Route`: path and component.

The next step is to create a root component that will contain the links for navigating between the Home and Product Details views. The root `AppComponent` will be located in the app.component.ts file.

> **Listing 3.4 app.component.ts**

```
import {Component} from '@angular/core';
@Component({
    selector: 'app',
    template: `
      <a [routerLink]="['/']">Home</a>
      <a [routerLink]="['/product']">Product Details</a>
      <router-outlet></router-outlet>
    `
})
export class AppComponent {}
```

Creates a link that binds routerLink to the empty path

Creates a link that binds routerLink to the path /product

The `<router-outlet>` specifies the area on the page where the router will render the components (one at a time).

Note the use of brackets in the `<a>` tags. The square brackets around `routerLink` denote property binding, and the brackets on the right represent an array with one element (for example, `['/']`). We'll show you examples of an array with two or more elements later in this chapter. The second anchor tag has the `routerLink` property bound to the component configured for the /product path. The matched components will be rendered in the area marked with `<router-outlet>`, which in this app is located below the anchor tags.

None of the components are aware of the router configuration, because it's the module's business. Let's declare and bootstrap the root module. For simplicity, implement these two actions in the same main.ts file.

Listing 3.5   main.ts

```
import { platformBrowserDynamic } from '@angular/platform-browser-dynamic';
import { NgModule }       from '@angular/core';
import { BrowserModule } from '@angular/platform-browser';
import { AppComponent }  from './components/app.component';
import {HomeComponent} from "./components/home";
import {ProductDetailComponent} from "./components/product";
import {LocationStrategy, HashLocationStrategy} from '@angular/common';
import {routing} from './components/app.routing';              ⟵─┐ Imports the routes
                                                                   │ configuration
@NgModule({
    imports:       [ BrowserModule,
                     routing ],                   ⟵─┐ Adds the routes configuration
    declarations: [ AppComponent,                    │ to @NgModule
                    HomeComponent,
                    ProductDetailComponent],
    providers:[{provide: LocationStrategy, useClass: HashLocationStrategy}], ⟵─┐
    bootstrap:    [ AppComponent ]
})                                              Lets the dependency injection mechanism
class AppModule { }                             know that you want HashLocationStrategy

platformBrowserDynamic().bootstrapModule(AppModule);     ⟵──── Loads the app
```

The module's `providers` property is an array of registered providers (there's just one in this example) for dependency injection, which will be covered in chapter 4. At this point, you just need to know that although the default location strategy is `PathLocationStrategy`, you want Angular to use the `HashLocationStrategy` class for routing (note the hash sign in the URL in figure 3.4).

NOTE Angular removes trailing slashes from URLs. You can see how the URLs for these routes look in figures 3.3 and 3.4. Child components may have their own route configurations, as we'll discuss later in this chapter.

Running the sample applications in this book

Typically the code that comes with each chapter has several sample applications. To run a particular application, you'll need to make a one-line change in the configuration file of SystemJS to specify the name of the main script that you want to run.

To run this application using the code that comes with the book, make sure that the main script that bootstraps your root module is properly mapped in systemjs.config.js. For example, this is how to specify that the main script is located in the main-param.ts file:

```
packages: {
   'app': {main: 'main-param', defaultExtension: 'ts'}
}
```

The same applies to the other sample applications in this and other chapters.

The main script of this application is located in the main.ts file in the directory samples. To run this app, make sure that the systemjs.config.js file lists main.ts in the app package, and then start the live-server from the project root directory.

SystemJS and on-the-fly transpiling

TypeScript offers an elegant declarative syntax for implementing many Angular features, including routing. We use SystemJS in our code samples, and the transpiling of TypeScript into JavaScript is done on the fly when the application code is loaded into the browser.

But what if the application doesn't work as expected? If you open the Developer Tools panel in your browser, you'll see that each file with the extension .ts has a corresponding .ts!transpiled file. This is a transpiled version of the code that may be handy if you need to see the actual JavaScript code that runs in the browser. The following figure shows the Chrome Developer Tools panel with the source code of product.ts!transpiled.

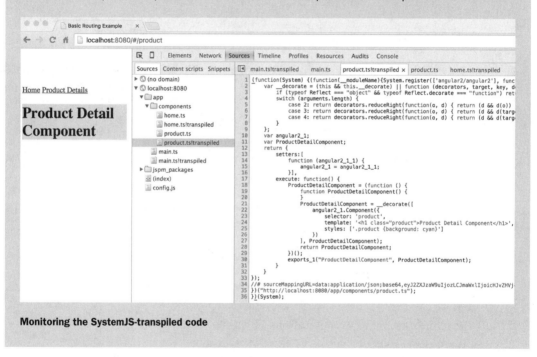

Monitoring the SystemJS-transpiled code

NOTE Angular comes with a Location class that allows you to navigate to an absolute URL by invoking its go(), forward(), and back() methods, along with some others. Location should be used only if you need to interact with the URL outside of the Angular router. You'll see an example of using Location in chapter 9, where you'll write scripts for unit testing.

3.1.3 *Navigating to routes with navigate()*

In the basic_routing code example in the previous section, you arranged the navigation using routerLink in HTML anchor tags. But what if you need to arrange navigation programmatically without asking the user to click a link? Let's modify that code sample to navigate by using the navigate() method. You'll add a button that will also navigate to the ProductDetailComponent, but this time no HTML anchors will be used.

Listing 3.6 (main-navigate.ts) will invoke the navigate() method on the Router instance that will be injected into the RootComponent via its constructor. For simplicity, you place the module and routes declaration, the bootstrap, and the AppComponent in the same file, but in real-world projects you should keep them separate as you did in the previous section.

Listing 3.6 main-navigate.ts

```
import {Component} from '@angular/core';
import { platformBrowserDynamic } from '@angular/platform-browser-dynamic';
import { NgModule }        from '@angular/core';
import { BrowserModule } from '@angular/platform-browser';
import {LocationStrategy, HashLocationStrategy} from '@angular/common';
import { Router, Routes, RouterModule } from '@angular/router';
import {HomeComponent} from "./components/home";
import {ProductDetailComponent} from "./components/product";

const routes: Routes = [
    {path: '',        component: HomeComponent},
    {path: 'product', component: ProductDetailComponent}
];

@Component({
    selector: 'app',
    template: `
        <a [routerLink]="['/']">Home</a>
        <a [routerLink]="['/product']">Product Details!!!</a>
        <input type="button" value="Product Details"
               (click)="navigateToProductDetail()" />      ⟵  Clicking this button invokes
        <router-outlet></router-outlet>                         the navigateToProductDetail()
    `                                                           method.
})
class AppComponent {

    constructor(private _router: Router){}      ⟵  Angular will inject the instance of
                                                    Router into the router variable.
    navigateToProductDetail(){
        this._router.navigate(["/product"]);    ⟵  Navigates to the configured product
    }                                               route programmatically
}

@NgModule({
    imports:      [ BrowserModule, RouterModule.forRoot(routes)],
    declarations: [ AppComponent, HomeComponent, ProductDetailComponent],
```

```
    providers:[{provide: LocationStrategy, useClass: HashLocationStrategy}],
    bootstrap:     [ AppComponent ]
})
class AppModule { }

platformBrowserDynamic().bootstrapModule(AppModule);
```

This example uses a button to navigate to the product route, but this can be done programmatically without requiring user actions. Just invoke the navigate() method (or navigateByUrl()) from your application code when necessary. You'll see another example of using this API in chapter 9, where we'll explain how to unit-test the router.

> **TIP** Having a reference to the Router instance allows you to check if a particular route is active by calling isRouteActive().

Handling 404 errors

If the user enters a nonexistent URL in your application, the router won't be able to find a matching route and will print an error message on the browser's console, leaving the user to wonder why no navigation is happening. Consider creating an application component that will be displayed whenever the application can't find the matching component.

For example, you could create a component named _404Component and configure it with the wildcard path **:

```
[
  {path: '',            component: HomeComponent},
  {path: 'product', component: ProductDetailComponent},
  {path: '**', component: _404Component}
])
```

Now whenever the router can't match the URL to any component, it'll render the content of _404Component instead. You can see it in action by running the application main-with-404.ts that comes with the book. Just enter a nonexistent URL in the browser, such as http://localhost:8080/#/wrong.

The wildcard route configuration has to be the last element in the array of routes. The router always treats the wildcard route as a match, so any routes listed after the wildcard one won't be considered.

3.2   *Passing data to routes*

The basic routing application showed how you can display different components in a predefined outlet on the window, but you often need not only to display a component, but also to pass some data to it. For example, if you navigate from the Home to the Product Details route, you need to pass the product ID to the component that represents the destination route, such as ProductDetailComponent.

The component that represents the destination route can receive passed parameters via its constructor argument of type `ActivatedRoute`. Besides the passed parameters, `ActivatedRoute` stores the route's URL segment, the outlet. We'll show you how to extract route parameters from an `ActivatedRoute` object in this section.

3.2.1 *Extracting parameters from ActivatedRoute*

When the user navigates to the Product Details route, you need to pass the product ID to this route to display details for the particular product. Let's modify the code of the application in the previous section so `RootComponent` can pass the product ID to `ProductDetailComponent`.

The new version of this component will be called `ProductDetailComponentParam`, and Angular will inject an object of type `ActivatedRoute` into it. The `ActivatedRoute` object will contain the information about the component loaded into the outlet.

Listing 3.7 `ProductDetailComponentParam`

```
import {Component} from '@angular/core';
import {ActivatedRoute} from '@angular/router';

@Component({
  selector: 'product',
  template: `<h1 class="product">Product Details for Product:
  ➥ {{productID}}</h1>`,
  styles: ['.product {background: cyan}']
})
export class ProductDetailComponentParam {
  productID: string;

  constructor(route: ActivatedRoute) {
    this.productID = route.snapshot.params['id'];
  }
}
```

Displays the received product ID using binding

The constructor of this component asks Angular to inject the ActivatedRoute object.

Gets the value of the parameter named id and assigns it to the productID class variable, which is used in the template via binding

The `ActivatedRoute` object will contain all the parameters that are being passed to the component. You just need to declare the constructor's argument, specifying its type, and Angular will know how to instantiate and inject this object. We'll cover dependency injection in detail in chapter 4.

In listing 3.8, you'll change the configuration of the `product` route and `router-Link` to ensure that the value of the product ID will be passed to the `ProductDetail-ComponentParam` component if the user choses to go this route. The new version of the app is called main-param.ts.

Listing 3.8 main-param.ts

```
import {Component} from '@angular/core';
import { platformBrowserDynamic } from '@angular/platform-browser-dynamic';
import { NgModule }      from '@angular/core';
```

```
import { BrowserModule } from '@angular/platform-browser';
import {LocationStrategy, HashLocationStrategy} from '@angular/common';
import { Routes, RouterModule } from '@angular/router';
import {HomeComponent} from "./components/home";
import {ProductDetailComponentParam} from "./components/product-param";

const routes: Routes = [
    {path: '',            component: HomeComponent},
    {path: 'product/:id', component: ProductDetailComponentParam}    ◁──────┐
];
```

**The path property has an
additional URL segment, /:id.**

```
@Component({
    selector: 'app',
    template: `
        <a [routerLink]="['/']">Home</a>
        <a [routerLink]="['/product', 1234]">Product Details</a>    ◁──────┐
        <router-outlet></router-outlet>
    `
})
class AppComponent {}
```

**This time there are two elements in the
array given to routerLink: the path that
the route starts with, and the number
that represents the product ID.**

```
@NgModule({
    imports:        [ BrowserModule, RouterModule.forRoot(routes)],
    declarations: [ AppComponent, HomeComponent, ProductDetailComponentParam],
    providers:[{provide: LocationStrategy, useClass: HashLocationStrategy}],
    bootstrap:      [ AppComponent ]
})
class AppModule { }

platformBrowserDynamic().bootstrapModule(AppModule);
```

The routerLink property for the Product Details link is initialized with a two-element array. The elements of the array build up the path specified in the routes configuration given to the RouterModule.forRoot() method. The first element of the array represents the static part of the route's path: product. The second element represents the variable part of the path: /:id.

For simplicity, you hardcode the ID to be 1234, but if the RootComponent class had a productID variable pointing at the appropriate object, you could write { productID} instead of 1234. For the Product Details route, Angular will construct the URL segment /product/1234. Figure 3.5 shows how the Product Details view will be rendered in the browser. Note the URL: the router replaced the product/:id path with /product/1234.

Let's review the steps that Angular performed under the hood to render the main page of the application:

1 Check the content of each routerLink to find the corresponding route configurations.
2 Parse the URLs, and replace the parameter names with actual values where specified.
3 Build the <a href=""> tags that the browser understands.

Figure 3.5   The Product Details route received the product ID `1234`**.**

Figure 3.6 shows a snapshot of the home page of the application with the Chrome Developer Tools panel open. Because the `path` property of the configured Home route had an empty string, Angular didn't add anything to the base URL of the page. But the anchor under the Product Details link has already been converted into a regular HTML tag. When the user clicks the Product Details link, the router will attach a hash sign and add /product/1234 to the base URL so that the absolute URL of the Product Details view will become http://localhost:8080/#/product/1234.

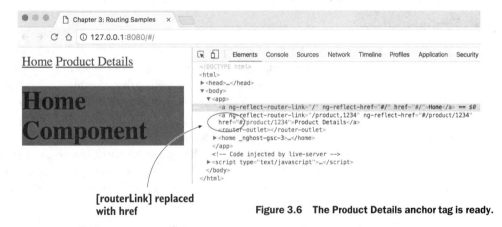

Figure 3.6   The Product Details anchor tag is ready.

3.2.2   *Passing static data to a route*

Parent components will usually pass data to their children, but Angular also offers a mechanism to pass arbitrary data to components at the time of route configuration. For example, besides dynamic data like a product ID, you may need to pass a flag indicating whether the application is running in a production environment. This can be done by using the `data` property of your route configuration.

The route for the product details can be configured as follows:

```
{path: 'product/:id', component: ProductDetailComponentParam , data:
➥ [{isProd: true}]}
```

The data property can contain an array of arbitrary key-value pairs. When the router opens ProductDetailComponentParam, the data value will be located in the data property of the ActivatedRoute.snapshot:

```
export class ProductDetailComponentParam {
  productID: string;
  isProdEnvironment: string;

  constructor(route: ActivatedRoute) {
    this.productID = route.snapshot.params['id'];

    this.isProdEnvironment = route.snapshot.data[0]['isProd'];
    console.log("this.isProdEnvironment = " + this.isProdEnvironment);
  }
}
```

Passing data to a route via the data property isn't an alternative to configuring parameters in the path property, as in path: 'product/:id', but it can come in handy when you need to pass some data to a route during the configuration phase, such as whether it's a production or QA environment. The application that implements this functionality is located in the main-param-data.ts file.

3.3   *Child routes*

An Angular application is a tree of components that have parent-child relations. Each component is well encapsulated, and you have full control over what you expose to the rest of the application's scripts and what you keep private within the component. Any component can have its own styles that won't mix with the parent's styles. A component can also have its own dependency injectors. A child component can have its own routes, but all routes are configured outside of any component.

In the previous section, you configured the routes to show the content of either HomeComponent or ProductDetailComponent in the router-outlet of AppComponent. Imagine now that you want to enable ProductDetailComponent (the child) to show either the product description or the seller's info.

This means that you want to add the configuration of child routes for Product-DetailComponent. You'll use the children property of the Route interface for this:

```
[ {path: '',              component: HomeComponent},
  {path: 'product/:id', component: ProductDetailComponent,
    children: [
      {path: '', component: ProductDescriptionComponent},
      {path: 'seller/:id', component: SellerInfoComponent}
    ]}
]
```

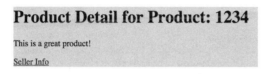

Home Product Details

Product Detail for Product: 1234

This is a great product!

Seller Info

Figure 3.7   The Product Description route

Figure 3.7 shows how the application will look once the user clicks the Product Details link on the root component, which renders `ProductDetailComponent` (the child) showing `ProductDescription`. This is the default route of the child, because its `path` property has an empty string.

Figure 3.8 shows the application after the user clicks the Product Details link and then on Seller Info.

Home Product Details

Product Detail for Product: 1234

The seller of this product is Mary Lou (98%)

Seller Info

Figure 3.8   The child route renders
`SellerInfo.`

> **NOTE** If you read the electronic version of this book, you'll see that the seller's info is shown on a yellow background. We did this on purpose to discuss the styling of components a bit later in this chapter.

To implement the views shown in figures 3.7 and 3.8, you'll modify `ProductDetail-Component` so it also has two children, `SellerInfoComponent` and `ProductDescrip-tionComponent`, and its own `<router-outlet>`. Figure 3.9 shows the hierarchy of components that you're going to implement.

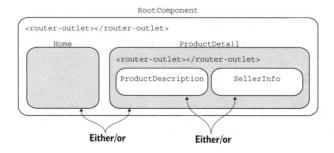

Figure 3.9   The routes hierarchy in the basic_routing app

The entire code of this example with the child routes is located in main-child.ts, shown next.

```
import {Component} from '@angular/core';
import { platformBrowserDynamic } from '@angular/platform-browser-dynamic';
import { NgModule }       from '@angular/core';
import { BrowserModule } from '@angular/platform-browser';
import {LocationStrategy, HashLocationStrategy} from '@angular/common';
import { Routes, RouterModule } from '@angular/router';
import {HomeComponent} from "./components/home";
import {ProductDetailComponent} from './components/product-child';
import {ProductDescriptionComponent} from './components/product-description';
import {SellerInfoComponent} from './components/seller';

const routes: Routes = [
    {path: '',               component: HomeComponent},
    {path: 'product/:id', component: ProductDetailComponent,
        children: [
          {path: '',              component: ProductDescriptionComponent},
          {path: 'seller/:id', component: SellerInfoComponent}
        ]}
];

@Component({
    selector: 'app',
    template: `
        <a [routerLink]="['/']">Home</a>
        <a [routerLink]="['/product', 1234]">Product Details</a>
        <router-outlet></router-outlet>
    `
})
class AppComponent {}

@NgModule({
    imports:      [ BrowserModule, RouterModule.forRoot(routes)],
    declarations: [ AppComponent, HomeComponent, ProductDetailComponent,
                    ProductDescriptionComponent, SellerInfoComponent],
    providers:[{provide: LocationStrategy, useClass: HashLocationStrategy}],
    bootstrap:    [ AppComponent ]
})
class AppModule { }

platformBrowserDynamic().bootstrapModule(AppModule);
```

Take another look at the URL in figure 3.8. When the user clicks the Product Details link, the product/1234 segment is added to the URL. The router finds a match to this path in the configuration object and renders ProductDetailComponent in the outlet.

The new version of ProductDetailComponent (product-child.ts) has its own outlet, where it can display either ProductDescriptionComponent (the default) or Seller-InfoComponent.

Listing 3.10 `ProductDetailComponent`

```
import {Component} from '@angular/core';
import {ActivatedRoute} from '@angular/router';

@Component({
    selector: 'product',
    styles: ['.product {background: cyan}'],
    template: `
      <div class="product">
        <h1>Product Details for Product: {{productID}}</h1>
        <router-outlet></router-outlet>
        <p><a [routerLink]="['./seller', 5678]">Seller Info</a></p>
      </div>
    `
})
export class ProductDetailComponent {
  productID: string;

  constructor(route: ActivatedRoute) {
    this.productID = route.snapshot.params['id'];
  }
}
```

> **ProductDetailComponent has its own router-outlet to render its child components one at a time.**

> **When the user clicks this link, Angular adds the /seller/5678 segment to the existing URL and renders SellerInfoComponent.**

> **NOTE** Child components don't need to be imported. Neither Product-DescriptionComponent nor SellerInfoComponent is explicitly mentioned in the template of ProductDetailComponent, and there's no need to list them in the directives property. They're included in AppModule.

By looking at the route configuration for SellerInfoComponent, you'll see that it expects to receive the seller's ID as a parameter. You'll be passing a hard-coded value of 5678 as the seller's ID.

When the user clicks the Seller Info link, the URL will include the product/1234/seller/5678 segment (see figure 3.8). The router will find a match in the configuration object and will display SellerInfoComponent.

> **NOTE** This version of ProductDetailComponent has only one link to open the seller's info. To navigate from the seller route back to /product, the user can just click the web browser's Back button.

ProductDescriptionComponent is trivial.

Listing 3.11 `ProductDescriptionComponent`

```
import {Component} from '@angular/core';

@Component({
    selector: 'product-description',
    template: '<p>This is a great product!</p>'
})
export class ProductDescriptionComponent {}
```

Because `SellerInfoComponent` expects to receive the seller's ID, its constructor needs an argument of type `ActivatedRoute` to get the seller ID, as you did in `Product-DetailComponent`.

Listing 3.12   `SellerInfoComponent`

```
import {Component} from '@angular/core';
import {ActivatedRoute} from '@angular/router';

@Component({
    selector: 'seller',
    template: 'The seller of this product is Mary Lou (98%)',
    styles: [':host {background: yellow}']
})
export class SellerInfoComponent {
   sellerID: string;

   constructor(route: ActivatedRoute){
     this.sellerID = route.snapshot.params['id'];
     console.log(`The SellerInfoComponent got the seller id ${this.sellerID}`);
   }
}
```

You use a pseudoclass `:host` to display the content of this component on a yellow background. This will serve as a good segue to a brief discussion of Shadow DOM.

The `:host` pseudoclass selector can be used with elements that are created using Shadow DOM, which provides better encapsulation for components (see the "Shadow DOM Support in Angular" sidebar). Although not all web browsers support Shadow DOM yet, Angular emulates Shadow DOM by default and creates a shadow root. The HTML element associated with this shadow root is called the shadow host.

In listing 3.12, you use `:host` to apply the yellow background color to `SellerInfo-Component`, which serves as a shadow host. Shadow DOM styles of the components aren't merged with the styles of the global DOM, and the IDs of the component's HTML tags won't overlap with the IDs of the DOM.

Deep linking

Deep linking is the ability to create a link to specific content inside a web page rather than to the entire page. In the basic routing applications, you've seen examples of deep linking:

- The URL http://localhost:8080/#/product/1234 links not just to the Product Details page, but to a specific view representing the product with an ID of 1234.
- The URL http://localhost:8080/#/product/1234/seller/5678 links even deeper. It shows the information about the seller with an ID of 5678 who sells the product whose ID is 1234.

You can easily see deep linking in action by copying the link http://localhost:8080/#/product/1234/seller/5678 from the application running in Chrome and pasting it into Firefox or Safari.

Shadow DOM support in Angular

Shadow DOM is a part of the Web Components standards. Every web page is represented by a tree of DOM objects, but Shadow DOM allows you to encapsulate a subtree of HTML elements to create a boundary between one component and another. Such a subtree is rendered as part of the HTML document, but its elements aren't attached to the main DOM tree. In other words, the Shadow DOM places a wall between the DOM content and the internals of the HTML component.

When you add a custom tag to a web page, it includes an HTML fragment, and with Shadow DOM this fragment is scoped to the component without merging with the DOM of the web page. With Shadow DOM, the CSS styles of the custom component won't be merged with the main DOM CSS, preventing possible conflicts in rendering styles.

Open any YouTube video in the Chrome browser, which natively supports Shadow DOM. At the time of this writing, the video player is represented by the tag `video`, which you can find by opening the Developer Tools and browsing the content under the Elements tab as shown in the following figure.

```
▼<video class="video-stream html5-main-video" style="width: 640px; height: 360px;
caedbe13-d34a-400c-adb1-82a713307b24">
  ▼ #shadow-root (user-agent)
    ▼<div pseudo="-webkit-media-controls">
      ▼<div pseudo="-webkit-media-controls-overlay-enclosure">
        ▼<input type="button" style="display: none;">
          ▼ #shadow-root (user-agent)
            ""
        </input>
      </div>
      ►<div pseudo="-webkit-media-controls-enclosure">…</div>
    </div>
</video>
```

The <video> tag on a YouTube page

Although the video player consists of the content area and a toolbar with a dozen controls (the Play button, the audio slider, and so on), they're all encapsulated inside the shadow root. From the main DOM perspective, this page contains a "Lego block" `<video>`. To peek inside of this tag, you'd need to select the Show User Agent Shadow DOM option in the Developer Tools settings.

In Angular components, you specify the HTML markup in the `template` or `template-Url` property of the `@Component` annotation. If a web browser supports Shadow DOM natively, or you requested that Angular should emulate it, the component's HTML isn't merged with the global DOM object of the web page. In Angular, you can specify Shadow DOM mode by setting the `encapsulation` property in the `@Component` annotation to one of the following values:

- `ViewEncapsulation.Emulated`—Emulates encapsulation of Shadow DOM (the default). This instructs Angular to generate unique attributes for the styles of the component and won't merge its styles with the styles of the web page's DOM. For example, if you open Developer Tools in Chrome while navigating to `Seller-InfoComponent`, its HTML markup will look like this:

(continued)

```
<head>
...
  <style>[_nghost-yls-7] {background: yellow;}</style>
</head>
...
<seller _nghost-yls-7="" _ngcontent-yls-6="">
  <p _ngcontent-yls-7=""></p>
  The seller of this product is Mary Lou (98% positive feedback)
</seller>
```

- `ViewEncapsulation.Native`—Uses the Shadow DOM that's natively supported by the browser. The HTML and styles aren't merged with the DOM of the web page. You should use this option only if you're sure that the user's browser supports Shadow DOM; otherwise an error is thrown. In this mode, the styles of `SellerInfoComponent` won't be added to the `<head>` section of the page, but all styles of the component and its parents will be encapsulated inside the component.

```
▼<seller _ngcontent-jme-8>
  ▼#shadow-root
      <style>:host {background: yellow}</style>
      <p></p>
      "The seller of this product is Mary Lou (98% positive feedback) "
      <style>.home[_ngcontent-jme-3] {
      background: red;
      }</style>
      <style>.product[_ngcontent-jme-5] {
      background: cyan;
      }</style>
</seller>
```

The shadow root encapsulates all styles.

- `ViewEncapsulation.None`—Doesn't use Shadow DOM encapsulation. All the markup and styles will be integrated into the global web page DOM. The `:host` selector won't work in this mode, because there won't be any shadow host. You can still style the `SellerInfoComponent`, referring to the component by its selector:

```
import {Component, ViewEncapsulation} from '@angular/core';

@Component({
    selector: 'seller',
    template: 'The seller of this product is Mary Lou (98%)',
    styles: ['seller {background: yellow}'],
    encapsulation: ViewEncapsulation.None
})
export class SellerInfoComponent {}
```

Angular won't generate any additional style attributes and will add the following line to the `<head>` section of the page:

```
<style>seller {background: yellow}</style>
```

In section 6.2.3, you'll see how `ViewEncapsulation` affects the UI rendering with and without Shadow DOM.

3.4   Guarding routes

Now that you know how to arrange basic navigation using the router, let's consider some scenarios that require validation to be performed to decide if the user (or a program) is allowed to navigate to or leave the route:

- Open the route only if the user is authenticated and authorized to do so.
- Display a multipart form that consists of several components, and the user is allowed to navigate to the next section of the form only if the data entered in the current section is valid.
- Remind the user about unsaved changes if they try to navigate from the route.

The router has hooks that give you more control over the navigation to and from a route. You can use these hooks to implement any of preceding scenarios to *guard* the routes.

> **NOTE** Angular includes a number of component lifecycle hooks that allow you to handle important events in the life of a component. We'll cover them in chapter 6.

In section 3.1, we mentioned that the `Routes` type is an array of items that conforms to the `Route` interface, shown here:

```
export interface Route {
    path?: string;
    pathMatch?: string;
    component?: Type | string;
    redirectTo?: string;
    outlet?: string;
    canActivate?: any[];
    canActivateChild?: any[];
    canDeactivate?: any[];
    canLoad?: any[];
    data?: Data;
    resolve?: ResolveData;
    children?: Route[];
    loadChildren?: string;
}
```

While configuring the previous routes, you used three properties from this interface: path, component, and data. Now let's get familiar with the canActivate and can-Deactivate properties, which allow you to hook up the routes with guards. Basically, you need to write a function implementing the validating logic that will return either true or false, and assign it to one of these properties. If canActivate() of the guard returns true, the user can navigate to the route. If canDeactivate() returns true, the user can navigate away from the route. Because both the canActivate and can-Deactivate properties of Route accept an array as a value, you can assign multiple functions (guards) if you need to check more than one condition to allow or forbid the navigation.

Let's update the example from section 3.1.2 (the one with the Home and Product Details links) to illustrate how you can protect the product route from users who aren't logged in. To keep the example simple, you won't use an actual login service but will generate the login status randomly.

You'll create a guard class that implements the interface CanActivate, which declares only one function to implement: canActivate(). This function should contain application logic that returns true or false. If the function returns false (the user isn't logged in), the application won't navigate to the route and will print an error message on the console.

Listing 3.13   LoginGuard class

```
import {CanActivate} from "@angular/router";
import {Injectable} from "@angular/core";

@Injectable()
export class LoginGuard implements CanActivate{

  canActivate() {
      return this.checkIfLoggedIn();
  }

  private checkIfLoggedIn(): boolean{

      // A call to the actual login service would go here
      // For now we'll just randomly return true or false

      let loggedIn:boolean = Math.random() <0.5;

      if(!loggedIn){
          console.log("LoginGuard:
          ➡ The user is not logged in and can't navigate product details");
      }

      return loggedIn;
  }
}
```

As you can see, this implementation of the `canActivate()` function will randomly return `true` or `false`, emulating the user's logged-in status.

The next step is to update the router configuration so it uses your guard. The following code snippet shows how the routes could be configured for an app that has Home and Product Details routes. The latter is protected by `LoginGuard`:

```
[
  {path: '',          component: HomeComponent},
  {path: 'product', component: ProductDetailComponent, canActivate:
➥ [LoginGuard] }
]
```

Adding one or more guards to the array given to the `canActivate` property will automatically invoke all the guards, one after the other. If any of the guards returns `false`, navigating to the route will be prohibited.

But who will instantiate the `LoginGuard` class? Angular will do it for you using its dependency injection mechanism (described in chapter 4), but you have to mention this class in the list of providers that are needed for injection to work. Add the name `LoginGuard` to the list of providers in `@NgModule`:

```
@NgModule({
    imports:      [ BrowserModule, RouterModule.forRoot(routes)],
    declarations: [ AppComponent, HomeComponent, ProductDetailComponent],
    providers:[{provide: LocationStrategy, useClass: HashLocationStrategy}
              LoginGuard],
    bootstrap:    [ AppComponent ]
})
```

The complete code of the main app script (main-with-guard.ts) follows.

Listing 3.14   main-with-guard.ts

```
import {Component} from '@angular/core';
import { platformBrowserDynamic } from '@angular/platform-browser-dynamic';
import { NgModule }      from '@angular/core';
import { BrowserModule } from '@angular/platform-browser';
import {LocationStrategy, HashLocationStrategy} from '@angular/common';
import { Routes, RouterModule } from '@angular/router';
import {HomeComponent} from "./components/home";
import {ProductDetailComponent} from "./components/product";
import {LoginGuard} from "./guards/login.guard";

const routes: Routes = [
    {path: '',          component: HomeComponent},
    {path: 'product', component: ProductDetailComponent,
        canActivate:[LoginGuard] }
];

@Component({
    selector: 'app',
    template: `
```

```
        <a [routerLink]="['/']">Home</a>
        <a [routerLink]="['/product']">Product Details</a>
        <router-outlet></router-outlet>
})
class AppComponent {}

@NgModule({
    imports:      [ BrowserModule, RouterModule.forRoot(routes)],
    declarations: [ AppComponent, HomeComponent, ProductDetailComponent],
    providers:[{provide: LocationStrategy, useClass: HashLocationStrategy},
              LoginGuard],
    bootstrap:    [ AppComponent ]
})
class AppModule { }

platformBrowserDynamic().bootstrapModule(AppModule);
```

If you run this app and click the Product Details link, it'll either navigate to this route or print the error message on the browser console, depending on the randomly generated value in `LoginGuard`. Figure 3.10 shows a screenshot taken after the user clicked the Product Details link but `LoginGuards` decided that the user wasn't logged in.

In this example, you implemented the `canActivate()` method without providing any arguments to it. But this method can be used with the following signature:

```
canActivate(destination: ActivatedRouteSnapshot, state: RouterStateSnapshot)
```

The values of `ActivatedRouteSnapshot` and `RouterStateSnapshot` will be injected by Angular automatically, and this may be quite handy if you want to analyze the current state of the router. For example, if you'd like to know the name of the route the user tried to navigate to, this is how you can do it:

```
canActivate(destination: ActivatedRouteSnapshot, state: RouterStateSnapshot)
    {
      console.log(destination.component.name);
    ...
}
```

Figure 3.10   Clicking the Product Details link is guarded.

TIP If you want to wait for some async data to arrive before navigating to a route, use the `resolve` property while configuring the route. There you can specify a class that implements the `Resolve` interface with the function `resolve()`. The router won't instantiate the configured component until this function returns.

Implementing the `CanDeactivate` interface that controls the process of navigating from a route works similarly. Just create a guard class that implements the method `canDeactivate()`, like this:

```
import {CanDeactivate, Router} from "@angular/router";
import {Injectable} from "@angular/core";

@Injectable()
export class UnsavedChangesGuard implements CanDeactivate{

    constructor(private _router:Router){}

    canDeactivate(){
        return window.confirm("You have unsaved changes.
    ➥ Still want to leave?");

    }
}
```

Don't forget to add the `canDeactivate` property to the route configuration, and to include the new guard in the providers list in the module:

```
@NgModule({
    imports:       [ BrowserModule, RouterModule.forRoot(routes)],
    declarations: [ AppComponent, HomeComponent, ProductDetailComponent],
    providers:[{provide: LocationStrategy, useClass: HashLocationStrategy},
               LoginGuard, UnsavedChangesGuard],
    bootstrap:       [ AppComponent ]
})
```

TIP For a fancier way of displaying alerts and confirmation dialogs, use the `MdDialog` component from the Material Design 2 library (https://github.com/angular/material2).

For more details about the component lifecycle hooks applicable to navigation, refer to the `@angular/router` section in the Angular API documentation (https://angular.io/docs/ts/latest/api/). We'll discuss component lifecycles in chapter 6.

3.5 *Developing a SPA with multiple router outlets*

In the previous section you learned that a child route is represented by a URL consisting of parent and child segments. Your single-page app had a single tag, `<router-outlet>`, where Angular would render the component configured for either the parent or the child. Now we'll discuss how to configure and render sibling routes, meaning routes that are rendered in separate outlets at the same time. Let's see some use cases:

- Suppose a Gmail web client displays the list of emails in your inbox, and you decide to compose a new email. The new view will be displayed on the right side of the window, and you'll be able to switch between the inbox and the draft of the new email without closing either view.
- Imagine a dashboard-like SPA that has several dedicated areas (outlets), and each area can render more than one component (but one at a time). Outlet A can display your stock portfolio either as a table or as a chart, while outlet B shows either the latest news or an advertisement.
- Say you want to add a chat area to a SPA so the user can communicate with a customer service representative while keeping the current route active as well. Basically, you want to add an independent chat route allowing the user to use both routes at the same time and to switch from one route to another.

In Angular, you can implement any of these scenarios by having not only a *primary* outlet, but also named *auxiliary* outlets, which are displayed at the same time as the primary one.

To separate the rendering of components for primary and auxiliary routes, you'll need to add yet another `<router-outlet>` tag, but this outlet must have a name. For example, the following code snippet defines primary and chat outlets:

```
<router-outlet></router-outlet>
<router-outlet name="chat"></router-outlet>
```

Let's add a named route for a chat to the sample application. Figure 3.11 illustrates two routes opened at the same time after the user clicked the Home link and then the Open Chat link. The left side shows the rendering of `HomeComponent` in the primary outlet, and the right side shows `ChatComponent` rendered in a named outlet. Clicking the Close Chat link will remove the content of the named outlet. (We added an HTML `<input>` field to `HomeComponent` and a `<textarea>` to `ChatComponent` so it's easier to see which component has the focus when the user switches between the Home and Chat routes.)

Figure 3.11
Rendering a chat view
with an auxiliary route

Note the parentheses in the URL of the auxiliary route, http://localhost:8080/#home/(chat). Whereas a child route is separated from the parent using the forward slash, an auxiliary route is represented as a URL segment in parentheses. This URL tells you that home and chat are sibling routes.

The code that implements this sample is located in the main_aux.ts file, and it's shown in listing 3.15. We've kept all the required components in the same file for simplicity. Both `HomeComponent` and `ChatComponent` have inlined styles to place them next to each other in the window. `HomeComponent` is styled to get 70% of the available viewport width, and `ChatComponent` will get the remaining 30%.

Listing 3.15 main_aux.ts

```
import {Component} from '@angular/core';
import { platformBrowserDynamic } from '@angular/platform-browser-dynamic';
import { NgModule }       from '@angular/core';
import { BrowserModule } from '@angular/platform-browser';
import {LocationStrategy, HashLocationStrategy} from '@angular/common';
import { Routes, RouterModule } from '@angular/router';

@Component({
    selector: 'home',
    template: `<div class="home">Home Component
               <input type="text" placeholder="Type something here"/>
            ➥ </div>`,
    styles: [`.home {background: red; padding: 15px 0 0 30px;  height: 80px;
         ➥ width:70%;
                    font-size: 30px; float:left; box-sizing:border-box;}`]})
export class HomeComponent {}

@Component({
    selector: 'chat',
    template: `<textarea placeholder="Chat with customer service"
                    class="chat"></textarea>`,
    styles: [`.chat {background: #eee; height: 80px;width:30%;
         ➥ font-size: 24px;
                    float:left; display:block; box-sizing:border-box;} `]})
export class ChatComponent {}

const routes: Routes = [
    {path: '',  redirectTo: 'home', pathMatch: 'full'},
    {path: 'home', component: HomeComponent},
    {path: 'chat', component: ChatComponent, outlet:"aux"}
];

@Component({
    selector: 'app',
    template: `
        <a [routerLink]="['']">Home</a>
        <a [routerLink]="[{outlets: {primary: 'home', aux: 'chat'}}]">
         ➥ Open Chat</a>
        <a [routerLink]="[{outlets: {aux: null}}]">Close Chat</a>
        <br/>
```

Configures the route for the Home component. Because no outlet is specified, the component will be rendered in the primary one.

Configures the route for the Chat component to be rendered in the outlet named aux

Renders the Home component in the primary outlet and Chat in the outlet called aux

To remove the named outlet with its content, give it a null value.

```
        <router-outlet></router-outlet>
        <router-outlet name="aux"></router-outlet>
})
class AppComponent {}
```

Declares the primary outlet

Declares an additional named outlet, <router-outlet>. Here you name it aux.

```
@NgModule({
    imports:      [ BrowserModule, RouterModule.forRoot(routes)],
    declarations: [ AppComponent, HomeComponent, ChatComponent],
    providers:[{provide: LocationStrategy, useClass: HashLocationStrategy}],
    bootstrap:    [ AppComponent ]
})
class AppModule { }

platformBrowserDynamic().bootstrapModule(AppModule);
```

> **NOTE** Because class declarations aren't hoisted (hoisting is explained in appendix A), make sure you declare your components before using them with routerLink.

If you want to navigate to (or close) the named outlets programmatically, use the Router.navigate() method, as explained in section 3.1.3. Here's an example:

```
navigate([{outlets: {aux: 'chat'}}]);
```

Let's take a breather and recap what we've covered so far in this chapter:

- Routes are configured on the module level.
- Each route has a path mapped to a component.
- The area where the route content is rendered is defined by the placement of the <router-outlet> area in the component's template.
- The routerLink can be used for navigating to a named route.
- The navigate() method can be used for navigating to a named route.
- If a route requires a parameter, you have to configure it in the path property of the route configuration and pass its value in routerLink or in the navigate() method.
- If a route expects a parameter, the underlying component must have a constructor with an argument of type ActivatedRoute.
- If a child component has its own route configuration, it's called a a child route, and it's configured using the children property defined in the Route interface.
- An application can show more than one route at the same time using named routes.

We're almost done covering the router. We'll discuss one more topic: how to implement lazy loading of components for rarely used routes. This is an important technique that will allow you to minimize the amount of code loaded for the landing page of your app. After that, you'll implement routing in the online auction.

3.6 Splitting an app into modules

Angular modules allow you to split an application into more than one module, where each module implements certain functionality. As a matter of fact, each of the code samples in this chapter already has more than one module, such as AppModule, BrowserModule, and RouterModule. AppModule is the root module of an application, but BrowserModule and RouterModule are feature modules. Note the main difference between them: the root module is bootstrapped, whereas feature modules are imported, as shown in the following code snippet:

```
@NgModule({
    imports:[ BrowserModule,
            RouterModule.forRoot(routes)],
    ...
})
class AppModule { }

platformBrowserDynamic().bootstrapModule(AppModule);
```

Each module can expose and hide certain functionality, and all modules are executed in the same context, so they can share objects if need be. RootModule and BrowserModule were created by the Angular team, but you can split your application into modules too.

In a feature module, the @NgModule decorator has to import CommonModule instead of BrowserModule. Let's take the app with two links—Home and Product Details—and add one more: Luxury Items. Imagine that luxury items have to be processed differently than regular products, and you want to separate this functionality into a feature module called LuxuryModule, which will have one component called LuxuryComponent. It's recommended that a feature module and its supporting components, services, and other resources be placed in a separate directory. In the sample app, it'll be a directory named luxury.

The code of LuxuryModule is located in the luxury.module.ts file, shown next.

Listing 3.16 luxury.model.ts

```
import { NgModule }       from '@angular/core';
import { CommonModule } from '@angular/common';
import {RouterModule} from '@angular/router';
import {LuxuryComponent} from "./luxury.component";

@NgModule({
    imports:       [ CommonModule,
        RouterModule.forChild([
        {path: 'luxury', component: LuxuryComponent}
    ]) ],
    declarations: [ LuxuryComponent ]
})

export class LuxuryModule { }
```

Imports CommonModule as required for feature modules

Configures the route for this module using the forChild() method

This module will have just one component.

When the URL has the luxury segment, renders LuxuryComponent.

When you configure the root module, use the `forRoot` method, and for feature modules use `forChild()`.

The code of `LuxuryComponent` will just display the text "Luxury Component" on a yellow (for gold) background:

```
import {Component} from '@angular/core';

@Component({
    selector: 'luxury',
    template: `<h1 class="gold">Luxury Component</h1>`,
    styles: ['.gold {background: yellow}']
})
export class LuxuryComponent {}
```

Note that you're exporting `LuxuryComponent` to make it available to other members of the root module. The code of `AppComponent`, `AppModule`, and the bootstrap function is located in the main-luxury.ts file.

Listing 3.17   main-luxury.ts

```
import { platformBrowserDynamic } from '@angular/platform-browser-dynamic';
import { NgModule, Component } from '@angular/core';
import { BrowserModule } from '@angular/platform-browser';
import {LocationStrategy, HashLocationStrategy} from '@angular/common';
import {RouterModule} from "@angular/router";
import {HomeComponent} from "./components/home";
import {ProductDetailComponent} from "./components/product";
import {LuxuryModule} from "./components/luxury/luxury.module";

@Component({
    selector: 'app',
    template: `
        <a [routerLink]="['/']">Home</a>
        <a [routerLink]="['/product']">Product Details</a>
        <a [routerLink]="['/luxury']">Luxury Items</a>          ◁─┐  Adds the link to the
        <router-outlet></router-outlet>                           │  main app to navigate
    `                                                             └  to the luxury path
})
export class AppComponent {}

@NgModule({
    imports: [ BrowserModule,                    ┐ Declares the
               LuxuryModule,              ◁──────┘ feature module
               RouterModule.forRoot([
Configures ┌─▷      {path: '',          component: HomeComponent},
the route for│      {path: 'product',   component: ProductDetailComponent}
 the root    │      ])
 module  └          ],
    declarations: [ AppComponent, HomeComponent, ProductDetailComponent],
    providers:[{provide: LocationStrategy, useClass: HashLocationStrategy}],
    bootstrap:     [ AppComponent ]
})
```

```
class AppModule { }

platformBrowserDynamic().bootstrapModule(AppModule);
```

Note that the root module doesn't know about the internals of `LuxuryModule`, and it doesn't even mention `LuxuryComponent`. When the router parses the routes configuration from both root and feature modules, it'll properly map the `luxury` path to the `LuxuryComponent` that's exported by `LuxuryModule`. If you run this application and click the Luxury Items link, you'll see the window shown in figure 3.12.

Figure 3.12   Rendering `LuxuryModule`

This was an example of splitting a chunk of functionality into a module. Should you decide to stop selling luxury items, you'll only need to remove the references to `LuxuryModule` from the root module and one link from `AppComponent`. This is pretty easy refactoring, compared to the process of removing functionality from a monolithic single-module app.

Moving a feature module from one app to another becomes easier as well. Not that every app needs to be able to sell luxury items, but many apps in a commercial portal may need, say, a payment module that can be reused across apps with minimal effort.

This is all good, but keep in mind that even though you encapsulated some functionality into a separate module, the code of this module is loaded on the application's launch. Do you really want to load the luxury module code into the browser when the application starts? Let's discuss this next.

3.7   *Lazy-loading modules*

In large applications, you want to minimize the amount of code that needs to be downloaded to render the landing page of your application. The less code your app initially downloads, the faster the user will see it. This is especially important for mobile apps when they're used in a poor connection area. If your application has modules that are rarely used, you can make them downloadable on demand, or *lazy-loaded*.

Angular allows you to easily split your app into modules: one root module and one or more feature modules. The latter can be loaded either eagerly, as you did in the previous section, or lazily.

After implementing the functionality for luxury items, suppose you realize that most users rarely click the Luxury Items link. Why load the code that handles luxury items on the initial bootstrap of the app? Let's refactor the app to load the luxury module on demand.

Listing 3.18 implements lazy loading of the module. This sample will look a lot like listing 3.17, but you'll make a small change in the main module and change the way `LuxuryModule` is exported. This code is located in the main-luxury-lazy.ts file.

Listing 3.18 main-luxury-lazy.ts

```
import { platformBrowserDynamic } from '@angular/platform-browser-dynamic';
import { NgModule, Component }      from '@angular/core';
import { BrowserModule } from '@angular/platform-browser';
import {LocationStrategy, HashLocationStrategy} from '@angular/common';
import {RouterModule} from "@angular/router";
import {HomeComponent} from "./components/home";
import {ProductDetailComponent} from "./components/product";

@Component({
    selector: 'app',
    template: `
        <a [routerLink]="['/']">Home</a>
        <a [routerLink]="['/product']">Product Details</a>
        <a [routerLink]="['/luxury']">Luxury Items</a>
        <router-outlet></router-outlet>
    `
})
export class AppComponent {}

@NgModule({
    imports: [ BrowserModule,
               RouterModule.forRoot([
                    {path: '',         component: HomeComponent},
                    {path: 'product', component: ProductDetailComponent},
                    {path: 'luxury', loadChildren:
                    ➥ 'app/components/luxury/luxury.lazy.module'}
                    ])
               ],
    declarations: [ AppComponent, HomeComponent, ProductDetailComponent],
    providers:[{provide: LocationStrategy, useClass: HashLocationStrategy}],
    bootstrap:    [ AppComponent ]
})
class AppModule { }

platformBrowserDynamic().bootstrapModule(AppModule);
```

Note that this time you aren't explicitly importing LuxuryModule. Also, you changed
the route configuration for the luxury path, which now looks like this:

```
{path: 'luxury', loadChildren: 'app/components/luxury/luxury.lazy.module'}
```

Instead of mapping the path to a component, you use the loadChildren property,
providing the path to the module to be loaded. Note that the value of loadChildren
isn't a typed module name, but a string. The root module doesn't know about the
LuxuryModule type; but when the user clicks the Luxury Items link, the module loader
will parse this string and load LuxuryModule from the luxury.lazy.module.ts file, which
looks a little different than the version presented in the previous section.

Listing 3.19 luxury.lazy.module.ts

```
import { NgModule }        from '@angular/core';
import { CommonModule } from '@angular/common';
import {RouterModule} from '@angular/router';
import {LuxuryComponent} from "./luxury.component";

@NgModule({
    imports:        [ CommonModule,
        RouterModule.forChild([
        {path: '', component: LuxuryComponent}
    ]) ],
    declarations: [ LuxuryComponent ]
})

export default class LuxuryModule { }
```

Here you configure an empty path to be used as a default route. Because this module will be lazy-loaded, and you we didn't declare the `LuxuryModule` type in the root module, you have to use the `default` keyword while exporting this class. When the user clicks the Luxury Items link in the root module, the loader will load the content of the luxury.lazy.module.ts file and will figure out that `LuxuryModule` is a default entry point to the script from this file.

Now if you run the main-luxury-lazy application with the Developer Tools panel open to the Network tab, you won't see the luxury module in the list of downloaded files. Click the Luxury Items link, and you'll see that the browser makes an additional request to the server to download `LuxuryModule` and `LuxuryComponent`.

This super-simple example reduced the size of the initial download only by 1 KB. But architecting large applications using lazy-loading techniques can lower the initial size of the downloadable code by hundreds of kilobytes or more, improving the perceived performance of your application. Perceived performance is what the user *thinks* of the performance of your application, and improving it is important, especially when the app is being loaded from a mobile device on a slow network.

3.8 Hands-on: adding navigation to the online auction

This hands-on exercise starts where you left off in chapter 2. So far, you have just the home page of the auction (see figure 2.3). The goal of this project is to add navigation so the user can click the product name, which should replace the view that shows the carousel and product thumbnails with a `ProductItemComponent` view.

You won't see the final version of the Product Details view in this chapter. Even though the code from chapter 2 has `ProductService` with all the product details, we'll use it in chapter 4 to illustrate dependency injection. Figure 3.13 shows what the online auction will look like in this chapter, after the user clicks the First Product title on the home page.

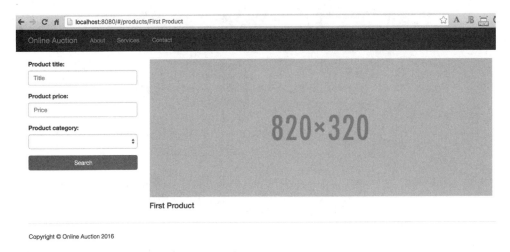

Figure 3.13   Navigating the Product Details route

In this hands-on section, you'll need to perform the following steps:

1 Create a `ProductDetailComponent` that displays only the product title.
2 Refactor the code to introduce a `HomeComponent` that encapsulates the carousel and a grid with product items.
3 Configure the route for the `products` path that takes a product title. This route has to navigate to `ProductDetailComponent`, which will receive the product title via the `ActivatedRoute` object.
4 Modify the `ApplicationComponent` code to render either `HomeComponent` or `ProductDetailComponent` depending on the selected route.
5 Add `<route-outlet>` to the main application to render either `HomeComponent` or `ProductDetailComponent`.
6 Add a link with `[routerLink]` to the template of `ProductItemComponent` so when the user clicks the product's title, the application will navigate to the Product Details route.

NOTE   If you prefer skip ahead to see the final version of this project in action, open the command window in the auction folder and run `npm install` followed by `npm start`. Otherwise, copy the auction folder from chapter 2 to a separate location, and follow the instructions in the next subsections.

3.8.1   Creating ProductDetailComponent

Create a new app/components/product-detail folder and add a product-detail.ts file to that folder with the following content.

Listing 3.20 product-detail.ts

```typescript
import {Component} from '@angular/core';
import {ActivatedRoute} from '@angular/router';

@Component({
  selector: 'auction-product-page',
  template: `
    <div>
      <img src="http://placehold.it/820x320">
      <h4>{{productTitle}}</h4>
    </div>
  `
})
export default class ProductDetailComponent {
  productTitle: string;

  constructor(route: ActivatedRoute){
    this.productTitle = route.snapshot.params['prodTitle'];
  }
}
```

3.8.2 *Creating HomeComponent and code refactoring*

In chapter 2, you created a main page for the auction that contained a number of components. You'll need to refactor the code so the new version of the main page will use routing. You'll define an area with the tag <router-outlet> where you'll display either HomeComponent or ProductDetailComponent. HomeComponent will encapsulate the existing CarouselComponent and a grid with ProductItemComponents. Here are the steps:

1 Create a new app/components/home folder, and in it add a home.ts file with the following content.

Listing 3.21 home.ts

```typescript
import {Component} from '@angular/core';

@Component({
  selector: 'auction-home-page',
  styleUrls: ['/home.css'],
  template: `
    <div class="row carousel-holder">
      <div class="col-md-12">
        <auction-carousel></auction-carousel>
      </div>
    </div>
    <div class="row">
      <div *ngFor="let product of products"
        class="col-sm-4 col-lg-4 col-md-4">
        <auction-product-item [product]="product">
          </auction-product-item>
```

```
      </div>
    </div>
  `
})
export default class HomeComponent {
  products: Product[] = [];

  constructor(private productService: ProductService) {
    this.products = this.productService.getProducts();
  }
}
```

Angular injects into this component `ProductService`, and the provider for this service is declared in `AppModule`. You'll learn about providers in the next chapter.

In chapter 2, the preceding code was located in the application.ts file. But you want to encapsulate this code inside `HomeComponent`, and you'll configure a route for it in `AppModule`. In the next step, you'll remove the corresponding code from application.ts.

If you see styles that aren't explicitly defined in the code, they come from the CSS that comes with the Bootstrap library. You can customize them as needed.

2   Create the home.css file to specify styles for placing the Bootstrap carousel component inside `HomeComponent`.

Listing 3.22   home.css

```
.slide-image {
    width: 100%;
}

.carousel-holder {
    margin-bottom: 30px;
}

.carousel-control,.item {
    border-radius: 4px;
}
```

3.8.3   *Simplifying ApplicationComponent*

Now that you've encapsulated a large portion of the code inside `HomeComponent`, the code of `ApplicationComponent` will become shorter:

1   Replace the content of the application.ts file with the following code.

Listing 3.23   application.ts

```
import {Component, ViewEncapsulation} from '@angular/core';

@Component({
  selector: 'auction-application',
```

```
templateUrl: 'app/components/application/application.html',
styleUrls: ['app/components/application/application.css'],
encapsulation:ViewEncapsulation.None
})
export default class ApplicationComponent {}
```

In the `templateUrl` and `styleUrls` properties, you use the full path to the HTML and CSS files. In chapter 10, in the sidebar "Using relative paths in templates," you'll learn how to use a relative path while specifying HTML and CSS files.

In a book, it's easier to describe shorter code snippets, so you'll place the markup of `ApplicationComponent` into a separate application.html file.

2 Modify the content of application.html to look like this.

Listing 3.24   application.html

```
<auction-navbar></auction-navbar>

<div class="container">
  <div class="row">
    <div class="col-md-3">
      <auction-search></auction-search>
    </div>

    <div class="col-md-9">
      <router-outlet></router-outlet>
    </div>
  </div>
</div>

<auction-footer></auction-footer>
```

The main change here is the replacement of the carousel and product item components with the tag `<router-outlet>`. When the router renders `HomeComponent`, the carousel and product item components will be rendered as well.

The top portion of the auction window is taken up by the navigation bar, the bottom portion is the footer, and the area in the middle is split into two sections: the search component and the router outlet. According to Bootstrap's grid system, the entire width of the window is divided into 12 equal columns. you allocate 3 of them to `<auction-search>`, and 9 will go to `<router-outlet>`. In other words, 25% of the screen width is allocated for the search, and 75% is for the routes. You'll implement search in chapter 7, which covers working with forms.

3.8.4   Adding a RouterLink to ProductItemComponent

`HomeComponent` includes multiple instances of `ProductItemComponent`. Each of them should have a `routerLink` to navigate to the `ProductDetailComponent` passing the product title as a parameter. Follow these steps:

1 Modify the code of the product-item.ts file to reference a CSS file, as shown here.

Listing 3.25 product-item.ts

```
import {Component, Input} from '@angular/core';
import {Product} from '../../services/product-service';

@Component({
  selector: 'auction-product-item',
  styleUrls: ['app/components/product-item/product-item.css'],
  templateUrl: 'app/components/product-item/product-item.html',
})
export default class ProductItemComponent {
  @Input() product: Product;
}
```

The product-item.html file needs an anchor tag with the `routerLink` directive, which should navigate to the route mapped to the path `products/:prodTitle`. You'll configure it in `AppModule` a bit later.

2 Modify the content of product-item.html to look like this.

Listing 3.26 product-item.html

```
<div class="thumbnail">
  <img src="http://placehold.it/320x150">
  <div class="caption">
    <h4 class="pull-right">{{ product.price | currency }}</h4>
    <h4><a [routerLink]="['/
products', product.title]">{{ product.title }}</a></h4>
    <p>{{ product.description }}</p>
  </div>
  <div class="ratings">
    <auction-stars [rating]="product.rating"></auction-stars>
  </div>
</div>
```

You use the currency pipe (a pipe is specified after the vertical bar) for formatting the product price. If this pipe doesn't work in your browser, read the workaround in section 5.3.

3 Create a product-item.css file with the following content.

Listing 3.27 product-item.css

```
.caption {
  height: 130px;
  overflow: hidden;
}
```

```
.caption h4 { white-space: nowrap; }

.thumbnail { padding: 0; }

.thumbnail img { width: 100%; }

.thumbnail .caption-full {
  padding: 9px;
  color: #333;
}

.ratings {
  color: #d17581;
  padding-left: 10px;
  padding-right: 10px;
}
```

3.8.5 *Modifying the root module to add routing*

Finally, you need to update the app.module.ts file to add the RouterModule and location strategy, and to configure routes.

Listing 3.28 app.module.ts

```
import { NgModule }        from '@angular/core';
import { BrowserModule } from '@angular/platform-browser';
import { RouterModule } from '@angular/router';
import {LocationStrategy, HashLocationStrategy} from '@angular/common';
import ApplicationComponent from './components/application/application';
import CarouselComponent from "./components/carousel/carousel";
import FooterComponent from "./components/footer/footer";
import NavbarComponent from "./components/navbar/navbar";
import ProductItemComponent from "./components/product-item/product-item";
import SearchComponent from "./components/search/search";
import StarsComponent from "./components/stars/stars";
import {ProductService} from "./services/product-service";
import HomeComponent from "./components/home/home";
import ProductDetailComponent from "./components/product-detail/
➥ product-detail";

@NgModule({
    imports:      [ BrowserModule,
                    RouterModule.forRoot([
                        {path: '',                    component:
                        ➥ HomeComponent},
                        {path: 'products/:prodTitle',
                        ➥ component: ProductDetailComponent}
    ]) ],
    declarations: [ ApplicationComponent, CarouselComponent,
                    FooterComponent, NavbarComponent,
                    HomeComponent, ProductDetailComponent,
                    ProductItemComponent, SearchComponent, StarsComponent],
    providers:    [ProductService,
```

```
                        {provide: LocationStrategy, useClass:
                        ⮡ HashLocationStrategy}],
    bootstrap:    [ ApplicationComponent ]
})
export class AppModule { }
```

Here you configure two routes: the base URL (the empty path) will navigate to HomeComponent, and the products/:prodTitle path is for rendering ProductDetailComponent, which will get the value of the product title as a parameter. The value for prodTitle will be provided in ProductItemComponent, where the routerLink was defined.

3.8.6   *Running the auction*

Switch to the auction directory in the command window, and start the server by entering npm start (the start script is configured in package.json, as explained in chapter 2). The browser will open the home page of the auction, which looks the same as in chapter 2. Now click the title of any product, and you should see its simplified Product Details page as shown in figure 3.13. In chapter 4, you'll inject additional product details into this view.

Applying the spread operator

As your application grows, the number of components that you declare in AppModule can make your code less readable. Using the ES6 spread operator (discussed in appendix A) may help. Consider creating a separate file where you list all your components, like this:

```
export const myComponents = [
    ApplicationComponent,
    CarouselComponent,
    FooterComponent,
    NavbarComponent,
    HomeComponent,
    ProductDetailComponent,
    ProductItemComponent,
    SearchComponent,
    StarsComponent];
```

Then your @NgModule decorator can use the spread operator as follows:

```
@NgModule({
    // other code goes here

    declarations: [ ...myComponents],

    // other code goes here
})
```

3.9 *Summary*

In this chapter, you've learned how to implement navigation in a SPA using the Angular router. These are the main takeaways from this chapter:

- Configure routes for your application using `RouterModule`.
- By selecting a location strategy, you can control what the URL of each view looks like.
- While navigating an application, the router renders the underlying component in the content area defined by the `<router-outlet>` tags. There could be one or more such areas.
- To navigate to the route, add anchor tags to your application. The anchor tags should use the `routerLink` property instead of the `href` attribute. You can pass parameters to the route at this point.
- To minimize the initial size of your app, see if some of the modules can be loaded later on demand by implementing lazy-loading techniques.

Dependency injection 4

This chapter covers

- Introducing Dependency Injection (DI) as a design pattern
- Benefits of DI
- How Angular implements DI
- Registering object providers and using injectors
- The hierarchy of injectors
- Applying DI in the online auction application

In the previous chapter, we discussed the router, and now your online auction application knows how to navigate from the Home view to an almost-empty Product Details view. In this chapter, you'll continue working on the online auction, but this time we'll concentrate on how to use Angular to automate the process of creating objects and assembling the application from its building blocks.

Any Angular application is a collection of components, directives, and classes that may depend on each other. Although each component can explicitly instantiate its dependencies, Angular can do this job using its dependency injection (DI) mechanism.

We'll start this chapter by identifying the problem that DI solves and reviewing the benefits of DI as a software engineering design pattern. Then we'll go over the specifics of how Angular implements the DI pattern using an example `ProductComponent` that depends on a `ProductService`. You'll see how to write an injectable service and how to inject it into another component.

Then you'll see a sample application that demonstrates how Angular DI allows you to easily replace one component dependency with another by changing just one line of code. After that, we'll introduce a more advanced concept: a hierarchy of injectors. At the end of the chapter, we'll go through a hands-on exercise to build the next version of the online auction that uses the techniques covered in the chapter.

4.1 The Dependency Injection and Inversion of Control patterns

Design patterns are recommendations for how to solve certain common tasks. A given design pattern can be implemented differently depending on the software you use. In this section, we'll briefly introduce two design patterns: Dependency Injection (DI) and Inversion of Control (IoC).

4.1.1 The Dependency Injection pattern

If you've ever written a function that takes an object as an argument, you can say that you wrote a program that instantiates this object and *injects* it into the function. Imagine a fulfillment center that ships products. An application that keeps track of shipped products can create a product object and invoke a function that creates and saves a shipment record:

```
var product = new Product();
createShipment(product);
```

The `createShipment()` function depends on the existence of an instance of the `Product` object. In other words, the `createShipment()` function has a dependency: `Product`. But the function itself doesn't know how to create `Product`. The calling script should somehow create and give (think *inject*) this object as an argument to the function.

Technically, you're decoupling the creation of the `Product` object from its use—but both of the preceding lines of code are located in the same script, so it's not real decoupling. If you need to replace `Product` with `MockProduct`, it's a small code change in this simple example.

What if the `createShipment()` function had three dependencies (such as product, shipping company, and fulfillment center), and each of those dependencies had its own dependencies? In that case, creating a different set of objects for `createShipment()` would require many more manual code changes. Would it be possible to ask someone to create instances of dependencies (with their dependencies) for you?

This is what the Dependency Injection pattern is about: if object A depends on an object of type B, object A won't explicitly instantiate object B (as with the `new` operator in the previous example). Rather, it will have B *injected* from the operational environment. Object A just needs to declare, "I need an object of type B; could someone please give it to me?" The words *of type* are important here. Object A doesn't request a specific implementation of the object and will be happy as long as the injected object is of type B.

4.1.2   *The Inversion of Control pattern*

Inversion of Control (IoC) is a more general pattern than DI. Rather than making your application use some API from a framework (or a software container), the framework creates and supplies the objects that the application needs. The IoC pattern can be implemented in different ways, and DI is one of the ways of providing the required objects. Angular plays the role of the IoC container and can provide the required objects according to your component's declarations.

4.1.3   *Benefits of dependency injection*

Before we explore the syntax of Angular's implementation of DI, let's look at the benefits of having objects injected versus instantiating them with a new operator. Angular offers a mechanism that helps with registering and instantiating component dependencies. In short, DI helps you write code in a loosely coupled way and makes your code more testable and reusable.

LOOSE COUPLING AND REUSABILITY

Say you have a ProductComponent that gets product details using the ProductService class. Without DI, your ProductComponent needs to know how to instantiate the ProductService class. This can be done multiple ways, such as using new, calling getInstance() on a singleton object, or invoking createProductService() on some factory class. In any case, ProductComponent becomes *tightly coupled* with ProductService.

  If you need to reuse ProductComponent in another application that uses a different service to get product details, you must modify the code (for example, productService = new AnotherProductService()). DI allows you to decouple application components by sparing them from the need to know how to create their dependencies.

  Consider the following ProductComponent example:

```
@Component({
  providers: [ProductService]
})
class ProductComponent {
  product: Product;

  constructor(productService: ProductService) {

    this.product = productService.getProduct();
  }
}
```

In Angular applications, you register objects for DI by specifying providers. A *provider* is an instruction to Angular about *how* to create an instance of an object for future injection into a target component or directive. In the preceding code snippet, the line `providers: [ProductService]` is shorthand for `providers: [{provide:ProductService, useClass:ProductService}]`.

> **NOTE** You saw the `providers` property in chapter 3, but it was defined not on the component but on the module level.

Angular uses the concept of a *token*, which is an arbitrary name representing an object to be injected. Usually the token's name matches the type of the object to be injected, so the preceding code snippet instructs Angular to provide a `ProductService` token using the class of the same name. Using an object with the property `provide`, you can map the same token to different values or objects (such as to emulate the functionality of the `ProductService` while someone else is developing a real service class).

> **NOTE** In section 4.4.1, you'll see how to declare a token with an arbitrary name.

Now that you've added the `providers` property to the `@Component` annotation of `ProductComponent`, Angular's DI module will know that it has to instantiate an object *of type* `ProductService`. `ProductComponent` doesn't need to know which concrete implementation of the `ProductService` type to use—it'll use whatever object is specified as a provider. The reference to the `ProductService` object will be injected via the constructor's argument, and there's no need to explicitly instantiate `ProductService` in `ProductComponent`. Just use it as in the preceding code, which calls the service method `getProduct()` on the `ProductService` instance magically created by Angular.

If you need to reuse the same `ProductComponent` in a different application with a different implementation of the type `ProductService`, change the `providers` line, as in the following example:

```
providers: [{provide: ProductService, useClass: AnotherProductService}]
```

Now Angular will instantiate `AnotherProductService`, but the code using the type `ProductService` won't break. In this example, using DI increases the reusability of `ProductComponent` and eliminates its tight coupling with `ProductService`. If one object is tightly coupled with another, this may require substantial code modifications if you want to reuse just one of them in another application.

TESTABILITY

DI increases the testability of your components in isolation. You can easily inject mock objects if their real implementations aren't available or you want to unit-test your code.

Say you need to add a login feature to your application. You can create a `Login-Component` (to render ID and password fields) that uses a `LoginService` component, which should connect to a certain authorization server and check the user's privileges. The authorization server has to be provided by a different department, but it's not ready yet. You finish coding the `LoginComponent`, but you can't test it for reasons that are out of your control, such as a dependency on another component developed by someone else.

In testing, we often use mock objects that mimic the behavior of real objects. With a DI framework, you can create a mock object, `MockLoginService`, that doesn't connect to an authorization server but rather has hard-coded access privileges assigned to the users with certain ID/password combinations. Using DI, you can write a single line that injects `MockLoginService` into your application's Login view without needing to wait until the authorization server is ready. Later, when that server is ready, you can modify the `providers` line so Angular will inject the real `LoginService` component, as shown in figure 4.1.

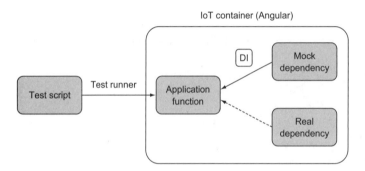

Figure 4.1   DI in testing

> **NOTE**   In the hands-on section of chapter 9, you'll see how to unit-test inject-able services.

4.2   *Injectors and providers*

Now that you've had a brief introduction to Dependency Injection as a general software engineering design pattern, let's go over the specifics of implementing DI in Angular. In particular, we'll go over such concepts as injectors and providers.

Each component can have an `Injector` instance capable of injecting objects or primitive values into a component or service. Any Angular application has a root injector available to all of its modules. To let the injector know *what* to inject, you specify the provider. An injector will inject the object or value specified in the provider into the constructor of a component.

> **NOTE**   Although eagerly loaded modules don't have their own injectors, a lazy-loaded module has its own sub-root injector that's a direct child of the application root injector.

Providers allow you to map a custom type (or a token) to a concrete implementation of this type (or value). You can specify the provider(s) either inside the component's @Component decorator or as a property of @NgModule, as in every code sample so far.

> **TIP** In Angular, you can inject data only via a constructor's arguments. If you see a class with a no-argument constructor, it's a guarantee that nothing is injected into this component.

You'll be using ProductComponent and ProductService for all the code samples in this chapter. If your application has a class implementing a particular type (such as Product-Service), you can specify a provider object for this class during the AppModule bootstrap, like this:

```
@NgModule({
  . . .
  providers: [{provide:ProductService,useClass:ProductService}]
})
```

When the token name is the same as the class name, you can use the shorter notation to specify the provider in the module:

```
@NgModule({
  . . .
  providers: [ProductService]
})
```

The providers property can be specified in the @Component annotation. The short notation of the ProductService provider in @Component looks like this:

```
providers:[ProductService]
```

No instance of ProductService is created at this point. The providers line instructs the injector as follows: "When you need to construct an object that has an argument of type ProductService, create an instance of the registered class for injection into this object."

> **NOTE** Angular also has the viewProviders property, which is used when you don't want the child components to use providers declared in the parent. You'll see an example of using viewProviders in section 4.5.

If you need to inject a different implementation of a particular type, use the longer notation:

```
@NgModule({
  . . .
  providers: [{provide:ProductService,useClass:MockProductService}]
})
```

Here it is on the component level:

```
@Component({
   ...
   providers: [{provide:ProductService, useClass:MockProductService}]
})
```

This gives the following instruction to the injector: "When you need to inject an object of type `ProductService` into a component, create an instance of the class `MockProductService`."

Thanks to the provider, the injector knows *what* to inject; now you need to specify *where* to inject the object. In TypeScript, it comes down to declaring a constructor argument specifying its type. The following line shows how to inject an object of type `ProductService` into the constructor of a component:

```
constructor(productService: ProductService)
```

> **Injection with TypeScript vs. ES6**
>
> TypeScript simplifies the syntax of injection into a component because it doesn't require you to use any DI annotations with the constructor arguments. All you need to do is specify the type of the constructor's argument:
>
> ```
> constructor(productService: ProductService)
> ```
>
> This works because any component has an annotation `@Component`. And because the TypeScript compiler is configured with the option `"emitDecoratorMetadata":` `true`, Angular will automatically generate all required metadata for the object to be injected.
>
> Because you use SystemJS for on-the-fly TypeScript transpiling, you can add the following TypeScript compiler option in systemjs.config.js:
>
> ```
> typescriptOptions: {
>     "emitDecoratorMetadata": true
>   }
> ```
>
> If you're writing the class in ES6, add the `@Inject` annotation with an explicit type to the constructor's arguments:
>
> ```
> constructor(@Inject(ProductService) productService)
> ```

The constructor will remain the same regardless of which concrete implementation of `ProductService` is specified as a provider. Figure 4.2 shows a sample sequence diagram of the injection process.

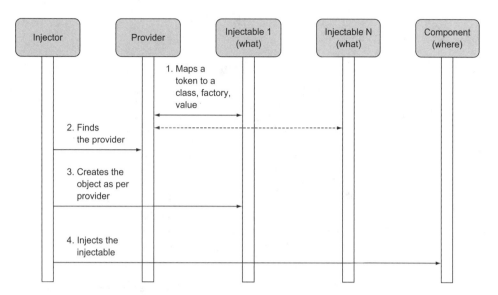

Figure 4.2   Injecting in time

4.2.1   *How to declare a provider*

You can declare custom providers as an array of objects that contain a `provide` property. Such an array can be specified in the `providers` property of the module or on the component level.

Here's an example of a single-element array that specifies the provider object for the `ProductService` token:

```
[{provide:ProductService, useClass:MockProductService}]
```

The `provide` property maps the token to the method of instantiating the injectable object. This example instructs Angular to create an instance of the `MockProduct-Service` class wherever the `ProductService` token is used as a dependency. But the object creator (Angular's injector) can use a class, a factory function, a string, or a special `OpaqueToken` class for instantiation and injection:

- To map a token to an implementation of a class, use the object with the `useClass` property, as shown in the preceding example.
- If you have a factory function that instantiates objects based on certain criteria, use an object with the `useFactory` property, which specifies a factory function (or a fat-arrow expression) that knows how to instantiate required objects. The factory function can have an optional argument with dependencies, if they exist.
- To provide a `string` with a simple injectable value (such as the URL of a service), use the object with the `useValue` property.

In the next section, you'll use the `useClass` property while reviewing a basic application. Section 4.4 will illustrate `useFactory` and `useValue`.

4.3   A sample application with Angular DI

Now that you've seen a number of code snippets related to Angular DI, let's build a small application that will bring all the pieces together. We want to prepare you for using DI in the online auction application.

4.3.1   Injecting a product service

Let's create a simple application that uses `ProductComponent` to render product details and `ProductService` to supply data about the product. If you use the downloadable code that comes with the book, this app is located in the main-basic.ts file in the di_samples directory. In this section, you'll build an application that produces the page shown in figure 4.3.

> **Basic Dependency Injection Sample**
> **Product Details**
> Title: iPhone 7
> Description: The latest iPhone, 7-inch screen
> Price: $249.99

Figure 4.3   A sample DI application

`ProductComponent` can request the injection of the `ProductService` object by declaring the constructor argument with a type:

```
constructor(productService: ProductService)
```

Figure 4.4 shows a sample application that uses these components.

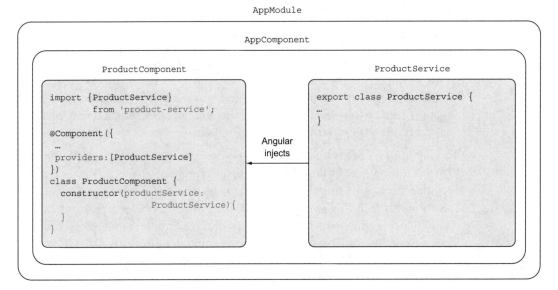

Figure 4.4   Injecting `ProductService` into `ProductComponent`

AppModule bootstraps AppComponent, which includes ProductComponent, which is dependent on ProductService. Note the import and export statements. The class definition of ProductService starts with the export statement, to enable other components to access its content. ProductComponent includes the import statement providing the name of the class (ProductService) and the module being imported (located in the file product-service.ts).

The providers attribute defined on the component level instructs Angular to provide an instance of the ProductService class when requested. ProductService may communicate with some server, requesting details for the product selected on the web page, but we'll skip this part for now and concentrate on how this service can be injected into ProductComponent. Let's implement the components from figure 4.4.

In addition to index.html, you'll be creating the following files:

- The main-basic.ts file will contain the code to load the AppModule, which includes AppComponent, which hosts ProductComponent.
- ProductComponent will be implemented in the product.ts file.
- ProductService will be implemented in a single product-service.ts file.

Each of these is pretty simple. The main-basic.ts file, shown in the following listing, contains the code of the module and root component, which hosts the ProductComponent child component. The module imports and declares ProductComponent.

Listing 4.1 main-basic.ts

```
import {Component} from '@angular/core';
import ProductComponent from './components/product';
import { platformBrowserDynamic } from '@angular/platform-browser-dynamic';
import { NgModule }      from '@angular/core';
import { BrowserModule } from '@angular/platform-browser';

@Component({
    selector: 'app',
    template: `<h1> Basic Dependency Injection Sample</h1>
            <di-product-page></di-product-page>`
})
class AppComponent {}

@NgModule({
    imports:      [ BrowserModule],
    declarations: [ AppComponent, ProductComponent],
    bootstrap:    [ AppComponent ]
})
class AppModule { }

platformBrowserDynamic().bootstrapModule(AppModule);
```

Based on the tag <di-product-page>, it's easy to guess that there's a component with the selector having this value. This selector is declared in ProductComponent, whose dependency (ProductService) is injected via the constructor.

Listing 4.2   product.ts

```
import {Component, bind} from '@angular/core';
import {ProductService, Product} from "../services/product-service";

@Component({
  selector: 'di-product-page',
  template: `<div>
  <h1>Product Details</h1>
  <h2>Title: {{product.title}}</h2>
  <h2>Description: {{product.description}}</h2>
  <h2>Price: \${{product.price}}</h2>
</div>`,
  providers:[ProductService]
})

export default class ProductComponent {
  product: Product;

  constructor( productService: ProductService) {

    this.product = productService.getProduct();
  }
}
```

The short notation of the providers property tells the injector to instantiate the ProductService class.

Angular instantiates ProductService and injects it here.

In listing 4.2, the name of the type is the same as the name of the class—Product-Service—so you use a short notation without the need to explicitly map the `provide` and `useClass` properties. When specifying providers, you separate the name (a token) of the injectable object from its implementation. In this case, the name of the token is the same as the name of the type: `ProductService`. The actual implementation of this service can be located in a class called `ProductService`, `OtherProductService`, or something else. Replacing one implementation with another comes down to changing the `providers` line.

The constructor of `ProductComponent` invokes `getProduct()` on the service and places a reference to the returned `Product` object in the `product` class variable, which is used in the HTML template. By using double curly braces, listing 4.2 lets you bind the `title`, `description`, and `price` properties of the `Product` class.

The product-service.ts file includes the declaration of two classes: `Product` and `ProductService`.

Listing 4.3   product-service.ts

```
export class Product {
  constructor(
    public id: number,
    public title: string,
    public price: number,
    public description: string) {
  }
}
```

The Product class represents a product (a value object). It's used outside of this script, so you export it.

```
export class ProductService {

  getProduct(): Product {
    return new Product(0, "iPhone 7", 249.99, "The latest iPhone,
    ➥ 7-inch screen");
  }
}
```

For simplicity, the getProduct() method always returns the same product with hard-coded values.

In a real-world application, the getProduct() method would have to get the product information from an external data source, such as by making an HTTP request to a remote server.

To run this example, open a command window in the project folder and execute the command npm start. The live-server will open the window, as shown earlier in figure 4.3. The instance of ProductService is injected into ProductComponent, which renders product details provided by the server.

In the next section, you'll see a ProductService decorated with the @Injectable annotation, which can be used to generate DI metadata when the service itself has dependencies. The @Injectable annotation isn't needed here because Product-Service doesn't have any other service injected into it, and Angular doesn't need additional metadata to inject ProductService into components.

4.3.2 *Injecting the Http service*

Often, a service will need to make an HTTP request to get the requested data. Product-Component depends on ProductService, which is injected using the Angular DI mechanism. If ProductService needs to make an HTTP request, it'll have an Http object as its own dependency. ProductService will need to import the Http object for injection; @NgModule must import HttpModule, which defines Http providers. The ProductService class should have a constructor for injecting the Http object. Figure 4.5 shows ProductComponent depending on ProductService, which has its own dependency: Http.

Figure 4.5 A dependency can have its own dependency.

The following code snippet illustrates the Http object's injection into ProductService and the retrieval of products from the products.json file:

```
import {Http} from '@angular/http';
import {Injectable} from "@angular/core";

@Injectable()
```

```
export class ProductService {
    constructor(private http:Http){
        let products = http.get('products.json');
    }
    // other app code goes here
}
```

The class constructor is the injection point, but where do you declare the provider for injecting the Http type object? All the providers required to inject various flavors of Http objects are declared in HttpModule. You just need to add it to your AppModule, like this:

```
import { HttpModule} from '@angular/http';
...
@NgModule({
    imports: [
        BrowserModule,
        HttpModule
    ],
    declarations: [ AppComponent ],
    bootstrap: [ AppComponent ]
})
export class AppModule { }
```

> **NOTE** In section 8.3.4, you'll write an application illustrating the architecture shown in figure 4.5.

Now that you've seen how to inject an object into a component, let's look at what it takes to replace one implementation of the service with another using Angular DI.

4.4   *Switching injectables made easy*

Earlier in this chapter, we stated that the DI pattern allows you to decouple components from their dependencies. In the previous section, you decoupled Product-Component from ProductService. Now let's simulate another scenario.

Suppose you've started development with a ProductService that's supposed to get data from a remote server, but the server's feed isn't ready. Rather than modify the code in ProductService to introduce hard-coded data for testing, you'll create another class: MockProductService.

Moreover, to illustrate how easy it is to switch from one service to another, you'll create a small application that uses two instances of ProductComponent. Initially, the first one will use MockProductService and the second ProductService. Then, with a one-line change, you'll make both of them use the same service. Figure 4.6 shows how the multiple _injectors application will render product components in the browser.

Figure 4.6   Rendering two products

The iPhone 7 product is rendered by `Product1Component`, and the Samsung 7 is rendered by `Product2Component`. This application focuses on switching product services using Angular DI, so we've kept the components and services simple. Toward this end, all of the TypeScript code is located in one main.ts file.

A class playing the role of an interface

In appendix B, we explain the TypeScript interfaces, which are a useful way to ensure that an object being passed to a function is valid or that a class implementing an interface sticks to a declared contract. A class can implement an interface using the keyword `implements`, but there's more: in TypeScript, all classes can be used as interfaces (although we don't encourage using this feature), so `ClassA` can implement `ClassB`. Even if the code isn't initially written with interfaces, you can still use a concrete class as if it were declared as an interface.

The content of main.ts is shown in listing 4.4. We'd like to draw your attention to the following line:

```
class MockProductService implements ProductService
```

This shows one class "implementing" another as if the latter was declared as an interface.

Listing 4.4 main.ts

```
import { platformBrowserDynamic } from '@angular/platform-browser-dynamic';
import { NgModule, Component } from '@angular/core';
import { BrowserModule } from '@angular/platform-browser'

class Product {
  constructor(public title: string) {}
}

class ProductService {                              Initially, you developed
  getProduct(): Product {                           ProductService as a class.
    // Code making an HTTP request to get actual product details
    // would go here
    return new Product('iPhone 7');
  }                                                 Then you introduced
}                                                   another service,
                                                    MockProductService, that
class MockProductService implements ProductService {  implements ProductService
  getProduct(): Product {                           as an interface.
    return new Product('Samsung 7');
  }
}

@Component({
  selector: 'product1',
  template: '{{product.title}}'})
```

```
class Product1Component {
  product: Product;

  constructor(private productService: ProductService) {
    this.product = productService.getProduct();
  }
}
```

The constructor of **ProductComponentl** gets the instance of **ProductService** injected.

```
@Component({
  selector: 'product2',
  template: '{{product.title}}',
  providers: [{provide:ProductService, useClass:MockProductService}]
})
class Product2Component {
  product: Product;

  constructor(private productService: ProductService) {
    this.product = productService.getProduct();
  }
}
```

Declares a specific implementation of **ProductService** in the second component

There's no need to change the constructor. **ProductComponent2** gets **MockProductService** because its provider was specified at the component level.

```
@Component({
  selector: 'app',
  template: `
    <h2>A root component hosts two products<br>
    ➡ provided by different services</h2>
    <product1></product1>
    <br>
    <product2></product2>
    `
})
class AppComponent {}
```

AppComponent renders two child components, and each of them uses a different instance of **ProductService**.

```
@NgModule({
  imports:        [ BrowserModule],
  providers:      [ProductService],
  declarations:   [ AppComponent, Product1Component, Product2Component],
  bootstrap:      [ AppComponent ]
})
class AppModule { }
```

Registers a provider with an application-level injector

```
platformBrowserDynamic().bootstrapModule(AppModule);
```

If a component doesn't need a specific ProductService implementation, there's no need to explicitly declare a provider for each component, as long as a provider was specified at the parent's level. In listing 4.4, Product1Component doesn't declare its own providers, so Angular will find one on the application level. But each component is free to override the providers declaration made at the app or parent component level, as in Product2Component.

ProductService becomes a common token that both product components understand. Product2Component declares an explicit provider, which maps MockProduct-Service to the common ProductService custom type. This component-level provider will override the parent's one. If you decide that `Product1Component` should use `Mock-ProductService` as well, you can add the `providers` line to its `@Component` annotation, as in `Product2Component`.

Running this application renders product components in the browser, as shown earlier in figure 4.6. This all is good, but suppose you're notified by another team that the `ProductService` class (used as the app-level provider) won't be available for some time. How can you switch to using `MockProductService` exclusively for a while?

This requires a one-line change. Replacing the `providers` line in the module declaration will do the trick:

```
@NgModule({
...
providers: [{provide:ProductService, useClass:MockProductService}]
...
})
```

From now on, wherever the type `Product-Service` needs to be injected and no providers line is specified on the component level, Angular will instantiate and inject `Mock-ProductService`. Running the application after making the preceding change renders the components as shown in figure 4.7.

Imagine that your application had dozens of components using `ProductSer-

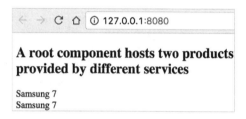

Figure 4.7   Rendering two products with `MockProductService`

vice`. If each of them instantiated this service with a `new` operator or a factory class, you'd need to make dozens of code changes. With Angular DI, you were able to switch the service by changing one line in the `providers` declaration.

> ## JavaScript hoisting and classes
>
> Class declarations aren't *hoisted* (hoisting is explained in appendix A). Typically, each class is declared in a separate file, and their declarations are imported on top of the script so all class declarations are available up front.
>
> If multiple classes are declared in one file, both `ProductService` and `MockProductService` must be declared before the components that use them. If you run into a situation where the objects are declared after the point of injection, consider using the function `forwardRef()` with the annotation `@Inject` (see the Angular documentation for `forwardRef()` at http://mng.bz/31YN).

4.4.1   Declaring providers with useFactory and useValue

Let's look at some examples that illustrate the factory and value providers. In general, factory functions are used when you need to implement application logic prior to instantiating an object. For example, you may need to decide which object to instantiate, or your object may have a constructor with arguments that you need to initialize before creating an instance.

The following listing, from the main-factory.ts file, shows how you can specify a factory function as a provider. This factory function creates either `ProductService` or `MockProductService` based on a `boolean` flag.

Listing 4.5 Specifying a factory function as a provider

```
const IS_DEV_ENVIRONMENT: boolean = true;

@Component({
  selector: 'product2',

  providers:[{
    provide: ProductService,
    useFactory: (isDev) => {
      if (isDev){
        return new MockProductService();
      } else{
        return new ProductService();
      }
    },
    deps: ["IS_DEV_ENVIRONMENT"]}],

  template: '{{product.title}}'
})
class Product2Component {
  product: Product;

  constructor(productService: ProductService) {
    this.product = productService.getProduct();
  }
}
```

First you declare a token with an arbitrary name (`IS_DEV_ENVIRONMENT` in this case) and set it to `true` to let the program know you're operating in the development environment (that is, you want to work with the mock product service). The factory uses the arrow expression that will instantiate `MockProductService`.

The constructor of `Product2Component` has an argument of type `ProductService`, and the service will be injected there. You could use such a factory for `Product1Component` as well; changing the value of `IS_DEV_ENVIRONMENT` to `false` would inject the instance of `ProductService` into both components.

Listing 4.5 isn't the best solution for switching environments: it reaches out to `IS_DEV_ENVIRONMENT`, which was declared *outside* of the component, breaking the component's encapsulation. You want the component to be self-contained, so let's try to inject the value of `IS_DEV_ENVIRONMENT` into the component; that way, it doesn't need to reach out to the external code.

Declaring a constant (or a variable) isn't enough to make it injectable. You need to register the value of IS_DEV_ENVIRONMENT with the injector, using provide with useValue, which lets you use it as an injectable parameter in the arrow expression in listing 4.5.

NOTE Both useFactory and useValue come from Angular Core. useValue is a special case of useFactory, for when the factory is represented by a single expression and doesn't need any other dependencies.

For an easy switch between development and other environments, you can specify the environment's value provider on the root component level, as shown in listing 4.6; then the service factory will know which service to construct. The value of the use-Factory property is a function with two arguments: the factory function itself and its dependencies (deps).

NOTE Listing 4.6 and many other code examples in this book use fat-arrow function expressions (described in appendix A). In essence, a fat-arrow function expression is a shorter notation for anonymous functions. For example, (isDev) => {…} is equivalent to function(isDev) {…}.

Listing 4.6 Specifying the environment's value provider

```
@Component({
  selector: 'product2',

  providers:[{
    provide: ProductService,
    useFactory: (isDev) => {
      if (isDev){
        return new MockProductService();
      } else{
        return new ProductService();
      }
    },
        deps:["IS_DEV_ENVIRONMENT"]})],
  template: '{{product.title}}'
}
class Product2Component {...}
...

@NgModule({
  ...
  providers: [ ProductService,
            {provide: "IS_DEV_ENVIRONMENT", useValue:true}]
})
```

The factory function has an
isDev argument, which is a
dependency that's injected
from outside.

The second property, deps,
defines the dependency of the
factory function (an injectable
value of **IS_DEV_ENVIRONMENT**
in this case).

To make the value of
IS_DEV_ENVIRONMENT injectable,
specify provide with useValue.

Because you inject the value into IS_DEV_ENVIRONMENT at the app level, any child component that uses this factory will be affected by a simple switch from false to true.

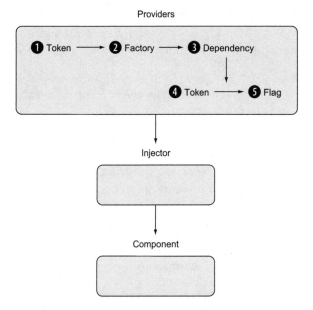

① The first token is ProductService.
② The factory is defined as an arrow function expression.
③ The factory has a dependency—IS_DEV_ENVIRONMENT.
④ The second token is IS_DEV_ENVIRONMENT.
⑤ The second token is mapped to the value false.

Figure 4.8   Binding a factory with dependencies

To recap, a provider maps the token to a class or a factory to let the injector know how to create objects. The class or factory may have its own dependencies, so the providers should specify all of them. Figure 4.8 illustrates the relationships between the providers and the injector in listing 4.6.

Angular prepares a tree of providers, finds the injector, and uses it for the Product2Component component. Angular will use either the component's injector or the parent's. We'll discuss the hierarchy of injectors next.

4.4.2   *Using OpaqueToken*

Injecting into a hard-coded string (such as IS_DEV_ENVIRONMENT) may cause problems if your application has more than one provider that uses a string with the same value for a different purpose. Angular offers an OpaqueToken class that's preferable to using strings as tokens.

Imagine that you want to create a component that can get data from different servers (such as dev, prod, and QA). The next listing illustrates how you can introduce an injectable value, BackendUrl, as an instance of OpaqueToken rather than as a string.

Listing 4.7 Using `OpaqueToken` instead of a string

```
import {Component, OpaqueToken, Inject, NgModule} from '@angular/core';
import { platformBrowserDynamic } from '@angular/platform-browser-dynamic';
import { BrowserModule } from '@angular/platform-browser';

export const BackendUrl  = new OpaqueToken('BackendUrl');

@Component({
  selector: 'app',
  template: 'URL: {{url}}'
})
class AppComponent {
  constructor(@Inject(BackendUrl) public url: string) {}
}

@NgModule({
  imports:        [ BrowserModule],
  declarations:   [ AppComponent],
  providers:      [ {provide:BackendUrl, useValue: 'myQAserver.com'}],
  bootstrap:      [ AppComponent ]
})
class AppModule { }

platformBrowserDynamic().bootstrapModule(AppModule);
```

You wrap the string "BackendUrl" into an instance of `OpaqueToken`. Then, in the constructor of this component, instead of injecting a vague `string` type, you inject a concrete `BACKEND_URL` type with the value provided in the module declaration.

4.5   *The hierarchy of injectors*

Any Angular application is a tree of nested components. When the web page loads, Angular creates an application object with its injector. It also creates a hierarchy of components with corresponding injectors, according to the application structure. For example, you may want a certain function to be executed when your application is initialized:

```
{provide:APP_INITIALIZER, useValue: myappInit}
```

The application's root component hosts other components. If you include, for example, component B in the template of component A, the latter becomes a parent of the former. In other words, a root component is a parent to other child components, which in turn can have their own children.

Consider the following HTML document, which includes a root component represented by the tag `<app>`:

```
<html>
  <body>
    <app></app>
  </body>
</html>
```

From the following code, you can see that app is a selector of the AppComponent, which is a parent of the <product1> and <product2> components:

```
@Component({
  selector: 'app',
  template: `
    <product1></product1>
    <product2></product2>
  `
})
class AppComponent {}
```

The parent component's injector creates an injector for each child component, so you have a hierarchy of components and a hierarchy of injectors. Also, the template markup of each component can have its own Shadow DOM with elements, and each element gets its own injector. Figure 4.9 shows the hierarchy of injectors.

When your code creates a component that requires a particular object to be injected, Angular looks for a provider of the requested object at the component level. If found, the component's injector is used. If it's not found, Angular checks whether the provider exists on one of the parent components. If the provider for the requested object isn't found at any level of the injectors hierarchy, Angular will throw an error.

> **NOTE** Angular creates an additional injector for a lazy-loaded module. Providers declared in the @NgModule of a lazy-loaded module are available in the module, but not to the entire application.

The example application injects only a service, and it doesn't illustrate the use of element injectors. In the browser, each component instance can be represented by a Shadow DOM, which has one or more elements depending on what's defined in the

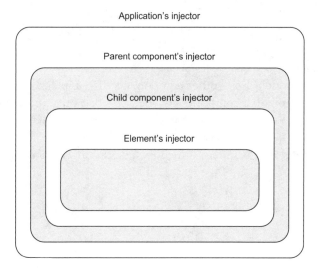

Figure 4.9   The hierarchy of injectors

component's template. Each element in the Shadow DOM has an ElementInjector that follows the same parent-child hierarchy as the DOM elements themselves.

Say you want to add an autocomplete feature to the HTML <input> element component. To do that, you can define a directive as follows:

```
@Directive({
  selector: '[autocomplete]'
})
class AutoCompleter {
  constructor(element: ElementRef) {
    // Implement the autocomplete logic here
  }
}
```

The square brackets mean autocomplete can be used as an attribute of the HTML element. The reference to this element will be automatically injected into the constructor of the AutoCompleter class by the element injector.

Now take another look at the code from section 4.4. The Product2Component class had a provider of MockProductService at the component level. The Product1-Component class didn't specify any providers for the type ProductService, so Angular performed the following actions:

- Checked its parent AppComponent—no providers there.
- Checked the AppModule and found providers: [ProductService] there.
- Used the app-level injector and created an instance of ProductService on the app level.

If you remove the providers line from Product2Component and rerun the application, it'll still work using the app-level injector and the same instance of the ProductService for both components. If providers for the same token were specified on both parent and child components, and each of these components had a constructor requesting an object represented by the token, two separate instances of such an object would be created: one for the parent and another for the child.

4.5.1 *viewProviders*

If you want to ensure that a particular injectable service won't be visible to the component's children or other components, use the viewProviders property instead of providers. Say you're writing a reusable library that internally uses a service that you don't want to be visible from the applications that use this library. Using viewProviders instead of providers will allow you to make such a service private for the library.

Here's another example. Imagine that you have the following hierarchy of components:

```
<root>
  <product2>
    <luxury-product></luxury-product>
  </product2>
</root>
```

Both `AppModule` and `Product2Component` have providers defined using the token `ProductService`, but `Product2Component` uses a special class that you don't want to be visible to its children. In this case, you can use the `viewProviders` property with the `Product2Component` class; when the injector of `LuxuryProductComponent` doesn't find a provider, it'll go up the hierarchy. It won't see the provider in `Product2Component`, and it will use the provider for `ProductService` defined in `RootComponent`.

> **NOTE** An instance of the injectable object is created and destroyed at the same time as the component that defines the provider for this object.

4.6   *Hands-on: using DI in the online auction application*

In chapter 3, you added routing to the online auction action so it can render a simplified Product Details view. In this hands-on exercise, you'll implement the `Product-Detail` component to show actual product details.

The Home page of the auction is shown in figure 4.10. If you click any of the links, such as First Product or Second Product, the app will show you a pretty basic detail view, as we showed in figure 3.16.

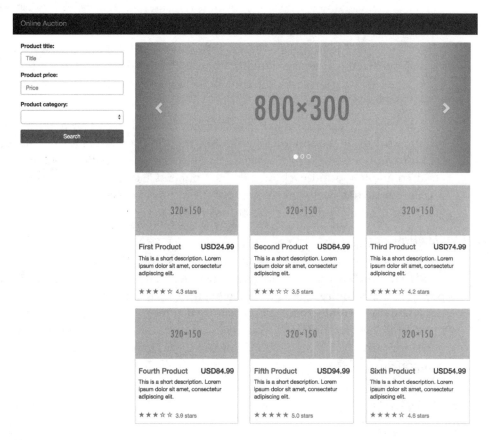

Figure 4.10   The auction Home page

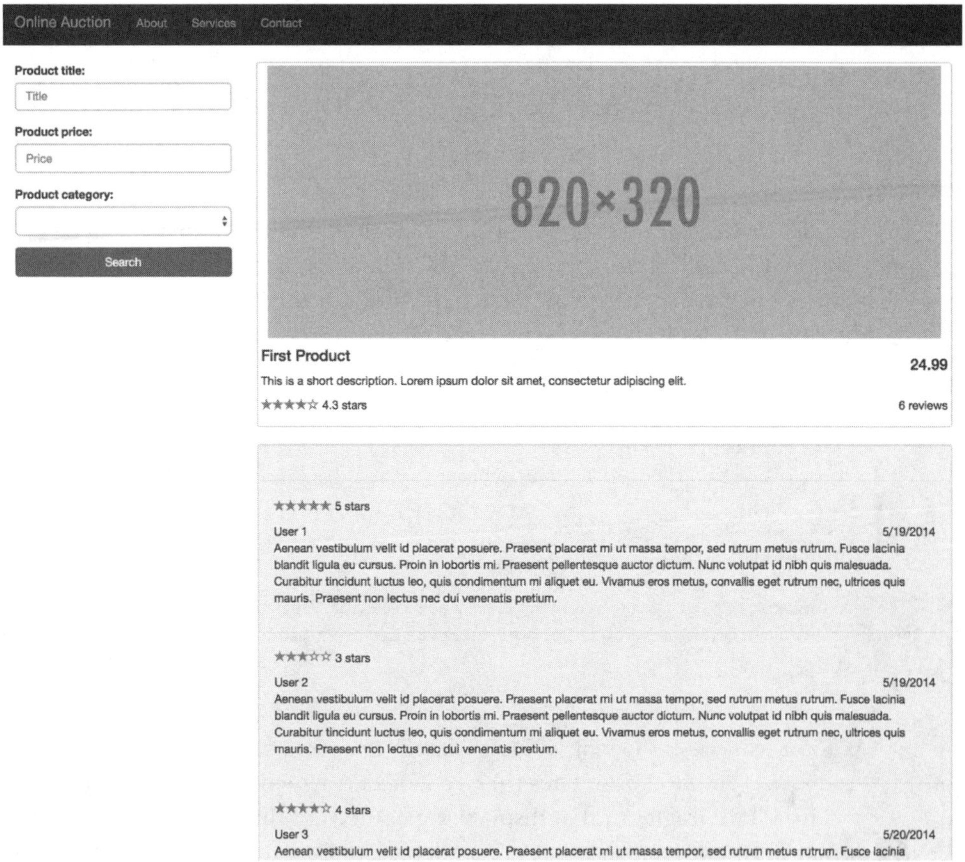

Figure 4.11   The auction Product Details view

Your goal is to render the details of the selected product, providing yet another illustration of DI in action. Figure 4.11 shows how the Product Details view will look at the end of this hands-on exercise when First Product is selected.

> **TIP** We'll use the auction application developed in chapter 3 as a starting point for this exercise. If you prefer to see the final version of this project, browse the source code in the auction folder from chapter 4. Otherwise, copy the auction folder from chapter 3 to a separate location, run `npm install`, and follow the instructions in this section.

Now that you've learned about provider and dependency injection, let's quickly review some code fragments from the auction created in the previous chapter, focusing on the DI-related code. The script in the app.module.ts file specifies the app-level service providers, as shown here:

```
@NgModule({
    ...
    providers:    [ProductService,
                  {provide: LocationStrategy, useClass: HashLocationStrategy}],
    bootstrap:    [ ApplicationComponent ]
})
export class AppModule { }
```

Because the `ProductService` provider is specified in the module, it can be reused by all children of `ApplicationComponent`. The following fragment from `HomeComponent` (see home.ts) doesn't specify `providers` to be used for the injection of `ProductService` via the constructor—it reuses the instance of `ProductService` created in its parent:

```
@Component({
  selector: 'auction-home-page',
  styleUrls: ['/home.css'],
  template: `...`
})
export default class HomeComponent {
  products: Product[] = [];

  constructor(private productService: ProductService) {
    this.products = this.productService.getProducts();
  }
}
```

As soon as `HomeComponent` is instantiated, `ProductService` is injected, and its `get-Products()` method populates the `products` array, which is bound to the view.

The HTML fragment that displays the content of this array uses the `*ngFor` loop to display one `<auction-product-item>` template for each element of the array:

```
<div class="row">
  <div *ngFor="let product of products" class="col-sm-4 col-lg-4 col-md-4">
    <auction-product-item [product]="product"></auction-product-item>
  </div>
</div>
```

The template for `<auction-product-item>` contains the following line:

```
<h4><a [routerLink]="['/products', product.title]">{{ product.title }}</a>
➥ </h4>
```

Clicking this link instructs the router to render `ProductDetailComponent` and provides the value of `product.title` as the route parameter. You want to modify this code to pass the product ID instead of the title.

This brief overview of the existing code was intended to remind you how the Product Details page is requested. Next, let's implement the code to produce the view shown in figure 4.11.

4.6.1 Changing the code to pass the product ID as a parameter

Open the product-item.html file, and modify the line with [routerLink] so it looks
like this:

```
<h4><a [routerLink]="['/products', product.id]">{{ product.title }}</a></h4>
```

The product-item.html file contains the template used to display products in the
Home view. Now, clicking the product title will pass the product.id to the route configured for the path products.

4.6.2 Modifying ProductDetailComponent

Before you begin coding, look at figure 4.12, which shows the parent-child relationship
between the components of the auction. Understanding parent-child relations can help
you decide whether some of the parent injectors can be reused by their children.

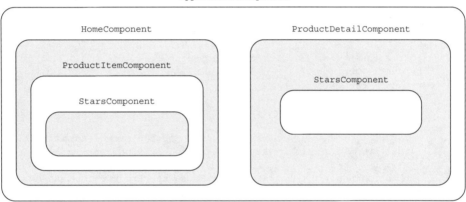

Figure 4.12   Parent-child relations in the auction

In chapter 3, you injected an instance of ProductService in HomeComponent, but
you'll need it in ProductDetailComponent as well. You can define the provider of
ProductService during the bootstrap of the application to make it available in all
children of ApplicationComponent. To do so, follow these steps:

1 Modify the code in app.module.ts to change the route configuration from
products/:prodTitle to products/:productId. The first lines of the @NgMod-
ule decorator should look like this.

Listing 4.8   Modifications in app.module.ts

```
@NgModule({
    imports:[ BrowserModule,
```

```
        RouterModule.forRoot([
           {path: '',   component: HomeComponent},
           {path: 'products/:productId',
               ➥ component: ProductDetailComponent}
   ])],
```

Because you're passing the product ID to `ProductDetailComponent`, its code should be modified accordingly.

2 Open the product-detail.ts file, and modify its code as shown next.

Listing 4.9   Modifications in product-detail.ts

```
import {Component} from '@angular/core';
import { ActivatedRoute} from '@angular/router';
import {Product, Review, ProductService} from
➥ '../../services/product-service';

@Component({
  selector: 'auction-product-page',
  templateUrl: 'app/components/product-detail/product-detail.html'
})
export default class ProductDetailComponent {
  product: Product;
  reviews: Review[];

  constructor(route: ActivatedRoute, productService: ProductService) {

     let prodId: number = parseInt(route.snapshot.params['productId']);
     this.product = productService.getProductById(prodId);

     this.reviews = productService.getReviewsForProduct(this.product.id);
  }
}
```

Angular will inject the `ProductService` instance into `ProductDetailComponent`. When `ProductDetailComponent` is created, it invokes the `getProductsById()` method, which returns one product with an `id` that matches the `productId` passed from the Home view via the constructor's argument of type `Activated-Route`. This is how you populate the `product` variable.

Then the constructor calls the `getReviewsForProduct()` method to populate the `reviews` array. You'll see the declaration of this method as well as the `Review` class later in this section.

3 Create the following product-detail.html file in the product-detail folder.

Listing 4.10   product-detail.html

```
<div class="thumbnail">
    <img src="http://placehold.it/820x320">
    <div>
```

```
        <h4 class="pull-right">{{ product.price }}</h4>
        <h4>{{ product.title }}</h4>
        <p>{{ product.description }}</p>
    </div>
    <div class="ratings">
        <p class="pull-right">{{ reviews.length }} reviews</p>
        <p><auction-stars [rating]="product.rating"></auction-stars></p>
    </div>
</div>
<div class="well" id="reviews-anchor">
    <div class="row">
        <div class="col-md-12"></div>
    </div>
     <div class="row" *ngFor="let review of reviews">
        <hr>
        <div class="col-md-12">
            <auction-stars [rating]="review.rating"></auction-stars>
            <span>{{ review.user }}</span>
            <span class="pull-right">
            ➥ {{ review.timestamp | date: 'shortDate' }}</span>
            <p>{{ review.comment }}</p>
        </div>
    </div>
</div>
```

This HTML template uses local binding to the properties of the product variable. Note how you use square brackets to pass the rating input to Stars-Component (represented by <auction-stars>), introduced in chapter 2. In this version of the auction, the user can only see the reviews; you'll implement the Leave a Review functionality in chapter 6.

The pipe operator (|) allows you to create filters that can transform a value. The expression review.timestamp | date: 'shortDate' takes the timestamp from a Review object and displays it in a shortDate form. You can find other date formats in the Angular documentation at http://mng.bz/CX8F. Angular comes with several classes that can be used with the pipe operator, and you can create custom filters (explained in chapter 5). In chapter 8, you'll see how to use the async pipe to automatically unwrap the server's responses.

4 To save you some typing, copy into your project the app/services/product-service.ts file provided with the code of the auction application for this chapter. This file contains three classes—Product, Review, and ProductService—and hard-coded data for products and reviews. The HTML template from listing 4.10 uses the following Product and Review classes.

Listing 4.11 Product and Review classes

```
export class Product {
  constructor(
    public id: number,
    public title: string,
```

```typescript
    public price: number,
    public rating: number,
    public description: string,
    public categories: string[]) {
  }
}

export class Review {
  constructor(
    public id: number,
    public productId: number,
    public timestamp: Date,
    public user: string,
    public rating: number,
    public comment: string) {
  }
}
```

The `ProductService` class is shown in the next listing.

Listing 4.12   `ProductService` class

```typescript
export class ProductService {
  getProducts(): Product[] {
    return products.map(p => new Product(p.id, p.title, p.price, p.rating,
    ➥ p.description, p.categories));
  }

  getProductById(productId: number): Product {
    return products.find(p => p.id === productId);
  }

  getReviewsForProduct(productId: number): Review[] {
    return reviews
      .filter(r => r.productId === productId)
      .map(r => new Review(r.id, r.productId, Date.parse(r.timestamp),
      ➥ r.user, r.rating, r.comment));
  }
}

var products = [
  {
    "id": 0,
    "title": "First Product",
    "price": 24.99,
    "rating": 4.3,
    "description": "This is a short description.""" Lorem ipsum dolor sit
    ➥ amet, consectetur adipiscing elit.",
    "categories": ["electronics", "hardware"]},
  {
    "id": 1,
    "title": "Second Product",
    "price": 64.99,
```

```
    "rating": 3.5,
    "description": "This is a short description. Lorem ipsum dolor sit
➥ amet, consectetur adipiscing elit.",
    "categories": ["books"]}];

var reviews = [
  {
    "id": 0,
    "productId": 0,
    "timestamp": "2014-05-20T02:17:00+00:00",
    "user": "User 1",
    "rating": 5,
    "comment": "Aenean vestibulum velit id placerat posuere. Praesent..."},
  {
    "id": 1,
    "productId": 0,
    "timestamp": "2014-05-20T02:53:00+00:00",
    "user": "User 2",
    "rating": 3,
    "comment": "Aenean vestibulum velit id placerat posuere. Praesent... "
}];
```

This class has three methods: getProducts(), which returns an array of Product objects; getProductById(), which returns one product; and getReviews-ForProduct(), which returns an array of Review objects for the selected product. All the data for products and reviews is hard-coded in the products and reviews arrays, respectively. (For brevity, we've shown fragments of these arrays.) The getReviewsForProduct() method filters the reviews array to find reviews for the specified productId. Then it uses the map() function to turn an array of Object elements into a new array of Review objects.

Using the ES6 API while compiling into ES5 syntax

If your IDE shows the find() function in red, it's because your tsconfig.json file specifies ES5 as a target for compilation, and find() wasn't supported in ES5 arrays. To remove the red, you can install the type definition file for ES6 shim:

```
npm i @types/es6-shim --save-dev
```

For details, see section B.10.1.

---

5 Start the server in the auction directory by entering the command npm start. When you see the auction's home page, click the product title to see the Product Details view shown in figure 4.11.

4.7   *Summary*

In this chapter, you've learned what the Dependency Injection pattern is and how Angular implements it. The online auction will use DI on every page. These are the main takeaways from this chapter:

- Providers register objects for future injection.
- You can create a provider not only for an object, but for a string value as well.
- Injectors form a hierarchy, and if Angular can't find the provider for the requested type at the component level, it'll try to find it by traversing parent injectors.
- The value of the `providers` property is visible in the child components, whereas `viewProviders` is only visible at the component level.

5
Bindings, observables, and pipes

This chapter covers

- Working with flavors of data binding
- Binding to attributes vs. properties
- Understanding observable data streams
- Treating events as observable data streams
- Minimizing network load by canceling unwanted HTTP requests
- Minimizing manual coding with pipes

The goal of the first four chapters of this book was to jump-start application development with Angular. In those chapters, we discussed how to use property bindings, handle events, and apply directives without providing detailed explanations. In this chapter, we want to take a breather and cover some of these techniques in more detail. You'll continue writing code in TypeScript, and you'll see an example of using destructuring syntax while handing events.

5.1   *Data binding*

Data binding allows you to connect the data from your application with the UI. The data-binding syntax lowers the amount of manual coding. Chapter 2 briefly introduced the data-binding syntax, and you used it in almost every example in the previous chapters. In particular, you've seen the following cases:

```
<h1>Hello {{ name }}!</h1>
```
Displays a value or an expression as a string in a template

```
<span [hidden]="isValid">This field is required</span>
```
Uses square brackets to bind an HTML element's properties

```
<button (click)="placeBid()">Place Bid</button>
```
Binds to events with parentheses

In Angular, data binding is implemented in a unidirectional way (also known as *one-way* data binding). The "one way" could mean either applying data changes from the component's properties to the UI or binding UI events with the component's methods. For example, whenever a component's `productTitle` property is updated, the view (the template) is automatically updated by using the following syntax in the template: `{{productTitle}}`. Similarly, when a user types in an `<input>` field, the event binding (denoted by parentheses) invokes an event handler on the right side of the equal sign:

```
(input) = "onInput()"
```

> **NOTE** In templates, both double curly braces in the text and square brackets in HTML elements' attributes result in property binding. Angular binds the interpolated value (a string with injected expression values) to the `text-Content` property of the corresponding DOM node. It's not just a one-time assignment—the text is constantly updated as the value of the corresponding expression changes.

What's wrong with AngularJS two-way binding?

In AngularJS, data changes on the view automatically update the underlying data (one direction), which also triggers an update of the view (another direction). In other words, AngularJS uses two-way data binding under the hood.

Although having two-way data binding in forms simplifies coding, using it to bind values in various application scripts may substantially slow performance in large applications. That's because AngularJS internally keeps a list of all data-binding expressions on the page, and a browser event can result in AngularJS checking the list of the expressions over and over again until it ensures that everything is in sync. During this process, a single property can be updated multiple times.

Although Angular doesn't use two-way data binding by default, you can still implement it. Now it's your choice, not the framework's. In this section, we'll go over several flavors of data binding:

- Event binding to invoke a function that handles this event
- Attribute binding to update the text value of an HTML element's attribute
- Property binding to update the value of the DOM element's property
- Template binding to transform the view template
- Two-way data binding with `ngModel`

5.1.1   *Binding to events*

To assign an event-handler function to an event, you need to put the event name in parentheses in the component's template. The following code snippet shows how to bind the function `onClickEvent()` to the `click` event, and the function `onInputEvent()` to the `input` event:

```
<button (click)="onClickEvent()">Get Products</button>

<input placeholder="Product name" (input)="onInputEvent()">
```

When the event specified in parentheses is triggered, the expression in double quotes is reevaluated. In the preceding example, the expressions are functions, so they're invoked each time the corresponding event is triggered.

   If you're interested in analyzing the properties of the event object, add the `$event` argument to the handler function. In particular, the `target` property of the event object represents the DOM node where the event occurred. The instance of the event object will be available only within the binding scope (that is, in the event-handler function). Figure 5.1 shows how to read the event-binding syntax.

   The event in parentheses is called *the target of binding*. You can bind functions to any standard DOM events that exist today (see "Event reference" in the Mozilla Developer Network documentation, http://mzl.la/1JcBR22) or that will be introduced in the future. You can also create custom events and bind function handlers to them the same way (see "Output properties and custom events" in section 6.1.1).

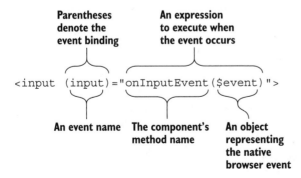

Figure 5.1   Event-binding syntax

5.1.2   *Binding to properties and attributes*

Each HTML element is represented by a tag with *attributes*, and the browser creates a DOM object with *properties* for each tag. The user sees DOM objects on the screen as they're rendered by the browser. You should have a good understanding of what exists at any given moment in three distinct areas:

- The HTML document
- The DOM object
- The rendered UI

An *HTML document* consists of elements represented by tags with attributes, which are always strings. The browser instantiates HTML elements as *DOM objects* (nodes) that have properties and are rendered on the web page as a UI. Whenever the values of the DOM nodes' properties change, the page is re-rendered.

PROPERTIES

Consider the following `<input>` tag:

```
<input type="text" value="John" required>
```

The browser uses this string to create a node in the DOM tree, which is a JavaScript object of type `HTMLInputElement`. Each DOM object has an API in the form of methods and *properties* (see "HTMLInputElement" in the Mozilla Developer Network documentation, http://mzl.la/1QqMBgQ). In particular, the `HTMLInputElement` object includes the properties `type` and `value` of type `DOMString`, and `required` of type `Boolean`. The browser renders this DOM node.

> **NOTE**   The browser will synchronize the rendered values with the values of the corresponding DOM object's properties, regardless of the synchronization features offered by a particular framework.

In Angular, you denote property binding by enclosing the property name in square brackets and assigning an expression (or a class variable) to it. Figure 5.2 illustrates how Angular's property-binding mechanism works. Imagine a component, `MyComponent`, that has a class with a `greeting` variable. The template of this component includes an `<input>` tag with the class variable `greeting` bound to the `value` property.

An application component may have a data structure that serves as a model. Application code may also change the model's property (such as a function that calculates something, or data coming from a server), which will trigger the property-binding mechanism, resulting in UI updates.

When property binding is used

Property binding is used in these two scenarios:

- A component needs to reflect the state of the model in the view.
- A parent component needs to update a property of its child (see the "Input Properties" section in chapter 6).

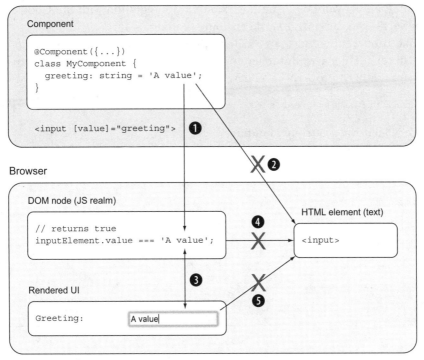

① Angular updates the **DOM** using the one-way property binding (from greeting to the DOM object's property). If a script assigns a reference to this <input> element to the variable inputElement, it's going to be equal to A value. Note that we use dot notation to access the value of the node's property.

② Angular's property binding doesn't update the attribute of the **HTML** element after the value of inputElement.value changes.

③ The DOM node's value property is displayed on the UI. Angular updated the DOM node, and the browser rendered the new value to keep the DOM and UI in sync.

④ The DOM node's value property doesn't change the attribute of the corresponding HTML element.

⑤ The browser doesn't sync the HTML element's attribute with the UI when the user types in the <input>. The user sees the new values coming from the DOM and not from the HTML document.

Figure 5.2 Property binding

ATTRIBUTES

We use the word *attributes* in the context of the HTML document (not the DOM object). Attribute bindings are rarely used, because the browser uses HTML to build the DOM tree; after that, it works mainly with properties of the DOM object. But there are some cases when you may need to use attribute bindings. For example, the hidden attribute isn't supported in Internet Explorer 10, and it won't create a corresponding

DOM attribute, so if you need to toggle the visibility of a component using CSS styles, attribute binding will help. Another example is integration with the Google Polymer framework—you can only do it via attribute binding.

Like property bindings, an attribute binding is denoted by placing an attribute name in square brackets. But to let Angular know that you want to bind to an attribute (and not the DOM property), you have to add the prefix `attr.`:

```
<input [attr.value]="greeting">
```

Figure 5.3 illustrates attribute binding.

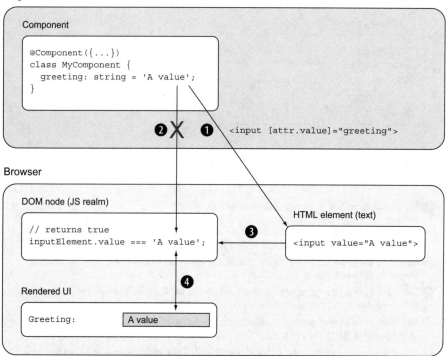

❶ Angular updates the HTML element using the one-way attribute binding (from greeting to the HTML element's attribute). Note the attr. in the binding expression.

❷ Angular's attribute binding doesn't update the DOM's node.

❸ In this case, the DOM's object got A value because the browser synchronized the value attribute between the HTML element and the DOM.

❹ The DOM node's value property is displayed on the UI because the browser keeps the UI and DOM in sync.

Figure 5.3 Attribute binding

Let's see how property and attribute bindings work in a simple example. Listing 5.1 shows an `<input>` element that uses binding with the value attribute and the value property. This code sample is located in the attribute-vs-property.ts file.

Listing 5.1 attribute-vs-property.ts

```
import { platformBrowserDynamic } from '@angular/platform-browser-dynamic';
import { NgModule, Component }       from '@angular/core';
import { BrowserModule } from '@angular/platform-browser';

@Component({
  selector: 'app',
  template: `
    <h3>Property vs attribute binding:</h3>
    <input [value]="greeting"
    [attr.value] = "greeting"
    (input)="onInputEvent($event)">
  `
})
class AppComponent {

  greeting: string = 'A value';

  onInputEvent(event: Event): void {
    let inputElement: HTMLInputElement = <HTMLInputElement> event.target;

    console.log(`The input property value = ${inputElement.value}`);
    console.log(`The input attribute value = ${inputElement
    .getAttribute('value')}`);
    console.log(`The greeting property value = ${this.greeting}`);
  }
}

@NgModule({
  imports:      [ BrowserModule],
  declarations: [ AppComponent],
  bootstrap:    [ AppComponent ]
})
class AppModule { }

platformBrowserDynamic().bootstrapModule(AppModule);
```

Attribute binding (annotation pointing to `[attr.value] = "greeting"`)

Property binding (annotation pointing to `<input [value]="greeting"`)

Binds a standard DOM input event, which is fired when the value of the `<input>` element is changed. (annotation pointing to `(input)="onInputEvent($event)"`)

The onInputEvent() event handler receives the Event object, and its target property has a reference to the element where this event occurs. (annotation pointing to `let inputElement: HTMLInputElement = <HTMLInputElement> event.target;`)

You use getAttribute() to get the attribute's value, whereas properties are accessible using the dot notation.

If you run this program and start typing in the input field, it'll print on the browser console the content of the DOM's value property, the value attribute of the HTML `<input>` element, and the content of the greeting property of MyComponent. Figure 5.4 shows the console output after we started this program and typed 3 in the `<input>` field.

The value of the value attribute didn't change. The value of greeting isn't changed either, which proves that Angular doesn't use two-way data binding. In AngularJS, changing the model (greeting) would update the view; and if the user changed the data on the view, it would automatically update the model.

Figure 5.4   Running the attribute-vs-property example

Simplifying code with destructuring

In appendix A, we'll cover the ES6 destructuring feature, which is also supported by TypeScript. Destructuring could simplify the code of the event-handler function `onInputEvent()` in listing 5.1.

The `onInputEvent()` function receives the `Event` object, and then a line extracts the value from the `target` property. With destructuring syntax, you can eliminate the line that extracts the value of `event.target`:

```
onInputEvent({target}): void {

  console.log(`The input property value = ${target.value}`);
  console.log(`The input attribute value =
  ➥ ${target.getAttribute('value')}`);
  console.log(`The greeting property value = ${this.greeting}`);
}
```

Using the curly braces in the argument of this function sends the following instruction to this function: "You'll get an object that has a `target` property. Just give me the value of this property."

5.1.3   Binding in templates

Say you need to conditionally hide or show a certain HTML element. You can do so by binding a Boolean flag to a `hidden` attribute or a `display` style of the element. Depending on the flag's value, this element will be either shown or hidden, but the object that represents this element remains in the DOM tree.

Angular offers *structural directives* (NgIf, NgSwitch, and NgFor) that change the DOM's structure by removing elements from or adding elements to it. NgIf can conditionally remove an element from or add one to the DOM tree. NgFor loops through an array and adds an element to the DOM tree for each array element. NgSwitch adds one element to the DOM tree from a set of possible elements, based on some condition. Using template binding, you can instruct Angular to do this for you. Removing elements can be better than hiding them if you want to ensure that your application won't waste time supporting the behavior of these elements (such as processing events or monitoring change detection).

HTML templates and Angular directives

The HTML `<template>` tag (see "<template>" in the Mozilla Developer Network documentation, http://mzl.la/1OndeMV) isn't a typical tag, because the browser ignores its content unless the application includes a script to parse and add it to the DOM. Angular offers so-called *shortcut syntaxes* for directives—they start with an asterisk, such as `*ngIf` or `*ngFor`. When Angular's parser sees a directive that starts with an asterisk, it converts this directive into an HTML fragment that uses a `<template>` tag and is recognizable by browsers.

Listing 5.2 includes one `<span>` and one `<template>` and illustrates two flavors of template binding using the `NgIf` directive. Depending on the flag's value (which is toggled by the button click), the `<span>` elements either add to the DOM or remove from it.

> **Listing 5.2   template-binding.ts**

```
import { platformBrowserDynamic } from '@angular/platform-browser-dynamic';
import { NgModule, Component }      from '@angular/core';
import { BrowserModule } from '@angular/platform-browser';

@Component({
    selector: 'app',
    template: `
    <button (click)="flag = !flag">Toggle flag's value</button>

    <p>
      Flag's value: {{flag}}
    </p>

    <p>
      1. span with *ngIf="flag": <span *ngIf="flag">Flag is true</span>
    </p>

    <p>
      2. template with [ngIf]="flag": <template [ngIf]="flag">Flag is true
      ➥ </template>
    </p>
    `
})
class AppComponent {
    flag: boolean = true;
}

@NgModule({
    imports:       [ BrowserModule],
    declarations: [ AppComponent],
```

```
    bootstrap:    [ AppComponent ]
})
class AppModule { }

platformBrowserDynamic().bootstrapModule(AppModule);
```

Unlike other Angular bindings, the template binding transforms the view template. The code in listing 5.2 conditionally adds the message about the flag's value to or removes it from the DOM tree. You use both the shortcut syntax, `*ngIf="flag"`, to handle the `<span>` element and a fully expanded version, `[ngIf]="flag"`, to handle the content of the `<template>` tag.

Figure 5.5 shows that when the flag is `true`, the DOM tree includes the content of both `<span>` and `<template>`. Figure 5.6 shows that when the flag is `false`, the DOM tree doesn't include either `<span>` or `<template>`.

Figure 5.5 Template binding: flag is `true`.

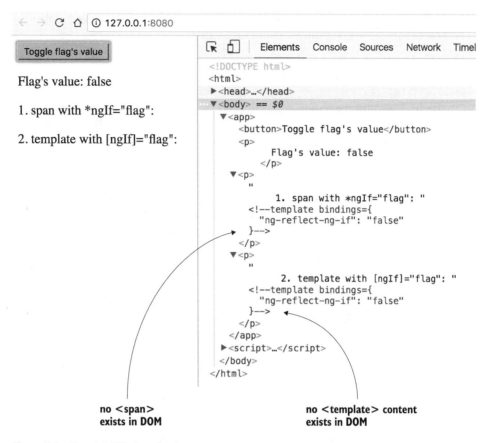

Figure 5.6 Template binding: flag is `false`.

All the binding examples you've seen so far illustrate binding in one direction: either from the UI to the application code, or from the code to the UI. But there's another scenario in which binding works in both directions, and we'll discuss it next.

5.1.4 *Two-way data binding*

Two-way data binding is a simple way to keep the view and the model in sync. Whether the view or the model change first, both are immediately synchronized.

You've learned that one-way binding from the UI to an Angular component is arranged by surrounding an event name with parentheses:

```
<input (input)="onInputEvent($event)">
```

One-way binding from a component to the UI is denoted by surrounding an HTML attribute with square brackets:

```
<input [value]="myComponentProperty" >
```

In some cases, you may still want to use two-way binding. The longer way of combining the two preceding examples would be as follows:

```
<input [value]="myComponentProperty"
       (input)="onInputEvent($event)>
```

Angular also offers a shorter, combined notation: `[()]`. In particular, Angular has a `NgModel` directive that you can use for two-way binding (note that when `NgModel` is used in templates, its name isn't capitalized):

```
<input [(ngModel)] = "myComponentProperty">
```

You can still see `myComponentProperty`, but which event does it handle? In this example, the `NgModel` directive is used with the `<input>` element. This event is the default trigger for synchronizing UI changes in the HTML `<input>` element with the underlying model. But the driving event can be different, depending on the UI control being used with `ngModel`. This is controlled internally by a special `ControlValueAccessor` Angular interface, which serves as a bridge between a control and a native element. `ControlValueAccessor` is used to create custom form controls.

Two-way binding was popular with forms where we needed to synchronize values from the form fields with the properties of underlying model object. In chapter 7, we'll cover the use of the `NgModel` directive in greater detail. You'll learn how to handle forms without needing to use `[(ngModel)]` for each form's control; but there are some cases where it can be handy, so let's get familiar with the syntax.

Suppose the landing page of a financial application allows the user to check the latest prices of a stock by entering its symbol in an input field. Users often enter the same stocks that they own or follow, such as `AAPL` for Apple. You can save the last-entered symbol as a cookie (or in HTML5 local storage), and the next time the user opens this page, the program can read the cookie and populate the input field. The user should still be able to type in this field, and the entered value should be synchronized with a `lastStockSymbol` variable, which plays the role of the model. The following listing implements this functionality.

Listing 5.3   two-way-binding.ts

```
import { platformBrowserDynamic } from '@angular/platform-browser-dynamic';
import { NgModule, Component }       from '@angular/core';
import { BrowserModule } from '@angular/platform-browser';
import { FormsModule } from '@angular/forms';

@Component({                                    Requests the two-way binding to synchronize
    selector: 'stock-search',                           the changes with lastStockSymbol
    template: `<input type='text' placeholder= "Enter stock symbol"
    ➥ [(ngModel)] = "lastStockSymbol" />                                    ◁─┐
            <br>The value of lastStockSymbol is {{lastStockSymbol}}`
})
```

```
class StockComponent {

    lastStockSymbol: string;                    ⊲──┐

    constructor() {
        setTimeout(() => {                               ⊲──┐
            // Code to get the last entered stock from
            // local history goes here (not implemented)

            this.lastStockSymbol="AAPL";
        }, 2000);
    }
}
@Component({
    selector: 'app',
    directives: [StockComponent],
    template:`<stock-search></stock-search>`

})
class AppComponent {}

@NgModule({
    imports:        [ BrowserModule, FormsModule],    ⊲──┐
    declarations:   [ AppComponent],
    bootstrap:      [ AppComponent ]
})
class AppModule { }

platformBrowserDynamic().bootstrapModule(AppModule);
```

lastStockSymbol is the model, and it can be modified either by the user typing in the input field or programmatically.

To emulate the scenario of reading the last stock symbol from a cookie, you arrange a one-second delay, after which the value of lastStockSymbol is changed to AAPL and the input field shows it.

Imports FormsModule so you can use NgModel

The `lastStockSymbol` variable and the value of the `<input>` field are always in sync. You can see this in action by running the script in the two-way-binding.ts file.

> **NOTE** Listing 5.3 uses Angular's `NgModel` directive to implement two-way data binding, but you can use application-specific properties for this as well. You'll need to name the properties using a special suffix, `Change`. In the hands-on section of chapter 6, you'll see how to modify a product rating using two-way binding with the `[(rating)]` syntax.

In AngularJS, two-way binding was the default mode of operation, which seems like a simple and elegant solution for synchronizing a view and a model. But on a complex UI containing dozens of controls, changing the value in one place could cause a chain of binding updates, and performance could suffer.

With two-way binding, debugging could also be more difficult, because there could be many reasons why a particular value was changed. Was it because of the user's input, or was it the result of a modified value in some variable?

Implementing change detection in the Angular framework wasn't trivial, either. With a unidirectional data flow, you always know where the change to a particular UI element or component property comes from, because only one property in the component's code can change a particular value on the UI.

5.2   *Reactive programming and observables*

Reactive programming is about creating responsive (fast) event-driven applications, where an observable event stream is pushed to subscribers. In software engineering, Observer/Observable is a well-known pattern, and it's a good fit in any asynchronous processing scenario. But reactive programming is a lot more than just an implementation of the Observer/Observable pattern. The observable streams can be canceled, they can notify about the end of a stream, and the data pushed to the subscriber can be transformed on the way from the source to the subscriber by applying various operators (functions).

> **NOTE** One of the most important characteristics of observables is that they implement the *push model* of data processing. In contrast, the *pull model* is implemented by looping through an array, by an Iterable, or by using ES6 generator functions.

Multiple libraries implement reactive extensions that support observable streams, and RxJS (https://github.com/Reactive-Extensions/RxJS) is one such library. The RxJS library is integrated in Angular.

5.2.1   *What are observables and observers?*

An *observer* is an object that handles a data stream pushed by an *observable* function. There are two main types of observables: hot and cold. A *cold* observable starts streaming data when some code invokes a subscribe() function on it. A *hot* observable streams data even if there's no subscriber interested in the data. In this book, we'll use only cold observables.

A script that subscribes to an observable provides the observer object that knows what to do with the stream elements:

```
let mySubscription: Subscription = someObservable.subscribe(myObserver);
```

To cancel the stream subscription, invoke the unsubscribe() method:

```
mySubscription.unsubscribe();
```

An *observable* is an object that streams elements from some data source (a socket, an array, UI events) one element at a time. To be precise, an observable stream knows how to do three things:

- Emit the next element
- Throw an error
- Send a signal that the streaming is over (that the last element has been served)

Accordingly, an observer object provides up to three callbacks:

- The function to handle the next element emitted by the observable
- The function to handle errors in the observable
- The function to be invoked when the stream of data finishes

NOTE In appendix A, we'll discuss using the `Promise` object, which can invoke an event handler specified in the `then()` function only once. The `subscribe()` method is like a sequence of `then()` invocations: one invocation for each arriving data element.

Application code can apply a sequence of operators, transforming each element prior to supplying it to the handler function. Figure 5.7 shows a sample data flow from an observable that emits data to a subscriber (which implements the observer). This data flow applies two operators: `map()` and `filter()`. The emitter (the producer) creates an original stream of data (rectangles). The `map()` operator transfers each rectangle into a triangle, which is given to a `filter()` operator that filters out the stream to push only selected triangles to the subscriber.

Figure 5.7   From observable to subscriber

A more realistic example would be a stream of `Customer` objects that's mapped to another stream containing only the `age` property of each customer. The first stream could be filtered to keep only those customer objects where `age < 50`.

NOTE Each operator accepts an observable object as an argument and returns an observable as well. This allows for chaining operators.

The documentation of reactive extensions (see "Operators" in the ReactiveX documentation, http://reactivex.io/documentation/operators.html) uses *marble* diagrams to illustrate operators. For example, the `map()` operator is represented as the marble diagram shown in figure 5.8.

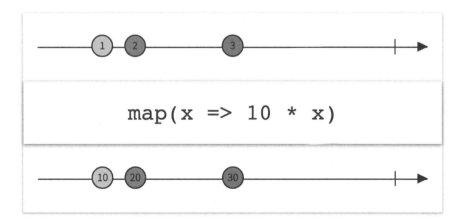

Figure 5.8   A marble diagram for `map`

This figure illustrates a map operator that applies a function multiplying each element of the stream by 10. The vertical bars on the right represent the ends of the respective streams. In marble diagrams, errors are represented by red cross signs.

TIP   Check out the RxMarbles website (http://rxmarbles.com), which offers interactive marble diagrams for a variety of Rx operators.

From arrays to iterables and observables

JavaScript has a number of useful methods for working with arrays of data, such as these:

- `map()`—Allows you to apply a function to each element of the array. With `map()`, you can transform one array into another without changing the number of elements. For example, `myArray.map(convertToJSON)`.
- `filter()`—Allows you to apply a function to each element of an array, filtering out elements by applying some business logic. For example, `myArray.filter (priceIsLessThan100)`. The resulting array may have fewer elements than the original.
- `reduce()`—Allows you to produce an aggregate value from an array's elements. For example, `myArray.reduce((x,y) => x+y)`. The result of `reduce()` is always a single value.

A stream is a collection of data given to your application over time. ES6 introduces the concept of *iterables* and *iterators* that let you treat an array as a data collection and iterate through its elements one at time.

The source of the iterable data doesn't have to be an array. You can write an ES6 generator function (see appendix A) that returns a reference to its iterator, and then you can start *pulling* the data (one at a time) from this iterator: `myIterator .next().value`. For each value, you can apply some business logic and then reach out for the next element.

An observable object is a more advanced version of an iterator. Iterators use the pull model to retrieve the data, whereas observables push the data to subscribers.

It's probably easier to understand the concept of an observable stream by visualizing asynchronous data coming from the server. You'll see such an example later in this chapter, and more in chapter 8 when you learn how to work with HTTP requests and WebSockets, but the concept of an observable stream can be applied to events as well. Is an event a one-time deal that just needs a handler function? Can you think of an event as a sequence of elements provided over time? We'll discuss event streams next.

NOTE   You'll see how to turn any service into an observable in chapter 8.

5.2.2   *Observable event streams*

Earlier in this chapter, you learned about the syntax of event binding in templates. Now let's take a closer look at event handling.

Each event is represented by the Event object (or a descendant) containing properties describing the event. Angular applications can handle standard DOM events and can create and *emit* (dispatch) custom events as well.

A handler function for an event can be declared with an optional $event parameter that contains a JavaScript object with properties describing the event. With standard DOM events, you can use any functions or properties of the browser's Event object (see "Event" in the Mozilla Developer Network documentation, http://mzl.la/1EAG6iw).

In some cases, you won't be interested in reading the event object's properties, such as when the only button on a page is clicked, and this is all that matters. In other cases, you may want to know specific information, such as what character was entered in the <input> field when the keyup event was dispatched:

```
template:`<input (keyup)="onKey($event)">`
...

onKey(event:any) {
  console.log("You have entered " + event.target.value);
}
```

The preceding code snippet accesses the value property of the <input> element by using event.target, which points at the element that dispatched the event. But Angular allows you to get the HTML element (and its properties) right in the template by declaring a *template local variable* that will always hold a reference to its HTML element.

The following code fragment declares a mySearchField local template variable (the name must start with a hash sign), extracts the value of the hosting HTML element (<input> in this case), and passes it to the event-handler function rather than the reference to the Event object. Note that the hash sign is needed only to declare a local variable in the template; you don't need the hash when using this variable in the JavaScript portion of the code:

```
template:`<input #mySearchField (keyup)="onKey(mySearchField.value)">`
...

onKey(value: string) {
  console.log("You have entered " + value);
}
```

> **NOTE** If your code dispatches a custom event, it can carry application-specific data, and the event object can be strongly typed (not just be of the type any). You'll see how to do this in chapter 6, in the section "Output properties and custom events."

A traditional JavaScript application treats a dispatched event as a one-time deal; for example, one click results in one function invocation. Angular offers another approach where you consider events observable streams of data happening over time. Handling observable streams is an important technique to master, so let's see what it's all about.

By subscribing to a stream, your code expresses an interest in receiving the stream's elements. During subscription, you specify the code to be invoked when the next element is emitted, and optionally the code for error processing and stream completion. Often you'll specify a number of chained operators and then invoke the `subscribe()` method.

How does all this apply to events coming from the UI? You could use event binding that handles multiple `keyup` events and handles the value of `lastStockSymbol`:

```
<input type='text' (keyup) = "getStockPrice($event)">
```

Isn't this technique good enough for handling multiple events? Imagine that the preceding code is used to get a price quote for the AAPL stock. After the user types the first *A*, the `getStockPrice()` function will make a promise-based request to the server, which will return the price of A, if there is such a stock. Then the user enters the second *A*, which results in another server request for the AA price quote. The process repeats for *AAP* and *AAPL*.

This isn't what you want, so you can arrange a 500-millisecond delay to give the user enough time to type several letters. The `setTimeout()` function comes to the rescue!

What if the user types slowly, and during the 500-millisecond interval manages only to enter *AAP*? The first request for AAP goes to the server, and 500 milliseconds later the second request for AAPL is sent. A program can't cancel the first HTTP request if the server returns a `Promise` object, so you'll keep your fingers crossed that your users type quickly and don't overload the server with unwanted requests.

With observable streams, there's a better solution to this problem, and some of the Angular UI components can generate them. For example, `FormControl` class is one of the fundamental blocks of forms processing and represents form elements. Each form element has its own `FormControl` object. By default, whenever the value of the form element changes, `FormControl` emits the `valueChanges` event, which produces an observable stream you can subscribe to.

Let's write a small app that uses a simple form with one input field that generates an observable stream. To understand the next example, you need to know that form elements are bound to Angular component properties via the `formControl` attribute.

> **NOTE**   There's a way to program forms by using directives in the component's template: these are *template-driven forms*. You can also program forms by creating form-related objects in the TypeScript code of your components. These are *reactive forms*. We'll cover Angular forms in chapter 7.

Listing 5.4 applies just one operator, `debounceTime()`, prior to invoking `subscribe()`. RxJS supports dozens of operators that you can use with observable streams (see the RxJS documentation, http://mng.bz/ZxZT), but Angular didn't reimplement all of them in the framework. That's why you need to import additional operators from

RxJS, which is a peer dependency of Angular. The `debounceTime()` operator lets you specify a delay in emitting data elements of a stream.

Listing 5.4 observable-events.ts

```
import { platformBrowserDynamic } from '@angular/platform-browser-dynamic';
import { NgModule, Component }      from '@angular/core';
import { BrowserModule } from '@angular/platform-browser';
import { FormControl,  ReactiveFormsModule} from '@angular/forms';
import 'rxjs/add/operator/debounceTime';

@Component({
    selector: "app",
    template: `
      <h2>Observable events demo</h2>
      <input type="text" placeholder="Enter stock" [formControl]="searchInput">
    `
})
class AppComponent {

    searchInput: FormControl = new FormControl('');

    constructor(){

        this.searchInput.valueChanges
            .debounceTime(500)
            .subscribe(stock => this.getStockQuoteFromServer(stock));
    }

    getStockQuoteFromServer(stock: string) {

        console.log(`The price of ${stock} is ${100*Math.random()
        ➥ .toFixed(4)}`);
    }
}

@NgModule({
    imports:       [ BrowserModule,  ReactiveFormsModule],
    declarations: [ AppComponent],
    bootstrap:     [ AppComponent ]
})
class AppModule { }

platformBrowserDynamic().bootstrapModule(AppModule);
```

You can either import the implementation of specific operators, as is done here, or import all of them using import 'rxjs/Rx';.

This <input> element is represented by the ngFormControl named search.

Waits 500 milliseconds before emitting the next event with the content of the <input> element

Subscribes to the observable stream

Imports the module supporting reactive forms

The `subscribe()` method creates the instance of `Observer`, which in this case passes each value from the stream generated by the `searchInput` to the `getStockQuote-FromServer()` method. In a real-world scenario, this method would issue a request to the server, and you'll see such an app in the next section; but for now, this function just generates a random number.

If you didn't use the `debounceTime()` operator, the `valueChanges` event would be emitted after each character typed by the user. To prevent processing each keystroke, you instruct `searchInput` to emit the data with a 500-millisecond delay, which allows the user to enter several characters before the content of the input field is emitted into the stream. Figure 5.9 shows a screenshot taken after we started this application and entered `AAPL` in the input field.

TIP   No matter how many operators you chain together, none of them will be invoked on the stream until you invoke `subscribe()`.

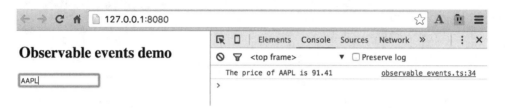

Figure 5.9   Getting the price for AAPL

NOTE   Listing 5.4 handles an observable stream that the `FormControl` object provided when the DOM object emitted the `change` event. If you prefer to generate an observable stream based on another event (such as on `keyup`), you can use the RxJS `Observable.fromEvent()` API (see the RxJS documentation on GitHub, http://mng.bz/8K8l).

You may argue that you could implement the preceding example by handling the `input` event, which would be dispatched when the user finished entering the stock symbol and moved the focus out of the input field. This is true, but there are many scenarios where you'll want an immediate response from the server, such as retrieving and filtering a data collection as the user types.

Listing 5.4 doesn't really make any network requests to the server for price quotes—you generate random numbers on the user's computer. Even if the user enters a wrong stock symbol, this example will result in a local invocation of `Math.random()`, which has a negligible effect on the application's performance. In a real-world application, the user's typos may generate network requests that introduce delays while returning quotes for mistakenly entered stock symbols. In the next section, we'll show you how to cancel pending server requests with observable streams.

5.2.3   *Cancelling observables*

One of the benefits of observables over promises is that the former can be canceled. In the previous section, we offered one scenario in which a typo might result in useless server requests. Implementing master-detail views is another use case for a request cancellation. Say a user clicks a row in a list of products to see the product details that must be retrieved from the server. Then they change their mind and click another row, which issues another server request; in that case, the pending request should ideally be canceled.

Let's look at how you can cancel pending requests by creating an application that issues HTTP requests as the user types in the input field. You'll handle two observable streams:

- The observable stream produced by the search field
- The observable stream produced by the HTTP requests issued while the user is typing in the search field

For this example (observable-events-http.ts), you'll use the free weather service at http://openweathermap.org, which provides an API for making weather requests for cities around the world. It returns the weather information as a JSON-formatted string. For example, to get the current temperature in London in Fahrenheit (units=imperial), the URL looks like this:

```
http://api.openweathermap.org/data/2.5/
➥ find?q=London&units=imperial&appid=12345
```

To use this service, you go to openweathermap.org and receive an application ID (appid). The code in listing 5.5 constructs the request URL by concatenating the base URL with the entered city name and the application ID. As the user enters the characters of the city name, the code subscribes to the event stream and issues HTTP requests. If a new request is issued before the response from the previous one comes back, the switchMap() operator cancels the previous request and sends the new one to this weather service. Canceling pending requests can't be done with promises. This example also uses the FormControl directive to generate an observable stream from the input field where the user enters the name of the city.

Listing 5.5   observable-events-http.ts

```
import { platformBrowserDynamic } from '@angular/platform-browser-dynamic';
import { NgModule, Component }       from '@angular/core';
import { BrowserModule } from '@angular/platform-browser';
import { FormControl,  ReactiveFormsModule} from '@angular/forms';
import {HttpModule, Http} from '@angular/http';              ⟵┐ Imports the required
                                                             │ HTTP support
import {Observable} from 'rxjs/Rx';
import 'rxjs/add/operator/switchMap';
import 'rxjs/add/operator/map';
import 'rxjs/add/operator/debounceTime';

@Component({
    selector: "app",
    template: `
      <h2>Observable weather</h2>
      <input type="text" placeholder="Enter city" [formControl]="searchInput">
      <h3>{{temperature}}</h3>
    `
})
```

```
class AppComponent {
  private baseWeatherURL: string=
➡ 'http://api.openweathermap.org/data/2.5/find?q=';
  private urlSuffix: string =
    ➡ "&units=imperial&appid=ca3f6d6ca3973a518834983d0b318f73";

  searchInput: FormControl = new FormControl('');
  temperature: string;

  constructor(private http:Http) {

      this.searchInput.valueChanges
        .debounceTime(200)
        .switchMap(city => this.getWeather(city))    ◀──┐
        .subscribe(
          res => {
              if (res['cod'] === '404') return;
              if (!res.main) {
                      this.temperature ='City is not found';
              } else {

                      this.temperature =
                          `Current temperature is  ${res.main.temp}F, ` +
                          `humidity: ${res.main.humidity}%`;
              }
          },
          err => console.log(`Can't get weather. Error code: %s, URL: %s`,
            ➡ err.message, err.url),
              () => console.log(`Weather is retrieved`)    ◀──┐
      );
  }

  getWeather(city: string): Observable<Array<string>> {
    return this.http.get(this.baseWeatherURL + city + this.urlSuffix)  ◀──┐
        .map(res => {
              console.log(res);
              return res.json()});    ◀──┐
  }
}
@NgModule({
    imports:        [ BrowserModule,   ReactiveFormsModule,
                      HttpModule],    ◀──
    declarations: [ AppComponent],        │ Adds HttpModule
    bootstrap:      [ AppComponent ]
})
class AppModule { }

platformBrowserDynamic().bootstrapModule(AppModule);
```

The switchMap() operator takes the entered value from the input field (the first observable) and passes it to the getWeather() method, which issues the HTTP request to the weather service.

The subscribe() method is needed to start the observable emitting its data, in this case at 200-millisecond intervals.

The second argument of subscribe() is a callback that's invoked in the case of an error.

The third argument of subscribe() is invoked after the stream is complete.

The getWeather() method constructs the URL and defines the HTTP GET request.

The map() operator takes the data that arrives in JSON form wrapped in the response object and converts it to an object.

We'd like you to recognize two observables in listing 5.5:

- The FormControl directive creates an observable from the input field events (this.searchInput.valueChanges).
- getWeather() also returns an observable.

You use the switchMap() operator instead of subscribe when the function that handles data generated by observable can also return an observable. Then you use subscribe() for the second observable:

Observable1 → switchMap(function) → Observable2 → subscribe()

You're switching over from the first observable to the second one. If Observable1 pushes the new value but the function that creates Observable2 hasn't finished yet, it's killed; switchMap() unsubscribes and resubscribes to Observable1 and starts handling the new value from this stream.

If the observable stream from the UI pushes the next value before getWeather() has returned its observable value, switchMap() kills the running getWeather(), gets the new value for the city from the UI, and invokes getWeather() again. While killing getWeather(), it also aborts the HTTP request that was slow and didn't complete in time.

The first argument of subscribe() contains a callback for handling data coming from the server. The code in this arrow expression is specific to the API provided by the weather service. You just extract the temperature and humidity from the returned JSON. The API offered by this particular weather service stores the error codes in the response, so you manually handle the status 404 here and not in the error-handler callback.

Now let's verify that canceling previous requests works. Typing the word London takes more than the 200 milliseconds specified in debounceTime(), which means the valueChanges event will emit the observable data more than once. To ensure that the request to the server takes more than 200 milliseconds, you need a slow internet connection.

> **NOTE** Listing 5.5 has lots of code in the constructor, which may look like a red flag to developers who prefer using constructors only to initialize variables and not to execute any code that takes time to complete. If you take a closer look, though, you'll notice that it just creates a subscription to two observable streams (UI events and HTTP service). No actual processing is done until the user starts entering the name of a city, which happens after the component is already rendered.

We ran the preceding example and then turned on throttling in Chrome Developer Tools, emulating a slow GPRS connection. Typing the word *London* resulted in four getWeather() invocations: for *Lo, Lon, Lond*, and *London*. Accordingly, four HTTP requests were sent over the slow connection, and three of them were automatically canceled by the switchMap() operator, as shown in figure 5.10.

With very little programming, you saved bandwidth by eliminating the need for the server to send four HTTP responses for cities you're not interested in and that may not even exist. As we stated in chapter 1, a good framework is one that allows you to write less code.

Pipes are yet another Angular feature that let you achieve more with less manual coding.

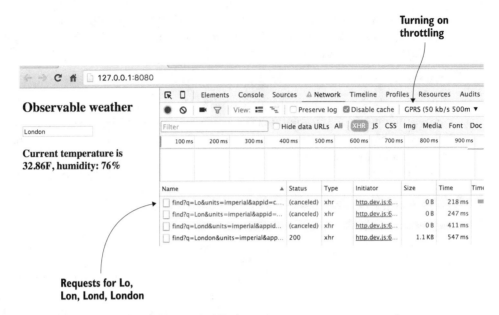

Figure 5.10   Running observable_events_http.ts

NOTE   Chapter 9 contains a refactored version of the weather application.

5.3   *Pipes*

A *pipe* is a template element that allows you to transform a value into a desired output. A pipe is specified by adding the vertical bar (|) and the pipe name right after the value to be transformed:

```
template: `<p>Your birthday is {{ birthday | date }}</p>`
```

Angular comes with a number of predefined pipes, and each pipe has a class that implements its functionality (such as `DatePipe`) as well as the name you can use in the template (such as `date`):

- `UpperCasePipe` allows you to convert an input string into uppercase by using | uppercase in the template.
- `DatePipe` lets you display a date in different formats by using | date.
- `CurrencyPipe` transforms a number into a desired currency by using | currency.
- `AsyncPipe` will unwrap the data from the provided observable stream by using | async. You'll see a code sample that uses `async` in chapter 8.

Some pipes don't require input parameters (such as `uppercase`), and some do (such as `date:'medium'`). You can chain as many pipes as you want. The next code snippet shows how to display the value of the `birthday` variable in a medium date format and in uppercase (for example, JUN 15, 2001, 9:43:11 PM):

```
template=
  `<p>
    {{ birthday | date:'medium' | uppercase}}
  </p>`
```

As you can see, with literally no coding, you can convert a date into the required format as well as show it in uppercase (see the date formats in the Angular `DatePipe` documentation, http://mng.bz/78lD).

A workaround for broken pipes

At the time of writing, pipes such as `date`, `number`, and `currency` don't work in all browsers. There are two workarounds for this issue:

- Add the polyfill service to your index.html:

  ```
  <script src="https://cdn.polyfill.io/v2/
  ➥ polyfill.min.js?features=Intl.~locale.en"></script>
  ```

  This service will polyfill just what your browser needs.

- If you don't want (or aren't allowed) to load scripts from CDNs, add the internationalization package to your project:

  ```
  npm install intl@1.1.0 --save
  ```

  Then add the following lines to your index.html:

  ```
  <script src="node_modules/intl/dist/Intl.min.js"></script>
  <script src="node_modules/intl/locale-data/jsonp/en.js"></script>
  ```

The second solution will increase the size of your application by 33 KB.

You can read more about pipes in the Angular documentation at https://angular.io/docs/ts/latest/guide/pipes.html, which includes the name of the class implementing a particular pipe as well as examples of its use.

5.3.1 Custom pipes

In addition to predefined pipes, Angular offers a simple way to create custom pipes, which can include code specific to your application. You need to create a `@Pipe` annotated class that implements the `PipeTransform` interface. The `PipeTransform` interface has the following signature:

```
export interface PipeTransform {
  transform(value: any, ...args: any[]): any;
}
```

This tells you that a custom pipe class must implement just one method with the preceding signature. The first parameter of transform takes a value to be transformed, and the second defines zero or more parameters required for your transformation algorithm. The @Pipe annotation is where you specify the name of the pipe to be used in the template. If your component uses custom pipes, they have to be explicitly listed in its @Component annotation in the pipes property.

In the previous section, the weather example displayed the temperature in London in Fahrenheit. But most countries use the metric system and show temperature in Celsius. Let's create a custom pipe that can convert the temperature from Fahrenheit to Celsius and back. The code of the custom TemperaturePipe pipe (see the following listing) can be used in a template as temperature.

Listing 5.6 temperature-pipe.ts

A custom pipe implements the PipeTransform interface, so you must add the transform method.

The name of the pipe is temperature, and it can be used in the component's template.

If this pipe is used without providing a format, you throw an error. An alternative approach would be to return the provided value without transformation.

```
import {Pipe, PipeTransform} from '@angular/core';

@Pipe({name: 'temperature'})
export class TemperaturePipe implements PipeTransform {

    transform(value: any[], fromTo: string): any {

        if (!fromTo) {
            throw "Temperature pipe requires parameter FtoC or CtoF ";
        }

        return (fromTo == 'FtoC') ?
                (value - 32) * 5.0/9.0:  // F to C
                value * 9.0 / 5.0 + 32;  // C to F

    }
}
```

Next comes the code of the component (pipe-tester.ts) that uses the temperature pipe. Initially this program will convert the temperature from Fahrenheit to Celsius (the FtoC format). By clicking the toggle button, you can change the direction of the temperature conversion.

Listing 5.7 pipe-tester.ts

```
import { platformBrowserDynamic } from '@angular/platform-browser-dynamic';
import { NgModule, Component }     from '@angular/core';
import { BrowserModule } from '@angular/platform-browser';
import { FormsModule } from '@angular/forms';
import {TemperaturePipe} from './temperature-pipe';

@Component({
```

```
    selector: 'app',

    template:`<input type='text' value="0"
            placeholder= "Enter temperature" [(ngModel)] = "temp">
            <button (click)="toggleFormat()">Toggle Format</button>
            <br>In {{targetFormat}} this temperature is {{temp | temperature:
        ➥ format | number:'1.1-2'}}`
})
class AppComponent {

    temp: number;
    toCelsius: boolean=true;
    targetFormat: string ='Celsius';
    format: string='FtoC';

    toggleFormat(){

        this.toCelsius = !this.toCelsius;
        this.format = this.toCelsius? 'FtoC': 'CtoF';

        this.targetFormat = this.toCelsius?'Celsius':'Fahrenheit';
    }
}
@NgModule({
    imports:       [ BrowserModule, FormsModule],
    declarations: [ AppComponent, TemperaturePipe],
    bootstrap:     [ AppComponent ]
})
class AppModule { }

platformBrowserDynamic().bootstrapModule(AppModule);
```

Chains the temperature pipe with Angular's number pipe to display the resulting temperature as a number that has at least one digit before the decimal point and up to two digits after

The initial value, FtoC, is passed as a parameter to the temperature pipe.

When the user clicks the toggle button, switches the conversion direction and changes the output text accordingly

Imports FormsModule, which is required for ngModel support

Explicitly lists the custom pipe in the module declarations

In the following section, you'll create yet another custom pipe to filter auctioned products.

5.4 *Hands-on: filtering products in the online auction*

In this exercise, you'll use observable event streams to filter featured products on the home page of the online auction. An auction (or any online store) may display many products, which complicates finding a specific product.

For example, auction users may remember just a couple of letters in a product title. To spare them scrolling through pages of products, you'll let them start typing the product title to filter out products that don't match. Most important, the rendered product list must change as the user types.

This is a good use case for applying reactive observable event streams. The user types a letter, which emits the next element of the stream that represents the current content of the search field. The subscriber of this stream provides immediate filtering and re-rendering of the products on the UI. In this scenario, you won't make any requests to the server.

NOTE   We'll use the auction application developed in chapter 4 as a starting point for this exercise. If you prefer to see the final version of this project, you can browse the source code in the auction folder for chapter 5. Otherwise, copy the auction folder from chapter 4 to a separate location, run `npm install`, and follow the instructions in this section.

Follow these steps:

1 Create a custom pipe, `FilterPipe`. To do so, create a new pipes subdirectory under app, and in it create the following filter-pipe.ts file, implementing the custom pipe `FilterPipe`.

Listing 5.8   filter-pipe.ts

```
import { Pipe, PipeTransform} from '@angular/core';

@Pipe({name: 'filter'})
export class FilterPipe implements PipeTransform {

  transform(list: any[], filterByField: string, filterValue: string): any {

    if (!filterByField || !filterValue) {          ◁─── If either the field name
        return list;                                     or the filter's value isn't
    }                                                    provided, don't filter.

    return list.filter(item => {                   ◁───
        const field = item[filterByField].toLowerCase();
        const filter = filterValue.toLocaleLowerCase();
        return field.indexOf(filter) >= 0;
    });
  }
}
```

Filters the array of Product objects by the property passed in the filterByField parameter. It returns true only for those array elements that have characters provided as a filterValue.

2 Modify `HomeComponent` to use `FilterPipe`. `HomeComponent` is the parent of `<auction-product-item>` components, and it also has a `products` variable that stores an array of products provided by `ProductService`. `FilterPipe` will filter out the elements of this array.

You need to add an `<input>` element where the user can enter a filter criterion. `HomeComponent` will subscribe to the observable stream of events from this input field to get the value for the pipe.

Finally, you need to use the custom pipe, which requires the following:

- Import the `FilterPipe`.
- Include `FilterPipe` in the `declarations` section of the `@NgModule` annotation.
- Apply the filter in the `*ngFor` loop to each array element.

Modify the code of the home.ts file so it looks like the following listing.

Listing 5.9 home.ts

```
import {Component} from '@angular/core';
import {FormControl} from '@angular/forms';
import {Product, ProductService} from '../../services/product-service';
import CarouselComponent from '../carousel/carousel';
import ProductItemComponent from '../product-item/product-item';
import {FilterPipe} from '../pipes/filter-pipe'         ◁──────┐  Imports the pipe
import 'rxjs/add/operator/debounceTime';

@Component({
  selector: 'auction-home-page',
  styleUrls: ['app/components/home/home.css'],
  template: `
    <div class="row carousel-holder">
      <div class="col-md-12">
        <auction-carousel></auction-carousel>
      </div>
    </div>
    <div class="row">
      <div class="col-md-12">
        <div class="form-group">
          <input placeholder="Filter products by title"
                 class="form-control" type="text"
                 [formControl]="titleFilter">     ◁──────┐  Addx the input element
        </div>                                            where the user can type
      </div>
    </div>
    <div class="row">
      <div *ngFor="let product of products | filter:'title':filterCriteria"
class="col-sm-4 col-lg-4 col-md-4">                       ◁──────┐
        <auction-product-item [product]="product"></auction-product-item>
      </div>
    </div>
    `
})
export default class HomeComponent {
  products: Product[] = [];
  titleFilter: FormControl = new FormControl();
  filterCriteria: string;

  constructor(private productService: ProductService) {
    this.products = this.productService.getProducts();
    this.titleFilter.valueChanges
      .debounceTime(100)
      .subscribe(                                 ◁──────┐
        value => this.filterCriteria = value,
        error => console.error(error));
  }
}
```

Applies the filter pipe. filter is the name of the custom pipe, title is the product property to filter by, and filterCriteria is the name of the property that holds the current filter criterion entered by the user.

Subscribes to the input's events stream, and assigns the filter value to match the current value of the <input> element.

3 Add `ReactiveFormsModule` to the `imports` section of `@NgModule` in app.module
.ts. You need it to support the filter `<input>` element.

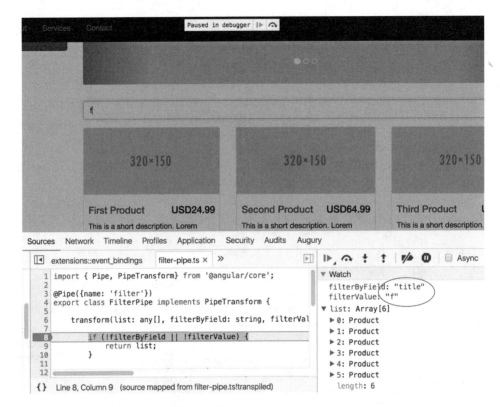

Figure 5.11   `FilterPipe` **receives the values.**

4   Run the application by entering `npm start` in the Command window. Start typing any letters from the product title in the filter field, and you'll see that only products that meet the filter criteria are rendered by the browser.

For reference, we ran the auction application and paused it in the debugger after typing the letter f in the filter field. Figure 5.11 shows the input received by `FilterPipe` before the filtering is complete.

In the Watch panel, you can see the values received by `FilterPipe` as parameters. The arrows illustrate TypeScript destructuring in action. After the filtering is complete, this window shows only products that have "f" in their titles. In this hands-on exercise, you implemented the event observable stream and the custom pipe.

5.5   *Summary*

From a binding perspective, there's a separation of responsibilities between a software developer and Angular. The developer is responsible for providing bindings between the component's template and the supporting code. Angular applies its change-detection mechanism to ensure that bindings are immediately updated to reflect the current state of the application.

Observable streams are a fundamental concept of the *reactive* programming style, which is being practiced by developers in multiple programming languages. RxJS 5, the JavaScript library of reactive extensions, is integrated into the Angular framework.

These are the main takeaways from this chapter:

- Binding to a component's properties propagates the data in one direction: from DOM to UI.
- Binding to events propagates actions from the UI to the component.
- Two-way binding is denoted with the `[()]` notation.
- You can use a structural directive, `ngIf`, to add nodes to and remove nodes from the browser's DOM.
- Using observable data streams simplifies asynchronous programming. You can subscribe to and unsubscribe from a stream as well as cancel pending requests for data.

Implementing
component
communications

This chapter covers

- Creating loosely coupled components
- How a parent component should pass data to its child, and vice versa
- Implementing the Mediator design pattern to create reusable components
- A component lifecycle
- Understanding change detection

We've established that any Angular application is a tree of components. While designing components, you need to ensure that they're reusable and self-contained and at the same time have some means for communicating with each other. In this chapter, we'll focus on how components can pass data to each other in a loosely coupled manner.

First, we'll show you how a parent component can pass data to its child by binding to the input properties of the child. Then you'll see how a child component can send data to its parent by emitting events via its output properties.

We'll continue with an example that applies the Mediator design pattern to arrange data exchange between components that don't have parent-child relationships. The Mediator pattern is probably the most important pattern in any component-based framework. Finally, we'll discuss the lifecycle of an Angular component and the hooks you can use to provide application-specific code that intercepts important events during a component's creation, lifespan, and destruction.

6.1 Inter-component communication

Figure 6.1 shows a view that consists of a number of components that are numbered and have different shapes for easier reference. Some of the components contain other components (let's call the outer ones *containers*), and others are peers. To abstract this from any particular UI framework, we avoided using HTML elements like input fields, drop-downs, and buttons, but you can extrapolate this into a view of your real-world application.

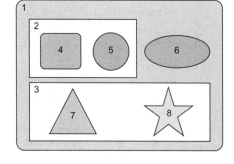

Figure 6.1 A view consists of components.

When you design a view that consists of multiple components, the less they know about each other, the better. Say a user clicks the button in component 4, which has to initiate some actions in component 5. Is it possible to implement this scenario without component 4 knowing that component 5 exists? Yes, it is.

You've seen already examples of loosely coupling components by using dependency injection. Now we'll show you a different technique for achieving the same goal, using bindings and events.

6.1.1 Input and output properties

Think of an Angular component as a black box with outlets. Some of them are marked as `@Input()`, and others are marked as `@Output()`. You can create a component with as many inputs and outputs as you want.

If an Angular component needs to receive values from the outside world, you can bind the producers of these values to the corresponding inputs of the component. Whom are they received from? The component doesn't have to know. The component just needs to know *what* to do with these values when they're provided.

If a component needs to communicate values to the outside world, it can *emit events* through its outputs. Whom are they emitted to? The component doesn't have to know. Whoever is interested can listen or subscribe to the events that a component emits.

Let's implement these principles. First you'll create an `OrderComponent` that can receive order requests from the outside world.

INPUT PROPERTIES

The input properties of a component are decorated with `@Input` and are used to get data from the parent component. Imagine that you want to create a UI component for placing orders to buy stocks. It will know how to connect to the stock exchange, but that's irrelevant in the context of this discussion of input properties. You want to ensure that `OrderComponent` receives data from other components via its properties marked with `@Input` annotations.

Listing 6.1 includes two components: `AppComponent` (the parent) and `Order-Component` (the child). The latter has two properties, `stockSymbol` and `quantity`, marked with `@Input` annotations. The `AppComponent` allows users to enter a stock symbol, which is passed to the `OrderComponent` via bindings.

You'll also pass `quantity` to the `OrderComponent`; but you won't use binding with `quantity`, so you can see the case when a parent needs to pass to the child a value that won't be changing. You'll leave off the binding mechanism by not surrounding the `quantity` attribute in the `<order-processor>` tag with square brackets.

Listing 6.1   input_property_binding.ts

```
import { platformBrowserDynamic } from '@angular/platform-browser-dynamic';
import { NgModule, Component, Input } from '@angular/core';
import { BrowserModule } from '@angular/platform-browser';

@Component({
    selector: 'order-processor',
    template: `
    Buying {{quantity}} shares of {{stockSymbol}}
    `,
    styles:[`:host {background: cyan;}`]
})
class OrderComponent {

    @Input() stockSymbol: string;        Declares two
    @Input() quantity: number;           input properties
}
@Component({
    selector: 'app',
    template: `
    <input type="text" placeholder="Enter stock (e.g. IBM)"
    ➡   (change)="onInputEvent($event)">
    <br/>
    <order-processor [stockSymbol]="stock"          ◁──  Binds the value of the stock
            quantity="100"></order-processor>       ◁──  property of AppComponent
                                                         to the input property of
                                                         OrderComponent
})
class AppComponent {             Assigns the value 100 to the input
    stock: string;               property of OrderComponent.
                                 There's no binding here.
```

```
onInputEvent({target}):void{
    this.stock=target.value;
}
}
@NgModule({
    imports:        [ BrowserModule],
    declarations:   [ AppComponent, OrderComponent],
    bootstrap:      [ AppComponent ]
})
class AppModule { }

platformBrowserDynamic().bootstrapModule(AppModule);
```

As soon as the user moves the focus from the AppComponent input field, the change event is dispatched, and OrderComponent gets a new stock symbol for processing.

TIP Because you don't use binding for the quantity attribute, the value 100 arrives in OrderComponent as a string (all values in HTML attributes are strings). If you want to preserve the types, use bindings, like this: [quantity]="100".

NOTE If you change the value of stockSymbol or quantity in the Order-Component, the change won't affect the property values of the parent component. Property binding is unidirectional: from parent to child.

Figure 6.2 shows the browser's window after the user types IBM in the input field. The OrderComponent received the input values.

The next question is, how can a component intercept the moment when one of its input properties changes? A simple way is to change the input property to a setter. You use stockSymbol in the template of the component, so you need the getter as well. Because you have a public setter, rename the variable to _stockSymbol and make it private.

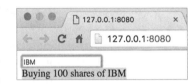

Figure 6.2 OrderComponent got the values.

Listing 6.2   Adding the setter and getter

```
private _stockSymbol: string;

@Input()
set stockSymbol(value: string) {
    this._stockSymbol = value;
    if (this._stockSymbol != undefined) {
      console.log(`Sending a Buy order to NASDAQ:
      ➥ ${this.stockSymbol} ${this.quantity}`);
    }
}

get stockSymbol(): string {
    return this._stockSymbol;
}
```

When this application starts, all input variables are initialized with default values, and the change-detection mechanism qualifies the initialization as a change of the bound variable stockSymbol. The setter is invoked, and, to avoid sending an order for the undefinedstockSymbol, you check its value in the setter.

NOTE   In section 6.2.1, we'll show you how to intercept the changes in input properties without using setters.

In chapter 3, we showed you how to pass parameters to a component using Activated-Route. In this scenario, parameters are passed via constructor. Binding to @Input() parameters is a solution for passing data from parent to child, and it works only for components located within the same route.

OUTPUT PROPERTIES AND CUSTOM EVENTS

Angular components can dispatch custom events using the EventEmitter object. These events can be handled either in the component or by its parents. EventEmitter is a subclass of Subject (implemented in RxJS) that can serve as both observable and observer. In other words, EventEmitter can dispatch custom events using its emit() method as well as consume observables using its subscribe() method. Because this section is about sending data from a component to the outside world, we'll focus on dispatching custom events here.

Let's say you need to write a UI component that's connected to a stock exchange and displays changing stock prices. This component may be used in a financial dashboard application in a brokerage firm. In addition to displaying prices, the component should also send events with the latest prices to the outside world so other components can apply business logic to the changing prices.

Let's create a PriceQuoterComponent that implements such functionality. For this example, you won't connect to any servers but will rather emulate the changing prices using a random number generator. Displaying changing prices in PriceQuoterComponent is pretty straightforward—you'll bind the stockSymbol and lastPrice properties to the component's template.

You'll notify the outside world by emitting custom events via the @Output property of the component. Not only will you fire the event as soon as the price changes, but this event will also carry a payload: an object with the stock symbol and the latest price. The following script implements this functionality.

Listing 6.3   output-property-binding.ts

```
import { platformBrowserDynamic } from '@angular/platform-browser-dynamic';
import { NgModule, Component, Output, EventEmitter }
        from '@angular/core';
import { BrowserModule } from '@angular/platform-browser';

interface IPriceQuote {
    stockSymbol: string;
```

◁──── **Declares a TypeScript interface to represent a price quote. This will help your IDE with error checking and type-ahead prompts.**

Displays the stock symbol and price in the component's UI. You use CurrencyPipe for currency formatting.

```
    lastPrice: number;
}

@Component({
    selector: 'price-quoter',
    template: `<strong>Inside PriceQuoterComponent: {{stockSymbol}}
 {{price | currency:'USD':true:'1.2-2'}}</strong>`,
    styles:[`:host {background: pink;}`]
})
class PriceQuoterComponent {
    @Output() lastPrice: EventEmitter <IPriceQuote> = new EventEmitter();
    stockSymbol: string = "IBM";
    price:number;

    constructor() {
      setInterval(() => {
          let priceQuote: IPriceQuote = {
              stockSymbol: this.stockSymbol,
              lastPrice: 100*Math.random()
          };

          this.price = priceQuote.lastPrice;

          this.lastPrice.emit(priceQuote)
      }, 1000);
    }
}
@Component({
    selector: 'app',
    template: `
    <price-quoter (lastPrice)="priceQuoteHandler($event)"></price-quoter><br>
    AppComponent received: {{stockSymbol}} {{price |
 currency:'USD':true:'1.2-2'}}`
})
@NgModule({
    imports:       [ BrowserModule],
    declarations: [ AppComponent, PriceQuoterComponent],
    bootstrap:     [ AppComponent ]
})
class AppModule { }

platformBrowserDynamic().bootstrapModule(AppModule);
```

The output property, lastPrice, is represented by the EventEmitter object, which emits lastPrice events to the parents of this component.

This example uses a hard-coded value, IBM, as a stock symbol.

Emulates changing prices by invoking a function that generates a random number every second and populates the priceQuote object

Sends each new price to whomever is interested via the output property by emitting an event, which carries the priceQuote object as a payload

This tag represents the PriceQuoterComponent child component, which internally updates the price quotes in its template. On the application level, the event handler for the last-price event is invoked to display the price quote that arrives with the event object.

Displays the price quotes in the application's template as well

The event handler receives the object of type IPriceQuote, and you extract the values of stockSymbol and lastPrice from it. If you run this example, you'll see the prices update every second in both PriceQuoterComponent (shaded background) as well as AppComponent (white background), as shown in figure 6.3.

Figure 6.3   Running the output properties example

TIP By default, the name of a custom event is the same as the name of the output property, which is `lastPrice` in this case. If you want to emit an event with a different name, specify the name of the event as an argument to the `@Output` annotation. For example, to emit an event called `last-price`, declare the output property as `@Output('last-price') lastPrice;`.

In listing 5.3, you create `PriceQuoterComponent` as an Angular component because it includes the UI. But the business may require the functionality for price-quote retrieval without the UI, in order to reuse it both in trader applications and on large dashboards. You could implement the same functionality as an injectable service, as you did with `ProductService` in the online auction project.

Event bubbling

As we write this, Angular doesn't offer a syntax to support event bubbling. For `Price-QuoterComponent`, this means if you try to listen to the `last-price` event not on this component but on its parent, the event won't bubble up there. In the following code snippet, the `last-price` event won't reach the `<div>` because it's the parent of `<price-quoter>`:

```
<div (last-price)="priceQuoteHandler($event)">
  <price-quoter ></price-quoter>
</div>
```

If event bubbling is important to your application, don't use `EventEmitter`; use native DOM events, instead. The following example is another version of `PriceQuoter-Component` that handles event bubbling without using Angular's `EventEmitter`:

```
import { platformBrowserDynamic } from '@angular/platform-browser-dynamic';
import { NgModule, Component, ElementRef }      from '@angular/core';
import { BrowserModule } from '@angular/platform-browser';

interface IPriceQuote {
  stockSymbol: string,
  lastPrice: number
}

@Component({
  selector: 'price-quoter',
  template: `PriceQuoter: {{stockSymbol}} \${{price}}`,
  styles:[`:host {background: pink;}`]
})
class PriceQuoterComponent {
  stockSymbol: string = "IBM";
  price:number;

  constructor(element: ElementRef) {
    setInterval(() => {
```

(continued)

```
      let priceQuote: IPriceQuote = {
        stockSymbol: this.stockSymbol,
        lastPrice: 100*Math.random()
      };

      this.price = priceQuote.lastPrice;

      element.nativeElement
          .dispatchEvent(new CustomEvent('last-price', {
            detail: priceQuote,
            bubbles: true
          }));
    }, 1000);
  }
}

@Component({
  selector: 'app',
  template: `
    <div (last-price)="priceQuoteHandler($event)">
      <price-quoter></price-quoter>
    </div>
    <br>
    AppComponent received: {{stockSymbol}} \${{price}}
  `
})
class AppComponent {

  stockSymbol: string;
  price:number;

  priceQuoteHandler(event: CustomEvent) {
    this.stockSymbol = event.detail.stockSymbol;
    this.price = event.detail.lastPrice;
  }
}
@NgModule({
  imports:      [ BrowserModule],
  declarations: [ AppComponent, PriceQuoterComponent],
  bootstrap:    [ AppComponent ]
})
class AppModule { }

platformBrowserDynamic().bootstrapModule(AppModule);
```

In the preceding application, Angular injects a reference to the DOM element that represents `<price-quoter>` using `ElementRef`, and then the custom event is dispatched by invoking `element.nativeElement.dispatchEvent()`. Event bubbling will work here, but keep in mind that this code becomes browser-specific and won't work with non-HTML renderers.

6.1.2   *The Mediator pattern*

When you design a component-based UI, each component should be self-contained, and components shouldn't rely on the existence of other UI components. Such loosely coupled components can be implemented using the Mediator design pattern, which according to Wikipedia "defines how a set of objects interact" (https://en.wikipedia.org/wiki/Mediator_pattern). We'll explain what this means by analogy with toy interconnecting bricks.

Imagine a child playing with building bricks (think *components*) that "don't know" about each other. Today this child (the *mediator*) can use some blocks to build a house, and tomorrow they'll construct a boat from the same components.

> **NOTE**   The role of the mediator is to ensure that components properly fit together according to the task at hand while remaining loosely coupled.

Let's revisit figure 6.1. Each component except 1 has a parent (a container) that can play the role of mediator. The top-level mediator is container 1, which is responsible for making sure components 2, 3, and 6 can communicate if need be. On the other hand, component 2 is a mediator for 4 and 5. Component 3 is the mediator for 7 and 8.

The mediator needs to receive data from one component and pass it to another. Let's go back to examples of monitoring stock prices.

Imagine a trader monitoring the prices of several stocks. At some point, the trader clicks the Buy button next to a stock symbol to place a purchase order with the stock exchange. You can easily add a Buy button to `PriceQuoterComponent` from the previous section, but this component doesn't know how to place orders to buy stocks. `PriceQuoterComponent` will notify the mediator (`AppComponent`) that the trader wants to purchase a particular stock at that very moment.

The mediator should know which component can place purchase orders and how to pass the stock symbol and quantity to it. Figure 6.4 shows how an `AppComponent` can mediate the communication between `PriceQuoterComponent` and `OrderComponent`.

> **NOTE**   Emitting events works like broadcasting. `PriceQuoterComponent` emits events via the `@Output` property without knowing who will receive the events. `OrderComponent` waits for the value of the `@Input` property to change as a signal for placing an order.

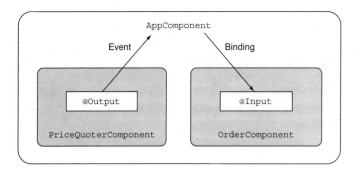

Figure 6.4   Mediating communications

To demonstrate the Mediator pattern in action, let's write a small application that consists of the two components shown in figure 6.4. You can find this application in the mediator directory, which has the following files:

- *stock.ts*—The interface defining a value object that represents a stock
- *price-quoter.ts*—PriceQuoterComponent
- *order.ts*—OrderComponent
- *mediator.ts*—PriceQuoterComponent and OrderComponent

You'll use the Stock interface in two scenarios:

- To represent the payload of the event emitted by PriceQuoteComponent
- To represent the data given to the OrderComponent via binding

The content of the stock.ts file is as follows.

Listing 6.4 stock.ts

```
export interface Stock {
  stockSymbol: string;
  bidPrice: number;
}
```

Suppose you use SystemJS to transpile the TypeScript on the fly. By default, SystemJS will turn the content of the stock.ts file into an empty stock.js module, and you'll get an error when the SystemJS loader tries to import it. You need to let SystemJS know that it has to treat Stock as a module. This can be done while configuring SystemJS by using the meta annotation, as shown in the following code extract from systemjs.config.js:

```
packages: {...},
meta: {
  'app/mediator/stock.ts': {
    format: 'es6'
  }
}
```

The PriceQuoteComponent, shown next, has a Buy button and the buy output property. It emits the buy event only when the user clicks the Buy button.

Listing 6.5 price-quoter.ts

```
import {Component, Output, Directive, EventEmitter} from '@angular/core';
import {Stock} from './stock';

@Component({
    selector: 'price-quoter',
    template: `<strong><input type="button" value="Buy"
➥      (click)="buyStocks($event)">
        {{stockSymbol}} \${{lastPrice | currency:'USD':true:'1.2-2'}}
```

```
    ➥ </strong>
                  `,
    styles:[`:host {background: pink; padding: 5px 15px 15px 15px;}`]
})
export class PriceQuoterComponent {
    @Output() buy: EventEmitter <Stock> = new EventEmitter();

    stockSymbol: string = "IBM";
    lastPrice:number;

    constructor() {
        setInterval(() => {
            this.lastPrice = 100*Math.random();
        }, 2000);
    }

    buyStocks(): void{

        let stockToBuy: Stock = {
            stockSymbol: this.stockSymbol,
            bidPrice: this.lastPrice
        };

        this.buy.emit(stockToBuy);
    }
}
```

When the mediator (AppComponent) receives the buy event from <price-quoter>, it
extracts the payload from this event and assigns it to the stock variable, which is
bound to the input parameter of <order-processor>. The code is shown next.

Listing 6.6   mediator.ts

```
import { platformBrowserDynamic } from '@angular/platform-browser-dynamic';
import { NgModule, Component} from '@angular/core';
import { BrowserModule } from '@angular/platform-browser';

import {OrderComponent} from './order';
import {PriceQuoterComponent} from './price-quoter';
import {Stock} from './stock';

@Component({
    selector: 'app',
    template: `
    <price-quoter (buy)="priceQuoteHandler($event)"></price-quoter><br>
    <br/>
    <order-processor [stock]="stock"></order-processor>
    `
})
class AppComponent {
    stock: Stock;

    priceQuoteHandler(event:Stock) {
```

```
        this.stock = event;
    }
}
@NgModule({
    imports:       [ BrowserModule],
    declarations:  [ AppComponent, OrderComponent,
                     PriceQuoterComponent],
    bootstrap:     [ AppComponent ]
})
class AppModule { }

platformBrowserDynamic().bootstrapModule(AppModule);
```

When the value of the buy input property on OrderComponent changes, its setter displays the message "Placed order ...", showing the stockSymbol and the bidPrice.

```
import {Component, Input} from '@angular/core';
import {Stock} from './stock';

@Component({
    selector: 'order-processor',
    template: `{{message}}`,
    styles:[`:host {background: cyan;}`]
})
export class OrderComponent {

    message:string = "Waiting for the orders...";

    private _stock: Stock;

    @Input() set stock(value: Stock ){
        if (value && value.bidPrice != undefined) {
            this.message = `Placed order to buy 100 shares of
        ➥ ${value.stockSymbol} at \$${value.bidPrice.toFixed(2)}`;
        }
    }

    get stock(): Stock{
        return this._stock;
    }
}
```

The screenshot in figure 6.5 was taken after the user clicked the Buy button when the price of the IBM stock was $12.17. PriceQuote-Component is rendered on top, and Order-Component is at the bottom. They're self-contained and loosely coupled.

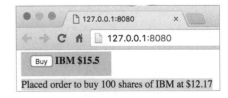

Figure 6.5   Running the mediator example

TIP Don't start implementing the UI components of your application until you've identified your mediators, the custom reusable components, and the means of communication between them.

The Mediator design pattern is a good fit for the online auction as well. Imagine the last minutes of a bidding war for a hot item. Users monitor frequently updated bids and click the button to increase their bids.

> **An alternative implementation of Mediator**
>
> In this section, you saw how sibling components use their parent as a mediator. If components don't have the same parent or aren't displayed at the same time (the router may not display the required component at the moment), you can use an injectable service as a mediator. Whenever the component is created, the mediator service is injected, and the component can subscribe to events emitted by the service (as opposed to using @Input() parameters like OrderComponent did).
>
> If you'd like to see this in action, read the "Providing search results to HomeComponent" section in the hands-on exercise in chapter 8. Check the code of the ProductService that plays the role of the mediator. This service defines the searchEvent: EventEmitter variable, which is used by SearchComponent to emit the data entered by the user. HomeComponent subscribes to the searchEvent variable to receive the text entered by the user in the search form.

6.1.3 *Changing templates at runtime with ngContent*

In some cases, you'll want to be able to dynamically change the content of a component's template at runtime. In AngularJS, this was known as *transclusion*, but the new term for it is *projection*. In Angular, you can project a fragment of the parent component's template onto its child by using the ngContent directive. The syntax is pretty simple and requires two steps:

1 In the child component's template, include the tags <ng-content></ng-content> (the *insertion point*).

2 In the parent component, include the HTML fragment that you want to project into the child's insertion point between tags representing the child component (such as <my-child>):

```
template: `
  ...
  <my-child>
    <div>Passing this div to the child</div>
  </my-child>
  ...
  `
```

In this example, the parent component won't render the content placed between <my-child> and </my-child>. The following listing illustrates this technique.

Listing 6.8 basic-ng-content.ts

```ts
import { platformBrowserDynamic } from '@angular/platform-browser-dynamic';
import { NgModule, Component, ViewEncapsulation}      from '@angular/core';
import { BrowserModule } from '@angular/platform-browser';

@Component({
  selector: 'child',
  styles: ['.wrapper {background: lightgreen;}'],
  template: `
    <div class="wrapper">
     <h2>Child</h2>
       <div>This div is defined in the child's template</div>
       <ng-content></ng-content>
     </div>
  `,
  encapsulation: ViewEncapsulation.Native
})
class ChildComponent {}

@Component({
  selector: 'app',
  styles: ['.wrapper {background: cyan;}'],
  template: `
    <div class="wrapper">
     <h2>Parent</h2>
       <div>This div is defined in the Parent's template</div>
       <child>
         <div>Parent projects this div onto the child </div>
       </child>
     </div>
  `,
  encapsulation: ViewEncapsulation.Native
})
class AppComponent {}

@NgModule({
  imports:      [ BrowserModule],
  declarations: [ AppComponent, ChildComponent],
  bootstrap:    [ AppComponent ]
})
class AppModule { }

platformBrowserDynamic().bootstrapModule(AppModule);
```

The content that comes from the parent is displayed here.

By default, Angular uses the ViewEncapsulation.Emulated mode (see the "Shadow DOM support in Angular" sidebar in chapter 3). You'll start with Native, and then you'll rerun this program in Emulated and None modes.

This content isn't rendered by AppComponent but is passed ChildComponent instead.

We'll also use this example to illustrate how the Shadow DOM and Angular's View-Encapsulation work. Have you noticed that both parent and child components use the .wrapper style in their outermost <div> elements? In a regular HTML page, this would mean both parent and child would be rendered with the same style. We'll show that it's possible to encapsulate styles in child components so they don't conflict with parent styles if their names are the same.

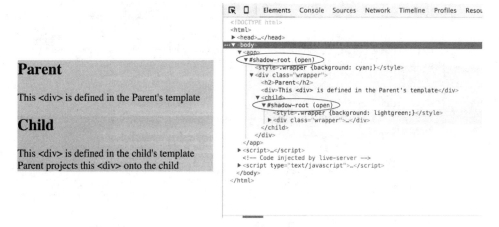

Figure 6.6   Running basic-ng-content.ts with `ViewEncapsulation.Native`

Figure 6.6 shows the running application in `ViewEncapsulation.Native` mode with the Developer Tools panel open. The `ChildComponent` got the HTML content from `AppComponent` and created Shadow DOM nodes for parent and child (see #shadow-root on the right). Note that the `.wrapper` style from the parent's `<div>` (cyan background, if you're reading this book in color) wasn't applied to the child's `<div>` also using the `.wrapper` style, which is rendered in a light green background. The child's #shadow-root acts as a wall protecting the child's styles from inheriting the parent's styles.

The screenshot in figure 6.7 was taken after changing encapsulation to `ViewEncapsulation.Emulated`. The DOM structure is different, and there are no longer any #shadow-root nodes. Angular generated additional attributes for the parent's and child's elements to implement encapsulation, but the UI is rendered the same way.

Figure 6.8 shows the same example running with encapsulation set to `ViewEncapsulation.None`. In this case, all of the parent's and child's elements were merged into

Figure 6.7   Running basic-ng-content.ts with `ViewEncapsulation.Emulated`

Figure 6.8   Running basic-ng-content.ts with `ViewEncapsulation.None`

the main DOM tree, and the styles weren't encapsulated—the entire window is shown with the parent's light green background.

PROJECTING INTO MULTIPLE AREAS

A component can have more than one `<ng-content>` tag in its template. Let's consider an example where a child component's template is split into three areas: header, content, and footer. The HTML markup for the header and footer could be projected by the parent component, and the content area could be defined in the child component. To implement this, the child component needs to include two separate pairs of `<ng-content></ng-content>` populated by the parent (header and footer).

To ensure that the header and footer content will be rendered in the proper `<ng-content>` areas, you'll use the `select` attribute, which can be any valid selector (a CSS class, a tag name, and so on). The child's template could look like this:

```
<ng-content select=".header"></ng-content>
<div>This content is defined in child</div>
<ng-content select=".footer"></ng-content>
```

The content that arrives from the parent will be matched by the selector and rendered in the corresponding area. Here's the complete code to implement this.

Listing 6.9   ng-content-selector.ts

```
import { platformBrowserDynamic } from '@angular/platform-browser-dynamic';
import { NgModule, Component}      from '@angular/core';
import { BrowserModule } from '@angular/platform-browser';

@Component({
  selector: 'child',
  styles: ['.child {background: lightgreen;}'],
```

```
    template: `
      <div class="child">
       <h2>Child</h2>
        <ng-content select=".header" ></ng-content>
        <div>This content is defined in child</div>
        <ng-content select=".footer"></ng-content>
      </div>
      `
})
class ChildComponent {}

@Component({
  selector: 'app',
  styles: ['.app {background: cyan;}'],
  template: `
    <div class="app">
     <h2>Parent</h2>
      <div>This div is defined in the Parent's template</div>
      <child>
        <div class="header" >Child got this header from parent {{todaysDate}}
        </div>
        <div class="footer">Child got this footer from parent</div>
      </child>
    </div>
    `
})
class AppComponent {
  todaysDate: string = new Date().toLocaleDateString();
}

@NgModule({
  imports:      [ BrowserModule],
  declarations: [ AppComponent, ChildComponent],
  bootstrap:    [ AppComponent ]
})
class AppModule { }

platformBrowserDynamic().bootstrapModule(AppModule);
```

Note that you use property binding in App-Component to include today's date in the header. The projected HTML can only bind the properties visible in the parent's scope, so you can't use the child's properties in the parent's binding expression.

Running this example will render the page shown in figure 6.9. The ngContent directive with the select attribute allows you to create a universal component with a view divided into several areas that get their markup from the outside.

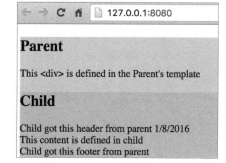

Parent

This \<div\> is defined in the Parent's template

Child

Child got this header from parent 1/8/2016
This content is defined in child
Child got this footer from parent

Figure 6.9   Running ng-content-select.ts

Direct binding to innerHTML

You can bind a component property with HTML content directly to `template`, as in this example:

```
<p [innerHTML]="myComponentProperty"></p>
```

But using `ngContent` is preferable to binding to `innerHTML` for the following reasons:

- `innerHTML` is a browser-specific API, whereas `ngContent` is platform independent.
- With `ng-content`, you can define multiple slots where the HTML fragments will be inserted.
- `ngContent` allows you to bind the parent component's properties into projected HTML.

6.2   *Component lifecycle*

Various events happen during the lifecycle of an Angular component. When a component is created, the change-detection mechanism (explained in the next section) begins monitoring the component. The component is initialized, added to the DOM, and rendered so the user can see it. After that, the state of the component (the values of its properties) may change, causing re-rendering of the UI; and finally, the component is destroyed.

Figure 6.10 shows the lifecycle hooks (callbacks) where you can add custom code if need be. The callbacks shown on the light gray background will be invoked only once, and those on the darker background multiple times.

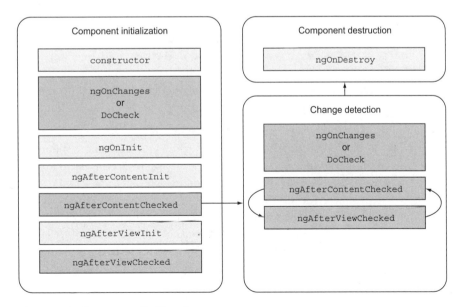

Figure 6.10   A component's lifecycle

The user sees the component after the initialization phase is complete. Then the change-detection mechanism ensures that the component's properties stay in sync with its UI. If the component is removed from the DOM tree as a result of the router's navigation or a structural directive (such as `ngIf`), Angular initiates the destroy phase.

The constructor is invoked first when the instance of the component is being created, but the component's properties aren't initialized yet in the constructor. After the constructor's code is complete, Angular will invoke the following callbacks *if you implemented them*:

- `ngOnChanges()`—Called when a parent component modifies (or initializes) the values bound to the input properties of a child. If the component has no input properties, `ngOnChanges()` isn't invoked. If you wish to implement a custom change-detection algorithm, it must be placed in `DoCheck()`. But implementing manual change detection there may be costly, because `DoCheck()` is invoked after every change-detection cycle.

- `ngOnInit()`—Invoked after the first invocation of `ngOnChanges()`, if any. Although you might initialize some component variables in the constructor, the properties of the component aren't ready yet. By the time `ngOnInit()` is invoked, the component's properties will have been initialized.

- `ngAfterContentInit()`—Invoked when the child component's state is initialized, if you used the `ngContent` directive to pass some HTML code to it.

- `ngAfterContentChecked()`—Invoked on the child component that used `ngContent` after it gets the content from the parent (or during the change-detection phase), if the bindings used in `ngContent` change.

- `ngAfterViewInit()`—Invoked when the binding on the component's template is complete. The parent component is initialized first, and, if it has children, this callback is invoked after all children are ready.

- `ngAfterViewChecked()`—Invoked when the change-detection mechanism checks whether there are any changes in the component template's bindings. This callback may be called more than once as the result of modifications in this or other components.

Whenever you see the word `Content` in the name of the lifecycle callback method, that method is applied if content is projected using `<ng-content>`. When you see the word `View` in the name of the callback method, it applies to the template of the component. The word `Checked` means the component's changes are applied and the component is synchronized with the DOM.

Some applications may need to invoke specific business logic whenever the value of a property changes. For example, financial applications need to log each of a trader's steps, so if a trader places a buy order at $101 and then immediately changes the price to $100, this must be tracked in a log file. This may be a good use case for adding logging in the `DoCheck()` callback.

During the destruction phase, your application may clean up system resources. Say your component is subscribed to an application-level service that keeps track of the

When not to write code in constructors

In the online auction application, you inject `ProductService` in the constructor of `HomeComponent` and invoke the `getProducts()` method right there. If the `getProducts()` method needed to use values of the component's properties, you'd move the invocation of this method to `ngOnInit()` to ensure that all properties were initialized by the time you called `getProducts()`. The other reason to move code from the constructor to `ngOnInit()` is to keep the constructor's code light without starting any long-running synchronous functions from there.

application state (such as an application store offered by the Redux library). When Angular destroys this component, it should unsubscribe from the state service in the `ngOnDestroy()` callback.

> **NOTE** Each lifecycle callback is declared in the interface with a name that matches the name of the callback without the prefix `ng`. For example, if you're planning to implement functionality in the `ngOnChanges()` callback, add `implements OnChanges` to your class declaration.

For more information about the component lifecycle, read the Angular documentation on lifecycle hooks at http://mng.bz/6huZ. In the next section, you'll see an example that uses one of the lifecycle hooks.

6.2.1 *Using ngOnChanges*

Let's illustrate component lifecycle hooks using `ngOnChanges()`. This example will include parent and child components, and the latter will have two input properties: `greeting` and `user`. The first property is a `string`, and the second is an `Object` with one property, `name`. To understand why the `ngOnChanges()` callback may or may not be invoked, you need to be familiar with the concept of mutable versus immutable objects.

Mutable vs. immutable

JavaScript strings are immutable, which means when a string value is created in memory, it will never change. Consider the following code snippet:

```
var greeting = "Hello";
greeting = "Hello Mary";
```

The first line creates the value `Hello` at a certain memory location, such as `@287651`. The second line doesn't change the value at that address but creates the new string `Hello Mary` at a different location, such as `@286777`. Now you have two strings in memory, and each of them is immutable.

What happens to the variable `greeting`? Its value changed, because it pointed initially at one memory location and then to another.

> **(continued)**
> JavaScript objects are mutable, which means after the object instance is created at a certain memory location, it stays there even if the values of its properties change. Consider the following code:
>
> ```
> var user = {name: "John"};
> user.name = "Mary";
> ```
>
> After the first line, the object is created, and the user variable points at a certain memory location, such as @277500. The string John has been created at another memory location, such as @287600, and the user.name variable stores the reference to this address.
>
> After the second line is executed, the new string Mary is created at another location, such as @287700, and the user.name variable stores the reference to this new address. But the user variable still stores the memory address @277500. In other words, you mutated the content of the object @277500.

Let's add the hook ngOnChanges() to the child component to demonstrate how it intercepts modifications of the input properties. This application has parent and child components. The child has two input properties (greetings and user) and one regular property (message). The user can modify the values of the input properties of the child. Let's demonstrate what property values will be given to the ngOnChanges() method if it's invoked.

Listing 6.10   ng-onchanges-with-param.ts

```
import { platformBrowserDynamic } from '@angular/platform-browser-dynamic';
import { NgModule, Component, Input,  OnChanges, SimpleChange,
  enableProdMode } from '@angular/core';
import { BrowserModule } from '@angular/platform-browser';
import {FormsModule} from '@angular/forms';

interface IChanges {[key: string]: SimpleChange};          ⟵  Declares a structural
                                                                type for the object to
@Component({                                                    store changes. It's used
  selector: 'child',                                            in ngOnChanges().
  styles: ['.child{background:lightgreen}'],
  template: `
    <div class="child">
      <h2>Child</h2>
      <div>Greeting: {{greeting}}</div>
      <div>User name: {{user.name}}</div>
      <div>Message: <input [(ngModel)]="message"></div>
    </div>
  `
})
class ChildComponent implements OnChanges {
```

The input properties of
ChildComponent get their
values from AppComponent.

The message property doesn't have
the @Input annotation. We've added
it to show that modifying its value
won't result in an invocation of the
ngOnChanges callback.

```
@Input() greeting: string;
@Input() user: {name: string};
message: string = 'Initial message';

  ngOnChanges(changes: IChanges) {
    console.log(JSON.stringify(changes, null, 2));
  }
}
```

Angular invokes ngOnChanges()
when the bindings to input
properties change.

```
@Component({
  selector: 'app',
  styles: ['.parent {background: lightblue}'],
  template: `
    <div class="parent">
      <h2>Parent</h2>
      <div>Greeting: <input type="text" [value]="greeting"
      (change)="greeting = $event.target.value"></div> //
      <div>User name: <input type="text" [value]="user.name"
      (change)="user.name = $event.target.value"></div>

      <child [greeting]="greeting" [user]="user"></child>
    </div>
  `
})
class AppComponent {
  greeting: string = 'Hello';
  user: {name: string} = {name: 'John'};
}

enableProdMode();

@NgModule({
  imports:      [ BrowserModule, FormsModule],
  declarations: [ AppComponent, ChildComponent],
  bootstrap:    [ AppComponent ]
})
class AppModule { }

platformBrowserDynamic().bootstrapModule(AppModule);
```

In the parent component, you
modify the values of greeting
and user.name on the change
event, which is dispatched
when these fields lose focus.

The values of the
parent's greeting
and user are bound
to the child's input
properties.

Enables production mode (see the
sidebar "Enabling production mode")

When Angular invokes ngOnChanges(), it provides the values of each modified input property. Each modified value is represented by an instance of the SimpleChange object that contains the current and previous values of the modified input property. The Simple.change.isFirstChange() method allows you to determine whether the value was set for the first time or if it's being updated. You use JSON.stringify() to pretty-print the received values.

NOTE TypeScript has a structural type system, so the type of the argument `changes` of `ngOnChanges()` is specified by including a description of the expected data. As an alternative, you could declare an interface (such as `interface IChanges {[key: string]: SimpleChange};`), and the function signature would look like `ngOnChanges(changes: IChanges)`. The preceding declaration of the `user` property in `AppComponent` is yet another example of using the structural type.

Let's see if changing `greeting` and `user.name` in the UI results in the invocation of `ngOnChanges()` on the child component. Figure 6.11 shows a screenshot after we ran listing 6.10 with the Chrome Developer Tools open.

Initially, when the application applied the binding to the child component's input properties, they had no values. The `ngOnChanges()` callback was invoked, and the previous values of both `greeting` and `user` were changed from {} to `Hello` and {name: "John"}, respectively.

Enabling production mode

In figure 6.11, you can see a message stating that Angular 2 is running in development mode, which performs assertions and other checks within the framework. One such assertion verifies that a change-detection pass doesn't result in additional changes to any bindings (for example, your code doesn't modify the UI in lifecycle callbacks).

To enable production mode, invoke `enableProdMode()` in your application before invoking the `bootstrap()` method. Enabling production mode will result in better performance in the browser.

Let's have the user change the values in all the input fields. After adding the word *dear* to the Greeting field and moving the focus away, Angular's change-detection mechanism refreshes the binding to the child's *immutable* input property, `greeting`; invokes

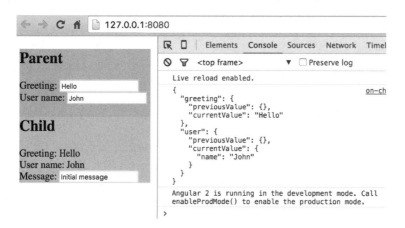

Figure 6.11   Initial invocation of `ngOnChanges()`

```
        "previousValue": {},
        "currentValue": "Hello"
      },
      "user": {
        "previousValue": {},
        "currentValue": {
          "name": "John"
        }
      }
    }
    {
      "greeting": {
        "previousValue": "Hello",
        "currentValue": "Hello dear"
      }
    }
```

Figure 6.12   **Invocation of** `ngOnChanges()` **after the greeting is changed**

the `ngOnChanges()` callback; and prints the previous value as `Hello` and the current one as `Hello dear`, as shown in figure 6.12.

Now suppose the user adds the word *Smith* in the User Name field and moves the focus from this field: no new messages are printed on the console, as shown in figure 6.13. That's because the user changed only the `name` property of the *mutable* user object; the reference to the `user` object itself didn't change. This explains why `ngOnChanges()` wasn't invoked. Changing the value in the `message` property of the `ChildComponent` didn't invoke `ngOnChanges()` either, because this property wasn't annotated with `@Input`.

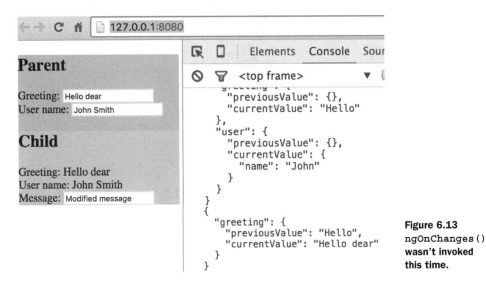

```
        "previousValue": {},
        "currentValue": "Hello"
      },
      "user": {
        "previousValue": {},
        "currentValue": {
          "name": "John"
        }
      }
    }
    {
      "greeting": {
        "previousValue": "Hello",
        "currentValue": "Hello dear"
      }
    }
```

Figure 6.13
`ngOnChanges()`
**wasn't invoked
this time.**

> **NOTE** Although Angular doesn't update bindings to input properties if the object reference hasn't changed, the change-detection mechanism still catches property updates on each object property. This is why John Smith, the new value of the User Name in the child component, has been rendered.

Earlier, in section 6.1.1, you used a setter to intercept the moment when the value of the input parameter changed. You could have used ngOnChanges() instead of the setters there. There are use cases when using ngOnChanges() instead of a setter isn't an option, and you'll see why in the hands-on section of this chapter.

6.3 *A high-level overview of change detection*

Angular's change-detection (CD) mechanism is implemented in zone.js (a.k.a. the Zone). Its main purpose is to keep the changes in the component properties (the model) and the UI in sync. CD is initiated by any asynchronous event that happens in the browser (the user clicked a button, data is received from a server, a script invoked the setTimeout() function, and so on).

  When CD runs its cycle, it checks all the bindings in the component's template. Why might binding expressions need to be updated? Because one of the component's properties changed.

> **NOTE** The CD mechanism applies changes from a component's property to the UI. CD never changes the value of the component's property.

You can think of an application as a tree of components with the root component on the top of this tree. When Angular compiles component templates, each component gets its own change detector. When CD is initiated by the Zone, it makes one pass starting from the root down to the leaf components, trying to see whether the UI of each component needs to be updated.

  Angular implements two CD strategies: Default and OnPush. If all components use the Default strategy, the Zone checks the entire component tree regardless of where the change happened. If a particular component declares the OnPush strategy, the Zone checks this component and its children only if the bindings to the component's input properties have changed. To declare the OnPush strategy, you just need to add the following line to the component's template:

```
changeDetection: ChangeDetectionStrategy.OnPush
```

Let's get familiar with these strategies using three components: the parent, child, and grandchild shown in figure 6.14.

  Let's say a property of the parent was modified. CD will begin checking the component and all of its descendants. The left side of figure 6.14 illustrates the default CD strategy: all three components are checked for changes.

  The right side of figure 6.14 illustrates what happens when the child component has the OnPush CD strategy. CD starts from the top, but it sees that the child component has

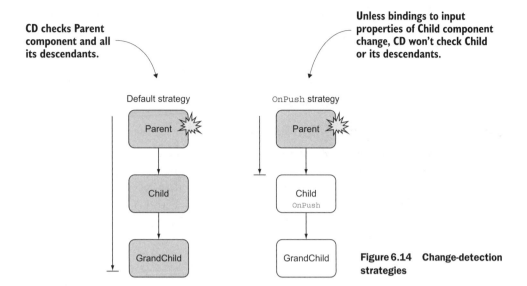

CD checks Parent component and all its descendants.

Unless bindings to input properties of Child component change, CD won't check Child or its descendants.

Figure 6.14 Change-detection strategies

declared the OnPush strategy. If no bindings to the input properties of the child component have changed, CD doesn't check either the child or the grandchild.

Figure 6.14 shows a small application with only three components, but real-world apps can have hundreds of components. With the OnPush strategy, you can opt out of CD for specific branches of the tree.

Figure 6.15 shows a CD cycle caused by an event in the GrandChild1 component. Even though this event happened in the leaf component, the CD cycle starts from the top; it's performed on each branch except the branches that originate from a component with the OnPush CD strategy and that has no changes in the bindings to its input properties. Components excluded from this CD cycle are shown on the white background.

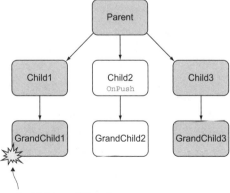

Event in the descendant triggers CD cycle, starting from top. Child2 and its descendants are excluded from CD cycle unless bindings to input properties of Child2 change.

Figure 6.15 Excluding a branch from a CD cycle

This was a brief overview of the CD mechanism, which is probably the most sophisticated module of Angular. You should learn about CD in depth only if you need to work on performance-tuning a UI-intensive application, such as a data grid containing hundreds of cells with constantly changing values. For more details about change detection in Angular, read the article "Change Detection in Angular 2" by Victor Savkin at http://mng.bz/bD6v.

6.4   *Exposing a child component's API*

You've learned how a parent component can pass data to its child using bindings to input properties. But there are other cases when the parent just needs to use the API exposed by the child. We'll show you an example that illustrates how a parent component can use the child's API from both the template and the TypeScript code.

Let's create a simple application in which a child component has a `greet()` method that will be invoked by the parent. To illustrate different techniques, the parent will use two instances of the same child component. These instances have different template variable names:

```
<child #child1></child>
<child #child2></child>
```

Now you can declare a variable in your TypeScript code, annotated with `@ViewChild`. This annotation is provided by Angular to get a reference to a child component, and you'll use it with the first child:

```
@ViewChild('child1')
firstChild: ChildComponent;
...
this.firstChild.greet('Child 1');
```

This code instructs Angular to find the child component identified by the template variable `child1` and place the reference to this component into the `firstChild` variable.

To illustrate another technique, you can access the second child component not from the TypeScript code but from the parent's template. It's as simple as this:

```
<button (click)="child2.greet('Child 2')">Invoke greet() on child 2</button>
```

The full code illustrating both techniques follows.

Listing 6.11   exposing-child-api.ts

```
import { platformBrowserDynamic } from '@angular/platform-browser-dynamic';
import { NgModule, Component, ViewChild, AfterViewInit } from
➥ '@angular/core';
import { BrowserModule } from '@angular/platform-browser';

@Component({
    selector: 'child',
    template: `<h3>Child</h3>`

})
```

```
class ChildComponent {
    greet(name) {
        console.log(`Hello from ${name}.`);
    }
}

@Component({
    selector: 'app',
    template: `
    <h1>Parent</h1>
    <child #child1></child>
    <child #child2></child>

    <button (click)="child2.greet('Child 2')">Invoke greet() on child 2
    ➥ </button>
    `
})
class AppComponent implements AfterViewInit {
    @ViewChild('child1')
    firstChild: ChildComponent;

    ngAfterViewInit() {
        this.firstChild.greet('Child 1');
    }
}

@NgModule({
    imports:      [ BrowserModule],
    declarations: [ AppComponent, ChildComponent],
    bootstrap:    [ AppComponent ]
})
class AppModule { }

platformBrowserDynamic().bootstrapModule(AppModule);
```

When you run this app, it prints "Hello from Child 1." on the console. Click the button, and it will print "Hello from Child 2." as shown in figure 6.16.

Figure 6.16 Accessing the child's API

> **Updating the UI from lifecycle hooks**
>
> Listing 6.11 uses the `ngAfterViewInit()` component lifecycle hook to invoke the API on the child. If the child's `greet()` method doesn't change the UI, this code works fine; but if you try to change the UI from `greet()`, Angular will throw an exception because the UI is changed after `ngAfterViewInit()` was fired. That's because this hook is called in the same event loop for both parent and child components.
>
> There are two ways to deal with this issue. You can run the application in production mode so Angular won't do the additional bindings check, or you can use `setTimeout()` for the code updating the UI so it runs in the next event loop.

6.5   *Hands-on: adding a rating feature to the online auction*

In this section, you'll add a rating feature to the auction. Previous versions of this application just displayed the rating, but now you want to let users rate a product. In chapter 4, you created the Produce Details view; here you'll add the Leave a Review button, which allows users to navigate to a view where they can assign one to five stars to a product and enter a review. A fragment of the new Produce Details view is shown in figure 6.17.

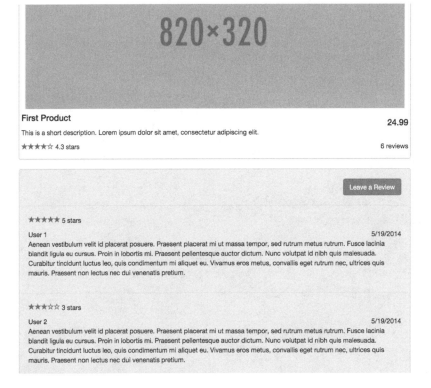

Figure 6.17   The Produce Details view

`StarsComponent` will have an input property, which will be modified. The newly added rating's value needs to be communicated to its parent `ProductItemComponent`.

> **NOTE** We'll use the auction application developed in chapter 5 as a starting point for this exercise. If you prefer to see the final version of this project, browse the source code in the auction folder for chapter 6. Otherwise, copy the auction folder from chapter 5 to a separate location. Then copy the package.json file from the auction folder for chapter 6, run `npm install`, and follow the instructions in this section.

Installing a type-definition file

In this version of the app, you want to use the `Array.fill()` method in the `Stars-Component`; but this API is available only in ES6, and the TypeScript compiler will complain. You already have the ES6 shim installed locally as a part of the `core.js` package. But because you want to keep ES5 as a target for transpiling, you need an ES6 shim type-declaration file so this API can be recognized by the TypeScript compiler.

You'll install an additional type definition file (see appendix B) from the npm repository. In general, you'll need to install type-definition files whenever you add a third-party JavaScript library.

Follow these steps:

1 Install the type-definition file for ES6 shim. To do so, open a command window and run the following command:

```
npm install @types/es6-shim --save-dev
```

This command installs the es6-shim.d.ts file in the node_modules/@types directory and saves this configuration in the `devDependencies` section of package.json file. You should be using TypeScript 2.0, which knows to look for type-definition files in the @types directory.

2 Modify the code of `StarsComponent`. The new version should work in two modes: read-only for displaying stars based on the data provided by `ProductService`, and writable for allowing users to click stars to set a new rating value.

Figure 6.17 shows the rendering of `ProductDetailComponent` (the parent) where `StarsComponent` (the child) is in read-only mode. If the user clicks the Leave a Review button, read-only mode should be turned off. You'll add a `readonly` input variable to toggle this mode.

The second input variable, `rating`, is for assigning ratings. You'll also add one output variable, `ratingChange`, that will emit an event with the newly set rating; this will be used by the parent component to recalculate the average rating.

When the user clicks one of the stars, it will invoke the `fillStarsWith-Color()` method, which will assign the value to `rating` and emit the rating's value by dispatching an event. Modify the code of the stars.ts file so it looks like the following listing.

Listing 6.12   stars.ts

```
import {Component, EventEmitter, Input, Output} from '@angular/core';

@Component({
  selector: 'auction-stars',
  styles: [`.starrating { color: #d17581; }`],
  templateUrl: 'app/components/stars/stars.html'
})
export default class StarsComponent {
  private _rating: number;
  private stars: boolean[];

  private maxStars: number =5;

  @Input() readonly: boolean = true;

  @Input() get rating(): number {
    return this._rating;
  }

  set rating(value: number) {
    this._rating = value || 0;
    this.stars = Array(this.maxStars).fill(true, 0, this.rating);
  }

  @Output() ratingChange: EventEmitter<number> = new EventEmitter();

  fillStarsWithColor(index) {

    if (!this.readonly) {
      this.rating = index + 1;
      this.ratingChange.emit(this.rating);
    }
  }
}
```

You use the setter for the input `rating`. This setter can be invoked either from within `StarsComponent` (to render an existing rating) or from its parent (when the user clicks the stars). In this application, using `ngOnChanges()` wouldn't work, because it would be invoked only once by the parent when `StarsComponent` was created.

Note the use of the ES6 method `fill()` in the `rating()` setter. You populate the `stars` array with the value `true` from element zero to whatever the rating value is. For each star that has to be filled with color, you store the value `true`; and for empty stars, you store `false`.

3 Modify the template of StarsComponent in the stars.html file as shown in list-ing 6.13. Using the ngFor directive, you loop through the stars array, which stores Boolean values. You'll use the stock images that come with the Bootstrap library for filled and empty stars (see http://getbootstrap.com/components). Based on the value of the array's element, you render either a star filled with color or an empty one. When the user clicks the star, you pass its index to the function fillStarsWithColor().

Listing 6.13 Revised stars.html

```
<p>
  <span *ngFor="let star of stars; let i = index"
        class="starrating glyphicon glyphicon-star"
        [class.glyphicon-star-empty]="!star"
        (click)="fillStarsWithColor(i)">
  </span>
  <span *ngIf="rating">{{rating | number:'.0-2'}} stars</span>
</p>
```

The number pipe formats the rating's value to show two digits after the decimal point.

4 Modify the template of ProductDetailComponent. ProductDetailComponent has a Leave a Review button that should provide a means for rating a product and leaving a review. Clicking this button will toggle the visibility of a <div> that allows users to click stars and enter a review, as shown in figure 6.18.

Figure 6.18 The Leave a Review view

Here StarsComponent works in editable mode, and the user can give the selected product up to five stars. This is how the template implementing the view in figure 6.18 could look:

```
<div [hidden]="isReviewHidden">
    <div><auction-stars [(rating)]="newRating"
      [readonly]="false" class="large"></auction-stars></div>
    <div><textarea [(ngModel)]="newComment"></textarea></div>
    <div><button (click)="addReview()" class="btn">Add review
    ➥ </button></div>
  </div>
```

readonly mode is turned off. Note that you use two-way binding in two places: [(rating)] and [(ngModel)]. Earlier in this chapter, we discussed the use of the ngModel directive for two-way binding; but if you have an input property (such as rating) and an output property that has the same name plus the suffix Change (such as ratingChange), you're allowed to use the [()] syntax with such properties.

The Leave a Review button toggles the visibility of the preceding <div>. This is how it can be implemented:

```
<button (click)="isReviewHidden = !isReviewHidden"
            class="btn btn-success btn-green">Leave a Review</button>
```

Replace the content of the product-detail.html file with the following.

Listing 6.14 product-detail.html

```
<div class="thumbnail">
    <img src="http://placehold.it/820x320">
    <div>
        <h4 class="pull-right">{{ product.price }}</h4>
        <h4>{{ product.title }}</h4>
        <p>{{ product.description }}</p>
    </div>
    <div class="ratings">
        <p class="pull-right">{{ reviews.length }} reviews</p>
        <p><auction-stars [rating]="product.rating" ></auction-stars></p>
    </div>
</div>
<div class="well" id="reviews-anchor">
    <div class="row">
        <div class="col-md-12"></div>
    </div>
    <div class="text-right">
        <button (click)="isReviewHidden = !isReviewHidden"
                class="btn btn-success btn-green">Leave a Review</button>
    </div>

    <div [hidden]="isReviewHidden">
        <div><auction-stars [(rating)]="newRating"
          [readonly]="false" class="large"></auction-stars></div>
        <div><textarea [(ngModel)]="newComment"></textarea></div>
        <div><button (click)="addReview()" class="btn">Add review</button>
        ➥ </div>
    </div>

    <div class="row" *ngFor="#review of reviews">
        <hr>
        <div class="col-md-12">
            <auction-stars [rating]="review.rating"></auction-stars>
            <span>{{ review.user }}</span>
```

```
                <span class="pull-
    right">{{ review.timestamp | date: 'shortDate' }}</span>
                <p>{{ review.comment }}</p>
            </div>
        </div>
</div>
```

After typing a review and giving stars to a product, the user clicks the Add Review button, which invokes `addReview()` on the component. Let's implement it in TypeScript.

5 Modify the product-detail.ts file. Adding a review should do two things: send the newly entered review to the server and recalculate the average product rating on the UI. You'll recalculate the average on the UI, but you won't implement the communication with the server; you'll log the review on the browser's console. Then you'll add the new review to the array of existing reviews. The following code fragment from `ProductDetailComponent` implements this functionality:

```
addReview() {
    let review = new Review(0, this.product.id, new Date(), 'Anonymous',
        this.newRating, this.newComment);
    console.log("Adding review " + JSON.stringify(review));
    this.reviews = [...this.reviews, review];

    this.product.rating = this.averageRating(this.reviews);

    this.resetForm();
}

averageRating(reviews: Review[]) {
    let sum = reviews.reduce((average, review) => average + review.rating, 0);
    return sum / reviews.length;
}
```

After creating a new instance of the `Review` object, you need to add it to the reviews array. The spread operator lets you write it in an elegant way:

```
this.reviews = [...this.reviews, review];
```

The reviews array gets the values of all existing elements (...this.reviews) plus the new one (review). The recalculated average is assigned to the rating property, which is propagated to the UI via binding.

What's left? Replace the content of the product-detail.ts file with the following code, and this hands-on exercise is over!

Listing 6.15   product-detail.ts

```
import {Component} from '@angular/core';
import {ActivatedRoute} from '@angular/router';
import {Product, Review, ProductService} from
```

```
➥ '../../services/product-service';
import StarsComponent from '../stars/stars';

@Component({
  selector: 'auction-product-page',
  styles: ['auction-stars.large {font-size: 24px;}'],
  templateUrl: 'app/components/product-detail/product-detail.html'
})
export default class ProductDetailComponent {
  product: Product;
  reviews: Review[];

  newComment: string;
  newRating: number;

  isReviewHidden: boolean = true;

  constructor(route: ActivatedRoute, productService: ProductService) {

    let prodId: number = parseInt(route.snapshot.params['productId']);
    this.product = productService.getProductById(prodId);

    this.reviews = productService.getReviewsForProduct(this.product.id);
  }

  addReview() {
    let review = new Review(0, this.product.id, new Date(), 'Anonymous',
        this.newRating, this.newComment);
    console.log("Adding review " + JSON.stringify(review));
    this.reviews = [...this.reviews, review];
    this.product.rating = this.averageRating(this.reviews);

    this.resetForm();
  }

  averageRating(reviews: Review[]) {
    let sum = reviews.reduce((average, review) => average + review.rating,0);
    return sum / reviews.length;
  }

  resetForm() {
    this.newRating = 0;
    this.newComment = null;
    this.isReviewHidden = true;
  }
}
```

6.6   *Summary*

Any Angular application is a hierarchy of components that need to communicate with
each other. This chapter was dedicated to covering different ways of arranging such
communication. Binding to the component's input properties and dispatching events
via the output properties allow you to create loosely coupled components. By means

of its change-detection mechanism, Angular intercepts changes in components' properties to ensure that their bindings are updated.

Each component goes through a certain set of events during its lifecycle. Angular provides several lifecycle hooks where you can write code to intercept these events and apply custom logic there.

These are the main takeaways for this chapter:

- Parent and child components should avoid direct access to each other's internals but should communicate via input and output properties.
- A component can emit custom events via its output properties, and these events can carry an application-specific payload.
- Communications between unrelated components can be arranged by using the Mediator design pattern.
- A parent component can pass one or more template fragments to a child at runtime.
- Each Angular component lets you intercept major lifecycle events of a component and insert application-specific code there.
- The Angular change-detection mechanism automatically monitors changes to components' properties and updates the UI accordingly.
- You can mark selected branches of your app component tree to be excluded from the change-detection process.

*Working with forms*7

This chapter covers

- Understanding the Angular Forms API (NgModel, FormControl, FormGroup, form directives, FormBuilder)
- Working with template-driven forms
- Working with reactive forms
- Understanding form validation

Angular offers rich support for handling forms. It goes beyond regular data-binding by treating form fields as first-class citizens and providing fine-grained control over form data.

This chapter will start by demonstrating how you can implement a sample user registration form in pure HTML. While working on this form, we'll briefly discuss the standard HTML forms and their shortcomings. Then you'll see what the Angular Forms API brings to the table, and we'll cover the template-driven and reactive approaches to creating forms in Angular.

After covering the basics, you'll refactor the original version of the user registration form to use the template-driven approach, and we'll discuss its pros and cons. Then we'll do the same with the reactive approach. After that, we'll discuss form validation. At the end of the chapter, you'll apply this new knowledge to the online auction application and start implementing its search form component.

> **Template-driven vs. reactive approaches**
>
> In a *template-driven* approach, forms are fully programmed in the component's template. The template defines the structure of the form, the format of its fields, and the validation rules.
>
> In contrast, in a *reactive* approach, you create the form model programmatically in the code (in TypeScript, in this case). The template can be either statically defined and bound to an existing form model or dynamically generated based on the model.

By the end of the chapter, you'll be familiar with the Angular Forms API and the various ways of working with forms and applying data validation.

7.1 Overview of HTML forms

HTML provides basic features for displaying forms, validating entered values, and submitting the data to the server. But HTML forms may not be good enough for real-world business applications, which need a way to programmatically process the entered data, apply custom validation rules, display user-friendly error messages, transform the format of the entered data, and choose the way data is submitted to the server. For business applications, one of the most important considerations when choosing a web framework is how well it handles forms.

In this section, we'll evaluate standard HTML form features using a sample user registration form, and we'll define a set of requirements that a modern web application needs to fulfill users' expectations. We'll also look at the form features provided by Angular.

7.1.1 Standard browser features

You may be wondering what you need from an application framework other than data-binding, if HTML already allows you to validate and submit forms. To answer this question, let's review an HTML form that uses only standard browser features.

Listing 7.1 Plain HTML user registration form

```html
<form action="/register" method="POST">
  <div>Username:        <input type="text"></div>
  <div>SSN:             <input type="text"></div>
  <div>Password:        <input type="password"></div>
  <div>Confirm password: <input type="password"></div>
  <button type="submit">Submit</button>
</form>
```

The form contains a button and four input fields: username, SSN, password, and password confirmation. Users can enter whatever values they want: no input validation is applied here. When the user clicks the Submit button, the form's values are submitted to the server's /register endpoint using HTTP POST, and the page is refreshed.

The default HTML form behavior isn't a good fit for a SPA, which typically needs the following functionality:

- Validation rules should be applied to individual input fields.
- Error messages should be displayed next to the input fields that cause the problems.
- Dependent fields should be validated all together. This form has password and password-confirmation fields, so whenever either of them is changed, both fields should be revalidated.
- The application should be in control of the values submitted to the server. When the user clicks the Submit button, the application should invoke an event-handler function to pass the form values. The application can validate the values or change their format before sending the submit request.
- The application should decide how the data is submitted to the server, whether it's a regular HTTP request, an AJAX request, or a WebSocket message.

HTML's validation attributes and semantic input types partially satisfy the first two requirements.

HTML VALIDATION ATTRIBUTES

Several standard validation attributes allow you to validate individual input fields: required, pattern, maxlength, min, max, step, and so on. For example, you can request that username be a required field and its value should contain only letters and numbers:

```
<input id="username" type="text" required pattern="[a-zA-Z0-9]+">
```

Here you use a regular expression, [a-zA-Z0-9]+, to restrict what can be entered in this field. When the user clicks the Submit button, the form will be validated before the submit request is sent. In figure 7.1, you can see the default error message displayed in the Chrome browser when username doesn't conform to the specified pattern.

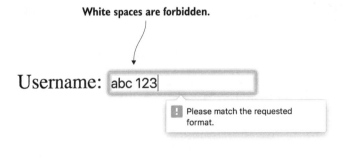

Figure 7.1   Validation error message

There are a number of problems with this message:

- It's too vague and doesn't help the user identify and fix the problem.
- As soon as the input field loses focus, the error message disappears.
- This message format likely won't match other styles in the application.

This input field prevents users from submitting invalid values, but it doesn't let you provide a decent user experience by helping the user with friendly client-side validation.

SEMANTIC INPUT TYPES

HTML supports multiple types of input elements: text, number, url, email, and so on. Choosing the right type for a form field may prevent users from entering an invalid value. But although this provides a better user experience, it's still not enough to satisfy application-specific validation needs.

Let's consider a ZIP code field (a U.S. postal code). It might be tempting to use the number input element, because a ZIP code is represented by a numeric value (at least, in the United States). To keep the values within a certain range, you could use the min and max attributes. For example, for a five-digit ZIP code, you could use following markup:

```
<input id="zipcode" type="number" min="10000" max="99999">
```

But not every five-digit number is a valid ZIP code. In a more complex example, you might also want to allow only a subset of ZIP codes from the user's state.

To support all these real-world scenarios, you need more advanced form support, and this is what an application framework can provide. Let's see what Angular has to offer.

7.1.2 Angular's Forms API

There are two approaches to working with forms in Angular: *template-driven* and *reactive*. These two approaches are exposed as two different APIs (sets of directives and TypeScript classes) in Angular.

With the template-driven approach, the form model is defined in the component's template using directives. Because you're limited to the HTML syntax while defining the form model, the template-driven approach suits only simple scenarios.

For complex forms, the reactive approach is a better option. With the reactive approach, you create an underlying data structure in the code (not in the template). After the model is created, you link the HTML template elements to the model using special directives prefixed with form*. Unlike template-driven forms, reactive forms can be tested without a web browser.

Let's highlight several important concepts to further clarify the difference between template-driven and reactive forms:

- Both types of forms have a *model*, which is an underlying data structure that stores the form's data. In the template-driven approach, the model is created implicitly by Angular based on the directives you attach to the template's elements. In the reactive approach, you create the model explicitly and then link the HTML template elements to that model.

- The model *is not* an arbitrary object. It's an object constructed using classes defined in the @angular/forms module: FormControl, FormGroup, and Form-Array. In the template-driven approach, you don't access these classes directly, whereas in the reactive approach you explicitly create instances of these classes.
- The reactive approach doesn't spare you from writing an HTML template. The view won't be generated for you by Angular.

Enabling Forms API support

Both types of forms—template-driven and reactive—need to be explicitly enabled before you start using them. To enable template-driven forms, add FormsModule from @angular/forms to the imports list of the NgModule that uses the Forms API. For reactive forms, use ReactiveFormsModule. Here's how to do it:

```
import { NgModule } from '@angular/core';
import { BrowserModule } from '@angular/platform-browser';
import { platformBrowserDynamic } from
  '@angular/platform-browser-dynamic';
import { FormsModule, ReactiveFormsModule } from '@angular/forms';

@NgModule({
    imports     : [ BrowserModule, FormsModule, ReactiveFormsModule ],
    declarations: [ AppComponent ],
    bootstrap   : [ AppComponent ]
})
class AppModule {}

platformBrowserDynamic().bootstrapModule(AppModule);
```

Both form modules can be imported in the same application module.

We won't repeat this code for each example in this chapter, but all of them assume the modules are imported. All the downloadable code samples for the book import the modules in AppModule.

7.2   *Template-driven forms*

As we mentioned earlier, you can use only *directives* to define a model in the template-driven approach. But what directives can you use? These directives come with Forms-Module: NgModel, NgModelGroup, and NgForm.

In chapter 5, we discussed how the NgModel directive can be used for two-way data binding. But in the Forms API, it plays a different role: it marks the HTML element that should become a part of the form model. Although these two roles are separate, they don't conflict and can be safely used at the same time on a single HTML element. You'll see examples later in this section. Let's briefly look at these directives and then apply the template-driven approach to the sample registration form.

7.2.1 Directives overview

Here we'll briefly describe the three main directives from FormsModule: NgModel, NgModelGroup, and NgForm. We'll show how they can be used in the template and highlight their most important features.

NGFORM

NgForm is the directive that represents the entire form. It's automatically attached to every <form> element. NgForm implicitly creates an instance of the FormGroup class that represents the model and stores the form's data (more on FormGroup later in this chapter). NgForm automatically discovers all child HTML elements marked with the NgModel directive and adds their values to the form model.

The NgForm directive has multiple selectors that you can use to attach NgForm to non-<form> elements:

```
<div ngForm></div>                    ◁———┐  Attribute selector
<ngForm></ngForm>                     ◁——— Element selector
```

This syntax comes in handy if you're using a CSS framework that requires a certain structure for the HTML elements, and you can't use the <form> element.

If you want to exclude a particular <form> from being handled by Angular, use the ngNoForm attribute:

```
<form ngNoForm></form>
```

The ngNoForm attribute prevents Angular from creating an instance of NgForm and attaching it to the <form> element.

NgForm has an exportAs property declared on its @Directive annotation, which allows you to use the value of this property to create a local template variable that references the instance of NgForm:

```
<form #f="ngForm"></form>
<pre>{{ f.value | json }}</pre>
```

First, you specify ngForm as the value of the exportAs property of NgForm; f points at the instance of NgForm attached to the <form>. Then you can use the f variable to access instance members of the NgForm object. One of them is value, which represents the current value of all form fields as a JavaScript object. You can pass it through the standard json pipe to display the form's value on the page.

NgForm intercepts the standard HTML form's submit event and prevents automatic form submission. Instead, it emits the custom ngSubmit event:

```
<form #f="ngForm" (ngSubmit)="onSubmit(f.value)"></form>
```

The code subscribes to the ngSubmit event using the event-binding syntax. onSubmit is an arbitrary name for the method defined in the component, and it's invoked when the ngSubmit event is fired. To pass all of the form's values as an argument to this method, use the f variable to access NgForm's value property.

NgModel

In the context of the Forms API, NgModel represents a single field on the form. It implicitly creates an instance of the FormControl class that represents the model and stores the fields' data (more on FormControl later in this chapter).

You attach the FormControl object to an HTML element using the ngModel attribute. Note that the Forms API doesn't require either a value assigned to ngModel or any kind of brackets around the attribute:

The name attribute is required when you add ngModel to an element.

```
<form>
   <input type="text"
          name="username"
          ngModel>
</form>
```

No value or brackets denote the data-binding syntax. ngModel serves as a marker for the NgForm directive that represents the form.

The NgForm.value property points at the JavaScript object that holds the values of all form fields. The value of the field's name attribute becomes the property name of the corresponding property in the JavaScript object in NgForm.value.

Like NgForm, the NgModel directive has an exportAs property, so you can create a variable in the template that will reference an instance of NgModel and its value property:

The value of the exportAs property of the NgModel directive is ngModel. You assign it to the local variable c.

```
<form>
   <input type="text"
          name="username"
          ngModel
          #c="ngModel">
   <pre>{{ c.value }}</pre>
</form>
```

The value property holds the current value entered in the previous <input> element.

NgModelGroup

NgModelGroup represents a part of the form and allows you to group form fields together. Like NgForm, it implicitly creates an instance of the FormGroup class. Basically, NgModelGroup creates a nested object in the object stored in NgForm.value. All the child fields of NgModelGroup become properties on the nested object.

Here's how you can use it:

The ngModelGroup attribute requires a string value, which becomes a property name that represents the nested object with values of the child fields.

```
<form #f="ngForm">
   <div ngModelGroup="fullName">
      <input type="text" name="firstName" ngModel>
      <input type="text" name="lastName" ngModel>
   </div>
</form>

<!-- Access the values from the nested object-->
<pre>First name: {{ f.value.fullName.firstName }}</pre>
<pre>Last name:  {{ f.value.fullName.lastName }}</pre>
```

To access the values of the firstName and lastName fields, use the nested fullName object.

7.2.2 *Enriching the HTML form*

Let's refactor the sample user registration form from listing 7.1. There, it was a plain HTML form that didn't use any Angular features. Now you'll wrap it into an Angular component, add validation logic, and enable programmatic handling of the submit event. Let's start by refactoring the template and then move on to the TypeScript part. First, modify the <form> element.

Listing 7.2   Angular-aware form

```
<form #f="ngForm" (ngSubmit)="onSubmit(f.value)">
      <!-- Form fields go here -->
</form>
```

You declare a local template variable f that points at the NgForm object attached to the <form> element. You need this variable to access the form's properties, such as value and valid, and to check whether the form has errors of a specific type.

You also configure the event handler for the ngSubmit event emitted by NgForm. You don't want to listen to the standard submit event, and NgForm intercepts the submit event and stops its propagation. This prevents the form from being automatically submitted to the server, resulting in a page reload. Instead, NgForm emits its own ngSubmit event.

The onSubmit() method is the event handler. It's defined as the component's instance method. In template-driven forms, onSubmit() takes one argument: the form's value, which is a plain JavaScript object that keeps the values of all the fields on the form. Next, you change the username and ssn fields.

Listing 7.3   Modified username and ssn fields

> The ngModel attribute attaches the NgModel directive to the <input> element and makes this field a part of the form. You also add the name attribute.

```
<div>Username: <input type="text" name="username" ngModel></div>
<div>SSN:      <input type="text" name="ssn"      ngModel></div>
```

> You make similar changes to the ssn field, but the value of the name attribute is different.

Now let's change the password fields. Because these fields are related and represent the same value, it's natural to combine them into a group. It will also be convenient to deal with both passwords as a single object when you implement form validation later in this chapter.

Listing 7.4   Modified password fields

The ngModelGroup directive instructs NgForm to create a nested
object within the form's value object that keeps the child fields.
passwordsGroup will become the property name for the nested object.

```
<div ngModelGroup="passwordsGroup">
  <div>Password:         <input type="password" name="password" ngModel>
  ➥ </div> 2((CO7-2))
  <div>Confirm password: <input type="password" name="pconfirm" ngModel>
  ➥ </div> 2((CO7-3))
</div>
```

Changes for the password and pconfirm fields
are similar to those for ngModelGroup, but
the values of the name attributes differ.

The Submit button is the only HTML element left in the template, but it remains the same as in the plain HTML version of the form:

```
<button type="submit">Submit</button>
```

Now that you're done with the template refactoring, let's wrap it into a component. Here's the code of the component:

Listing 7.5   HTML form component

```
@Component({
  selector: 'app',
  template: `...`
})
class AppComponent {
  onSubmit(formValue: any) {
    console.log(formValue);
  }
}
```

We haven't included the content of the template, to keep the listing terse, but the refactored version described earlier should be inlined here.

The onSubmit() event handler takes a single argument: the form's value. As you can see, the handler doesn't use any Angular-specific API. Depending on the validity flag, you can decide whether to post the formValue to the server. In this example, you print it to the console.

Figure 7.2 displays the sample registration form with the form directives applied to it. Each form directive is circled so you can see what the form is made up of. The complete

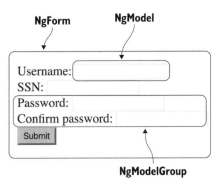

Figure 7.2   Form directives on the registration form

running application that illustrates how to use form directives is located in the 01
_template-driven.ts file, in the code that comes with the book.

7.3 *Reactive forms*

Unlike in the template-driven approach, creating a reactive form is a two-step process.
First you need to create a model programmatically in the code, and then you link
HTML elements to that model using directives in the template. Let's start with the first
step, creating a model.

7.3.1 *Form model*

The form model is an underlying data structure that keeps the form's data. It's constructed out of special classes defined in the `@angular/forms` module: `FormControl`,
`FormGroup`, and `FormArray`.

FORMCONTROL

`FormControl` is an atomic form unit. Usually it corresponds to a single `<input>` element, but it can also represent a more complex UI component like a calendar or a
slider. `FormControl` keeps the current value of the HTML element it corresponds to,
the element's validity status, and whether it's been modified.

Here's how you can create a control:

```
let username = new FormControl('initial value');
```
⟵ **Pass the control's initial value as the
first argument of the constructor.**

FORMGROUP

`FormGroup` usually represents a part of the form and is a collection of `FormControls`.
`FormGroup` aggregates the values and the statuses of each `FormControl` in the group. If
one of the controls in a group is invalid, the entire group becomes invalid. It's convenient for managing related fields on the form. `FormGroup` is also used to represent the
entire form. For example, if a date range is represented by two `date` input fields, they
can be combined into a single group to obtain the date range as a single value and display an error if either of the entered dates is invalid.

Here's how you can create a control group combining the `from` and `to` controls:

```
let formModel = new FormGroup({
  from: new FormControl(),
  to  : new FormControl()
});
```

FORMARRAY

`FormArray` is similar to `FormGroup`, but it has a variable length. Whereas `FormGroup`
represents an entire form or a fixed subset of a form's fields, `FormArray` usually represents a growable collection of fields. For example, you could use `FormArray` to allow
users to enter an arbitrary number of emails. Here's a model that would back such
a form:

```
                 ┌─▷  let formModel = new FormGroup({
FormGroup        │        emails: new FormArray([        ◁────
represents the   │          new FormControl(),          ◁──
entire form.     │          new FormControl()
                 │        ])
                 │      });
```

FormGroup represents the entire form.

Uses FormArray to represent the emails field, because you want to allow users to enter multiple emails

Unlike FormGroup, controls in FormArray aren't associated with keys, but you can reference them by index.

7.3.2 Form directives

The reactive approach uses a completely different set of directives than template-driven forms. The directives for reactive forms come with `ReactiveFormsModule` (see section 7.2).

All reactive directives are prefixed with the `form*` string, so you can easily distinguish the reactive from the template-driven approach just by looking at the template. Reactive directives aren't exportable, which means you can't create a variable in the template that references an instance of a directive. This is done intentionally to clearly separate the two approaches. In template-driven forms, you don't access the model classes; and in reactive forms, you can't operate the model in the template.

Table 7.1 shows how model classes correspond to form directives. The first column lists the model classes covered in the previous section. In the second column are the directives that bind a DOM element to an instance of a model class using the property-binding syntax. As you can see, `FormArray` can't be used with the property binding. The third column lists directives that link a DOM element to a model class by name. They must only be used in the `formGroup` directive.

Model class	Form directives	
	Bind	**Link**
FormGroup	formGroup	formGroupName
FormControl	formControl	formControlName
FormArray	—	formArrayName

Table 7.1 Correspondence of model classes to form directives

Let's look at the form directives.

FORMGROUP

`formGroup` often binds an instance of the `FormGroup` class that represents the entire form model to a top-level form's DOM element, usually a `<form>`. All directives attached to the child DOM elements will be in the scope of `formGroup` and can link model instances by name.

To use the `formGroup` directive, first create a `FormGroup` in the component:

```
@Component(...)
class FormComponent {
  formModel: FormGroup = new FormGroup({});
}
```

Then add the formGroup attribute to an HTML element. The value of the formGroup attribute references a component's property that keeps an instance of the FormGroup class:

```
<form [formGroup]="formModel"></form>
```

FORMGROUPNAME

formGroupName can be used to link nested groups in a form. It needs to be in the scope of a parent formGroup directive to link one of its child FormGroup instances. Here's how you'd define a form model that can be used with formGroupName.

Listing 7.6 Form model to use with `formGroupName`

A FormGroup without a name. It's bound to a DOM element using the formGroup directive and property-binding syntax.

```
@Component(...)
class FormComponent {
  formModel: FormGroup = new FormGroup({
    dateRange: new FormGroup({
      from: new FormControl(),
      to  : new FormControl()
    })
  })
}
```

A child FormGroup with the name dateRange. You can use formGroupName to link this group to a DOM element in the template.

Now let's look at the template.

Listing 7.7 `formGroup` template

```
<form [formGroup]="formModel">
  <div formGroupName="dateRange">...</div>
</form>
```

Binds the FormGroup that represents the entire form using property-binding syntax

Links the <div> element to the FormGroup called dateRange defined in formModel

In the formGroup scope, you can use formGroupName to link child model classes by names defined in the parent FormGroup. The value you assign to the formGroupName attribute must match the name you chose for the child FormGroup in listing 7.7 (in this case, it's dateRange).

> ### Property-binding shorthand syntax
> Because the value you assign to the *Name directive is a string literal, you can use a shorthand syntax and omit the square brackets around the attribute name. The long version would look like this:
>
> ```
> <div [formGroupName]="'dateRange'">...</div>
> ```
>
> Note the square brackets around the attribute name and single quotes around the attribute value.

FORMCONTROLNAME

formControlName must be used in the scope of the formGroup directive. It links one of its child FormControl instances to a DOM element.

Let's continue the example of the date-range model introduced when we explained the formGroupName directive. The component and form model remain the same. You only need to complete the template.

Listing 7.8   Completed `formGroup` template

```
<form [formGroup]="formModel">
  <div formGroupName="dateRange">
    <input type="date" formControlName="from">
    <input type="date" formControlName="to">
  </div>
</form>
```

As in the formGroupName directive, you just specify the name of a FormControl you want to link to the DOM element. Again, these are the names you chose while defining the form model.

FORMCONTROL

formControl can be used for single-field forms, when you don't want to create a form model with FormGroup but still want to use Forms API features like validation and the reactive behavior provided by the FormControl.valueChanges property. You saw an example in chapter 5 when we discussed observables. Here's the essence of that example.

Listing 7.9   FormControl

```
@Component({...})
class FormComponent {
  weatherControl: FormControl = new FormControl();   ⟵

  constructor() {
    this.weatherControl.valueChanges            ⟵
        .debounceTime(500)
        .switchMap(city => this.getWeather(city))
        .subscribe(weather => console.log(weather));
  }
}
```

> **Instead of defining a form model with FormGroup, as you saw earlier in this section, create a standalone instance of a FormControl.**

> **Uses valueChanges to get the value from the form**

You could use ngModel to sync the value entered by user with the component's property; but because you're using the Forms API, you can use its reactive features. In the preceding example, you apply several RxJS operators to the observable returned by the valueChanges property to improve the user experience. More details on this example can be found in chapter 5.

Here's the template of the `FormComponent` from listing 7.9:

```
<input type="text" [formControl]="weatherControl">
```

Because you're working with a standalone `FormControl` that's not a part of a Form-Group, you can't use the `formControlName` directive to link it by name. Instead you use `formControl` with the property-binding syntax.

FORMARRAYNAME

`formArrayName` must be used in the scope of a `formGroup` directive. It links one of its child `FormArray` instances to a DOM element. Because form controls in `FormArray` don't have names, you can link them to DOM elements only by index. Usually you render them in a loop, using the `ngFor` directive.

Let's look at an example that allows users to enter an arbitrary number of emails. We'll highlight the key parts of the code here, but you can find the full runnable example in 02_growable-items-form.ts in the code distributed with the book. First you define the model.

> **Listing 7.10   02_growable-items-form.ts file: defining the model**

```
                        @Component(...)
                        class AppComponent {
                          formModel: FormGroup = new FormGroup({
        Creates a  ┌──▷    emails: new FormArray([
   FormGroup that │         new FormControl()        ◁──  Uses a FormArray for the
  will represent  │       ])                              emails collection to allow
        the form  │     });                               users to enter multiple emails
                  │     //...
                        }
```

In the template, email fields are rendered in the loop using the `ngFor` directive.

> **Listing 7.11   02_growable-items-form.ts file: template**

```
                formArrayName links the           Loops through the emails array
                FormArray to the DOM element.       and creates an input field for
                                                               each entry
    <ul formArrayName="emails">                  ◁──┘
      <li *ngFor="let e of formModel.get('emails').controls; let i=index">  ◁──┘
        <input [formControlName]="i">            ◁─────┐
      </li>                                            │
┌──▷  <button type="button" (click)="addEmail()">Add Email</button>
│     </ul>                                        Links the <input>
│                                                  element to an instance
Defines the click event handler                    of FormControl by index
```

The `let i` notation in the `*ngFor` loop allows you to automatically bind the value of the array's `index` to the `i` variable available in the loop. The `formControlName` directive links the `FormControl` in `FormArray` to a DOM element; but instead of specifying a name, it uses the i variable that references the index of the current control. When users click the Add Email button, you push a new `FormControl` instance to the `FormArray`: `this.formModel.get('emails')` `.push(new FormControl())`.

Figure 7.3 shows the form with two email fields; an animated version, available at https://www.manning.com/books/angular-2-development-with-typescript, shows how it works. Every time the user clicks the Add Email button, a new `FormControl` instance is pushed to the emails `FormArray`, and through data-binding a new input field is rendered on the page. The form's value is updated below the form in real time via data-binding as well.

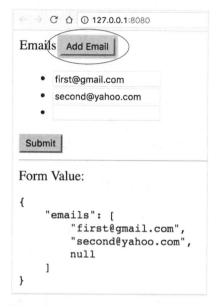

Figure 7.3 Form with a growable email collection

7.3.3 Refactoring the sample form

Now let's refactor the sample registration form from listing 7.1. Originally it was a plain HTML form, and then you applied a template-driven approach. Now it's time for a reactive version. You start reactive forms by defining a form model.

Listing 7.12   Defining a form model

```
@Component(...)
class AppComponent {
  formModel: FormGroup;          ⟵  Declares a component
                                      property that keeps the
                                      form's model
  constructor() {
    this.formModel = new FormGroup({   ⟵  Initializes the form model
                                            in the constructor
      'username': new FormControl(),
      'ssn': new FormControl(),
      'passwordsGroup': new FormGroup({   ⟵  Nested group for
                                               password fields
        'password': new FormControl(),
        'pconfirm': new FormControl()
      })
    });
  }

  onSubmit() {                           ⟵  Accesses the form's value
    console.log(this.formModel.value);        using the component's
  }                                           formModel property
}
```

The `formModel` property keeps an instance of the `FormGroup` type that defines the structure of the form. You'll use this property in the template to bind the model to the DOM element with the `formGroup` directive. It's initialized programmatically in the constructor by instantiating model classes. The names you give to form controls in the parent `FormGroup` are used in the template to link the model to the DOM elements with the `formControlName` and `formGroupName` directives.

`passwordsGroup` is a nested `FormGroup` to group the password and password-confirmation fields. It will be convenient to manage their values as a single object when you add form validation.

Because reactive form directives aren't exportable, you can't access them in the template and pass the form's value directly to the `onSubmit()` method as an argument. Instead, you access the value using the component's property that holds the form's model.

Now that the model is defined, you can write the HTML markup that binds to the model.

Listing 7.13 HTML binding to the model

> In the reactive approach, you don't pass any params to the method that handles the ngSubmit event.

> Binds the **<form>** element to the form model represented by a FormGroup class using the formGroup directive

> Uses the formControlName directive to link input fields to the FormControl instances defined in the parent FormGroup model

```
<form [formGroup]="formModel"
      (ngSubmit)="onSubmit()">
  <div>Username: <input type="text" formControlName="username"></div>
  <div>SSN:      <input type="text" formControlName="ssn"></div>

  <div formGroupName="passwordsGroup">
    <div>Password:        <input type="password" formControlName="password">
    </div>
    <div>Confirm password: <input type="password" formControlName="pconfirm">
    </div>
  </div>
  <button type="submit">Submit</button>
</form>
```

> Links password and pconfirm using the formControlName directive

> The HTML structure mimics the model structure you defined in the component. To link the FormGroup to the DOM element, use the formGroupName directive.

The behavior of this reactive version of the registration form is identical to the template-driven version, but the internal implementation differs. The complete application that illustrates how to create reactive forms is located in the 03_reactive.ts file, in the code that comes with the book.

7.3.4 *Using FormBuilder*

`FormBuilder` simplifies the creation of reactive forms. It doesn't provide any unique features compared to the direct use of the `FormControl`, `FormGroup`, and `FormArray` classes, but its API is more terse and saves you from the repetitive typing of class names.

Let's refactor the component class from the previous section to use `FormBuilder`. The template will remain exactly the same, but you'll change the way the `formModel` is constructed. Here's what it should look like.

Listing 7.14   Refactoring `formModel` with `FormBuilder`

FormBuilder is an injectable service provided by ReactiveFormsModule, so you can inject it into the constructor. Its methods will be used to configure formModel.

The FormBuilder.group() method creates a FormGroup using a configuration object passed as the first argument. The configuration object has the same format as the one that FormGroup's constructor accepts.

FormControl is instantiated using the configuration array.

Like FormGroup, FormBuilder allows you to create nested groups.

```
constructor(fb: FormBuilder) {
  this.formModel = fb.group({
    'username': [''],
    'ssn': [''],
    'passwordsGroup': fb.group({
      'password': [''],
      'pconfirm': ['']
    })
  });
}
```

The FormBuilder.group() method accepts an object with extra configuration parameters as the last argument. You can use it to specify group validators.

Unlike `FormGroup`, `FormBuilder` allows you to instantiate `FormControls` using an array. Each item of the array has a special meaning. The first item is `FormControl`'s initial value. The second is a validator function. It can also accept a third argument, which is an async validator function. The rest of the array's items are ignored.

As you can see, configuring a form model with `FormBuilder` is less verbose and is based on the configuration objects rather than requiring explicit instantiation of the control's classes. The complete application that illustrates how to use `FormBuilder` is located in the 04_form-builder.ts file in the code that comes with the book.

7.4   Form validation

One of the advantages of using the Forms API, compared to regular data binding, is that forms have validation capabilities. Validation is available for both types of forms: template-driven and reactive. You create validators as plain TypeScript functions. In the reactive approach, you use functions directly, and in the template-driven approach you wrap them into custom directives.

Let's start by validating reactive forms and then move to template-driven ones. We'll cover the basics and apply validation to the sample registration form.

7.4.1   Validating reactive forms

Validators are just functions that conform to the following interface:

```
interface ValidatorFn {
  (c: AbstractControl): {[key: string]: any};
}
```

The type declaration {[key: string]: any} describes an object literal, where the property names are strings and values can be of any type.

The validator function should declare a single parameter of type `AbstractControl` and return an object literal. There are no restrictions on the implementation of the function—it's up to the validator's author. `AbstractControl` is the superclass for `FormControl`, `Form-Group`, and `FormArray`, which means validators can be created for all model classes.

A number of predefined validators ship with Angular: `required`, `minLength`, `max-Length`, and `pattern`. They're defined as static methods of the `Validators` class declared in the `@angular/forms` module, and they match standard HTML5 validation attributes.

Once you have a validator, you need to configure the model to use it. In the reactive approach, you provide validators as arguments to the constructors of the model classes. Here's an example:

The first parameter is the default value, and the second is the validator function.

```
import { FormControl, Validators } from '@angular/forms';

let usernameControl = new FormControl('', Validators.required);
```

You can also provide a list of validators as the second argument:

```
let usernameControl = new FormControl('', [Validators.required,
➡ Validators.minLength(5)]);
```

To test the control's validity, use the `valid` property, which returns either `true` or `false`:

Indicates whether the value entered in the field passes or fails the validation rules configured for the control

```
let isValid: boolean = usernameControl.valid;
```

If any of the validation rules fails, you can get error objects generated by the validator functions:

```
let errors: {[key: string]: any} = usernameControl.errors;
```

> **The error object**
>
> The error returned by a validator is represented by a JavaScript object that has a property with the same name as the validator. Whether it's an object literal or an object with a complex prototypal chain doesn't matter for the validator.
>
> The property's value can be of any type and may provide additional error details. For example, the standard `Validators.minLength()` validator returns the following error object:
>
> ```
> {
>   minlength: {
>     requiredLength: 7,
>     actualLength: 5
>   }
> }
> ```

> **(continued)**
>
> The object has a top-level property that matches the validator's name, `minlength`. Its value is also an object with two fields: `requiredLength` and `actualLength`. These error details can be used to display a user-friendly error message.
>
> Not all validators provide the error details. Sometimes the top-level property just indicates that the error has occurred. In this case, the property is initialized with the value `true`. Here's an example of the standard `Validators.required()` error object:
>
> ```
> {
>    required: true
> }
> ```

CUSTOM VALIDATORS

Standard validators are good for validating basic data types, like strings and numbers. If you need to validate a more complex data type or application-specific logic, you may need to create a custom validator. Because validators in Angular are just functions with a certain signature, they're fairly easy to create. You need to declare a function that accepts an instance of one of the control types—FormControl, FormGroup, or FormArray—and returns an object that represents the validation error (see the sidebar "The error object").

Here's an example of a custom validator that checks whether the control's value is a valid Social Security number (SSN), which is a unique ID given to each U.S. citizen:

The type of the argument is FormControl, because you're testing an individual field.

Angular may invoke the validator even before a user enters a real value, so make sure it's not null.

```
function ssnValidator(control: FormControl): any {
    const value = control.value || '';
    const valid = value.match(/^\d{9}$/);
    return valid ? null : { ssn: true };
}
```

Matches the value against a regular expression that represents the SSN format. It's a trivial check, but it works for the example.

If the value is an invalid SSN, you return an error object. Otherwise null is returned, indicating that there are no errors. The error object doesn't provide any details.

Custom validators are used the same way as the standard ones:

```
let ssnControl = new FormControl('', ssnValidator);
```

The complete running application that illustrates how to create custom validators is located in the 05_custom-validator.ts file in the code that comes with the book.

GROUP VALIDATORS

You may want to validate not only individual fields but also groups of fields. Angular allows you to define validator functions for FormGroups as well.

Let's create a validator that will make sure the password and password-confirmation fields on the sample registration form have the same value. Here's one possible implementation:

Gets the names of all properties in the value object

```
function equalValidator({value}: FormGroup): {[key: string]: any} {
  const [first, ...rest] = Object.keys(value || {});
  const valid = rest.every(v => value[v] === value[first]);
  return valid ? null : {equal: true};
}
```

Returns either null or an error object

Iterates through all the values and makes sure they're equal

The signature of the function conforms to the `ValidatorFn` interface : the first parameter is of type `FormGroup`, which is a subclass of `AbstractControl`, and the return type is an object literal. Note that you use an ECMAScript feature called *destructuring* (see the "Destructuring" section in appendix A). You extract the `value` property from the instance of the `FormGroup` class that will be passed as an argument. This makes sense here because you never access any other `FormGroup` property in the validator's code.

Next you get the names of all properties in the value object and save them in two variables, `first` and `rest`. `first` is the name of a property that will be used as the reference value—values of all other properties must be equal to it to make validation pass. `rest` stores the names of all the other properties. Again, you're using the destructuring feature to extract references to the array items (see the section "Destructuring of arrays" in appendix A). Finally, you return either `null` if the values in the group are valid or an object that indicates the error state otherwise.

VALIDATING THE SAMPLE REGISTRATION FORM

Now that we've covered the basics, let's add validation to the sample registration form. You'll use the `ssnValidator` and `equalValidator` implemented earlier in this section. Here's the modified form model.

Listing 7.15 Modified form model

For the username control, you use the standard Validators.required validator. It makes sure a non-empty value is entered in the field.

For the ssn field, you use the ssnValidator implemented previously.

```
this.formModel = new FormGroup({
  'username': new FormControl('', Validators.required),
  'ssn': new FormControl('', ssnValidator),
  'passwordsGroup': new FormGroup({
    'password': new FormControl('', Validators.minLength(5)),
    'pconfirm': new FormControl('')
  }, {}, equalValidator)
});
```

Configures equalValidator for the passwordsGroup. It makes sure the values of all fields in the group are the same. Unlike FormControl, you pass validators as the third argument to the FormGroup constructor.

For the password field, you use the standard validators.minLength validator, which returns an error if the length of the entered string value is less than five characters.

Before printing the form's model to the console in the onSubmit() method, you check whether the form is valid:

```
onSubmit() {
  if (this.formModel.valid) {
    console.log(this.formModel.value);
  }
}
```

In the model-driven approach, configuring validators requires changes only in the code, but you still want to make some changes in the template. You want to display validation errors when the user enters an invalid value. Here's the modified version of the template.

Listing 7.16 Modified template

```
<form [formGroup]="formModel" (ngSubmit)="onSubmit()" novalidate>
  <div>Username:
    <input type="text" formControlName="username">
    <span [hidden]="!formModel.hasError('required', 'username')">Username is
    ➥ required</span>                              ◁──── Conditionally shows the error
  </div>                                                  message for the username field
  <div>SSN:
    <input type="text" formControlName="ssn">
    <span [hidden]="!formModel.hasError('ssn', 'ssn')">SSN is invalid
    ➥ </span>                                     ◁──── Adds an error message for the
  </div>                                                 ssn field as you did for the
                                                         username field
  <div formGroupName="passwordsGroup">
    <div>Password:
      <input type="password" formControlName="password">
      <span [hidden]="!formModel.hasError('minlength', ['passwordsGroup',
      ➥ 'password'])">                            ◁──── Conditionally shows the error
          Password is too short                         message for the password field
      </span>
    </div>
    <div>Confirm password:
      <input type="password" formControlName="pconfirm">
      <span [hidden]="!formModel.hasError('equal', 'passwordsGroup')">
          Passwords must be the same
      </span>
    </div>
  </div>
  <button type="submit">Submit</button>
</form>
```

Note how you access the hasError() method available on the form model when you conditionally show error messages. It takes two parameters: the name of the validation error you want to check, and the path to the field you're interested in in the form model. In the case of username, it's a direct child of the top-level FormGroup that represents the form model, so you specify just the name of the control. But the `password` field is a child of the nested `FormGroup`, so the path to the control is specified as an array of strings. The first element is the name of the nested group, and the second element is the name of the `password` field itself. Like the `username` field, `passwordsGroup` specifies the path as a string because it's a direct child of the top-level `FormGroup`.

The complete running application that illustrates how to use validator functions with reactive forms is located in the 09_reactive-with-validation.ts file in the code that comes with the book. In this example, you hardcoded the error messages in the template, but they can be provided by the validators. For the example that dynamically provides error messages, see the 07_custom-validator-error-message.ts file.

Configuring validators with FormBuilder

Validators can also be configured when you're using `FormBuilder` to define form models. Here's a modified version of the model for the sample registration form that uses `FormBuilder`:

```
@Component(...)
class AppComponent {
  formModel: FormGroup;

  constructor(fb: FormBuilder) {          ◁──┐   FormBuilder is a registered
    this.formModel = fb.group({                   provider, so you can inject it into
      'username': ['', Validators.required],      the component's constructor
      'ssn': ['', ssnValidator],        ◁──┐      instead of instantiating it directly
      'passwordsGroup': fb.group({               with the new keyword.
        'password': ['', Validators.minLength(5)],
        'pconfirm': ['']                          Validators are specified
      }, {validator: equalValidator})   ◁──┐      as the second array
    });                                            item while configuring
  }                                                FormControls.
}
```

FormBuilder is a registered provider, so you can inject it into the component's constructor instead of instantiating it directly with the new keyword.

Validators are specified as the second array item while configuring FormControls.

While configuring the FormGroup validators, you provide an options object as the second argument to the group() method, and you use the validator property on the object to specify the validators.

ASYNCHRONOUS VALIDATORS

The Forms API supports asynchronous validators. Async validators can be used to check form values against a remote server, which involves sending an HTTP request. Like regular validators, async validators are functions. The only difference is that async validators should return either an `Observable` or a `Promise` object. Here's an async version of the SSN validator.

Listing 7.17   Async SSN validator

> In this case, the return value
> is of the Observable type.

```
function asyncSsnValidator(control: FormControl): Observable<any> {    ⟵──┘
  const value: string = control.value || '';
  const valid = value.match(/^\d{9}$/);
  return Observable.of(valid ? null : { ssn: true }).delay(5000);    ⟵──┐
}
```

> To keep this example simple, you emulate asynchrony
> with the RxJS delay operator. The validation result
> arrives 5 seconds after the function is invoked.

Async validators are passed as the third argument to constructors of model classes:

```
let ssnControl = new FormControl('', null, asyncSsnValidator);
```

The complete running application that illustrates how to use async validators is located in the 08_async-validator.ts file in the code that comes with the book.

CHECKING A FIELD'S STATUS AND VALIDITY

You're already familiar with control properties such as `valid`, `invalid`, and `errors` for checking field statuses. In this section, we'll look at a number of other properties that help improve the user experience:

- *Touched and untouched fields*—In addition to checking a control's validity, you can also use the `touched` and `untouched` properties to check whether a field was visited by the user. If the user puts the focus into a field using the keyboard or mouse, the field becomes `touched`; otherwise it's `untouched`. This can be useful when displaying error messages—if the value in a field is invalid but it was never visited by the user, you can choose not to highlight it with red, because it's not a user mistake. Here's an example:

> Defines a CSS class that highlights an input field's
> border with red, for invalid fields

```
<style>.hasError {border: 1px solid red;}</style>    ⟵──┐
                                                          Adds the required
<input type="text" required                               validator for the
       name="username" ngModel #c="ngModel"         ⟵──  username field
       [class.hasError]="c.invalid && c.touched">    ⟵──┐
                                                          Conditionally applies
                                                          the hasError CSS
Enables Forms API support for the field, and              class to the <input>
saves a reference to the NgModel directive                element
instance in the template-locale c variable
```

NOTE   All the properties discussed here are available for the model classes `FormControl`, `FormGroup`, and `FormArray`, as well as for the template-driven directives `NgModel`, `NgModelGroup`, and `NgForm`.

Note the CSS class binding example on the last line. It conditionally applies the `hasError` CSS class to the element if the expression on the right side is `true`. If you used only `c.invalid`, the border would be highlighted as soon as the page was rendered; but this can confuse users, especially if the page has a lot of fields. Instead, you add one more condition: the field must be touched. Now the field is highlighted only after a user visits this field.

- *Pristine and dirty fields*—Another useful pair of properties are `pristine` and its counterpart `dirty`. `dirty` indicates that the field was modified after it was initialized with its original value. These properties can be used to prompt the user to save changed data before leaving the page or closing the dialog window.

NOTE All of the preceding properties have corresponding CSS classes (ng-touched and ng-untouched, ng-dirty and ng-pristine, ng-valid and ng-invalid) that are automatically added to HTML elements when the property is `true`. These can be useful to style elements in a certain state.

- *Pending fields*—If you have async validators configured for a control, you may also find the Boolean property `pending` to be useful. It indicates whether the validity status is currently unknown. This happens when an async validator is still in progress and you need to wait for the results. This property can be used for displaying a progress indicator.

For reactive forms, the `statusChanges` property of type `Observable` can be more convenient. It emits one of three values: `VALID`, `INVALID`, and `PENDING`.

VALIDATING TEMPLATE-DRIVEN FORMS

Directives are all you can use when you create template-driven forms, so you can wrap validator functions into directives to use them in the template. Let's create a directive that wraps the SSN validator implemented in listing 7.17.

Listing 7.18 SsnValidatorDirective

```
@Directive({
  selector: '[ssn]',
  providers: [{
    provide: NG_VALIDATORS,
    useValue: ssnValidator,
    multi: true
  }]
})
class SsnValidatorDirective {}
```

Defines the directive's selector as an HTML attribute

Declares a directive using the @Directive annotation from the @angular/core module

Registers ssnValidator as an NG_VALIDATORS provider

The square brackets around the `ssn` selector denote that the directive can be used as an attribute. This is convenient, because you can add the attribute to any `<input>` element or to an Angular component represented as a custom HTML element.

In this example, you register the validator function using the predefined NG_VALIDATORS Angular token. This token is in turn injected by the NgModel directive, and NgModel gets the list of all validators attached to the HTML element. Then NgModel passes validators to the FormControl instance it implicitly creates internally. The same mechanism is responsible for running validators; directives are just a different way to configure them. The multi property lets you associate multiple values with the same token. When the token is injected into the NgModel directive, NgModel gets a list of values instead of a single value. This enables you to pass multiple validators.

Here's how you can use SsnValidatorDirective:

```
<input type="text" name="my-ssn" ngModel ssn>
```

You can find the complete running application that illustrates directive validators in the 06_custom-validator-directive.ts file in the code that comes with the book.

VALIDATING THE SAMPLE REGISTRATION FORM

Now you can add form validation to the sample registration form. Let's start with the template.

> **Listing 7.19 Registration form validation template**

**Adds the validation directive
as the required attribute**

**Passes the form's value and validity
status to the onSubmit() method**

```
<form #f="ngForm" (ngSubmit)="onSubmit(f.value, f.valid)" novalidate>
  <div>Username:
    <input type="text" name="username" ngModel required>
    <span [hidden]="!f.form.hasError('required', 'username')">Username is
    ➥ required</span>
  </div>
  <div>SSN:
    <input type="text" name="ssn" ngModel ssn>
    <span [hidden]="!f.form.hasError('ssn', 'ssn')">SSN in invalid</span>
  </div>

  <div ngModelGroup="passwordsGroup" equal>
    <div>Password:
      <input type="password" name="password" ngModel minlength="5">
      <span [hidden]="!f.form.hasError('minlength', ['passwordsGroup',
      ➥ 'password'])">
      Password is too short
      </span>
    </div>
    <div>Confirm password:
      <input type="password" name="pconfirm" ngModel>
      <span [hidden]="!f.form.hasError('equal', 'passwordsGroup')">
      Passwords must be the same
      </span>
    </div>
  </div>
  <button type="submit">Submit</button>
</form>
```

**Conditionally shows and
hides error messages**

**equal is a directive wrapper for the
equalValidator you implemented earlier.
Custom validator directives are added the
same way as standard ones.**

In the template-driven approach, you don't have a model in the component. Only the template can inform the form's handler whether the form is valid, and that's why you pass the form's value and validity status as arguments to the onSubmit() method. You also add the novalidate attribute to prevent standard browser validation from interfering with the Angular validation.

Validation directives are added as attributes. The required directive is provided by Angular and is available once you register Forms API support with FormsModule. Similarly, you can use the minlength directive to validate the password field.

To conditionally show and hide validation errors, you use the same hasError() method you used in the reactive version. But to access this method, you need to use a form property of type FormGroup, available on the f variable that references an instance of the formGroup directive.

In the onSubmit() method, you check whether the form is valid before printing the value to the console.

Listing 7.20   Checking form validation

```
@Component({ template: '...' })
class AppComponent {
  onSubmit(formValue: any, isFormValid: boolean) {     ⟵   Adds the isFormValid
    if (isFormValid) {                                       parameter to the
      console.log(formValue);            ⟵                   method declaration
    }
  }                                         Prints the value of the form to
}                                           the console if the form is valid
```

Now for the last step: you need to add custom validator directives to the declarations list of the NgModule where you define AppComponent.

Listing 7.21   Adding validator directives

```
@NgModule({
  imports     : [ BrowserModule, FormsModule ],
  declarations: [ AppComponent, EqualValidatorDirective,
  ➥ SsnValidatorDirective ],             ⟵
  bootstrap   : [ AppComponent ]            Add directives in the
})                                          declarations list.
class AppModule {}
```

The complete running application that illustrates how to use validator directives with template-driven forms is located in the 10_template-driven-with-validation.ts file in the code that comes with the book.

7.5   *Hands-on: adding validation to the search form*

This hands-on exercise will start where you left off in chapter 6. You'll need to modify the code of the SearchComponent to enable form validation and collect the data entered in the form. When the search form is submitted, you'll print the form's value on the browser's console. Chapter 8 is about communication with the server, and in that chapter you'll refactor the code so the search form will make a real HTTP request.

In this section you'll perform the following steps:

1 Add a new method to the `ProductService` class that returns an array of all available product categories.
2 Create a model representing the search form using `FormBuilder`.
3 Configure validation rules for the model.
4 Refactor the template to properly bind to the model created in the previous step.
5 Implement the `onSearch()` method to handle the form's submit event.

Figure 7.4 shows what the search form will look like after you complete this hands-on exercise. It illustrates the validators in action.

If you prefer to see the final version of this project, browse the source code in the auction folder from chapter 7. Otherwise, copy the auction folder from chapter 6 to a separate location, and follow the instructions in this section.

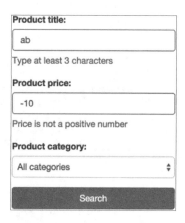

Figure 7.4 Search form with validators

7.5.1 *Modifying the root module to add Forms API support*

Update the app.module.ts file to enable reactive forms support for the application. Import `ReactiveFormsModule` from `@angular/forms`, and add it to the list of imported modules in the main application NgModule.

Listing 7.22 Updated app.module.ts file

```
import { ReactiveFormsModule } from '@angular/forms';

@NgModule({
  imports: [
    BrowserModule,
    FormsModule,
    ReactiveFormsModule,
    RouterModule.forRoot([ ... ])
  ],
```

7.5.2 *Adding a list of categories to the SearchComponent*

Each product has the `categories` property, represented by an array of strings, and a single product can relate to multiple categories. The form should allow users to select a category while searching for products; you need a way to provide a list of all available categories to the form so it can display them to users. In a real-world application, the categories would likely come from the server. In this online auction example, you'll add a method to the ProductService class that will return hardcoded categories:

1 Open the app/services/product-service.ts file, and add a getAllCategories() method that accepts no parameters and returns a list of strings:

```
getAllCategories(): string[] {
  return ['Books', 'Electronics', 'Hardware'];
}
```

2 Open the app/components/search/search.ts file, and add an import statement for ProductService:

```
import {ProductService} from '../../services/product-service';
```

3 Configure this service as a provider for SearchComponent:

```
@Component({
  selector: 'auction-search',
  providers: [ProductService],
  //...
})
```

4 Declare a categories: string[] class property as a reference to the list of categories. You'll use it for the data binding:

```
export default class SearchComponent {
  categories: string[];
}
```

5 Declare a constructor() with one parameter: ProductService. Angular will inject it when the component is instantiated. Initialize the categories property using the getAllCategories() method:

> **The private keyword automatically creates a class property with the same name as the parameter and initializes it with the provided value.**

```
constructor(private productService: ProductService) {          ⟵
  this.categories = this.productService.getAllCategories();
}
```

7.5.3 Creating a form model

Now let's define the model that will handle the search form:

1 Open the app/components/search/search.ts file, and add the Forms API-related imports. The import statement at the beginning of the file should look like this:

```
import {Component} from '@angular/core';
import {FormControl, FormGroup, FormBuilder, Validators} from
➥ '@angular/forms';
```

2   Declare a `formModel` class property of the `FormGroup` type:

```
export default class SearchComponent {
  formModel: FormGroup;
  //...
}
```

3   In the constructor, define the `formModel` using the `FormBuilder` class:

```
const fb = new FormBuilder();
this.formModel = fb.group({
  'title': [null, Validators.minLength(3)],
  'price': [null, positiveNumberValidator],
  'category': [-1]
})
```

4   Add a `positiveNumberValidator` function:

```
function positiveNumberValidator(control: FormControl): any {
  if (!control.value) return null;
  const price = parseInt(control.value);
  return price === null || typeof price === 'number' && price > 0
      ? null : {positivenumber: true};
}
```

`positiveNumberValidator()` attempts to parse an integer value from the Form-Control's value using the standard `parseInt()` function. If the parsed value is a valid positive number, the function returns `null`, meaning there are no errors. Otherwise the function returns an error object.

7.5.4   *Refactoring the template*

Let's add form directives to the template to bind the model defined in the previous step to the HTML elements:

1   You defined the form model in the code implementing the reactive approach, so in the template you should attach the `NgFormModel` directive to the `<form>` element:

Binds the form to the model already created in the component

Subscribes to the ngSubmit event. The onSearch() method will be invoked every time the user clicks the button. You'll define this method in the following steps.

```
<form [formGroup]="formModel"
      (ngSubmit)="onSearch()"
      novalidate>
```

Disables the native browser's form validation so it doesn't interfere with Angular's

2 Define the validation rules, and conditionally display error messages for the title field:

```
<div class="form-group"
     [class.has-error]="formModel.hasError('minlength', 'title')">
  <label for="title">Product title:</label>
  <input id="title"
         placeholder="Title"
         class="form-control"
         type="text"
         formControlName="title"
         minlength="3">
  <span class="help-block"
        [class.hidden]="!formModel.hasError('minlength', 'title')">
    Type at least 3 characters
  </span>
</div>
```

Here you use the `form-group`, `form-control`, `has-error`, and `help-block` CSS classes defined in the Twitter Bootstrap library. They're required to properly render the form and highlight the field with the red border in the case of a validation error. You can read more about these classes in the Bootstrap documentation, in the "Forms" section: http://getbootstrap.com/css/#forms.

3 Do the same for the product price field:

```
<div class="form-group"
     [class.has-error]="formModel.hasError('positivenumber', 'price')">
  <label for="price">Product price:</label>
  <input id="price"
         placeholder="Price"
         class="form-control"
         type="number"
         step="any"
         min="0"
         formControlName="price">
  <span class="help-block"
        [class.hidden]="!formModel.hasError('positivenumber', 'price')">
    Price is not a positive number
  </span>
</div>
```

4 Add validation rules and an error message for the product category field:

```
<div class="form-group">
  <label for="category">Product category:</label>
  <select id="category"
          class="form-control"
          formControlName="category">
    <option value="-1">All categories</option>
    <option *ngFor="let c of categories"
            [value]="c">{{c}}</option>
  </select>
</div>
```

The Submit button remains unchanged.

7.5.5   *Implementing the onSearch() method*

Add the following onSearch() method:

```
onSearch() {
  if (this.formModel.valid) {
    console.log(this.formModel.value);
  }
}
```

7.5.6   *Launching the online auction*

To launch the application, open a command window and start http-server in the root directory of the project. Enter http://localhost:8080 in a web browser, and you should see a Home page that includes the search form shown in 7.4. This version of the application illustrates form creation and validation without performing a search. You'll implement the search functionality in chapter 8, when we discuss communication with servers.

7.6   *Summary*

In this chapter, you've learned how to work with forms in Angular. These are the main takeaways from this chapter:

- There are two approaches to working with forms: template-driven and reactive. The template-driven approach is easier and quicker to configure, but the reactive one is easier to test, enables more flexibility, and provides more control over the form.
- The reactive approach offers advantages for applications that use not only the DOM renderer but another one (such as one from NativeScript) targeting non-browser environments. Reactive forms are programmed once and can be reused by more than one renderer.
- A number of standard validators ship with Angular, but you can also create custom ones. You should validate the user's input, but client-side validation isn't a replacement for performing additional validation on the server. Consider client-side validation as a way to provide instant feedback to the user, minimizing server requests involving invalid data.

Interacting
with servers using
HTTP and WebSockets

This chapter covers

- Creating a simple web server using the Node and Express frameworks
- Making server requests from Angular using the Http object API
- Communicating with the Node server from Angular clients using the HTTP protocol
- Wrapping a WebSocket client into an Angular service that generates an observable stream
- Broadcasting data from the server to multiple clients via WebSockets

Angular applications can communicate with any web server supporting HTTP or WebSocket protocols, regardless of what server-side platform is used. So far, we've been covering mostly the client side of Angular applications, with the weather service example in chapter 5 being the only exception. In this chapter, you'll learn how to communicate with web servers in more detail.

We'll first give you a brief overview of Angular's Http object, and then you'll create a web server using TypeScript and Node.js. This server will provide the data required for all of the code samples, including the online auction. Then you'll learn how the client code can make HTTP requests to web servers and consume the responses using *observables*, which we introduced in chapter 5. We'll also show you how to communicate with the server via WebSockets, focusing on the server-side data push.

In the hands-on section, you'll implement a product search function in which the data about auction products and reviews will come from the server via HTTP requests. You'll also implement product bid notifications, which will be sent by the server using the WebSocket protocol.

8.1   *A brief overview of the Http object's API*

Web applications run HTTP requests asynchronously so the UI remains responsive and the user can continue working with the application while the HTTP requests are being processed by the server. Asynchronous HTTP requests can be implemented using callbacks, promises, or observables. Although promises eliminate the callback hell (see appendix A), they have the following shortcomings:

- There's no way to cancel a pending request made with a promise.
- When a promise resolves or rejects, the client receives either the data or an error message, but in either case it'll just be a single piece of data. A promise doesn't offer a way to handle a continuous stream of chunks of data delivered over time.

Observables don't have these shortcomings. In section 5.2.2, we looked at a promise-based scenario that resulted in multiple unnecessary requests to get a price quote for a stock, generating unnecessary network traffic. Then, in the example with the weather services in section 5.2.3, we demonstrated how you can cancel HTTP requests made with observables.

Let's look at Angular's implementation of the Http class, which is included in the @angular/http package. This package includes several classes and interfaces, as described in the Angular HTTP client documentation at http://mng.bz/87C3.

If you peek inside the @angular/http/src/http.d.ts type definition file, you'll see the following APIs in the Http class:

```
import {Observable} from 'rxjs/Observable';
...
export declare class Http {
...
    constructor(_backend: ConnectionBackend, _defaultOptions: RequestOptions);

    request(url: string | Request, options?: RequestOptionsArgs):
    ➥ Observable<Response>;

    get(url: string, options?: RequestOptionsArgs): Observable<Response>;
```

```
  post(url: string, body: string, options?: RequestOptionsArgs):
➡ Observable<Response>;

  put(url: string, body: string, options?: RequestOptionsArgs):
➡ Observable<Response>;

 delete(url: string, options?: RequestOptionsArgs): Observable<Response>;

 patch(url: string, body: string, options?: RequestOptionsArgs):
➡ Observable<Response>;

 head(url: string, options?: RequestOptionsArgs): Observable<Response>;
}
```

This code is written in TypeScript, and each of the Http object's methods has url as a mandatory argument, which can be either a string or a Request object. You can also pass an optional object of type RequestOptionArgs. Each method returns an Observable that wraps an object of type Response.

The following code snippet illustrates one of the ways of using the get() API of the Http object, passing a URL as a string:

```
constructor(private http: Http) {
  this.http.get('/products').subscribe(...);
}
```

We haven't specified the full URL here (such as http://localhost:8000/products), assuming that the Angular application makes a request to the server where it was deployed, so the base portion of the URL can be omitted. The subscribe() method has to receive an observer object with the code for handling the received data and errors.

The Request object offers a more generic API, where you can separately create a Request instance, specify an HTTP method, and include the search parameters and a Header:

```
let myHeaders:Headers  = new Headers();
myHeaders.append('Authorization', 'Basic QWxhZGRpb');

this.http
    .request(new Request({
      headers: myHeaders,
      method: RequestMethod.Get,
      url: '/products',
      search: 'zipcode=10001'
    }))
    .subscribe(...);
```

RequestOptionsArgs is declared as a TypeScript interface:

```
export interface RequestOptionsArgs {
    url?: string;
    method?: string | RequestMethod;
```

```
    search?: string | URLSearchParams;
    headers?: Headers;
    body?: any;
    withCredentials?: boolean;
    responseType?: ResponseContentType;
}
```

All members of this interface are optional, but if you decide to use them, the TypeScript compiler will ensure that you provide values of the proper data types:

```
var myRequest: RequestOptionsArgs = {
    url: '/products',
    method: 'Get'
};

this.http
    .request(new Request(myRequest))
    .subscribe(...);
```

In the hands-on section, you'll see an example of using the `search` property of `RequestOptionsArgs` to make HTTP requests that have query string parameters.

What's the Fetch API?

There's an effort under way to unify the process of fetching resources on the web. The Fetch API (https://fetch.spec.whatwg.org/) can be used as a replacement for the `XMLHttpRequest` object. It defines generic `Request` and `Response` objects, which can be used not only with HTTP, but also with other emerging web technologies like Service Workers and the Cache API.

With the Fetch API, HTTP requests are made using the global function `fetch()`:

The URL of the resource you want to fetch is the only required parameter.

The fetch() call returns a promise that successfully resolves to the Response object regardless of the HTTP response code.

```
fetch('https://www.google.com/search?q=fetch+api')
  .then(response => response.text())
  .then(result => console.log(result));
```

When the requested data is received, you can apply your application's logic to the data. Here you just print the data on the console.

To extract the body's content from the response, you need to use one of the methods in the `Response` object. Each method expects the body to be in a certain format. You read the body as plain text using the `text()` method, which in turn returns a `Promise`.

Unlike Angular's observable-based `Http` service, the Fetch API is promise-based. The Fetch API is mentioned in Angular documentation because several of Angular's classes and interfaces are inspired by it (such as `Request`, `Response`, and `Request-OptionsArgs`).

Later in this chapter, you'll see how to make requests using the Http object's API and how to handle HTTP responses by subscribing to observable streams. In chapter 5, you used the public weather server, but here you'll create your own web server using the Node.js framework.

8.2 Creating a web server with Node and TypeScript

Many platforms allow you to develop and deploy web servers. In this book, we decided to use Node.js for the following reasons:

- There's no need to learn a new programming language to understand the code.
- Node allows you to create standalone applications (such as servers).
- Node does a great job in the area of communications using HTTP or WebSockets.
- Using Node lets you continue writing code in TypeScript, so we don't have to explain how to create a web server in Java, .NET, or Python.

In Node, a simple web server can be written with a few lines of code, and you'll start with a very basic one. Then you'll write a web server that can serve JSON data (product details, of course) using the HTTP protocol. A bit later, you'll create yet another version of the server that will communicate with the client over a WebSocket connection. Finally, in the hands-on project, we'll teach you how to write the client portion of the auction so it communicates with your web server.

8.2.1 Creating a simple web server

In this section, you'll create a standalone Node application that will run as a server supporting all the Angular code examples. When both the server and client sides are ready, the project's directory will have the structure shown in figure 8.1.

> **NOTE** If you've run the code samples from appendix B, you already have the TypeScript compiler installed on your computer. Otherwise, do that now.

Let's start by creating a directory named http_websocket_samples with a server subdirectory. Configure a new Node project there by running the following command:

```
npm init -y
```

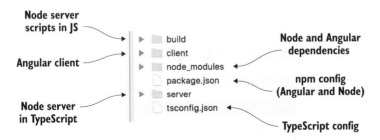

Figure 8.1 The project structure of an Angular-Node application

As you learned in chapter 2, the `-y` option instructs npm to create the package.json configuration file with default settings, without prompting you for any options.

Next, create the hello_server.ts file with the following content:

Listing 8.1   hello_server.ts

> Loads the Node module using the ES6 syntax import * as, which is supported by TypeScript as well

> This basic server will only know how to respond with HTTP status 200 and the text "Hello World!", regardless of what the client requests.

```
import * as http from 'http';

const server = http.createServer((request, response) => {
    response.writeHead(200, {'Content-Type': 'text/plain'});
    response.end('Hello World!\n');
});

const port = 8000;

server.listen(port);
console.log('Listening on http://localhost:' + port);
```

> The listen() function will make this script run infinitely.

Listing 8.1 needs to be transpiled, so create the tsconfig.json file in the http_websocket _samples directory to configure the tsc compiler.

Listing 8.2   tsconfig.json

> Instructs tsc to transpile modules according to the CommonJS spec. The import statement in hello_server.ts will be transpiled into var http = require('http');.

> The transpiler will put the .js files into the build directory.

> tsc shouldn't transpile the code located in the node_modules directory.

> Later, you'll create the client directory for the Angular part of the app, but that code doesn't need to be transpiled because SystemJS will do it on the fly.

```
{
    "compilerOptions": {
        "target": "es5",
        "module": "commonjs",
        "emitDecoratorMetadata": true,
        "experimentalDecorators": true,
        "outDir": "build"
    },
    "exclude": [
        "node_modules",
        "client"
    ]
}
```

After running the `npm run tsc` command, the transpiled hello_server.js file will be saved in the build directory, and you can start your web server:

```
node build/hello_server.js
```

Node will start the V8 JavaScript engine that will run the script from hello_server.js; it will create a web server and print the following message on the console: "Listening on http://localhost:8000". If you open your browser at this URL, you'll see a web page with the text "Hello World!"

> ### TypeScript 2.0 and @types
>
> In this project, you use a locally installed tsc compiler version 2.0, which uses the @types packages to install type-definition files. That's because older versions of tsc didn't support the types compiler option, and if you have an older version of tsc installed globally, running tsc will use that version, causing compilation errors.
>
> To ensure that you use the local version of tsc, configure it as a command ("tsc": "tsc") in the scripts section of package.json, and start the compiler by entering the npm run tsc command to transpile the server's files. Run this command from the same directory where the tsconfig.json file is located (the project root in the code samples for this chapter).

You need to have Node's type-definition files (see appendix B) to prevent TypeScript compilation errors. To install Node's type definitions for another project, run the following command from the root directory of your project:

```
npm i @types/node --save
```

If you use the code samples that come with this chapter, you can run the command npm install, because the package.json file includes the @types/node dependency for Node:

```
"@types/node": "^4.0.30"
```

8.2.2   *Serving JSON*

In all the auction code samples so far, the data about products and reviews has been hardcoded in the product-service.ts file as arrays of JSON-formatted objects. In the hands-on section, you'll move this data to the server, so the Node web server needs to know how to serve JSON.

To send JSON to the browser, you need to modify the header to specify a MIME type of application/json:

```
const server = http.createServer((request, response) => {
    response.writeHead(200, {'Content-Type': 'application/json'});
    response.end('{"message": "Hello Json!"}\n');
});
```

This snippet suffices as an illustration of sending JSON, but real-world servers perform more functions, such as reading files, routing, and handling various HTTP requests (GET, POST, and so on). Later, in the auction example, you'll need to respond with either product or review data depending on the request.

To minimize manual coding, let's install Express (http://expressjs.com), a Node framework that provides a set of features required by all web applications. You won't be using all of its functionality, but it will help with creating a RESTful web service that will return JSON-formatted data.

To install Express, run the following command from the http_websocket_samples directory:

```
npm install express --save
```

This downloads Express into the node_modules folder and updates the `dependencies` section in package.json.

Because this project's file has the entry `"@types/express": "^4.0.31"`, you already have all the type definitions for Express in your node_modules directory. But if you want to install them in any other project, run the following command:

```
npm i @types/express --save
```

Now you can import Express into your application and start using its API while writing code in TypeScript. The following listing shows the my-express-server.ts file that implements the server-side routing for HTTP GET requests.

Listing 8.3   my-express-server.ts

> You've implemented routing only for GET requests using the Express API's get(), but Express has the methods required to handle all HTTP methods. You can find their declarations in express.d.ts.

> Instantiates the Express object using the app constant as a reference

```
import * as express from "express";
const app = express();                    ◁

app.get('/', (req, res) => res.send('Hello from Express'));

app.get('/products', (req, res) => res.send('Got a request for products'));

app.get('/reviews', (req, res) => res.send('Got a request for reviews'));

const server = app.listen(8000, "localhost", () => {    ◁
  const {address, port} = server.address();

  console.log('Listening on http://localhost:' + port);
});
```

> You use destructuring here (see appendix A) to automatically extract the values of the address and port properties.

> Starts listening on port 8000 at the address localhost, and executes the code from the fat arrow function on startup

If you used the ES5 syntax instead of destructuring, you'd need to write two lines instead of one:

```
var address = server.address().address;
var port = server.address().port;
```

Transpile my-express-server.ts by running `npm run tsc`, and start this server (`node build/my-express-server.js`). You can request either products or services, depending on which URL you enter in the browser, as shown in figure 8.2.

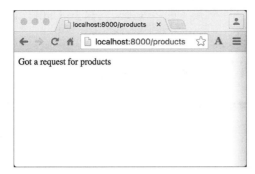 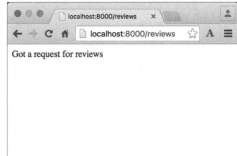

Figure 8.2 Server-side routing with Express

NOTE To debug Node applications, refer to your preferred IDE documentation. You can also use the node-inspector command-line tool (https://github.com/node-inspector/node-inspector).

8.2.3 Live TypeScript recompilation and code reload

The server-side examples are written in TypeScript, so you need to use tsc to transpile the code to JavaScript prior to deploying it in Node. In section B.3.1, in appendix B, we'll discuss the compilation option -w that runs tsc in watch mode; whenever a TypeScript file changes, it gets recompiled automatically. To set the auto-compilation mode for your code, open a separate command window in the directory with the sources, and run the following command there:

```
tsc -w
```

When no filenames are specified, tsc uses the tsconfig.json file for compilation options. Now, whenever you make a change in the TypeScript code and save the file, it'll generate a corresponding .js file in the build directory as specified in tsconfig.json. Accordingly, to start your web server with Node, you could use the following command:

```
node build/my-express-server.js
```

Live recompilation of the TypeScript code helps, but the Node server won't automatically pick up code changes after it has started. So that you don't need to manually restart the Node server to see your code changes in action, you can use a handy utility: Nodemon (http://nodemon.io). It will monitor for any changes in your source and, when it detects changes, will automatically restart your server and reload the code.

You can install Nodemon either globally or locally. For a global install, use the following command:

```
npm install -g nodemon
```

The following command will start your server in monitoring mode:

```
nodemon build/my-express-server.js
```

Install Nodemon locally (npm install nodemon --save-dev) and introduce npm scripts (https://docs.npmjs.com/misc/scripts) in the package.json file.

```
"scripts": {
  "tsc": "tsc",
  "start": "node build/my-express-server.js",
  "dev": "nodemon build/my-express-server.js"
},
"devDependencies": {
  "nodemon": "^1.8.1"
}
```

With this setup, you can start the server in development mode with npm run dev (auto restart/reload) or npm start in production (no restart/reload). We gave the name dev to the command that starts nodemon, but you can name it anything you want, such as startNodemon.

8.2.4   Adding the RESTful API for serving products

Your ultimate goal is to serve products and reviews for the auction application. In this section, we'll illustrate how to prepare a Node server with REST endpoints to serve products in JSON format when HTTP GET requests are received.

You'll modify the code in the my-express-server.ts file to serve either all products or a specific one (by ID). The modified version of this application, shown next, is located in the auction-rest-server.ts file.

```
import * as express from "express";
const app = express();

class Product {                                    Defines the
    constructor(                                   Product class
        public id: number,
        public title: string,
        public price: number){}
}
                                                   Creates an array of three
const products = [                                 Product instances with
    new Product(0, "First Product", 24.99),        the hardcoded data
    new Product(1, "Second Product", 64.99),
    new Product(2, "Third Product", 74.99)
];
                                                   This function returns the
                                                   entire array of Product
function getProducts(): Product[] {                instances.
    return products;
}
```

```
                                              ┌── Returns the text prompt as a response to
                                              │   the GET request coming from the base URL
app.get('/', (req, res) => {              <───┘
    res.send('The URL for products is http://localhost:8000/products');
});                                                 When Express receives the GET
                                                    request containing /products, it
app.get('/products', (req, res) => {       <─────   invokes the getProducts() function
    res.json(getProducts());                        and returns the result to the client
});                                                 in JSON format.

function getProductById(productId: number): Product {  <──  Returns the product by ID.
    return products.find(p => p.id === productId);          Here you use the new
}                                                           Array.prototype.find()
                                                            method introduced in ES6. If
app.get('/products/:id', (req, res) => {                    your IDE doesn't know about
    res.json(getProductById(parseInt(req.params.id)));      this method, install the type
});                                                         definition file for the es6-
                                                            shim polyfill: npm install
const server = app.listen(8000, "localhost", () => {        @types/es6-shim --save-dev.
    const {address, port} = server.address();
    console.log('Listening on %s %s', address, port);
});
```

**When Express receives GET requests with parameters, their values are stored in the
params property of the request object. You convert the product ID from a string to an
integer and invoke getProductById(). The result is sent to the client in JSON format.**

Now you can start the auction-rest-server.ts application in Node (run `nodemon build/
auction-rest-server.js`) and see if the browser receives all products or a selected
product. Figure 8.3 shows the browser window after we entered the URL http://local-
host:8000/products. Our server returned all the products in JSON format.

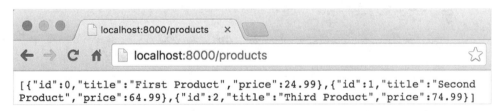

Figure 8.3   Node server response to http://localhost:8000/products

Figure 8.4 shows the browser window after we entered the URL http://local-
host:8000/products/1. This time, our server returned only data about the product
that has an `id` with the value of 1.

```
● ● ●      localhost:8000/products/1  ×

←  →  C  ⌂    localhost:8000/products/1                          ☆

{"id":1,"title":"Second Product","price":64.99}
```

Figure 8.4   Node server response to http://localhost:8000/products/1

The server is ready. Now you can learn how to initiate HTTP requests and handle responses in Angular applications.

8.3   *Bringing Angular and Node together*

Earlier in this chapter, you created the http_websocket_samples folder containing the auction-rest-server.ts file, which is a Node application that responds to HTTP GET requests and supplies product details. In this section, you'll write an Angular client that will issue HTTP requests and treat the product's data as an Observable object returned by your server. The code of the Angular application will be located in the client subdirectory (see figure 8.1).

8.3.1   *Static resources on the server*

A typical web application deployed on the server includes static resources (such as HTML, images, CSS, and JavaScript code) that have to be loaded in the browser when the user enters the application's URL. Because we're using SystemJS, which does on-the-fly transpiling, the TypeScript files are static resources as well.

From Node's perspective, the Angular portion of this application is considered static resources. Because Angular apps load dependencies from node_modules, this directory also belongs to the static resources required by the browser.

The Express framework has a special API to specify the directories with static resources, and you'll make slight modifications in the auction-rest-server.ts file shown in listing 8.5. In that file, you didn't specify the directory with static resources, because no client's app was deployed there. The new version of this file will be called auction-rest-server-angular.ts. First, add the following lines:

```
import * as path from "path";

app.use('/', express.static(path.join(__dirname, '..', 'client')));
app.use('/node_modules', express.static(path.join(__dirname, '..',
➥ 'node_modules')));
```

When the browser requests static resources, Node will look for them in the client and node_modules directories. Here you use Node's path.join API to ensure that the file path is created in a cross-platform way. You can use path.join when you need to build an absolute path for a specific file; you'll see examples later.

Let's keep the same REST endpoints on the server:

- / serves main.html, which is the landing page of the application.
- /products gets all products.
- /products/:id gets a product by its ID.

Unlike in the my_express_server.ts application, you don't want Node to handle the base URL; you want Node to send the main.html file to the browser. In the auction-rest-server-angular.ts file, change the route for the base URL / to look like this:

```
app.get('/', (req, res) => {
  res.sendFile(path.join(__dirname, '../client/main.html'));
});
```

Now, when the user enters the URL of the Node server in the browser, the main.html file will be served first. Then it'll load your Angular application with all dependencies.

THE COMMON NPM CONFIGURATION FILE

The new version of the package.json file will combine all dependencies required for both the Node-related code and your Angular application. Note that you declare several commands in the `script` section. The first command is for running the locally installed tsc, and the others are to start Node servers for the code samples included in this chapter.

Listing 8.6   Modified package.json file

```
{
  "private": true,
  "scripts": {
    "tsc": "tsc",
    "start": "node build/my-express-server.js",
    "dev": "nodemon build/my-express-server.js",
    "devRest": "nodemon build/auction-rest-server.js",
    "restServer": "nodemon build/auction-rest-server-angular.js",
    "simpleWsServer": "node build/simple-websocket-server.js",
    "twowayWsServer": "nodemon build/two-way-websocket-server.js",
    "bidServer": "nodemon build/bids/bid-server.js"
  },
  "dependencies": {
    "@angular/common": "^2.0.0",
    "@angular/compiler": "^2.0.0",
    "@angular/core": "^2.0.0",
    "@angular/forms": "^2.0.0",
    "@angular/http": "^2.0.0",
    "@angular/platform-browser": "^2.0.0",
    "@angular/platform-browser-dynamic": "^2.0.0",
    "@angular/router": "^3.0.0",

    "core-js": "^2.4.0",
    "rxjs": "5.0.0-beta.12",
    "systemjs": "0.19.37",
    "zone.js": "0.6.21",

    "@types/express": "^4.0.31",
    "@types/node": "^4.0.30",
    "express": "^4.14.0",
    "ws": "^1.1.1"
  },
  "devDependencies": {
    "@types/es6-shim": "0.0.30",
    "@types/ws": "0.0.29",
    "nodemon": "^1.8.1",
    "typescript": "^2.0.0"
  }
}
```

Note that you include the `@angular/http` package here, which includes Angular's support for the HTTP protocol. You also include `ws` and `@types/ws`—you'll need them for WebSocket support later in the chapter.

---

npm scripts

npm supports the `scripts` property in package.json with more than a dozen scripts available right out of the box (see the npm-scripts documentation for details, https://docs.npmjs.com/misc/scripts). You can also add new commands specific to your development and deployment workflow.

Some of these scripts need to be run manually (such as `npm start`), and some are invoked automatically (such as `postinstall`). In general, if any command in the `scripts` section starts with the `post` prefix, it'll run automatically after the command specified after this prefix. For example, if you define the command `"postinstall"` : `"myCustomIstall.js"`, each time you run `npm install`, the myCustomIstall.js script will run as well.

Similarly, if a command has a `pre` prefix, the command will run before the command named after this prefix. For example, in section 10.3.2, you'll see the following commands in the package.json file:

```
"prebuild": "npm run clean && npm run test",
 "build": "webpack --config webpack.prod.config.js --progress --profile
➥  --colors"
```

If you run the `build` command, npm will first run the script defined in `prebuild`; then it'll run the script defined in `build`.

So far, you've been using only two commands: `npm start` and `npm run dev`. But you can add any commands you like to the `scripts` section of your package.json file. For example, both the `build` and `prebuild` commands in the preceding example are custom commands.

Common vs. separate configuration files

In this chapter, all code samples for the client and server belong to a single npm project and share the same package.json file. All dependencies and typings are shared by the client and server applications. This setup may reduce the time for installing dependencies and save space on disk because some of the dependencies may be shared between the client and server.

But keeping the code for the client and server in a single project tends to complicate the build automation process for two reasons:

- Client and server may require conflicting versions of a particular dependency.
- You use build automation tools, which may require different configurations for client and server, and their node_modules directories won't be located in the root directory of the project.

In chapter 10, you'll separate the client and server portions of the online auction into two independent npm projects.

The next step is to add an Angular app to the client directory.

8.3.2 *Making GET requests with the Http object*

When Angular's `Http` object makes a request, the response comes back as `Observable`, and the client's code will handle it by using the `subscribe()` method. Let's start with a simple application (client/app/main.ts) that retrieves all products from the Node server and renders them using an HTML unordered list.

Listing 8.7 client/app/main.ts

```
import { platformBrowserDynamic } from '@angular/platform-browser-dynamic';
import { NgModule, Component }      from '@angular/core';
import { BrowserModule } from '@angular/platform-browser';
import {HttpModule, Http} from '@angular/http';
import { Observable} from "rxjs/Observable";
import 'rxjs/add/operator/map';

@Component({
  selector: 'http-client',
  template: `<h1>All Products</h1>
<ul>
  <li *ngFor="let product of products">
     {{product.title}}
  </li>
</ul>
`})
class AppComponent {

  products: Array = [];

  theDataSource: Observable;

  constructor(private http: Http) {

    this.theDataSource = this.http.get('/products')
       .map(res => res.json());
  }

  ngOnInit(){

    // Get the data from the server
    this.theDataSource.subscribe(
        data => {
           if (Array.isArray(data)){
              this.products=data;
           } else{
              this.products.push(data);
           }
        },
      err =>
           console.log("Can't get products. Error code: %s, URL: %s ",
           err.status, err.url),
```

Imports the HTTP module and the Http object that will be injected into AppComponent

There are more than 100 operators in RxJS; you just need map() in this example.

The instance of the Http service is injected into the component.

Doesn't send a GET request to the /products endpoint of the Node server yet, because no one subscribed to it

The map() operator converts the data into a JSON string and returns an Observable. No server requests are made until a subscribe() method is invoked.

The subscribe() method initiates the request to the server. subscribe() internally creates an Observer object, and this fat-arrow expression assigns the received data to the products array.

The error callback is invoked only if the server responds with an error.

```
                () => console.log('Product(s) are retrieved')
        );

    }
}
```

The final callback is invoked after the handling of the stream of data is complete.

```
@NgModule({
    imports:        [ BrowserModule,
                      HttpModule],
    declarations: [ AppComponent],
    bootstrap:      [ AppComponent ]
})
class AppModule { }
```

Declares HttpModule that defines providers required for injecting the Http object

```
platformBrowserDynamic().bootstrapModule(AppModule);
```

To see the error callback in action, change the endpoint from '/products' to something else. Your Angular application will print the following on the console: "Can't get products. Error code: 404, URL: http://localhost:8000/products".

NOTE   The HTTP GET request is sent to the server only when you invoke the subscribe() method and not when you call the get() method.

You're ready to start the server and enter its URL in the browser to see the Angular app served. You can start your Node server either by running the long command

```
node build/auction-rest-server-angular.js
```

or by using the npm script that you defined in the package.json file:

```
npm run restServer
```

Open the browser to http://localhost:8000, and you'll see the Angular app shown in figure 8.5.

NOTE   Make sure the client/systemjs.config .js file maps the app package to main.ts.

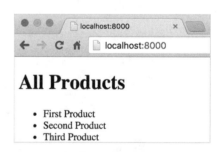

Figure 8.5   Retrieving all products from the Node server

TIP   You can make HTTP GET requests that pass parameters in the URL after the question mark (such as myserver.com?param1=val1&param2=val2). The Http.get() method can accept a second parameter, which is an object that implements RequestOptionsArgs. The search field of RequestOptionsArgs can be used to set either a string or a URLSearchParams object. You'll see an example of using URLSearchParams in the hands-on section.

8.3.3   *Unwrapping observables in templates with AsyncPipe*

In the previous section, you handled the observable stream of products in the TypeScript code by invoking the subscribe() method. Angular offers an alternative syntax that lets you handle observables right in the template of a component with pipes; it's covered in chapter 5.

Angular includes `AsyncPipe` (or async if used in templates), which can receive a `Promise` or `Observable` as input and subscribe to it automatically. To see this in action, let's make the following changes in the code from the previous section:

- Change the type of the `products` variable from `Array` to `Observable`.
- Remove the declaration of the `theDataSource` variable.
- Remove the invocation of `subscribe()` in the code. You'll assign the `Observable` returned by `http.get().map()` to `products`.
- Add the async pipe to the `*ngFor` loop in the template.

The following code (main-asyncpipe.ts) implements these changes.

Listing 8.8 main-asyncpipe.ts

```
import { platformBrowserDynamic } from '@angular/platform-browser-dynamic';
import { NgModule, Component }      from '@angular/core';
import { BrowserModule } from '@angular/platform-browser';
import {HttpModule, Http} from '@angular/http';
import 'rxjs/add/operator/map';
import { Observable} from "rxjs/Observable";

@Component({
  selector: 'http-client',
  template: `<h1>All Products</h1>
  <ul>
    <li *ngFor="let product of products | async">
      {{product.title}}
    </li>

  </ul>
  `})
class AppComponent {

  products: Observable<Array<string>>;

  constructor(private http: Http) {

    this.products = this.http.get('/products')
        .map(res => res.json());
  }
}

@NgModule({
  imports:      [ BrowserModule, HttpModule],
  declarations: [ AppComponent],
  bootstrap:    [ AppComponent ]
})
class AppModule { }

platformBrowserDynamic().bootstrapModule(AppModule);
```

The async pipe unwraps the array elements from the provided observable stream of products.

Now the products array has the type Observable, which wraps an array of strings.

Assigns an Observable that will be returned by map() to products

Running this application will produce the same output you saw in figure 8.5.

> **NOTE** This version of AppComponent with async is shorter than the version in listing 8.7. But the code that explicitly invokes subscribe() is easier to test.

8.3.4   *Injecting HTTP into a service*

In this section, you'll see an example of an injectable ProductService class that will encapsulate HTTP communications with the server. You'll create a small application in which the user can enter the product ID and have the application make a request to the server's /products/:id endpoint.

The user enters the product ID and clicks the button, which starts a subscription to the Observable property productDetails on the ProductService object. Figure 8.6 shows the injectable objects of the application you're going to build.

Figure 8.6   The client-server workflow

In chapter 7, you became familiar with the Forms API. Here you'll create an App-Component with a simple form that has an input field and a Find Product button. This application will communicate with the Node web server you created earlier, and you'll implement the client portion in two iterations. In the first version (main-form.ts), you won't use the ProductService class. The AppComponent will get the Http object injected and will make requests to the server.

Listing 8.9   main-form.ts

```
import { platformBrowserDynamic } from '@angular/platform-browser-dynamic';
import { NgModule, Component }       from '@angular/core';
import { BrowserModule } from '@angular/platform-browser';
import { FormsModule} from '@angular/forms';
import {HttpModule, Http} from '@angular/http';

@Component({
  selector: 'http-client',
  template: `<h1>Find Product By ID</h1>
    <form #f="ngForm" (ngSubmit) = "getProductByID(f.value)" >
      <label for="productID">Enter Product ID</label>
      <input id="productID" type="number" name = "productID" ngModel>
      <button type="submit">Find Product</button>
    </form>

    <h4>{{productTitle}} {{productPrice}}</h4>
`})
```

Defines the form that invokes getProductByID() when the user clicks the submit button

```
class AppComponent {

  productTitle: string;
  productPrice: string;

  constructor(private http: Http) {}

  getProductByID(formValue){
    this.http.get(`/products/${formValue.productID}`)
         .map(res => res.json())
         .subscribe(
            data => {this.productTitle= data.title;
                  this.productPrice=`$` + data.price;},
            err => console.log("Can't get product details. Error code: %s,
             URL: %s ",
               err.status, err.url),
            () =>    console.log( 'Done')
         );
  }
}

@NgModule({
    imports:      [ BrowserModule,  FormsModule, HttpModule],
    declarations: [ AppComponent],
    bootstrap:    [ AppComponent ]
})
class AppModule { }

platformBrowserDynamic().bootstrapModule(AppModule);
```

> **Uses string interpolation to attach the entered productID to the URL in the HTTP get() request. The HTTP GET request isn't issued yet at this point.**

> **In case of an error, prints the error code and the URL on the console**

> **subscribe() issues the GET request and assigns the received values to the productTitle and productPrice class variables, which are bound to the HTML template.**

Figure 8.7 shows a screenshot taken after we entered 2 as a product ID and clicked the Find Product button, which sent a request to the URL http://localhost:8000/products/2. The Node Express server matched /products/2 with the corresponding REST endpoint and routed this request to the method defined as app.get('/products/:id').

Figure 8.7　Getting product details by ID

INJECTING AN HTTP OBJECT INTO A SERVICE

Now let's introduce the `ProductService` class (product-service.ts). In listing 8.9, you injected `Http` into the constructor of the `AppComponent`; now you'll move the code that uses `Http` into `ProductService` so the code reflects the architecture in figure 8.6.

Listing 8.10   product-service.ts

You didn't use the @Injectable annotation in previous versions of ProductService because you didn't inject anything into the ProductService itself.

```
import { Http} from '@angular/http';
import { Injectable} from "@angular/core";
import {Observable} from 'rxjs/Observable';
import 'rxjs/add/operator/map';

@Injectable()
export class ProductService{

    constructor(private http: Http){}

    getProductByID(productID: string): Observable<any>{
        return this.http.get(`/products/${productID}`)
            .map(res => res.json());
    }
}
```

Angular injects the instance of the Http object, and the private qualifier results in implicit creation of the http instance variable.

The getProductByID() method forms the URL, but it doesn't invoke the subscribe() method. It returns an Observable object. The component that handles the data will provide an observer.

The `ProductService` class uses DI. The `@Injectable()` decorator instructs the TypeScript compiler to generate the metadata for `ProductService`, and using this decorator is required here. When you were injecting `Http` into the component that had another decorator (`@Component`), that was a signal to the TypeScript compiler to generate the metadata for the component required for DI. If the class `ProductService` didn't have any decorators, the TypeScript compiler wouldn't generate any metadata for it, and the Angular DI mechanism wouldn't know that it had some injection to do into `ProductService`. The mere existence of the `@Injectable()` decorator is required for classes that represent services, and you shouldn't forget to include `"emitDecoratorMetadata"`: true in the tsconfig.json file.

The new version of `AppComponent` (main-with-service.ts) will become a subscriber of the observable stream produced by `ProductService`.

Listing 8.11   main-with-service.ts

```
import { platformBrowserDynamic } from '@angular/platform-browser-dynamic';
import { NgModule, Component }      from '@angular/core';
import { BrowserModule } from '@angular/platform-browser';
import { FormsModule} from '@angular/forms';
import {HttpModule, Http} from '@angular/http';
import {ProductService} from './product-service';

@Component({
```

```
     selector: 'http-client',
     providers: [ProductService],
     template: `<h1>Find Product By ID Using ProductService</h1>
        <form #f="ngForm" (ngSubmit)="getProductByID(f.value)">
           <label for="productID">Enter Product ID</label>
           <input id="productID" type="number" ngControl="productID">
           <button type="submit">Find Product</button>
        </form>
        <h4>{{productTitle}} {{productPrice}}</h4>
     `})
class AppComponent {

     productTitle: string;
     productPrice: string;


     constructor(private productService: ProductService) {}

     getProductByID(formValue){
        this.productService.getProductByID(formValue.productID)
          .subscribe(
             data => {this.productTitle = data.title;
                      this.productPrice = `$` + data.price;},
             err => console.log("Can't get product details. Error code: %s,
             URL: %s ",
                        err.status, err.url),
             () => console.log('Done')
          );
     }
}

@NgModule({
    imports:      [ BrowserModule,  FormsModule, HttpModule],
    declarations: [ AppComponent],
    bootstrap:    [ AppComponent ]
})
class AppModule { }

platformBrowserDynamic().bootstrapModule(AppModule);
```

> **Now Angular injects the ProductService, whereas in the previous version of this component it injected the Http object.**

> **Invokes the method on ProductService that returns an Observable**

> **Subscribes to the Observable, and handles the results**

ProductService isn't a component, but a class, and Angular doesn't allow you to specify providers for classes. As a result, you specify the provider for Http in the AppComponent by including the providers property in the @Component decorator. The other choice would be to declare providers in @NgModule. In this particular application, it wouldn't make a difference.

In chapter 4, while discussing DI, we mentioned that Angular can inject objects, and, if they have their own dependencies, Angular will inject them as well. Listing 8.11 proves that Angular's DI module works as expected.

8.4 Client-server communication via WebSockets

WebSocket is a low-overhead binary protocol supported by all modern web browsers. With request-based HTTP, a client sends a request over a connection and waits for a response to come back (half-duplex), as shown in figure 8.8. On the other hand, the WebSocket protocol allows data to travel in both directions simultaneously (full-duplex) over the same connection, as shown in figure 8.9. The WebSocket connection is kept alive, which has an additional benefit: low latency in the interaction between the server and the client.

Whereas a typical HTTP request/response adds several hundred bytes (the headers) to the application data, with Web-Sockets the overhead is as low as a couple of bytes. If you're not familiar with Web-Sockets, refer to www.websocket.org or one of the many tutorials available online.

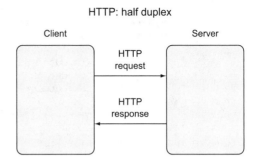

Figure 8.8   Half-duplex communication

8.4.1   *Pushing data from a Node server*

WebSockets are supported by most server-side platforms (Java, .NET, Python, and others), but you'll continue using Node to implement your WebSocket-based server. You'll implement one particular use case: the server will push data to a browser-

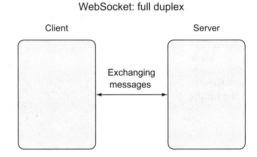

Figure 8.9   Full-duplex communication

based client as soon as the client connects to the socket. We purposely won't have you send a request for data from the client, to illustrate that WebSockets aren't about request-response communication. Either party can start sending the data over the Web-Socket connection.

Several Node packages implement the WebSocket protocol; here you'll use the npm package called `ws` (https://www.npmjs.com/package/ws). Install it by entering the following command in your project's directory:

```
npm install ws --save
```

Then install the type definition file for `ws`:

```
npm install @types/ws --save-dev
```

Now the TypeScript compiler won't complain when you use the API from the `ws` package. Besides, this file is handy for seeing the APIs and types available.

Your first WebSocket server will be pretty simple: it'll push the text "This message was pushed by the WebSocket server" to the client as soon as the connection is established. You purposely don't want the client to send any data request to the server, to illustrate that a socket is a two-way street and that the server can push the data without any request ceremony.

The application in listing 8.12 (simple-websocket-server.ts) creates two servers. The HTTP server will run on port 8000 and will be responsible for sending the initial HTML file to the client. The WebSocket server will run on port 8085 and will communicate with all connected clients through this port.

Listing 8.12   simple-websocket-server.ts

```
import * as express from "express";
import * as path from "path";
import {Server} from "ws";

const app = express();

app.use('/', express.static(path.join(__dirname, '..', 'client')));
app.use('/node_modules', express.static(path.join(__dirname, '..',
    'node_modules')));

// HTTP Server
app.get('/', (req, res) => {
    res.sendFile(path.join(__dirname, '..',
        'client/simple-websocket-client.html'));
});

const httpServer = app.listen(8000, "localhost", () => {

    console.log('HTTP Server is listening on port 8000');
});

// WebSocket Server
var wsServer: Server = new Server({port:8085});

console.log('WebSocket server is listening on port 8085');

wsServer.on('connection',
            websocket => websocket.send('This message was pushed by the
            WebSocket server'));
```

This example uses the Server type from the ws module for the explicit variable declaration. That's why you import only the Server definition.

Whenever the HTTP client connects to the base URL, the HTTP server will send back the client/simple-websocket-client.html file.

The HTTP Server starts listening on port 8000.

The WebSocket server starts listening on port 8085. The wsServer variable will know everything about this socket.

As soon as the client connects to the socket, the connection event is dispatched on the object represented by wsSocket to this particular client.

The send() method will push the message, "This message was pushed by the WebSocket server".

NOTE In listing 8.12, you import only the `Server` module from `ws`. If you used other exported members, you could write `import * as ws from "ws";`.

In listing 8.12, HTTP and WebSocket servers are running on different ports, but you could reuse the same port by providing the newly created `httpServer` instance to the constructor of `WsServer`:

```
const httpServer = app.listen(8000, "localhost", () => {...});

const wsServer: WsServer = new WsServer({server: httpServer});.
```

In the hands-on section, you'll reuse port 8000 for both HTTP and WebSocket communications (see the server/auction.ts file).

> **NOTE** As soon as the new client connects to the server, the reference to this connection is added to the `wsServer.clients` array so you can broadcast messages to all connected clients if needed: `wsServer.clients.forEach (client => client.send('…');`.

The content of the client's simple-websocket-client.html file is shown in listing 8.13. This client doesn't use either Angular or TypeScript. As soon as this file is downloaded to the browser, its script connects to your WebSocket server at ws://localhost:8085. Note that the protocol is ws and not `http`. For a secure socket connection, use the wss protocol.

Listing 8.13   simple-websocket-client.html

```html
<!DOCTYPE html>
<html>
<head>
    <meta charset="UTF-8">
</head>
<body>
<span id="messageGoesHere"></span>

<script type="text/javascript">
    var ws = new WebSocket("ws://localhost:8085");

    ws.onmessage = function(event) {
        var mySpan = document.getElementById("messageGoesHere");
        mySpan.innerHTML=event.data;
    };

    ws.onerror = function(event){
        console.log("Error ", event)
    }
</script>
</body>
</html>
```

Establishes the socket connection. At this point, the server upgrades the protocol from HTTP to WebSocket.

When the message arrives from the socket, you display its content in the <span> element.

In the case of an error, the browser logs the error message on the console.

To run the server that pushes data to the clients, start the Node server (`node build/ simple-websocket-server.js` or `npm simpleWsServer`). It will print the following messages on the console:

```
WebSocket server is listening on port 8085
HTTP Server is listening on 8000
```

> **NOTE** If you'll be modifying the code located in the server directory, don't forget to run `npm run tsc` in the root directory of your project to create a fresh version of your JavaScript code in the build directory. Otherwise the `node` command will load the old JavaScript file.

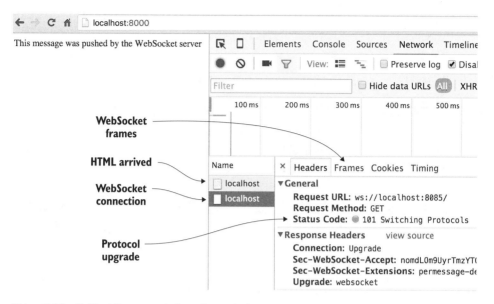

Figure 8.10   Getting the message from the socket

To receive the message pushed from the server, open the browser to http://local-host:8000. You'll see the message, as shown in figure 8.10.

In this example, the HTTP protocol is used only to initially load the HTML file. Then the client requests the protocol upgrade to WebSocket (status code 101), and from then on this application won't use HTTP.

TIP You can monitor messages going over the socket by using the Frames tab in Chrome Developer Tools.

8.4.2   Turning a WebSocket into an observable

In the previous section, you wrote a client in JavaScript (no Angular) using the browser's `WebSocket` object. Now we'll show you how to create a service that will wrap the browser's `WebSocket` object in an observable stream so Angular components can subscribe to messages coming from the server over the socket connection.

Earlier, in section 8.3.2, the code that received the product data was structured as follows (in pseudocode):

```
this.http.get('/products')
  .subscribe(
      data => handleNextDataElement(),
      err => handleErrors(),
      () => handleStreamCompletion()
);
```

Basically, your goal was to write the application code that would consume the observable stream provided by Angular's `Http` service. But Angular has no service that will produce an observable from a WebSocket connection, so you'll have to write such a service. This way, the Angular client will be able to subscribe to messages coming from the WebSocket the same way it did with the Http object.

WRAPPING ANY SERVICE IN AN OBSERVABLE STREAM

Now you'll create a small Angular application that won't use a WebSocket server but will illustrate how to wrap business logic into an Angular service that emits data via an observable stream. Let's start by creating an observable service that will emit hard-coded values without actually connecting to a socket. The following code creates a service that emits the current time every second.

Listing 8.14 **custom-observable-service.ts**

```
import {Observable} from 'rxjs/Rx';

export class CustomObservableService{

  createObservableService(): Observable<Date>{

      return new Observable(
          observer => {
              setInterval(() =>
                  observer.next(new Date())
              , 1000);
          }
      );
  }
}
```

In this code, you create an observable, assuming that the subscriber will provide an Observer object that knows what to do with the data pushed by the observable. Whenever the observable invokes the next() method on the observer, the subscriber will receive the value given as an argument (new Date() in this example). The data stream never throws an error and never completes.

> **NOTE** You can also create a subscriber for an observable by explicitly invoking Subscriber.create(). You'll see such an example in the hands-on section.

The AppComponent in listing 8.15 gets the CustomObservableService injected, invokes the createObservableService() method that returns Observable, and subscribes to it, creating an observer that knows what to do with the data. The observer in this application assigns the received time to the currentTime variable.

Listing 8.15 **custom-observable-service-subscriber.ts**

```
import { platformBrowserDynamic } from '@angular/platform-browser-dynamic';
import { NgModule, Component }     from '@angular/core';
import { BrowserModule } from '@angular/platform-browser';
```

```
import 'rxjs/add/operator/map';

import {CustomObservableService} from "./custom-observable-service";

@Component({
  selector: 'app',
  providers: [ CustomObservableService ],
  template: `<h1>Simple subscriber to a service</h1>
      Current time: {{currentTime | date: 'jms'}}
  `})
class AppComponent {

  currentTime: Date;

  constructor(private sampleService: CustomObservableService) {

      this.sampleService.createObservableService()
        .subscribe( data => this.currentTime = data );
  }
}

@NgModule({
  imports:        [ BrowserModule],
  declarations:   [ AppComponent],
  bootstrap:      [ AppComponent ]
})
class AppModule { }

platformBrowserDynamic().bootstrapModule(AppModule);
```

For this app, you create the index.html file in the root directory of the project. This app doesn't use any servers, and you can run it by entering the command live-server in the terminal window. In the browser's window, the current time will be updated every second. You use DatePipe here with the format 'jms', which displays only hours, minutes, and seconds (all date formats are described in the Angular DatePipe documentation at http://mng.bz/78lD).

This is a simple example, but it demonstrates a basic technique for wrapping any application logic in an observable stream and subscribing to it. In this case, you use setInterval(), but you could replace it with any application-specific code that generates one or more values and sends them as a stream.

Don't forget about error handling and completing the stream if need be. The following code snippet shows a sample observable that sends one element to the observer, may throw an error, and tells the observer that the streaming is complete:

```
return new Observable(
    observer => {
      try {
        observer.next('Hello from observable');

        //throw ("Got an error");
```

```
    } catch(err) {
      observer.error(err);
    } finally{
      observer.complete();
    }
  }
);
```

If you uncomment the line with `throw`, `observer.error()` is invoked, which results in the invocation of the error handler on the subscriber, if there is one.

Now let's teach the Angular service to communicate with the WebSocket server.

ANGULAR TALKING TO A WEBSOCKET SERVER

Let's create a small Angular application with a WebSocket service (on the client) that interacts with the Node WebSocket server. The server-side tier can be implemented with any technology that supports WebSockets. Figure 8.11 illustrates the architecture of such an application.

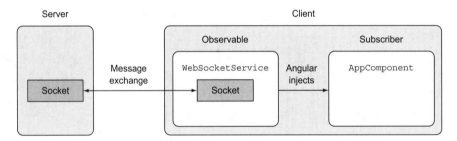

Figure 8.11   Angular interacting with a server via a socket

The code in listing 8.16 wraps the browser's `WebSocket` object into an observable stream. This service creates an instance of `WebSocket` that's connected to the server based on the provided URL, and this instance handles messages received from the server. The `WebSocketService` also has a `sendMessage()` method so the client can send messages to the server.

Listing 8.16   websocket-observable-service.ts

```
import {Observable} from 'rxjs/Rx';

export class WebSocketService{

    ws: WebSocket;

    createObservableSocket(url:string):Observable{

        this.ws = new WebSocket(url);

        return new Observable(
```

```
        observer => {

          this.ws.onmessage = (event) =>
                    observer.next(event.data);

          this.ws.onerror = (event) => observer.error(event);

          this.ws.onclose = (event) => observer.complete();

        }
    );
  }

  sendMessage(message: any){
      this.ws.send(message);
  }
}
```

NOTE   Listing 8.16 shows one way to create an observable from WebSocket. As an alternative, you can use the `Observable.webSocket()` method to do this.

Listing 8.17 shows the code of the `AppComponent` that subscribes to `WebSocketService`, which is injected into the `AppComponent` from figure 8.11. This component can also send messages to the server when the user clicks the Send Msg to Server button.

Listing 8.17   websocket-observable-service-subscriber.ts

```
import { platformBrowserDynamic } from '@angular/platform-browser-dynamic';
import { NgModule, Component } from '@angular/core';
import { BrowserModule } from '@angular/platform-browser';

import {WebSocketService} from "./websocket-observable-service";

@Component({
  selector: 'app',
  providers: [ WebSocketService ],
  template: `<h1>Angular subscriber to WebSocket service</h1>
      {{messageFromServer}}<br>
      <button (click)="sendMessageToServer()">Send msg to Server</button>
  `})
class AppComponent {

  messageFromServer: string;

  constructor(private wsService: WebSocketService) {

      this.wsService.createObservableSocket("ws://localhost:8085")
        .subscribe(
          data => {
            this.messageFromServer = data;
          },
          err => console.log( err),
          () => console.log( 'The observable stream is complete')
      );
```

```
    }

    sendMessageToServer(){
        console.log("Sending message to WebSocket server");

        this.wsService.sendMessage("Hello from client");
    }
}

@NgModule({
    imports:       [ BrowserModule],
    declarations:  [ AppComponent],
    bootstrap:     [ AppComponent ]
})
class AppModule { }

platformBrowserDynamic().bootstrapModule(AppModule);
```

The HTML file that renders this component is called two-way-websocket-client.html.
You need to make sure websocket-observable-service-subscriber is configured as the
main app script in systemjs.config.js.

Listing 8.18   two-way-websocket-client.html

```
<!DOCTYPE html>
<html>
<head>
  <title>Http samples</title>

  <script src="https://cdn.polyfill.io/v2/
    polyfill.js?features=Intl.~locale.en"></script>

  <script src="node_modules/zone.js/dist/zone.js"></script>
  <script src="node_modules/typescript/lib/typescript.js"></script>
  <script src="node_modules/reflect-metadata/Reflect.js"></script>
  <script src="node_modules/rxjs/bundles/Rx.js"></script>
  <script src="node_modules/systemjs/dist/system.src.js"></script>
  <script src="systemjs.config.js"></script>
  <script>
    System.import('app').catch(function (err) {console.error(err);});
  </script>
</head>
<body>
<app>Loading...</app>
</body>
</html>
```

Finally, you'll create another version of simple-websocket-server.ts to serve an HTML
file with a different Angular client. This server will be implemented in the two-way-
websocket-server.ts file and will have almost the same code, with two small changes:

1 When the server receives a request to the base URL, it needs to serve the preceding HTML to the client:

```
app.get('/', (req, res) => { res.sendFile(path.join(__dirname, '..',
➡ 'client/two-way-websocket-client.html'));
});
```

2 You need to add the `on('message')` handler to process messages arriving from the client:

```
wsServer.on('connection',
    websocket => {
        websocket.send('This message was pushed by the WebSocket server');

        websocket.on('message',
                    message => console.log("Server received: %s",
                    ➡ message));
    });
```

To see this application in action, run `nodemon build/two-way-websocket_server.js` (or use the `npm run twowayWsServer` command that's configured in package.json), and open your browser to localhost:8000. You'll see the window with the message pushed from Node, and if you click the button, a "Hello from client" message will be sent to the server. We took the screenshot in figure 8.12 after clicking the button once (Chrome Developer Tools was opened to the Frames tab under Network).

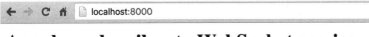

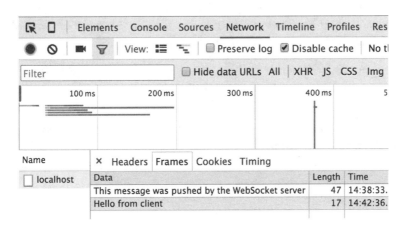

Figure 8.12 Getting the message in Angular from Node

Now that you know how to communicate with a server via the HTTP and WebSocket protocols, let's teach the online auction to interact with the Node server.

8.5   *Hands-on: implementing product search and bid notifications*

The amount of code added to this chapter's version of the auction is pretty substantial, so we decided to spare you from typing it all. In this hands-on exercise, we'll just review the new and modified code fragments in the new version of the auction app that comes with this chapter. This version of the application accomplishes two main goals:

- Implements product search functionality. The SearchComponent will connect the auction to the Node server via HTTP, and the data about products and reviews will come from the server.
- Adds server-pushed bid notifications using the WebSocket protocol, so the user can subscribe and watch bid prices for a selected product.

Figure 8.13 shows the main players involved in the product search implementation.

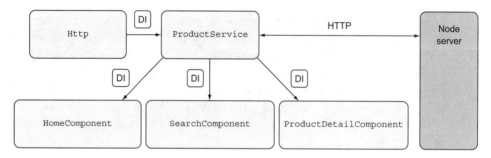

Figure 8.13   Product search implementation

The DI in the figure stands for *dependency injection*. Angular injects the Http object into ProductService, which in turn is injected into three components: HomeComponent, SearchComponent, and ProductDetailComponent. The ProductService object is responsible for all communications with the server.

> **NOTE**   You use the Node server in this project, but you can use any technology that supports the HTTP and WebSocket protocols, such as Java, .NET, Python, Ruby, and so on.

As we mentioned, we'll provide brief explanations about the code changes made in various scripts, but you should perform a detailed code review of the auction on your own. In this chapter's version of the auction, the scripts section looks like this:

```
"scripts": {
    "tsc": "tsc",
    "start": "node build/auction.js",
    "dev": "nodemon build/auction.js"
}
```

Running npm start will start your Node server loading the auction.js script. In this project, the tsconfig.json file specifies the build directory as an output for the TypeScript compiler; two files, auction.js and model.js, are created there when you run npm run tsc in the project root directory. If you have version 2.0 or later of the TypeScript compiler installed globally, you can just run the tsc command.

The TypeScript auction.ts source contains the code implementing the HTTP and WebSocket servers, and model.ts contains the data that now resides on the server. Running npm run dev will start your Node server in live reload mode.

8.5.1 *Implementing product search using HTTP*

The auction's home page has a Search form on the left side; the user can enter search criteria, click the button Search, and get matching products from the server. As shown in figure 8.13, ProductService is responsible for all HTTP communications with the server, including the initial load of product information or finding products that meet certain criteria.

MOVING PRODUCT AND REVIEW DATA TO THE SERVER

So far, data about products and reviews has been hardcoded in the client-side ProductService class; when the application starts, it shows all the hardcoded products in HomeComponent. When the user clicks a product, the router navigates to ProductDetailComponent, which shows product details and reviews, also hardcoded in ProductService.

Now you want the data about products and reviews to be located on the server. The server/auction.ts and server/model.ts files contain the code that will run as a Node application (the web server). The auction.ts file implements HTTP and WebSocket functionality, and the model.ts file declares the Product and Review classes and the products and reviews arrays with the data. These arrays were also removed from the client/app/services/product-service.ts file.

> **NOTE** The Product class has a new categories property, which will be used in the SearchComponent.

THE PRODUCTSERVICE CLASS

The ProductService class will get the Http object injected, and most of the methods of this class will return observable streams generated by HTTP requests. The following code fragment shows the new version of the getProducts() method:

```
getProducts(): Observable<Product[]> {
  return this.http.get('/products')
    .map(response => response.json());
}
```

As you'll recall, the preceding method won't issue the HTTP GET request until some object subscribes to getProducts() or a component's template uses an AsyncPipe with the data returned by this method (you can find an example in HomeComponent).

The getProductById() method looks similar:

```
getProductById(productId: number): Observable<Product> {
  return this.http.get(`/products/${productId}`)
    .map(response => response.json());
}
```

The getReviewsForProduct() method also returns an Observable:

```
getReviewsForProduct(productId: number): Observable<Review[]> {
  return this.http
    .get(`/products/${productId}/reviews`)
    .map(response => response.json())
    .map(reviews => reviews.map(
      (r: any) => new Review(r.id, r.productId, new Date(r.timestamp),
      ➥ r.user, r.rating, r.comment)));
}
```

The new ProductService.search() method is used when the user clicks the Search button in SearchComponent:

```
search(params: ProductSearchParams): Observable<Product[]> {
    return this.http
      .get('/products', {search: encodeParams(params)})
      .map(response => response.json());
  }
```

The preceding Http.get() method uses a second argument, which is an object with the search property for storing the query string parameters. As you saw in the RequestOptionsArgs interface earlier, the search property can hold either a string or an instance of URLSearchParams.

Following is the code of the ProductService.encodeParams() method, which turns a JavaScript object into an instance of URLSearchParams:

```
function encodeParams(params: any): URLSearchParams {
  return Object.keys(params)
    .filter(key => params[key])
    .reduce((accum: URLSearchParams, key: string) => {
      accum.append(key, params[key]);
      return accum;
    }, new URLSearchParams());
}
```

The new ProductService.getAllCategories() method is used to populate the Categories dropdown in the SearchComponent:

```
getAllCategories(): string[] {
  return ['Books', 'Electronics', 'Hardware'];
}
```

The `ProductService` class also defines a new `searchEvent` variable of type `EventEmitter`. We'll explain its use in the next section when we discuss how to pass the search results to the `HomeComponent`.

PROVIDING SEARCH RESULTS TO HOMECOMPONENT

Initially, `HomeComponent` displays all products by invoking the `ProductService.get-Products()` method. But if the user performs a search by some criteria, you need to make a request to the server, which may return a subset of products or an empty data set if none of the products meet the search criteria.

`SearchComponent` receives a result, which has to be passed to `HomeComponent`. If both of these components were children of the same parent (such as `AppComponent`), you could use the parent as a mediator (see chapter 6) and input/output parameters of the children for the data. But `HomeComponent` is added to `AppComponent` dynamically by the router, and currently Angular doesn't support cross-route input/output parameters. You need another mediator, and the `ProductService` object can become one, because it's injected into both `SearchComponent` and `HomeComponent`.

The `ProductService` class has a `searchEvent` variable that's declared as follows:

```
searchEvent: EventEmitter = new EventEmitter();
```

`SearchComponent` uses this variable to emit the `searchEvent` that carries the object with search parameters as the payload. `HomeComponent` subscribes to this event, as shown in figure 8.14.

`SearchComponent` is a form, and when the user clicks the Search button, it has to notify the world about which search parameters were entered. `Product-Service` does this by emitting the event with the search parameters:

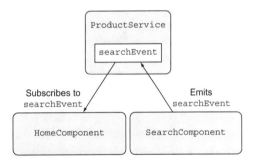

Figure 8.14   Component communication via events

```
onSearch() {
  if (this.formModel.valid) {
    this.productService.searchEvent.emit(this.formModel.value);
  }
}
```

`HomeComponent` is subscribed to the `searchEvent` that may arrive from `SearchComponent` with a payload of search parameters. As soon as that happens, the `ProductService.search()` method is invoked:

```
this.productService.searchEvent
  .subscribe(
    params => this.products = this.productService.search(params),
    console.error.bind(console),
    () => console.log('DONE')
  );
```

Search limitations

Our search solution assumes that HomeComponent is displayed on the screen when the user performs the product search. But if the user navigates to the Product Detail view, HomeComponent is removed from the DOM, and there are no listeners for the search-Event. This isn't a serious shortcoming for an example in a book, and an easy fix would be to disable the search button if the user navigated from the Home route. You can also inject the Router object into SearchComponent and, when the user clicks the Search button while the home route isn't active (if (!router.isActive(url))), navigate to it programmatically by invoking router.navigate('home'), which returns a Promise object. When the promise is resolved, you can emit the searchEvent from there.

HANDLING PRODUCT SEARCH ON THE SERVER

The following code fragment is from the auction.ts file that handles the product search request sent from the client. When the client hits the server's endpoint with query string parameters, you pass the received parameters as req.query to the get-Products() function, which performs a sequence of filters (as specified by the parameters) on the products array to filter out the non-matching products:

```
app.get('/products', (req, res) => {
  res.json(getProducts(req.query));
});

...

function getProducts(params): Product[] {
  let result = products;

  if (params.title) {
    result = result.filter(
      p => p.title.toLowerCase().indexOf(params.title.toLowerCase()) !== -1);
  }
  if ( result.length > 0 && parseInt(params.price)) {
    result = result.filter(
      p => p.price <= parseInt(params.price));
  }
  if ( result.length > 0 && params.category) {
    result = result.filter(
      p => p.categories.indexOf(params.category.toLowerCase()) !== -1);
  }

  return result;
}
```

TESTING THE PRODUCT SEARCH FUNCTIONALITY

Now that we've done a brief code review of the product search implementation, you can start the Node server using the command npm run dev and open the browser to localhost:8000. When the auction app loads, enter your search criteria in the form on the left, and see how HomeComponent re-renders its children (ProductItemComponent) that meet the search criteria.

8.5.2 Broadcasting auction bids using WebSockets

In real auctions, multiple users can bid on products. When the server receives a bid from a user, the bid server should broadcast the latest bid to all users who are interested in receiving such notifications (those who subscribed for notifications). You've emulated the bidding process by generating random bids from random users.

When users open the Product Details view, they should be able to subscribe to bid notifications made by other users on the selected product. You implement this functionality with a server-side push via WebSockets. Figure 8.15 shows the Product Details view with the Watch toggle button that starts and stops the current bid notifications pushed by the server over the socket. Next, we'll briefly highlight the changes in the auction app related to bid notifications.

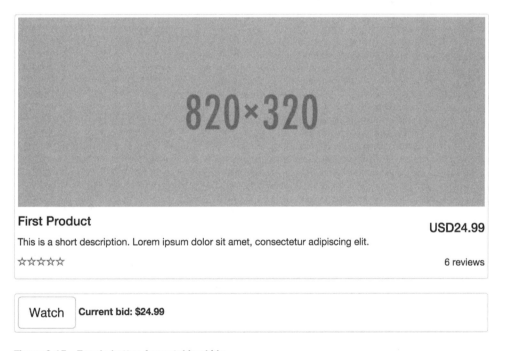

First Product   **USD24.99**

This is a short description. Lorem ipsum dolor sit amet, consectetur adipiscing elit.

☆☆☆☆☆   6 reviews

| Watch | **Current bid: $24.99** |

Figure 8.15 Toggle button for watching bids

THE CLIENT SIDE

Two new services are located in the client/app/services directory: BidService and WebSocketService. WebSocketService is an Observable wrapper for the WebSocket object. It's similar to the one you created earlier, in section 8.4.2.

BidService gets the WebSocketService injected:

```
@Injectable()
export class BidService {
  constructor(private webSocket: WebSocketService) {}

  watchProduct(productId: number): Observable {
    let openSubscriber = Subscriber.create(
      () => this.webSocket.send({productId: productId}));

    return this.webSocket.createObservableSocket('ws://
      localhost:8000', openSubscriber)
        .map(message => JSON.parse(message));
  }
}
```

BidService is injected into ProductDetailComponent. When the user clicks the
Watch toggle button, the BidService.watchProduct() method sends the product ID
to the server, indicating that this user wants to start or stop watching the selected
product:

```
toggleWatchProduct() {
  if (this.subscription) {
    this.subscription.unsubscribe();
    this.subscription = null;
    this.isWatching = false;
  } else {
    this.isWatching = true;
    this.subscription = this.bidService.watchProduct(this.product.id)
      .subscribe(
        products => this.currentBid = products.find((p: any) => p.productId
        ➥ === this.product.id).bid,
        error => console.log(error));
  }
}
```

The template of the ProductDetailComponent has the Watch toggle button, and the
latest bid received from the server is rendered as HTML label:

```
<button class="btn btn-default btn-lg"
        [ngClass]="{active: isWatching}"
        (click)="toggleWatchProduct()"
        role="button">
  {{ isWatching ? 'Stop watching' : 'Watch' }}
</button>

<label>Current bid: {{ currentBid | currency }}</label>
```

There's also a small new client/app/services/services.ts script, in which you declare
all the import statements and the array of services used for dependency injection:

```
import {BidService} from './bid-service';
import {ProductService} from './product-service';
import {WebSocketService} from './websocket-service';

export const ONLINE_AUCTION_SERVICES = [
  BidService,
  ProductService,
  WebSocketService
];
```

The providers declared in the ONLINE_AUCTION_SERVICES constant are used in the main.ts file that bootstraps the Angular portion of the auction:

```
@NgModule({
...
  providers:[ProductService,
             ONLINE_AUCTION_SERVICES,
             {provide: LocationStrategy, useClass: HashLocationStrategy}],
  bootstrap:[ ApplicationComponent ]
})
```

THE SERVER SIDE

The server/auction.ts script includes the code that maintains subscribed clients and generates random bids. Each generated bid can be up to five dollars higher than the last one. As soon as the new bid is generated, it's broadcast to all subscribed clients.

The following code from the server/auction.ts file handles bid notification requests and broadcasting bids to all subscribed clients:

```
const wsServer: WsServer = new WsServer({server: httpServer});
```
⟵ Creates the WebSocket server listening to the same port as the HTTP server

```
wsServer.on('connection', ws => {
  ws.on('message', message => {
    let subscriptionRequest = JSON.parse(message);
    subscribeToProductBids(ws, subscriptionRequest.productId);
  });
});
```
Stores references to bid subscriptions in a Map where the key is a reference to the WebSocket connection that represents the user, and the value is an array of product IDs for which the client wants to receive bid notifications

```
const subscriptions = new Map<any, number[]>();
```
⟵

```
function subscribeToProductBids(client, productId: number): void {
  let products = subscriptions.get(client) || [];
  subscriptions.set(client, [...products, productId]);
}
```
⟵ Finds the existing product subscriptions for the connected client, and adds a new product ID to the subscriptions array

```
setInterval(() => {
  generateNewBids();
  broadcastNewBidsToSubscribers();
}, 2000);
```
⟵ Every two seconds, generates a new bid and broadcasts it to all clients who subscribe to the specific product notifications

```
const currentBids = new Map<number, number>();
```

```
function generateNewBids() {
  getProducts().forEach(p => {
    const currentBid = currentBids.get(p.id) || p.price;
    const newBid = random(currentBid, currentBid + 5); //
      Max bid increase is $5
    currentBids.set(p.id, newBid);
  });
}

function broadcastNewBidsToSubscribers() {

  subscriptions.forEach((products: number[], ws: WebSocket) => {
    if (ws.readyState === 1) { // 1 - READY_STATE_OPEN
      let newBids = products.map(pid => ({
        productId: pid
        bid: currentBids.get(pid)
      }));
      ws.send(JSON.stringify(newBids));
    } else {
      subscriptions.delete(ws);
    }
  });
}
```

> **For each connected client, sends the current bids for the subscribed products**

Here you test the `readyState` property of the WebSocket object to make sure the client is still connected. For example, if the user closed the auction window, there would be no need to send bid notifications, so this socket connection is removed from the `subscriptions` map.

> **NOTE** Note the use of the spread operator (…) in the `subscribeToProduct-Bids()` method. You use it to copy an existing array of product IDs and add a new one.

We've covered the WebSocket-related code of the auction, and we encourage you to review the rest of the code on your own. To test the bid-notification functionality, you'll need to start the application, click a product title, and, on the product detail view, click the Watch button. You should see the new bids for this product that are pushed from the server. Open the auction application in more than one browser to test that each browser properly turns bid notifications on and off.

8.6   Summary

The main subject of this chapter was enabling client-server interaction, which is the reason web frameworks exist. Angular, combined with the RxJS extensions library, offers a unified approach for consuming data from the server: the client's code subscribes to the data stream coming from the server, whether it's an HTTP- or WebSocket-based interaction. The programming model is changed: instead of requesting the data as in AJAX-style applications, Angular consumes data that's *pushed* by observable streams. These are the main takeaways from this chapter:

- Angular comes with the `Http` object that supports HTTP communications with web servers.
- Providers for HTTP services are located in the `HttpModule` module. If your app uses HTTP, don't forget to include it in the `@NgModule` decorator.
- Public methods of `HttpObject` return `Observable`, and only when the client subscribes to it is the request to the server made.
- The WebSocket protocol is more efficient and concise than HTTP. It's bidirectional, and both client and server can initiate communication.
- Creating a web server with NodeJS and Express is relatively simple, but an Angular client can communicate with web servers implemented in different technologies.

Unit-testing
Angular applications

9

This chapter covers

- The basics of unit testing with the Jasmine framework
- The main artifacts from the Angular testing library
- Testing the main players of an Angular app: services, components, and the router
- Running unit tests against web browsers with the Karma test runner
- Implementing unit testing in the online auction example

To ensure that your software has no bugs, you need to test it. Even if your application has no bugs today, it may have them tomorrow, after you modify the existing code or introduce new code. Even if you don't change the code in a particular module, it may stop working properly as a result of changes in another module. Your application code has to be retested regularly, and this process should be automated. You

278

need to prepare test scripts and start running them as early as possible in your development cycle.

There are two main types of testing for the front end of web applications:

- *Unit testing* asserts that a small unit of code (such as a component or function) accepts the expected input data and returns the expected result. Unit testing is about testing isolated pieces of code, especially public interfaces. That's what we'll discuss in this chapter.
- *End-to-end testing* asserts that the entire application works as end users expect and that all units properly interact with each other. For end-to-end testing of Angular 2 applications, you can use the Protractor library (see https://angular.github.io/protractor).

NOTE *Load* or *stress testing* shows how many concurrent users can work with a web application while it maintains the expected response time. Load-testing tools are mainly about testing the server side of web applications.

Unit tests are for testing the business logic of separate units of code, and typically you'll be running unit tests a lot more often than end-to-end tests. End-to-end testing can emulate a user's actions (such as button clicks) and check the behavior of your application. During end-to-end testing, you shouldn't run the unit-testing scripts.

This chapter is about unit-testing Angular applications. Several frameworks have been specifically created for implementing and running unit tests, and our framework of choice is Jasmine. Actually, it's not only our choice—as we write this, Angular's testing library only works with Jasmine for unit testing. This is described in the "Jasmine Testing 101" section of the Angular documentation (http://mng.bz/0nv3).

We'll start by covering the basics of unit testing with Jasmine; toward the end of the chapter, you'll write and run test scripts to unit-test selected components in the online auction. We'll give you a brief overview of Jasmine so you can quickly start writing unit tests; for more details, see the Jasmine documentation (http://jasmine.github.io). For running tests, you'll use a test runner called Karma (https://karma-runner.github.io), which is an independent command-line utility that can run tests written in different test frameworks.

9.1 *Getting to know Jasmine*

Jasmine allows you to implement a behavior-driven development (BDD) process, which suggests that tests of any unit of software should be specified in terms of the desired behavior of the unit. With BDD, you use natural language constructs to describe what you think your code should be doing. You write unit-test specifications in the form of short sentences, such as "ApplicationComponent is successfully instantiated" or "StarsComponent emits the rating change event."

Because it's so easy to understand the meaning of the tests, they can serve as your program documentation. If other developers need to become familiar with your code, they can start by reading the code of the unit tests to understand your intentions.

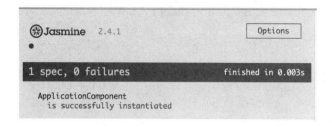

Figure 9.1   Running tests using Jasmine's test runner

Using natural language to describe tests has another advantage: it's easy to reason about the test results, as shown in figure 9.1.

> **TIP** As much as we'd like all of our tests to pass, make a habit of ensuring that your tests fail first, and see if the test results are easy to understand.

In Jasmine terminology, a test is called a *spec*, and a combination of one or more specs is called a *suite*. A test suite is defined with the describe() function —this is where you describe what you're testing. Each test spec in the suite is programmed as an it() function, which defines the expected behavior of the code under test and how to test it. Here's an example:

```
describe('MyCalculator', () => {
  it('should know how to multiply', () => {
    // The code that tests multiplication goes here
  });
  it('should not divide by zero', () => {
    // The code that tests division by zero goes here
  });

});
```

Testing frameworks have the notion of an *assertion*, which is a way of questioning whether an expression is true or false. If the assertion is false, the framework throws an error. In Jasmine, assertions are specified using the function expect(), followed by *matchers*: toBe(), toEqual(), and so on. It's as if you're writing a sentence. "I expect 2+2 to equal 4" looks like this:

```
expect(2 + 2).toEqual(4);
```

Matchers implement a Boolean comparison between the actual and expected values. If the matcher returns true, the spec passes. If you expect a test result not to have a certain value, just add the keyword not before the matcher:

```
expect(2 + 2).not.toEqual(5);
```

You can find the complete list of matchers at Jamie Mason's Jasmine-Matchers page on GitHub: https://github.com/JamieMason/Jasmine-Matchers.

We've given our test suites the same names as the files under test, adding the suffix *.spec* to the name, which is a standard practice; for example, application.spec.ts contains

the test script for application.ts. The following test suite is from the file application
.spec.ts; it tests that the instance of `ApplicationComponent` is created:

```
import AppComponent from './app';

describe('AppComponent', () => {
  it('is successfully instantiated', () => {

    const app = new AppComponent();

    expect(app instanceof AppComponent).toEqual(true);
  });
});
```

This is a test suite containing a single test. If you extract the texts from `describe()`
and `it()` and put them together, you'll get a sentence that clearly indicates what
you're testing here: "ApplicationComponent is successfully instantiated."

> **NOTE** If other developers need to know what your spec tests, they can read
> the texts in `describe()` and `it()`. Each test should be self-descriptive and
> serve as program documentation.

The preceding code instantiates `AppComponent` and expects the expression `app
instanceof AppComponent` to be evaluated to `true`. From the `import` statement, you
can guess that this test script is located in the same directory as `AppComponent`.

Where to store test files

The Jasmine framework is used to unit test JavaScript applications written in different
frameworks or in pure JavaScript. One of the approaches for storing test files is to
create a separate test directory and keep only test scripts there, so they aren't mixed
up with the application code.

In Angular applications, we prefer to keep each test script in the same directory as
the component or service under test. This is convenient for two reasons:

- All component-related files are located together in the same directory. Typically,
  we create a directory for storing the component's .ts, .html, and .css files; adding a .spec file there won't clutter the directory content.
- There's no need to change the configuration of the SystemJS loader, which
  already knows where the application files are located. It will load the tests from
  the same locations.

If you want some code to be executed before each test (such as to prepare test dependencies), you can specify it in the *setup* functions `beforeAll()` and `beforeEach()`,
which will run before the suite or each spec, respectively. If you want to execute some
code right after the suite or each spec is finished, use the *teardown* functions `after-
All()` and `afterEach()`.

TIP If you have a spec with multiple it() tests, and you want the runner to skip some tests, change them from it() to xit().

9.1.1   *What to test*

Now that you have an understanding of how to test, the question is what to test. In Angular applications written in TypeScript, you can test functions, classes, and components:

- *Test functions*—Say you have a function that converts the passed string to uppercase. You can write multiple tests just for this function, for cases where the argument is null, an empty string, undefined, a lowercase word, an uppercase word, a mixed-case word, a number, and so on.
- *Test classes*—If you have a class containing several methods (like Product-Service), you can write a test suite that includes all the tests needed to ensure that each of the class methods functions properly.
- *Test components*—You can test the public API of your services or components. In addition to testing them for correctness, we'll show you code samples that use publicly exposed properties or methods.

9.1.2   *How to install Jasmine*

You can get Jasmine by downloading its standalone distribution, but you'll install it using npm, as you've done for all other packages in this book. The npm repository has several Jasmine-related packages, but you just need jasmine-core. Open the command window in the root of your project, and run the following command:

```
npm install jasmine-core --save-dev
```

To make sure the TypeScript compiler knows about the Jasmine types, run the following command to install the Jasmine type-definition file:

```
npm i @types/jasmine --save-dev
```

When your tests are written, you need a test-runner application to run them. Jasmine comes with two runners: one is for the command line (see the npm package jasmine), and the other is HTML-based. You'll start by using the HTML-based runner, but to run tests from the command line, you'll use another test runner called Karma.

Although Jasmine comes with a preconfigured HTML-based runner as a sample app, you need to create an HTML file to test yours. This HTML file should include the following script tags that load Jasmine:

```
<link rel="stylesheet" href="node_modules/jasmine-core/lib/jasmine-core/
➥ jasmine.css">
  <script src="node_modules/jasmine-core/lib/jasmine-core/jasmine.js">
  </script>
  <script src="node_modules/jasmine-core/lib/jasmine-core/jasmine-html.js">
  </script>
  <script src="node_modules/jasmine-core/lib/jasmine-core/boot.js"></script>
```

Using the standalone Jasmine distribution

If you want to see the running Jasmine tests quickly, download the zip file with the standalone version of Jasmine from https://github.com/jasmine/jasmine/releases. Unzip this file, and open SpecRunner.html in your web browser. You'll see the window shown here.

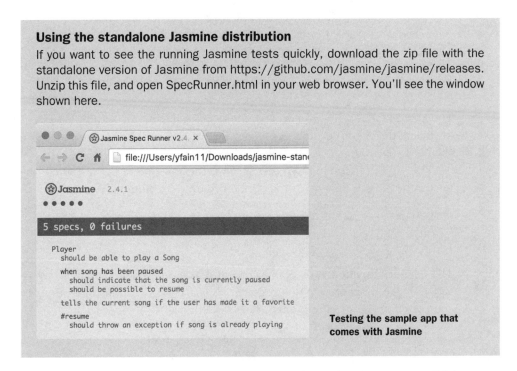

Testing the sample app that comes with Jasmine

You'll also need to add all required Angular dependencies, as you did in every index.html file in all the code samples in the book, plus the Angular testing library. You'll keep using the SystemJS loader, but this time you'll load the code of the unit tests (the .spec files), which will load the application code via `import` statements.

In this chapter, we'll show you how to write unit tests. You'll run them manually using the HTML-based runner first. Then we'll show you how to use Karma, which can run command-line tests that report possible errors in different browsers. In chapter 10, you'll integrate Karma into the application build process, so the unit tests will run automatically as part of the build.

9.2 *What comes with Angular's testing library*

Angular comes with a testing library that includes the wrappers for Jasmine's `describe()`, `it()`, and `xit()` functions and also adds such functions as `beforeEach()`, `async()`, `fakeAsync()`, and others.

Because you don't configure and bootstrap the application during test runs, Angular offers a `TestBed` helper class that allows you to declare modules, components, providers, and so on. `TestBed` includes such functions as `configureTestingModule()`, `createComponent()`, `inject()`, and others. For example, the syntax for configuring a testing module looks similar to configuring `@NgModule`:

```
beforeEach(() => {
    TestBed.configureTestingModule({
        imports: [ ReactiveFormsModule, RouterTestingModule,
```

```
                    RouterTestingModule.withRoutes(routes)],
        declarations: [AppComponent, HomeComponent, WeatherComponent],
        providers: [{provide: WeatherService, useValue: {} }
        ]
    })
 });
```

The `beforeEach()` function is used in test suites during the setup phase. It allows you to specify the required modules, components, and providers that may be needed by each test.

The `inject()` function creates an injector and injects the specified objects into tests, according to the app's providers configured for Angular DI:

```
inject([Router, Location], (router: Router, location: Location) => {
  // Do something
})
```

The `async()` function runs in the Zone and may be used with asynchronous services. `async()` doesn't complete the test until all of its asynchronous operations have been completed or the specified timeout has passed:

```
it(' does something', async(inject([AClass], object => {
  myPromise.then(() => { expect(true).toEqual(true); });
}), 3000));
```

The `fakeAsync()` function lets you speed up the testing of asynchronous services by simulating the passage of time:

```
it('...', fakeAsync(() => {
  // Do something

  tick(1000);          ◁────  Simulates the asynchronous
  expect(...);                passage of I second
}));
```

The Angular testing library has an `NgMatchers` interface that includes the following matchers:

- `toBePromise()`—Expects the value to be a promise
- `toBeAnInstanceOf()`—Expects the value to be an instance of a class
- `toHaveText()`—Expects the element to have exactly the given text
- `toHaveCssClass()`—Expects the element to have the given CSS class
- `toHaveCssStyle()`—Expects the element to have the given CSS styles
- `toImplement()`—Expects a class to implement the interface of the given class
- `toContainError()`—Expects an exception to contain the given error text
- `toThrowErrorWith()`—Expects a function to throw an error with the given error text when executed

The Angular Testing API for TypeScript is documented at http://mng.bz/ym8N. We'll show you how to test services, routers, event emitters, and components later in this chapter, but first let's go over some basics.

9.2.1 Testing services

Typically, Angular services are injected into components; to set up the injectors, you need to define providers for an `it()` block. Angular offers the `beforeEach()` setup method, which runs before each `it()` call. You can inject the service into `it()` using `inject()` to test synchronous functions in the service.

Real services may need some time to complete, and this may slow your tests. There are two ways to speed up tests:

- Create a class that implements a mock service by extending a class of the real service that returns hardcoded data quickly. For example, you can create a mock service for `WeatherService` that returns immediately without making any requests to the remote server that returns actual weather data:

```
class MockWeatherService implement WeatherService {
  getWeather() {
    return Observable.empty();
  }
}
```

- Use the `fakeAsync()` function, which automatically identifies asynchronous calls and replaces timeouts, callbacks, and promises with immediately executed functions. The `tick()` function allows you to fast-forward the time, so there's no need to wait until the timeout expires. You'll see examples of using `fakeAsync()` later in this chapter.

9.2.2 Testing navigation with the router

To test the router, your spec scripts can invoke such router methods as `navigate()` and `navigateByUrl()`. The `navigate()` method takes an array of configured routes (commands) that will construct the route as an argument, whereas `navigateByUrl()` takes a string representing the segment of the URL you want to navigate to.

If you use `navigate()`, you specify the configured path and route params, if any. If the router is properly configured, it should update the URL in the address bar of the browser.

The next code snippet shows how to programmatically navigate to the `product` route, pass 0 as a route param, and ensure that after the navigation, the URL (represented by the `Location` object) has a segment of `/product/0`:

```
it('should be able to navigate to product details using commands API',
    fakeAsync(inject([Router, Location], (router: Router, location:
    ➥ Location) => {
      TestBed.createComponent(AppComponent);
      router.navigate(['/products', 0]);
```

```
    tick();
    expect(location.path()).toBe('/product/0');
  })
));
```

When you provide an array of values to the router, it's called a *commands API*. For the preceding code fragment to work, the route with parameter /products/:productId has to be configured, as explained in chapter 3.

The it() function invokes the callback provided as the second argument. fake-Async() wraps a function provided as an argument (inject() in the previous example) and executes it in the Zone. The tick() function lets you manually fast-forward the time and advance tasks in the microtasks queue in the browser's event loop. In other words, you can emulate the time that asynchronous tasks take, and execute asynchronous code synchronously, which simplifies and speeds up execution of the unit tests.

With TestBed.createComponent() (explained in the next section), you create an instance of the component. Then you invoke the router's navigate() method, advance the async tasks that perform the navigation with tick(), and check whether the current location is the same as the expected one.

The navigateByUrl() function takes a specific URL segment and should properly build the Location.path that represents the client's portion in the address bar of the browser. This is what you'll test:

```
router.navigateByUrl('/products');
...
expect(location.path()).toBe('/products');
```

You'll see how to use navigateByUrl() in section 9.3.

While testing the router, you can use SpyLocation, which is a mock for the Location provider. It allows tests to fire simulated location events. For example, you can prepare a specific URL and simulate the change of the hash portion, the browser's Back and Forward buttons, and more.

9.2.3 *Testing components*

Components are classes with templates. If your class contains methods implementing the application's logic, you can test them as you would any other functions; but more often you'll be testing the templates. In particular, you're interested in testing that the bindings work properly and that they display the expected data.

Angular offers the TestBed.createComponent() method, which returns a ComponentFixture object that will be used to work with the component when it's created. This fixture gives you access to both the component and the native HTML element's instances, so you can assign values to the component's properties as well as find specific HTML elements in the component's template.

You can also trigger the change-detection cycle on the component by invoking the detectChanges() method on the fixture. After the change detection has updated the

UI, you can run the `expect()` function to check the rendered values. The following code snippet illustrates these actions using a `ProductComponent` that has a product property, assuming that it's bound to the template element `<h4>`:

```
let fixture = TestBed.createComponent(ProductDetailComponent);
let element = fixture.nativeElement;
let component = fixture.componentInstance;
component.product = {title: 'iPhone 7', price: 700};

fixture.detectChanges();
expect(element.querySelector('h4').innerHTML).toBe('iPhone 7');
```

Now let's write a sample application in which you'll implement unit tests for a component, a router, and a service.

9.3 Testing a sample weather application

Let's try testing Angular components and services using an application that has a main page with two links: Home and Weather. You'll use a router to navigate to the Weather page, which is a refactored version of the weather app you created in chapter 5 (observable-events-http.ts).

Figure 9.2 Checking the weather component in the test_samples project

In chapter 5, a large chunk of the code was placed in the constructor of `AppComponent`, which complicates testing because you can't invoke the code of the constructor after an object is created. Now `WeatherComponent` will get the `Weather-Service` injected, and `WeatherService` will use the remote server from chapter 5 to get the weather information. Figure 9.2 shows what the window looked like when we ran this application, navigated to the Weather route, and entered `New York` in the input field.

Figure 9.3 shows the structure of this project (see the test_weather directory). Note the .spec files, which contain the code for unit-testing the components and the weather service.

To run these tests, create the following test.html file that loads all the spec.ts files circled in figure 9.3

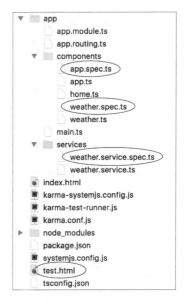

Figure 9.3 The structure of the test_samples project

Listing 9.1   test.html

```html
<!DOCTYPE html>
<html lang="en">
<head>
  <meta charset="utf-8">
  <title>Testing the Weather Application</title>
  <base href="/">

  <!-- TypeScript in-browser compiler -->
  <script src="node_modules/typescript/lib/typescript.js"></script>

  <!-- Polyfills -->
  <script src="node_modules/reflect-metadata/Reflect.js"></script>

  <!-- Jasmine -->
  <link rel="stylesheet" href="node_modules/jasmine-core/lib/jasmine-core/
  ➥ jasmine.css">
  <script src="node_modules/jasmine-core/lib/jasmine-core/jasmine.js">
  ➥ </script>
  <script src="node_modules/jasmine-core/lib/jasmine-core/jasmine-html.js">
  ➥ </script>
  <script src="node_modules/jasmine-core/lib/jasmine-core/boot.js"></script>

  <!-- Zone.js -->
  <script src="node_modules/zone.js/dist/zone.js"></script>
  <script src="node_modules/zone.js/dist/proxy.js"></script>
  <script src="node_modules/zone.js/dist/sync-test.js"></script>
  <script src="node_modules/zone.js/dist/jasmine-patch.js"></script>
  <script src="node_modules/zone.js/dist/async-test.js"></script>
  <script src="node_modules/zone.js/dist/fake-async-test.js"></script>
  <script src="node_modules/zone.js/dist/long-stack-trace-zone.js"></script>

  <!-- SystemJS -->
  <script src="node_modules/systemjs/dist/system.src.js"></script>
  <script src="systemjs.config.js"></script>
</head>
<body>
<script>
  var SPEC_MODULES = [
    'app/components/app.spec',
    'app/components/weather.spec',
    'app/services/weather.service.spec'
  ];

  Promise.all([
    System.import('@angular/core/testing'),
    System.import('@angular/platform-browser-dynamic/testing')
  ])
  .then(function (modules) {
    var testing = modules[0];
    var browser = modules[1];
```

Loads Jasmine files *(annotation, pointing to Jasmine section)*

Declares an array with the names of the specs to be loaded

Loads two Angular modules required for testing

When the testing modules are loaded, stores their references in the variables

```
        testing.TestBed.initTestEnvironment(        ◁─────┐
            browser.BrowserDynamicTestingModule,
            browser.platformBrowserDynamicTesting());
```

> **Initializes the test environment.
> If you configure AppModule in
> the app, you replace it with
> BrowserDynamicTestingModule
> in tests.**

```
    // Load all the spec files.
    return Promise.all(SPEC_MODULES.map(function (module) {
      return System.import(module);
    }));
  })
  .then(window.onload)        ◁─────┐
  .catch(console.error.bind(console));
</script>
</body>
</html>
```

> **After the frameworks and specs are
> loaded, initiates the event handler for the
> load event so Jasmine will run the tests**

9.3.1 Configuring SystemJS

To use an HTML-based test runner, you need to add Angular testing modules to your SystemJS configuration. Here's the fragment from the systemjs.config.js file that comes with this project.

Listing 9.2 systemjs.config.js fragment

```
'@angular/common/testing'                        : 'ng:common/bundles/
➥ common-testing.umd.js',
    '@angular/compiler/testing'                  : 'ng:compiler/bundles/
    ➥ compiler-testing.umd.js',
    '@angular/core/testing'                      : 'ng:core/bundles/
    ➥ core-testing.umd.js',
    '@angular/router/testing'                    : 'ng:router/bundles/
    ➥ router-testing.umd.js',
    '@angular/http/testing'                      : 'ng:http/bundles/
    ➥ http-testing.umd.js',
    '@angular/platform-browser/testing'          : 'ng:platform-browser/
    ➥ bundles/platform-browser-testing.umd.js',
    '@angular/platform-browser-dynamic/testing':
'ng:platform-browser-dynamic/bundles/platform-browser-dynamic-testing.umd.js',
  },
  paths: {
    'ng:': 'node_modules/@angular/'
  },
```

9.3.2 Testing the weather router

The router for this application is configured in the app.routing.ts file.

Listing 9.3 app.routing.ts

```
import { Routes, RouterModule } from '@angular/router';
import { HomeComponent } from './components/home';
import { WeatherComponent } from './components/weather';
```

```
export const routes: Routes = [
  { path: '',        component: HomeComponent },
  { path: 'weather', component: WeatherComponent }
];

export const routing = RouterModule.forRoot(routes);
```

Although you can configure the routes either in your app module or in a separate file, having the routes configured in a separate file is a best practice. Doing so allows you to reuse the route configuration to run both the application and the test scripts.

The script in app.module.ts of the weather app uses the `routes` constant in the declaration of `@NgModule`.

Listing 9.4   app.module.ts

```
@NgModule({
  imports: [BrowserModule, HttpModule, ReactiveFormsModule, routing],
  declarations: [AppComponent, HomeComponent, WeatherComponent],
  bootstrap: [AppComponent],
  providers: [
    { provide: LocationStrategy,   useClass: HashLocationStrategy },
    { provide: WEATHER_URL_BASE,   useValue: 'http://api.openweathermap.org/
➥  data/2.5/weather?q=' },
    { provide: WEATHER_URL_SUFFIX, useValue:
➥  '&units=imperial&appid=ca3f6d6ca3973a518834983d0b318f73' },
    WeatherService
  ]
})
```

The test script for the routes is located in the app.spec.ts file, and it reuses the same routes constant.

Listing 9.5   app.spec.ts

```
import { TestBed, fakeAsync, inject, tick } from '@angular/core/testing';
import { Location } from '@angular/common';
import { ReactiveFormsModule } from '@angular/forms';
import { provideRoutes, Router } from '@angular/router';
import { RouterTestingModule } from '@angular/router/testing';

import { routes } from '../app.routing';
import { WeatherService } from '../services/weather.service';
import { AppComponent } from './app';
import { HomeComponent } from '../components/home';
import { WeatherComponent } from '../components/weather';

describe('Router', () => {

  beforeEach(() => {
    TestBed.configureTestingModule({
```

Test suite for the routes defined in app.routing.ts

Before running each test, you configure the testing module to include the components and providers required for testing the router.

**Tests navigation to WeatherComponent, which gets the
WeatherService injected, so you need to register a
provider for the fake service here.**

**Provides
routes for the
router-testing
module**

```
    imports: [ ReactiveFormsModule, RouterTestingModule,
              RouterTestingModule.withRoutes(routes)],
    declarations: [AppComponent, HomeComponent, WeatherComponent],
    providers: [{provide: WeatherService, useValue: {} } )
    ]
  })
});
```

**Tests that the router can navigate to the route /.
The / route doesn't add anything to the base URL,
so you expect it to be an empty string.**

```
it('should be able to navigate to home using commands API',
   fakeAsync(inject([Router, Location], (router: Router, location:
   Location) => {
     TestBed.createComponent(AppComponent);
     router.navigate(['/']);
     tick();
     expect(location.path()).toBe('/');
   })
));
```

**You need to create AppComponent
because it declares <router-outlet>.**

**Fast-forwards the time required for the
asynchronous creation of AppComponent**

```
it('should be able to navigate to weather using commands API',
   fakeAsync(inject([Router, Location], (router: Router, location:
   Location) => {
     TestBed.createComponent(AppComponent);
     router.navigate(['/weather']);
     tick();
     expect(location.path()).toBe('/weather');
   })
));
```

**Tests whether the router can
navigate to the /weather route
using the navigate() method**

```
it('should be able to navigate to weather by URL',
   fakeAsync(inject([Router, Location], (router: Router, location:
   Location) =>
     TestBed.createComponent(AppComponent);
     router.navigateByUrl('/weather');
     tick();
     expect(location.path()).toEqual('/weather');
   })
));

});
```

**Tests whether the router
can navigate to the /
weather route using the
navigateByUrl() method**

Note that you import `ReactiveFormsModule` because `WeatherComponent` uses the
Forms API.

> **NOTE** Don't unit-test third-party code in your app. In listing 9.5, you use an
> empty object as a provider for `WeatherService`, which in the real app makes
> calls to a remote weather server. What if that remote server is down when you
> run your test specs? Unit tests should assert that your scripts work fine, not
> someone else's software. That's why you don't use an actual `WebService` and
> use an empty object instead.

When testing the client-side navigation of your application, you'll use the `Router` class and its `navigate()` and `navigateByUrl()` methods.

Listing 9.5 illustrates the use of both the `navigate()` and the `navigateByUrl()` methods for testing that the programmatic navigation properly updates the address bar of the application. But because you don't run that app during the test, there's no browser address bar, so it has to be emulated. That's why instead of `RouterModule`, you use `RouterTestingModule`, which knows how to check the expected content of the address bar using the `Location` class.

Now let's look at testing the injection of services. As a matter of fact, you've already been injecting services while testing routes:

```
fakeAsync(inject([Router, Location],...))
```

But in the next section, we'll show you a different way to initialize the required services: you'll get the `Injector` object and invoke its `get()` method.

9.3.3 *Testing the weather service*

The `WeatherService` class encapsulates communications with the weather server.

Listing 9.6 weather.service.ts

```
import {Inject, Injectable, OpaqueToken} from '@angular/core';
import {Http, Response} from '@angular/http';
import {Observable} from 'rxjs/Observable';
import 'rxjs/add/operator/filter';
import 'rxjs/add/operator/map';

export const WEATHER_URL_BASE = new OpaqueToken('WeatherUrlBase');
export const WEATHER_URL_SUFFIX = new OpaqueToken('WeatherUrlSuffix');

export interface WeatherResult {
  place: string;
  temperature: number;
  humidity: number;
}

@Injectable()
export class WeatherService {
  constructor(
      private http: Http,
      @Inject(WEATHER_URL_BASE) private urlBase: string,
      @Inject(WEATHER_URL_SUFFIX) private urlSuffix: string) {
  }

  getWeather(city: string): Observable<WeatherResult> {
    return this.http
        .get(this.urlBase + city + this.urlSuffix)
        .map((response: Response) => response.json())
        .filter(this._hasResult)
```

```
            .map(this._parseData);
    }

  private _hasResult(data): boolean {
    return data['cod'] !== '404' && data.main;
  }

  private _parseData(data): WeatherResult {
    let [first,] = data.list;
    return {
     place: data.name || 'unknown',
      temperature: data.main.temp,
      humidity: data.main.humidity
    };
  }
 }
}
```

Note the use of the OpaqueToken type mentioned in chapter 4. You use it twice to inject into urlBase and urlSuffix the values provided in the @NgModule decorator. Using dependency injection for urlBase and urlSuffix makes it simpler to replace the real weather server with a mock, if need be.

The getWeather() method in listing 9.6 forms the URL for the HTTP get() by concatenating urlBase, city, and urlSuffix. The result is processed by map(), filter(), and another map() so the observable will emit objects of type WeatherResult.

NOTE You aren't testing the _hasResult() and _parseData() methods because private methods can't be unit-tested. Should you decide to test them, change their access level to public.

To test WeatherService, you'll use the MockBackend class, which is one of Angular's implementations of the Http object. MockBackend doesn't make any HTTP requests but intercepts them and allows you to create and return hardcoded data in the format of the expected result.

Before each test, you'll get a reference to the Injector object, which will get you the new instances of MockBackend and WeatherService. The testing code for the WeatherService is located in the weather.service.spec.ts file.

Listing 9.7 weather.service.spec.ts

```
import {async, getTestBed, TestBed, Injector} from '@angular/core/testing';
import {Response, ResponseOptions, HttpModule, XHRBackend} from '@angular/
➥ http';
import {MockBackend, MockConnection} from '@angular/http/testing';
import {WeatherService, WEATHER_URL_BASE, WEATHER_URL_SUFFIX} from './
➥ weather.service';

describe('WeatherService', () => {
  let mockBackend: MockBackend;
```

```
    let service: WeatherService;

    let injector: Injector;

    beforeEach(() => {
      TestBed.configureTestingModule({
        imports: [HttpModule],
        providers: [
          { provide: XHRBackend, useClass: MockBackend },
          { provide: WEATHER_URL_BASE, useValue: '' },
          { provide: WEATHER_URL_SUFFIX, useValue: '' },
          WeatherService
        ]
      });

      injector = getTestBed();
    });
```

Gets an instance of the Injector. The TestBed class implements the Injector interface, and getTestBed() returns an object that implements the injector's API.

```
    beforeEach(() => {
      mockBackend = injector.get(XHRBackend);
      service = injector.get(WeatherService);
    });
```

Sets the providers that the test injector should use for the XHRBackend token

Sets the providers that the test injector should use for the WeatherService token

```
    it('getWeather() should return weather for New York', async(() => {
      let mockResponseData = {
        cod: '200',
        name: 'New York',
        main: {
          temp: 57,
          humidity: 44
        }
      };
```

The test starts by creating a mock object to represent the weather for New York. The structure of this object mimics the actual response data from the real web service.

Configures MockBackend by subscribing to "HTTP requests," and emulates the real response with the content of mockResponseData. The body of this response is created by instantiating ResponseOptions.

```
      mockBackend.connections.subscribe((connection: MockConnection) => {
        let responseOpts = new ResponseOptions({body:
          JSON.stringify(mockResponseData) });
        connection.mockRespond(new Response(responseOpts));
      });

      service.getWeather('New York').subscribe(weather => {
        expect(weather.place).toBe('New York');
        expect(weather.humidity).toBe(44);
        expect(weather.temperature).toBe(57);
      });
    }));
  });
```

The invocation of getWeather('New York') is expected to return the mock data for New York. The getWeather() method internally uses Http emulated by MockBackend.

These are the main takeaways from testing services injection:

- Prepare the providers.
- If you're using services that make requests to external servers, mock them up.

We've shown you how to test the navigation and services; now let's look at how you can test an Angular component.

9.3.4 *Testing the weather component*

`WeatherService` is injected into `WeatherComponent` (weather.ts) via constructor, where you subscribe to the observable's messages coming from the `WeatherService`. When the user starts entering the name of a city in the UI, the `getWeather()` method is invoked, and the returned weather data is displayed in the template via binding.

Listing 9.8   weather.ts

```
import {Component} from '@angular/core';
import {FormControl} from '@angular/forms';
import 'rxjs/add/operator/debounceTime';
import 'rxjs/add/operator/switchMap';

import {WeatherService, WeatherResult} from '../services/weather.service';

@Component({
  selector: 'my-weather',
  template: `
    <h2>Weather</h2>
    <input type="text" placeholder="Enter city" [formControl]="searchInput">
    <h3>Current weather in {{weather?.place}}:</h3>
    <ul>
      <li>Temperature: {{weather?.temperature}}F</li>
      <li>Humidity: {{weather?.humidity}}%</li>
    </ul>
  `
})
export class WeatherComponent {
  searchInput: FormControl;
  weather: WeatherResult;

  constructor(weatherService: WeatherService) {
    this.searchInput = new FormControl('');
    this.searchInput.valueChanges
        .debounceTime(300)
        .switchMap((place: string) => weatherService.getWeather(place))
        .subscribe(
            (wthr: WeatherResult) => this.weather = wthr,
            error => console.error(error),
            () => console.log('Weather is retrieved'));
  }
}
```

You want to write a test to check that when the `weather` property gets the values, the template is properly updated via bindings. You also want to test that when the value of the `searchInput` object changes, the observable emits data via its `valueChanges` property.

> ## The Elvis operator
>
> The template of `WeatherComponent` includes expressions with question marks, such as `weather?.place`. The question mark in this context is called the *Elvis operator*.
>
> The `weather` property is populated asynchronously, and if `weather` is `null` by the time the expression is evaluated, the `weather.place` expression would throw an error. To suppress null dereferencing, you use the Elvis operator to short-circuit further evaluation if `weather` is null. The Elvis operator offers an explicit notation to show which values could be null.

The test suite will contain one test to check that data bindings work as expected. `TestBed.createComponent(WeatherComponent);` will create a `ComponentFixture` that contains references to the `WeatherComponent` as well as the DOM object that represents this component. In listing 9.8, you use the `weather` property for bindings; you'll initialize this property with the object literal containing hardcoded values for `place`, `humidity`, and `temperature`.

After that, you'll force change-detection by invoking the `detectChanges()` method on the instance of `ComponentFixture`. You expect to see the values from `weather` in one `<h3>` and two `<li>` tags in the component's template. The code for this test is located in the weather.spec.ts file.

Listing 9.9   weather.spec.ts

```
import { TestBed} from '@angular/core/testing';
import { ReactiveFormsModule } from '@angular/forms';

import { WeatherComponent } from './weather';
import { WeatherService } from '../services/weather.service';

describe('WeatherComponent', () => {

  beforeEach(() => {
    TestBed.configureTestingModule({
      imports: [ ReactiveFormsModule ],
      declarations: [ WeatherComponent],
      providers: [{provide: WeatherService, useValue: {} }]
    })
  });

  it('should display the weather ', () => {
    let fixture = TestBed.createComponent(WeatherComponent);
    let element = fixture.nativeElement;
    let component = fixture.componentInstance;
    component.weather = {place: 'New York', humidity: 44, temperature: 57};
```

WeatherComponent expects WeatherService to be injected, and you replace the real service with an empty object.

Gets a reference to the component under test

Creates an instance of WeatherComponent, and gets a ComponentFixture back

Gets a reference to the HTML element rendered for this component

Initializes the component's weather property as if the data came from the server

Compares the text of the <h3> element with the expected value

```
fixture.detectChanges();              ⟵── Initiates change detection

expect(element.querySelector('h3').innerHTML).toBe('Current weather in
    ➡ New York:');
expect(element.querySelector('li:nth-of-
    type(1)').innerHTML).toBe('Temperature: 57F');   ⟵──
expect(element.querySelector('li:nth-of-
    type(2)').innerHTML).toBe('Humidity: 44%');
  });
});
```

Compares the text of the first and second <li> with the expected values. You use the CSS selector li:nth-of-type() to get the text of the <li> element by its position.

TIP Listing 9.9 uses an empty object to mock `WeatherService` because you don't plan to invoke any methods on it. You could define the mock service as `class MockWeatherService implements WeatherService` and provide implementations for the real methods, but they would return hardcoded values. When defining a mock service in real-world applications, it's advisable to create classes that implement the interfaces of the real services.

NOTE In chapter 7, you learned two approaches for creating forms in Angular. Although the template-driven approach requires little coding, using reactive forms makes them more testable without requiring the DOM object.

RUNNING TESTS IN THE HTML-BASED RUNNER

Let's run the test suite for the weather application in the HTML-based runner. Just run the live-server, and enter the URL http://localhost:8080/test.html in the browser. All the tests should pass, and the browser window should look like figure 9.4.

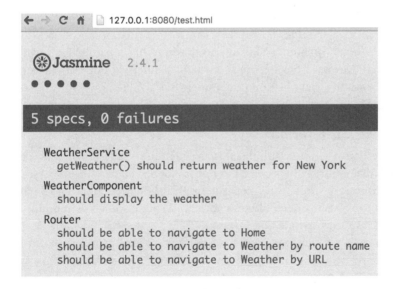

Figure 9.4   The test suite passed.

When you write tests, you want to see how they fail. Let's make one of the tests fail to see how it's reported. Change the temperature to 58 degrees on the line where you initialize the `weather` property:

```
component.weather = {place: 'New York', humidity: 44, temperature: 58};
```

The test still expects the UI to render the temperature as 57 degrees:

```
expect(element.querySelector('li:nth-of-type(1)').innerHTML)
    .toBe('Temperature: 57F');
```

The test output shown in figure 9.5 reports the failure of one of five tests.

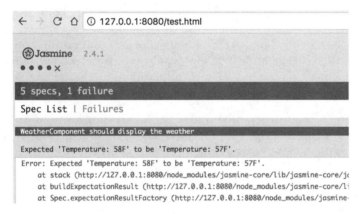

Figure 9.5 The test suite failed.

Manually running tests in the web browser isn't the best way to unit-test your code. You want a testing process that can be run as a script from a command line, so it can be integrated into the automated build process. Jasmine has a runner that can be used from a command prompt, but we prefer to use an independent test runner, Karma, that can work with a variety of unit-test frameworks. We'll show you how to use the Karma runner next.

9.4 Running tests with Karma

Karma (https://karma-runner.github.io) is a test runner that was originally created by the AngularJS team, but it's being used to test JavaScript code written with or without frameworks. Karma is built using Node.js, and although it doesn't run in a web browser, it can run tests to check whether your application will work in multiple browsers (you'll run tests for Chrome and Firefox).

For the Weather application, you'll install Karma and the plugins for Jasmine, Chrome, and Firefox, and save them in the `devDependencies` section of package.json:

```
npm install karma karma-jasmine karma-chrome-launcher karma-firefox-
    launcher --save-dev
```

To run Karma, configure the npm `test` command of the project as follows:

```
"scripts": {
  "test": "karma start karma.conf.js"
}
```

> **NOTE** The karma executable is a binary file located in the node_modules/ .bin directory.

You'll also create a small karma.conf.js configuration file to let Karma know about the project. This file is located in the root directory of the project and includes paths for Angular files as well as configuration options for the Karma runner.

Listing 9.10   karma.conf.js

Tests the application against the
Chrome and Firefox browsers

The unit tests are
written using Jasmine.

Runs the
tests once
and stops.
This option
is useful
when
Karma
runs as
part of an
automated
build.

Prints dots on the console to
indicate the tests' progress

Karma should know about files
from the Angular framework
(including the testing library).

```
module.exports = function (config) {
  config.set({
    browsers: ['Chrome', 'Firefox'],
    frameworks: ['jasmine'],
    reporters: ['dots'],
    singleRun: true,
    files: [
      // Paths loaded by Karma.
      'node_modules/typescript/lib/typescript.js',
      'node_modules/reflect-metadata/Reflect.js',
      'node_modules/systemjs/dist/system.src.js',
      'node_modules/zone.js/dist/zone.js',
      'node_modules/zone.js/dist/async-test.js',
      'node_modules/zone.js/dist/fake-async-test.js',
      'node_modules/zone.js/dist/long-stack-trace-zone.js',
      'node_modules/zone.js/dist/proxy.js',
      'node_modules/zone.js/dist/sync-test.js',
      'node_modules/zone.js/dist/jasmine-patch.js',

      // Paths loaded via module imports.
      {pattern: 'karma-systemjs.config.js', included: true,  watched: false},
      {pattern: 'karma-test-runner.js', included: true,  watched: false},
      {pattern: 'node_modules/@angular/**/
*.js', included: false, watched: false},
      {pattern: 'node_modules/@angular/**/
*.js.map', included: false, watched: false},
      {pattern: 'node_modules/rxjs/**/
*.js', included: false, watched: false},
      {pattern: 'node_modules/rxjs/**/
*.js.map', included: false, watched: false},
      {pattern: 'app/**/*.ts', included: false, watched: true}
    ],
```

Karma SystemJS
configuration. Identical to
the systemjs.config.js file
but additionally defines
baseURL: 'base'.

This script will run
the tests.

Files are loaded via module imports and can
contain either the test scripts or the application
code included in the import statements.

```
        proxies: {
          '/app/': '/base/app/'
        },
        plugins: [
          'karma-jasmine',
          'karma-chrome-launcher',
          'karma-firefox-launcher'
        ]
      })
    };
```

Plugins required for the run → `plugins: [`

← **Required for component assets fetched by Angular's compiler. Filenames that start with /app in the styleUrls and templateUrl properties (not used in the weather app) should be proxied via the Karma-generated /base/app path.**

Most of listing 9.10 lists the paths where required files are located. Karma generates a temporary HTML page that includes the files listed with `included: true`. Files listed with `included: false` will be dynamically loaded at runtime. All the Angular files, including the testing ones, are loaded dynamically by SystemJS.

You'll need to add one more file to the project: karma-test-runner.js. It's the script that actually runs the tests.

Listing 9.11   karma-test-runner.js

Finds all files with the spec.ts name extension

Lets the browser show full stack traces in case of errors

The default Jasmine timeout for the async function calls is 5 seconds, but this line changes it to 1 second.

```
Error.stackTraceLimit = Infinity;            ←

jasmine.DEFAULT_TIMEOUT_INTERVAL = 1000;     ←

__karma__.loaded = function () {};           ←

function resolveTestFiles() {
    return Object.keys(window.__karma__.files)
        .filter(function (path) { return /\.spec\.ts$/.test(path); })
        .map(function (moduleName) { return System.import(moduleName); });
}

Promise.all([
    System.import('@angular/core/testing'),
    System.import('@angular/platform-browser-dynamic/testing')
]).
    then(function (modules) {
        var testing = modules[0];
        var browser = modules[1];

        testing.TestBed.initTestEnvironment(
            browser.BrowserDynamicTestingModule,
            browser.platformBrowserDynamicTesting());
    }).
    then(function () { return Promise.all(resolveTestFiles()); })   ←
    .then(function () { __karma__.start(); },
        function (error) { __karma__.error(error.stack || error); });
```

← **Because the app code and specs are loaded asynchronously, don't run Karma on the loaded event. You'll call karma.start() later, once all the specs are loaded.**

Loads two Angular modules required for testing

← **After the modules are loaded, specifies the default Angular providers**

Loads the test specs

← **Initializes the test environment**

Runs the tests

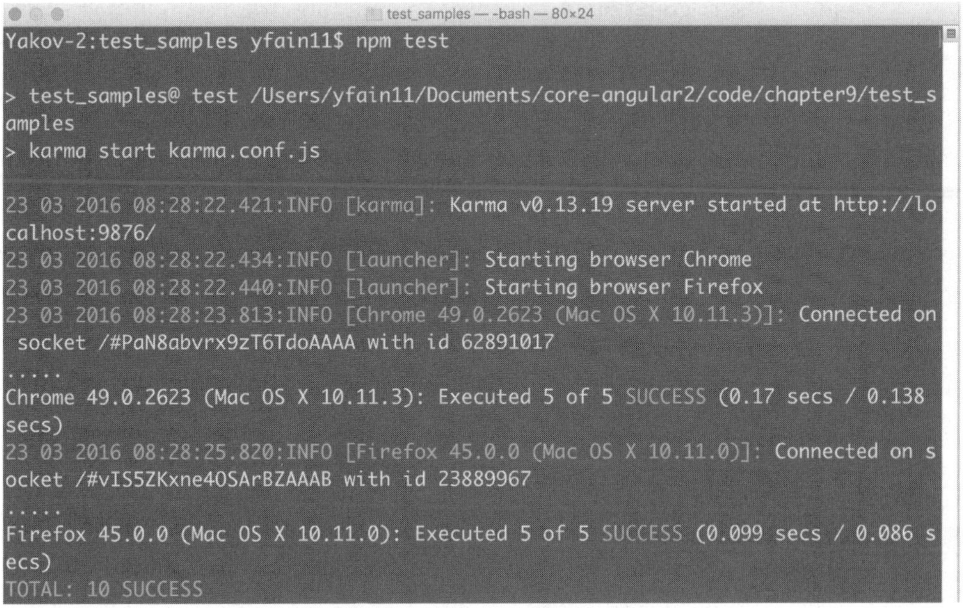

Figure 9.6 Testing the weather application with Karma

Now you're ready to run your tests using the command npm test from the command line. During the run, Karma will open and close each configured browser and print the test results, as shown in figure 9.6.

Developers tend to use the latest versions of the browser that has the best dev tools, which is Google Chrome. We've seen real-world projects in which a developer demos the application running perfectly in Chrome, and then users complain about an error in Safari. Make sure the development process uses Karma and tests the application against all browsers. Before giving your application to the QA team or showing it to your manager, make sure your Karma runner doesn't report any errors in all the required browsers.

Now that we've given you an overview of writing and running unit tests, let's implement tests for the online auction.

9.5   *Hands-on: unit-testing the online auction*

The goal of this exercise is to show you how to unit-test selected modules of the online auction application. In particular, you'll add unit tests for ApplicationComponent, StarsComponent, and ProductService. You'll run the tests using Jasmine's HTML-based runner and then Karma.

> **NOTE** We're going to use the auction application from chapter 8 as a starting point, so copy it to a separate directory and follow the instructions in this section. If you prefer to review the code instead of typing it, use the code that comes with chapter 9, and run the tests.

Install Jasmine, Karma, the type-definition files for Jasmine, and all Angular dependencies by running the following commands:

```
npm install jasmine-core karma karma-jasmine karma-chrome-launcher karma-
➥ firefox-launcher --save-dev

npm install @types/jasmine --save-dev
npm install
```

In the client directory, create a new auction-unit-tests.html file for loading Jasmine tests.

Listing 9.12 auction-unit-tests.html

```html
<!DOCTYPE html>
<html>
<head>
  <title>[TEST] Online Auction</title>

  <!-- TypeScript in-browser compiler -->
  <script src="node_modules/typescript/lib/typescript.js"></script>

  <!-- Polyfills -->
  <script src="node_modules/reflect-metadata/Reflect.js"></script>

  <!-- Jasmine -->
  <link rel="stylesheet" href="node_modules/jasmine-core/lib/jasmine-core/
  ➥ jasmine.css">
  <script src="node_modules/jasmine-core/lib/jasmine-core/jasmine.js">
  ➥ </script>
  <script src="node_modules/jasmine-core/lib/jasmine-core/jasmine-html.js">
  ➥ </script>
  <script src="node_modules/jasmine-core/lib/jasmine-core/boot.js"></script>

  <!-- Zone.js -->
  <script src="node_modules/zone.js/dist/zone.js"></script>
  <script src="node_modules/zone.js/dist/proxy.js"></script>
  <script src="node_modules/zone.js/dist/sync-test.js"></script>
  <script src="node_modules/zone.js/dist/jasmine-patch.js"></script>
  <script src="node_modules/zone.js/dist/async-test.js"></script>
  <script src="node_modules/zone.js/dist/fake-async-test.js"></script>
  <script src="node_modules/zone.js/dist/long-stack-trace-zone.js"></script>

  <!-- SystemJS -->
  <script src="node_modules/systemjs/dist/system.src.js"></script>
  <script src="systemjs.config.js"></script>
</head>
```

```html
<body>
<script>
  var SPEC_MODULES = [
    'app/components/application/application.spec',
    'app/components/stars/stars.spec',
    'app/services/product-service.spec'
  ];

  Promise.all([
    System.import('@angular/core/testing'),
    System.import('@angular/platform-browser-dynamic/testing')
  ])
        .then(function (modules) {
          var testing = modules[0];
          var browser = modules[1];

          testing.TestBed.initTestEnvironment(
                  browser.BrowserDynamicTestingModule,
                  browser.platformBrowserDynamicTesting());

          // Load all the spec files.
          return Promise.all(SPEC_MODULES.map(function (module) {
            return System.import(module);
          }));
        })
        .then(window.onload)
        .catch(console.error.bind(console));
</script>
</body>
</html>
```

The content of this file is similar to test.html from the weather application. The only difference is that you're loading different spec files here: application.spec, stars.spec, and product-service.spec.

9.5.1 *Testing ApplicationComponent*

Create an application.spec.ts file in the client/app/components/application directory to test that ApplicationComponent is successfully instantiated. This isn't an overly useful test, but it can serve as an illustration of testing whether an instance of a TypeScript class (not even one related to Angular) was successfully created.

> **Listing 9.13 application.spec.ts**

```typescript
import ApplicationComponent from './application';

describe('ApplicationComponent', () => {
  it('is successfully instantiated', () => {
    const app = new ApplicationComponent();
    expect(app instanceof ApplicationComponent).toEqual(true);
  });
});
```

9.5.2 *Testing ProductService*

To test `ProductService`, create a product-service.spec.ts file in the app/services directory. In this spec, you'll test the HTTP service, and although the `it()` function is rather small, there will be lots of preparation before the test runs.

Listing 9.14 product-service.spec.ts

```
import {async, getTestBed, TestBed, inject, Injector} from '@angular/core/
➥ testing';
import {Response, ResponseOptions, HttpModule, XHRBackend} from '@angular/
➥ http';
import {MockBackend, MockConnection} from '@angular/http/testing';          ◁────┐
import {ProductService} from './product-service';

describe('ProductService', () => {
  let mockBackend: MockBackend;
  let service: ProductService;

  let injector: Injector;

  beforeEach(() => {
    TestBed.configureTestingModule({
      imports: [HttpModule],
      providers: [
        { provide: XHRBackend, useClass: MockBackend },                     ◁────┐
        ProductService
      ]
    });
    injector = getTestBed();
  });

  beforeEach(inject([XHRBackend, ProductService], (_mockBackend,
  ➥ _service) => {
    mockBackend = _mockBackend;
    service = _service;
  }));

  it('getProductById() should return Product with ID=1', async(() => {
    let mockProduct = {id: 1};                                              ◁────┐
    mockBackend.connections.subscribe((connection: MockConnection) => {    ◁──┐
      let responseOpts = new ResponseOptions({body:
      ➥ JSON.stringify(mockProduct) });
      connection.mockRespond(new Response(responseOpts));
    });

    service.getProductById(1).subscribe(p => {
      expect(p.id).toBe(1);                                                ◁──
    });
  }));
});
```

> **MockBackend serves as an implementation of the HTTP service. MockConnection represents the connection.**

> **Keeps references to the injected services so the test can use them**

> **Overrides the default implementation of Http by explicitly instantiating this object and passing it the MockBackend as an argument. You don't change the BaseRequestOption, but it's a required argument.**

> **Prepares the fake data to be returned by the MockBackend**

> **Configures the mock back end**

> **Invoking getProductById(I) on the service should return the object with ID equal to I.**

First you create an object literal, mockProduct = {id: 1}, which is used to emulate the data that could come from the server as an HTTP response. You want mockBackend to mock and return an object with hardcoded values for each HTTP request. You could have created an instance of Product with more properties, but for this simple test, having just the ID suffices.

9.5.3 Testing StarsComponent

For the last test, we picked StarsComponent because it demonstrates how you can test a component's properties and the event emitter. StarsComponent loads its HTML from a file that requires special processing during testing. Angular loads the files specified in templateUrl asynchronously and performs just-in-time compilation on them. You'll need to do the same in the test spec by invoking TestBed.compileComponents(). This step is required for any component that uses the templateUrl property. In the client/ app/components/stars directory, create a stars.spec.ts file with the following content.

Listing 9.15 stars.spec.ts

```
import { TestBed, async, fakeAsync, inject } from '@angular/core/testing';
import StarsComponent from './stars';

describe('StarsComponent', () => {
  beforeEach(() => {
    TestBed.configureTestingModule({
      declarations: [ StarsComponent ]
    });
  });

  beforeEach(async(() => {
    TestBed.compileComponents();
  }));

  it('is successfully injected', () => {
    let component = TestBed.createComponent(StarsComponent).componentInstance;
    expect(component instanceof StarsComponent).toEqual(true);
  });

  it('readonly property is true by default', () => {
    let component = TestBed.createComponent(StarsComponent).componentInstance;
    expect(component.readonly).toEqual(true);
  });

  it('all stars are empty', () => {
    let fixture = TestBed.createComponent(StarsComponent);
    let element = fixture.nativeElement;
    let cmp = fixture.componentInstance;
    cmp.rating = 0;
```

Compiles the content of the file used in templateUrl

Checks that the instance was injected (compare with listing 9.13)

Creates a fixture, and gets the reference to the component's instance

Checks that the readonly input property of StarsComponent is true by default. The user should be able to click stars only in Leave Review mode.

Checks that all empty stars are rendered if the rating is equal to 0

```
      fixture.detectChanges();

      let selector = '.glyphicon-star-empty';
      expect(element.querySelectorAll(selector).length).toBe(5);
    });

    it('all stars are filled', () => {
      let fixture = TestBed.createComponent(StarsComponent);
      let element = fixture.nativeElement;
      let cmp = fixture.componentInstance;
      cmp.rating = 5;

      fixture.detectChanges();

      let selector = '.glyphicon-star:not(.glyphicon-star-empty)';
      expect(element.querySelectorAll(selector).length).toBe(5);
    });

    it('emits rating change event when readonly is false', async(() => {
      let component = TestBed.createComponent(StarsComponent).componentInstance;
      component.ratingChange.subscribe(r => {
        expect(r).toBe(3);
      });
      component.readonly = false;
      component.fillStarsWithColor(2);
    }));
  });
```

> **Checks that all filled stars are rendered if the rating is equal to 5**

> **Checks that EventEmitter works**

`TestBed` creates a new instance of `StarsComponent` (you don't use the injected one here) and gives you a fixture with references to the component and the native element. To test that all the stars are empty, you assign 0 to the input `rating` property on the component instance. The `rating` property is actually a setter on `StarsComponent` that modifies both `rating` and the `stars` array:

```
set rating(value: number) {
  this._rating = value || 0;
  this.stars = Array(this.maxStars).fill(true, 0, this.rating);
}
```

Then you start the change-detection cycle, which forces the *ngFor loop to re-render the star images in the template of the `StarsComponent`:

```
<p>
  <span *ngFor="let star of stars; let i = index"
        class="starrating glyphicon glyphicon-star"
        [class.glyphicon-star-empty]="!star"
        (click)="fillStarsWithColor(i)">
  </span>
  <span *ngIf="rating">{{rating | number:'.0-2'}} stars</span>
</p>
```

The CSS for the filled stars is `starrating glyphicon glyphicon-star`. The empty stars have an additional CSS class, `glyphicon-star-empty`. The test `'all stars are empty'` uses the `glyphicon-star-empty` selector and expects that there are exactly five native elements with this class.

The test `'all stars are filled'` assigns the rating 5. It uses the CSS selector `.glyphicon-star:not(.glyphicon-star-empty)`, which uses the `not` operator to ensure that the stars aren't empty.

The test `'emits rating change event when readonly is false'` uses the injected component. There you subscribe to the `ratingChange` event, expecting the values of the rating to be 3. When a user wants to change the rating, they click the third star (while leaving a review), which invokes the `fillStarsWithColor` method on the component, passing 3 as the `index` argument:

```
fillStarsWithColor(index) {
  if (!this.readonly) {
    this.rating = index + 1; // to prevent zero rating
    this.ratingChange.emit(this.rating);
  }
}
```

Because there's no user to do the clicking during the unit testing, you invoke this method programmatically:

```
component.readonly = false;
 component.fillStarsWithColor(2);
```

If you want to see how this test fails, change the argument of `fillStarsWithColor()` to any number other than 2.

Order of operations in testing events

The code of the test `'emits rating change event when readonly is false'` may make you wonder why you write the preceding two lines at the end of the test after `subscribe()` is invoked. The subscription to `Observable` is lazy, and it'll receive the next element only after the `fillStarsWithColor(2)` method is invoked, emitting the event. If you move the `subscribe()` method down, the event will be emitted before the subscriber is created, and the test will fail on timeout because the `done()` method will never be invoked.

9.5.4 *Running the tests*

To run the tests, first recompile the server's code by running `npm run tsc`. Then start the auction application by entering `npm start` on the console. It'll start the Node server on port 8000. Enter `http://localhost:8000/auction-unit-tests.html` in the browser, and the tests should run, producing the output shown in figure 9.7.

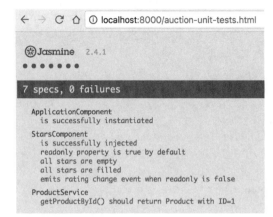

Figure 9.7   Testing the online auction with the HTML-based runner

To run the same tests using Karma, copy the files karma.conf and karma-test-runner from chapter 9's auction directory into the root directory of your project. (These files were explained in section 9.4.) Run `npm test`, and you should see the output shown in figure 9.8.

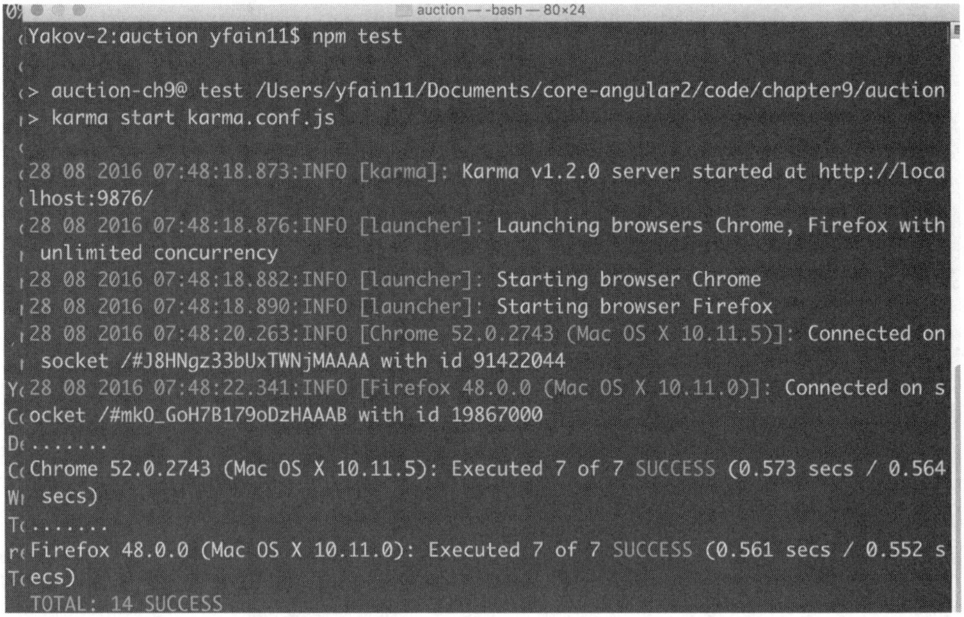

```
Yakov-2:auction yfain11$ npm test

> auction-ch9@ test /Users/yfain11/Documents/core-angular2/code/chapter9/auction
> karma start karma.conf.js

28 08 2016 07:48:18.873:INFO [karma]: Karma v1.2.0 server started at http://loca
lhost:9876/
28 08 2016 07:48:18.876:INFO [launcher]: Launching browsers Chrome, Firefox with
 unlimited concurrency
28 08 2016 07:48:18.882:INFO [launcher]: Starting browser Chrome
28 08 2016 07:48:18.890:INFO [launcher]: Starting browser Firefox
28 08 2016 07:48:20.263:INFO [Chrome 52.0.2743 (Mac OS X 10.11.5)]: Connected on
 socket /#J8HNgz33bUxTWNjMAAAA with id 91422044
28 08 2016 07:48:22.341:INFO [Firefox 48.0.0 (Mac OS X 10.11.0)]: Connected on s
ocket /#mkO_GoH7B179oDzHAAAB with id 19867000
.......
Chrome 52.0.2743 (Mac OS X 10.11.5): Executed 7 of 7 SUCCESS (0.573 secs / 0.564
 secs)
.......
Firefox 48.0.0 (Mac OS X 10.11.0): Executed 7 of 7 SUCCESS (0.561 secs / 0.552 s
ecs)
TOTAL: 14 SUCCESS
```

Figure 9.8   Testing the auction with Karma

9.6 *Summary*

We can't overstate the importance of running unit tests in your Angular applications. Unit tests let you ensure that each component or service of your application works as expected. In this chapter, we've demonstrated how to write unit tests using the Jasmine framework and how to run them with either Jasmine or Karma. These are the main takeaways for this chapter:

- A component or a service is a good candidate for writing a test suite.
- Although you can keep all test files separate from your application, it's more convenient to keep them next to the components they test.
- Unit tests run quickly, and most application business logic should be tested with unit tests.
- While you're writing tests, make them fail to see that their failure report is easy to understand.
- If you decide to implement end-to-end testing, don't rerun unit tests during this process.
- Running unit tests should be part of your automated build process. We'll show you how to do that in chapter 10.

Bundling and deploying applications with Webpack

This chapter covers

- Bundling apps for deployment using Webpack
- Configuring Webpack for bundling Angular apps in dev and prod
- Integrating the Karma test runner into the automated build process
- Creating a prod build for the online auction
- Automating project generation and bundling with Anguar CLI

Over the course of this book, you've written and deployed multiple versions of the online auction and lots of smaller applications. Web servers properly served your applications to the user. So why not just copy all the application files to the production server, run `npm install`, and be done with deployment?

No matter which programming language or framework you use, you'll want to achieve two goals:

- The deployed web application should be small in size (so it can load faster).
- The browser should make a minimal number of requests to the server on startup (so it can load faster).

When a browser makes requests to the server, it gets HTML documents, which may include additional files like CSS, images, videos, and so on. Let's take the online auction application as an example. On startup, it makes hundreds of requests to the server just to load Angular with its dependencies and the TypeScript compiler, which weigh 5.5 MB combined. Add to this the code you wrote, which is a couple of dozen HTML, TypeScript, and CSS files, let alone images! It's a lot of code to download, and way too many server requests for such a small application. Look at figure 10.1, which shows the content of the Network tab in Chrome Developer Tools after the auction was loaded into our browser: there are lots of network requests, and the app size is huge.

Real-world applications consist of hundreds or even thousands of files, and you want to minimize, optimize, and bundle them together during deployment. In addition, for production, you can precompile the code into JavaScript, so you don't need to load the 3 MB TypeScript compiler in the browser.

Several popular tools are used to deploy JavaScript web applications. All of them run using Node and are available as npm packages. These tools fit into two main categories:

- Task runners
- Module loaders and bundlers

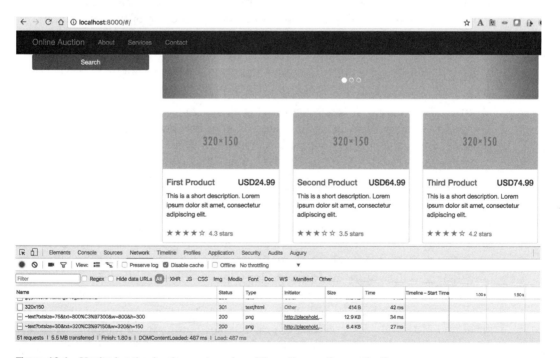

Figure 10.1 Monitoring the development version of the online auction application

Grunt (http://gruntjs.com) and Gulp (http://gulpjs.com) are widely used general-purpose task runners. They know nothing about JavaScript applications, but they allow you to configure and run the tasks required for deploying the applications. Grunt and Gulp aren't easy to maintain for build processes, because their configuration files are several hundred lines long.

In this book, you used npm scripts for running tasks, and a task is a script or a binary file that can be executed from a command line. Configuring npm scripts is simpler than using Grunt and Gulp, and you'll continue using them in this chapter. If the complexity of your project increases and the number of npm scripts becomes unmanageable, consider using Grunt or Gulp to run builds.

So far you've used SystemJS to load modules. Browserify (http://browserify.org), Webpack (http://webpack.github.io), Broccoli (www.npmjs.com/package/broccoli-system-builder), and Rollup (http://rollupjs.org) are all popular bundlers. Each of them can create code bundles to be consumed by the browsers. The simplest is Webpack, which allows you to convert and combine all your application assets into bundles with minimal configuration. A concise comparison of various bundlers is available on the Webpack site: http://mng.bz/136m.

The Webpack bundler was created specifically for web applications running in a browser, and many typical tasks required for preparing web application builds are supported out of the box with minimal configuration and without the need to install additional plugins. This chapter starts by introducing Webpack, and then you'll prepare two separate builds (dev and prod) for the online auction. Finally, you'll run an optimized version of the online auction and compare the size of the application with what's shown in figure 10.1.

You won't use SystemJS in this chapter—Webpack will invoke the TypeScript compiler while bundling the apps. The compilation will be controlled by a special loader that uses tsc internally to transpile TypeScript into JavaScript.

NOTE The Angular team has created Angular CLI (https://github.com/angular/angular-cli), which is a command-line interface for automating an application's creation, testing, and deployment. Angular CLI uses the Webpack bundler internally. We'll introduce Angular CLI later in this chapter.

10.1 Getting to know Webpack

While preparing for a trip, you may pack dozens of items into a couple of suitcases. Savvy travelers use special vacuum-seal bags that allow them to squeeze even more clothes into the same suitcase. Webpack is an equivalent tool. It's a module loader and a bundler that lets you group your application files into bundles; you can also optimize their sizes to fit more into the same bundle.

For example, you can prepare two bundles for deployment: all your application files are merged into one bundle, and all required third-party frameworks and libraries are in another. With Webpack, you can prepare separate bundles for development and production deployment, as shown in figure 10.2. In dev mode, you'll create the bundles in memory, whereas in production mode Webpack will generate actual files on disk.

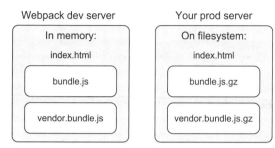

Figure 10.2   Dev and prod deployments

It's convenient to write an application as a set of small modules where one file is one module, but for deployment you'll need a tool to pack all of these files into a small number of bundles. This tool should know how to build the module dependencies tree, sparing you from manually maintaining the order of the loaded modules. Webpack is such a tool, and in the Webpack philosophy, everything can be a module, including CSS, images, and HTML.

The process of deployment with Webpack consists of two major steps:

1 Build the bundles (this step can include code optimization).
2 Copy the bundles to the desired server.

Webpack is distributed as an npm package, and, like all tools, you can install it either globally or locally. Let's start by installing Webpack globally:

```
npm install webpack -g
```

> **NOTE**   This chapter uses Webpack 2.1.0, which at the time of this writing is in beta. To install it globally, we used the command `npm i webpack@2.1.0-beta.25 -g`.

A bit later, you'll install Webpack locally by adding it into the `devDependencies` section of the package.json file. But installing it globally will let you quickly see the process of turning an application into a bundle.

> **TIP**   A curated list of Webpack resources (documentation, videos, libraries, and so on) is available on GitHub. Take a look at awesome-webpack: https://github.com/d3viant0ne/awesome-webpack.

10.1.1 *Hello World with Webpack*

Let's get familiar with Webpack via a very basic Hello World example consisting of two files: index.html and main.js. Here's the index.html file.

Listing 10.1   index.html

```
<!DOCTYPE html>
<html>
<body>
  <script src="main.js"></script>
</body>
</html>
```

The main.js file is even shorter.

Listing 10.2   main.js

```
document.write('Hello World!');
```

Open a command-prompt window in the directory where these file are located, and run the following command:

```
webpack main.js bundle.js
```

The main.js file is a source file, and bundle.js is the output file in the same directory. We usually include the word *bundle* in the output filename. Figure 10.3 shows the result of running the preceding command.

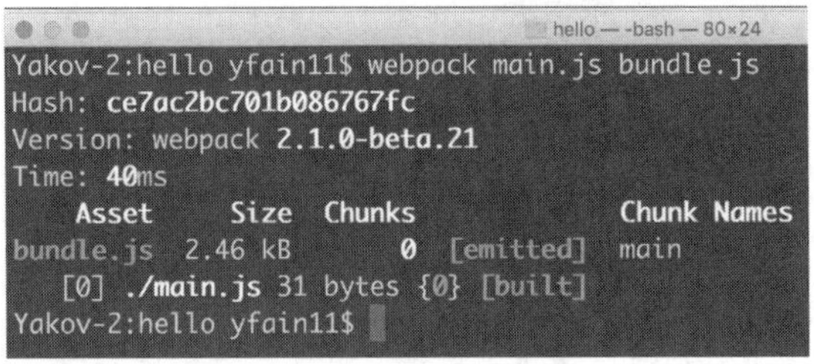

Figure 10.3   Creating the first bundle

Note that the size of the generated bundle.js is larger than that of main.js because Webpack didn't just copy one file into another but added other code required by this bundler. Creating a bundle from a single file isn't overly useful, because it increases the file size; but in a multi-file application, bundling files together makes sense. You'll see this as you read this chapter.

Now you need to modify the <script> tag in the HTML file to include bundle.js instead of main.js. This tiny application will render the same "Hello World!" message as the original.

Webpack allows you to specify various options on the command line, but it's better to configure the Webpack bundling process in webpack.config.js, which is a JavaScript file. A simple configuration file is shown here.

Listing 10.3   webpack.config.js

```
const path = require('path');

module.exports = {
  entry: "./main",
  output: {
    path: './dist',
    filename: 'bundle.js'
  }
};
```

To create a bundle, Webpack needs to know the main module (the *entry point*) of your application, which may have dependencies on other modules or third-party libraries (other entry points). By default, Webpack adds the .js extension to the name of the entry point specified in the `entry` property. Webpack loads the entry-point module and builds a memory tree of all dependent modules. By reading the configuration file in listing 10.3, Webpack will know that the application entry is located in the ./main.js file and that the resulting bundle.js file has to be saved in the ./dist directory, which is a common name for the distribution bundles.

> **TIP** Storing the output files in a separate directory will allow you to configure your version-control system to exclude the generated files. If you use a Git version-control system, add the dist directory to the .gitignore file.

You could specify more than one entry point by providing an array as a value for the `entry` property:

```
entry: ["./other-module", "./main"]
```

In this case, each of these modules will be loaded on startup.

> **NOTE** To create multiple bundles, you need to specify the values of the `entry` property not as strings, but as objects. You'll see such an example later in this chapter, when you instruct Webpack to put the Angular code in one bundle and the application code in another.

If the Webpack configuration file is present in the current directory, you don't need to provide any command-line parameters; you can run the `webpack` command to create your bundles. The other choice is to run Webpack in watch mode using the `--watch` or `-w` command-line option, so whenever you make a change to your application files, Webpack will automatically rebuild the bundle:

```
webpack --watch
```

You can also instruct Webpack to run in watch mode by adding the following entry to webpack.config.js:

```
watch: true
```

USING WEBPACK-DEV-SERVER

In previous chapters, you used live-server to serve your applications, but Webpack comes with its own webpack-dev-server that has to be installed separately. Usually you add Webpack to the existing npm project and install both Webpack and its development server locally by running the following command:

```
npm install webpack webpack-dev-server --save-dev
```

This command will install all required files in the node_modules subdirectory and will add webpack and webpack-dev-server to the `devDependencies` section of package.json.

The next version of Hello World is located in the directory hello-world-devserver and includes the index.html file shown next.

Listing 10.4   hello-world-devserver/index.html

```
<!DOCTYPE html>
<html>
<body>
  <script src="/bundle.js"></script>
</body>
</html>
```

The main.js JavaScript file remains the same:

```
document.write('Hello World!');
```

The package.json file in the hello-world-devserver project looks like this.

Listing 10.5   hello-world-devserver/package.json

```
{
  "name": "first-project",
  "version": "1.0.0",
  "description": "",
  "main": "main.js",
  "scripts": {
    "start": "webpack-dev-server"
  },
  "keywords": [],
  "author": "",
  "license": "ISC",
  "devDependencies": {
    "webpack": "^2.1.0-beta.25",
    "webpack-dev-server": "^2.1.0-beta.0"
  }
}
```

Note that you've configured the npm `start` command for running the local webpack-dev-server.

> **NOTE**   When you serve your application with webpack-dev-server, it'll run on the default port 8080 and will generate the bundles in memory without saving them in a file. Then webpack-dev-server will recompile and serve the new versions of the bundles every time you modify the code.

You can add the configuration section of webpack-dev-server in the `devServer` section of the webpack.config.js file. There you can put any options that webpack-dev-server allows on the command line (see the Webpack product documentation at http://mng.bz/gn4r). This is how you could specify that the files should be served from the current directory:

```
devServer: {
  contentBase: '.'
}
```

The complete configuration file for the hello-world-devserver project is shown here and can be reused by both the `webpack` and `webpack-dev-server` commands.

Listing 10.6 hello-world-devserver/webpack.config.js

```
const path = require('path');

module.exports = {
  entry: {
    'main': './main.js'
  },
  output: {
    path: './dist',
    filename: 'bundle.js'
  },
  watch: true,
  devServer: {
    contentBase: '.'
  }
};
```

In listing 10.6, two of the options are needed only if you're planning to run the webpack command in watch mode and generate output files on disk:

- The Node module `path` resolves relative paths in your project (in this case, it specifies the ./dist directory).
- `watch: true` starts Webpack in watch mode.

If you run the `webpack-dev-server` command, the preceding two options aren't used. `webpack-dev-server` always runs in watch mode, doesn't output files on disk, and builds bundles in memory. The `contentBase` property lets `webpack-dev-server` know where your index.html file is located.

Let's try to run the Hello World application by serving the application with webpack-dev-server. In the command window, run npm `start` to start webpack-dev-server. On the console, webpack-dev-server will log the output, which starts with the URL you can use with the browser, which by default is http://localhost:8080.

Open your browser to this URL, and you'll see a window that displays the message "Hello World". Modify the text of the message in main.js: Webpack will automatically rebuild the bundle, and the server will reload the fresh content.

RESOLVING FILENAMES

This is all good, but you've been writing code in TypeScript, which means you need to let Webpack know that your modules can be located not only in .js files, but in .ts files as well. In the webpack.config.js file in listing 10.6, you specified the filename with the extension: main.js. But you can specify just the filenames without any extensions as long webpack.config.js has the `resolve` section. The following code snippet shows how you can let Webpack know that your modules can be located in files with extension .js or .ts:

```
resolve: {
  extensions: ['.js', '.ts']
}
```

The TypeScript files also have to be preprocessed (transpiled). You need to tell Webpack to transpile your application's .ts files into .js files before creating bundles; you'll see how to do that in the next section.

Usually, build-automation tools provide you with a way to specify additional tasks that need to be performed during the build process. Webpack offers *loaders* and *plugins* that allow you to customize builds.

10.1.2 *How to use loaders*

Loaders are transformers that take a source file as input and produce another file as output (in memory or on disk), one at a time. A loader is a small JavaScript module with an exported function that performs a certain transformation. For example, `json-loader` takes an input file and parses it as JSON. `base64-loader` converts its input into a base64-encoded string. Loaders play a role similar to *tasks* in other build tools. Some loaders are included with Webpack so you don't need to install them separately; others can be installed from public repositories. Check the list of loaders in the Webpack docs on GitHub (http://mng.bz/U0Yv) to see how to install and use the loaders you need.

In essence, a loader is a function written in Node-compatible JavaScript. To use a loader that's not included with the Webpack distribution, you'll need to install it using npm and include it in your project's package.json file. You can either manually add the required loader to the `devDependencies` section of package.json or run the `npm install` command with the `--save-dev` option. In the case of ts-loader, the command would look like this:

```
npm install ts-loader --save-dev
```

Loaders are listed in the webpack.config.js file in the `module` section. For example, you can add the ts-loader as follows:

```
module: {
  loaders: [
    {
```

```
      test: /\.ts$/,
      exclude: /node_modules/,
      loader: 'ts-loader'
    },
  ]
}
```

This configuration tells Webpack to check (test) each filename and, if it matches the regular expression \.ts$, to preprocess it with ts-loader. In the syntax of regular expressions, the dollar sign at the end indicates that you're interested only in files having names that end with .ts. Because you don't want to include Angular's .ts files in the bundle, you exclude the node_modules directory. You can either reference loaders by their full name (such as ts-loader), or by their shorthand name, omitting the -loader suffix (for example, ts). If you use relative paths in your templates (for example, template: "./home.html"), you need to use angular2-template-loader.

> **NOTE** The SystemJS loader isn't used in any of the projects presented in this chapter. Webpack loads and transforms all project files using one or more loaders configured in webpack.config.js based on the file type.

USING LOADERS FOR HTML AND CSS FILES

In the previous chapters, Angular components that stored HTML and CSS in separate files were specified in the @Component annotation as templateUrl and styleUrls, respectively. Here's an example:

```
@Component({
  selector: 'my-home',
  styleUrls: ['app/components/home.css')],
  templateUrl: 'app/components/home.html'
})
```

We usually keep the HTML and CSS files in the same directory where the component code is located. Can you specify the path relative to the current directory?

Webpack allows you to do this:

```
@Component({
  selector: 'my-home',
  styles: [home.css'],
  templateUrl: 'home.html'
})
```

While creating bundles, Webpack automatically adds the require() statements for loading CSS and HTML files, replacing the preceding code with the following:

```
@Component({
  selector: 'my-home',
  styles: [require('./home.css')],
  templateUrl: require('./home.html')
})
```

Then Webpack checks every `require()` statement and replaces it with the content of the required file, applying the loaders specified for the respective file types. The `require()` statement used here isn't the one from CommonJS: it's the internal Webpack function that makes Webpack aware that these files are dependencies. Webpack's `require()` not only loads the files, but also can reload them when modified (if you run it in watch mode or use webpack-dev-server).

> ### Relative paths in templates with SystemJS
>
> It's great that Webpack supports relative paths. But what if you want to be able to load the same app with either SystemJS or Webpack?
>
> By default, in Angular you have to use the full path to external files, starting from the app root directory. This would require code changes if you decided to move the component into a different directory.
>
> But if you use SystemJS and keep the component's code and its HTML and CSS files in the same directory, you can use a special `moduleId` property. If you assign to this property a special `__moduleName` binding, SystemJS will load files relative to the current module without the need to specify the full path:
>
> ```
> declare var __moduleName: string;
> @Component({
>   selector: 'my-home',
>   moduleId:__moduleName,
>   templateUrl: './home.html',
>   styleUrls: ['./home.css']
> })
> ```
>
> You can read more about relative paths in the Angular documentation in the "Component-Relative Paths" section at http://mng.bz/47w0.

In dev mode, for HTML processing, you'll use `raw-loader`, which transforms .html files into strings. To install this loader and save it in the `devDependencies` section of package.json, run the following command:

```
npm install raw-loader --save-dev
```

In prod, you'll use `html-loader`, which removes extra spaces, newline characters, and comments from HTML files:

```
npm install html-loader --save-dev
```

For CSS processing, you use the loaders `css-loader` and `style-loader`; during the building process, all related CSS files will be inlined. `css-loader` parses CSS files and minifies the styles. `style-loader` inserts CSS as a `<style>` tag on the page; it does so dynamically in the runtime. To install these loaders and save them in the devDependencies section of package.json, run the following command:

```
npm install css-loader style-loader --save-dev
```

You can chain loaders using an exclamation point as a piping symbol. The following fragment is from a webpack-config.js file that includes an array of loaders. When loaders are specified as an array, they're executed from the bottom to the top (so the ts loader will be executed first in this example). This extract is from a sample project in the next section, where CSS files are located in two folders (src and node_modules):

**Transforms the content of
each .html file into a string**

**Excludes CSS files located in
the node_modules directory**

```
loaders: [
  {test: /\.css$/,  loader: 'to-string!css', exclude: /node_modules/},
  {test: /\.css$/,  loader: 'style!css', exclude: /src/},
  {test: /\.html$/, loader: 'raw'},
  {test: /\.ts$/,   loader: 'ts'}
]
```

**Adds <style> tags
for third-party CSS
files located in
node_modules**

**Transpiles each .ts
file using ts-loader**

First you exclude the CSS files located in the node_modules directory, so this transformation will apply only to application components. You chain the to-string and css loaders here. The css loader is executed first, turning the CSS into a JavaScript module, and then its output is piped to the to-string loader to extract the string from the generated JavaScript. The resulting string is inlined into the corresponding components in the @Component annotation, in place of require(), so Angular can apply the proper ViewEncapsulation strategy.

Then you want Webpack to inline the third-party CSS files located in node_modules (not in src). css-loader reads the CSS, generates a JavaScript module, and passes it to style-loader, which generates <style> tags with the loaded CSS and inserts them into the <head> section of the HTML document. Finally, you turn the HTML files into strings and transpile the TypeScript code.

TIP In Angular, you want the CSS to be encapsulated in the components to gain the benefits of ViewEncapsulation, as explained in chapter 6. That's why you inline CSS into the JavaScript code. But there's a way to build a separate bundle that contains just the CSS by using the ExtractTextPlugin plugin. If you use CSS preprocessors, install and use the sass-loader or less-loader.

WHAT PRELOADERS AND POSTLOADERS ARE FOR

Sometimes you may want to perform additional file processing even before the loaders start their transformations. For example, you may want to run your TypeScript files through a TSLint tool to check the code for readability, maintainability, and functional errors. For that, you need to add the `preLoaders` section in the Webpack configuration file:

```
preLoaders: [
  {
    test: /\.ts$/,
    exclude: /node_modules/,
    loader: "tslint"
  }
]
```

Preloaders always run before loaders; and if they run into any errors, those are reported on the command line. You can also configure some postprocessing by adding a `postLoaders` section to webpack.config.js.

10.1.3   *How to use plugins*

If Webpack loaders transform files one at a time, plugins have access to all files, and they can process them before or after the loaders kick in. For example, the Commons-ChunkPlugin plugin allows you to create a separate bundle for common modules required by various scripts in your application. The CopyWebpackPlugin plugin can copy either individual files or entire directories to the build directory. The UglifyJS-Plugin plugin performs code minification of all transpiled files.

Say you want to split your application code into two bundles, `main` and `admin`, and each of these modules uses the Angular framework. If you just specify two entry points (`main` and `admin`), each bundle will include the application code as well as its own copy of Angular. To prevent this from happening, you can process the code with the CommonsChunkPlugin. With this plugin, Webpack won't include any of the Angular code in the `main` and `admin` bundles; it will create a separate shareable bundle with the Angular code only. This will lower the total size of your application because it includes only one copy of Angular shared between two application modules. In this case, the HTML file should include the vendor bundle first, followed by the application bundle.

UglifyJSPlugin is a wrapper for the UglifyJS minifier, which takes the JavaScript code and performs various optimizations. For example, it compresses the code by joining consecutive `var` statements, removes unused variables and unreachable code, and optimizes `if` statements. Its mangler tool renames local variables to single letters. For a full description of UglifyJS, visit its GitHub page (https://github.com/mishoo/UglifyJS). You'll use these and other plugins in the following sections.

10.2   *Creating a basic Webpack configuration for Angular*

Now that we've covered the Webpack basics, let's see how to bundle a simple Angular application written in TypeScript. We've created a small application that consists of Home and About components and doesn't use external templates or CSS files. This project is located in the basic-webpack-starter directory, and its structure is shown in figure 10.4.

The main.ts script bootstraps the AppModule and MyApp components, which configure the router and have two links for navigating to either HomeComponent or AboutComponent. Each of these components displays a simple message—the actual functionality is irrelevant in the context of this chapter. You'll focus on creating two bundles: one for Angular and its dependencies, and the other for the application code.

The vendor.ts file is small—it just uses the import statements required by Angular. We did this to create a situation where there are two entry points (main.ts and vendor.ts) that contain common Angular code, which you'll put into a separate bundle.

Figure 10.4   The basic-webpack-starter project

Listing 10.7   basic-webpack-starter/vendor.ts

```
import 'zone.js/dist/zone';
import 'reflect-metadata/Reflect.js';
import '@angular/http';
import '@angular/router';
import '@angular/core';
import '@angular/common';
```

Because these import statements can also be used in main.ts, you'll use the Commons-ChunkPlugin to avoid including Angular code in both bundles. Instead, you'll build a separate Angular bundle that's shared by the main entry point and any other entry point if you decide to split the application code into smaller chunks.

> **NOTE** The vendor.ts file should import all the modules that you want included in the common bundle and removed from the application code. Webpack will inline into the common bundle all the code required for the imported modules.

The content of the webpack.config.js configuration file is shown here.

Listing 10.8   basic-webpack-starter/webpack.config.js

You use require to bring the path modules in to resolve the paths to files. Then you require two plugins: CommonsChunkPlugin and copy-webpack-plugin.

```
const path               = require('path');
const CommonsChunkPlugin = require('webpack/lib/optimize/
➥ CommonsChunkPlugin');
const CopyWebpackPlugin  = require('copy-webpack-plugin');

module.exports = {
  entry: {
    'main'  : './src/main.ts',
```

The value for the entry property is specified as an object, which tells Webpack to build two bundles: one for the main.ts entry and another for vendor.ts.

```
    'vendor': './src/vendor.ts'
  },
  output: {
    path    : './dist',
    filename: 'bundle.js'
  },
  plugins: [
    new CommonsChunkPlugin({ name: 'vendor', filename: 'vendor.bundle.js' }),
    new CopyWebpackPlugin([{from: './src/index.html', to: 'index.html'}])
  ],
  resolve: {
    extensions: ['', '.ts', '.js']
  },
  module: {
    loaders: [
      {test: /\.ts$/, loader: 'ts-loader'}
    ],
    noParse: [path.join(__dirname, 'node_modules', 'angular2', 'bundles')]
  },
  devServer: {
    contentBase: 'src',
    historyApiFallback: true
  },
  devtool: 'source-map'
};
```

The output bundles will be saved in the dist directory, and the name of the main entry point will go to the bundle.js file. The output for the second entry point will be configured in the plugins section.

Instructs Webpack to create a common vendor.bundle.js bundle with the content that can be shared by all application bundles

Copies the index.html file into the dist directory

To speed up the build process, you don't parse Angular minified files located in the node_modules/angular2/bundles directory.

Lets the dev server know that the application code is located in the src directory

Generates source maps

Because CommonsChunkPlugin comes with Webpack, there's no need to install it separately. After you install copy-webpack-plugin, Webpack will find it in the node_modules directory.

Listing 10.8 has two entry points: main.ts contains the app code plus Angular, and vendor.ts has only the Angular code. So the Angular code is common to both of these entry points, and this plugin will extract it from main and will keep it only in vendor .bundle.js.

Although it's nice to bundle all of your app code into one JavaScript file for deployment, it's easier to debug code in its original form of separate files. By adding source-map to webpack.config.js, you tell Webpack to generate source maps so you can see the sources of the JavaScript, CSS, and HTML files, even though the browser executes the code from bundle.js.

You use the option `"sourceMap": true` in the tsconfig.json file so the TypeScript source maps are generated. Web browsers load the source map files only if you have the developer console open, so generating source maps is a good idea even for production deployments. Keep in mind that `ts-loader` will perform the code transpilation, so you turn off tsc code generation by setting `"noEmit": true` in tsconfig.json.

Now let's see how npm's package.json file will change to include the Webpack-related content. In the basic version of package.json, you'll add two lines in the `scripts` section.

The devDependencies section will include webpack, webpack-dev-server, and the required loaders and plugins.

Listing 10.9   basic-webpack-starter/package.json

```
{
  "name": "basic-webpack-starter",
  "version": "1.0.0",
  "description": "A basic Webpack-based starter project for an Angular 2
    application",
  "homepage": "https://www.manning.com/books/angular-2-development-with-
    typescript",
  "private": true,
  "scripts": {
    "build": "webpack",
    "start": "webpack-dev-server --inline --progress --port 8080"
  },
  "dependencies": {
    "@angular/common": "^2.1.0",
    "@angular/compiler": "^2.1.0",
    "@angular/core": "^2.1.0",
    "@angular/http": "^2.1.0",
    "@angular/platform-browser": "^2.1.0",
    "@angular/platform-browser-dynamic": "^2.1.0",
    "@angular/router": "^3.0.0",
    "rxjs": "5.0.0-beta.12",
    "systemjs": "^0.19.37",
    "zone.js": "0.6.21"
  },
  "devDependencies": {
    "@types/es6-shim": "0.0.31",
    "copy-webpack-plugin": "^3.0.1",
    "ts-loader": "^0.8.2",
    "typescript": "^2.0.0",
    "webpack": "^2.1.0-beta.25",
    "webpack-dev-server": "^2.1.0-beta.0"
  }
}
```

Causes Webpack to write the bundles in the dist output directory

Creates the bundles in memory, and will serve them to the browser using webpack-dev-server

Adds copy-webpack-plugin as a development dependency. Note that you didn't need to add CommonsChunkPlugin, because it comes with Webpack.

Installs type definitions to support ES6 features. You'll also add the compiler option "types":["es6-shim"] in tsconfig.json.

Adds the loaded ts-loader as a development dependency

Adds Webpack development server as a development dependency

Includes Webpack as a development dependency

NOTE We use NPM packages from the @types namespace and the TypeScript compiler option @types to handle type-definition files. You need TypeScript 2.0. or later installed to use the @types option.

Both the start and build scripts use the same Webpack configuration from the webpack.config.js file. Let's see how these scripts differ.

10.2.1   *npm run build*

After running npm run build, the command window looks like what you see in figure 10.5. The application weighs 2.5 MB and makes just three network requests to load.

```
● ● ●              ▦ basic-webpack-starter — -bash — 80×24
Yakov-2:basic-webpack-starter yfain11$ npm run build

> basic-webpack-starter@1.0.0 build /Users/yfain11/Documents/core-angular2/code/
chapter10/basic-webpack-starter
> webpack

ts-loader: Using typescript@2.0.2 and /Users/yfain11/Documents/core-angular2/cod
e/chapter10/basic-webpack-starter/tsconfig.json
Hash: e66e00092da0a25822b9
Version: webpack 2.1.0-beta.21
Time: 5677ms
              Asset      Size  Chunks             Chunk Names
          bundle.js   6.34 kB       0  [emitted]  main
   vendor.bundle.js   2.56 MB       1  [emitted]  vendor
      bundle.js.map   3.93 kB       0  [emitted]  main
vendor.bundle.js.map    2.5 MB       1  [emitted]  vendor
         index.html  250 bytes         [emitted]
   + 358 hidden modules
Yakov-2:basic-webpack-starter yfain11$ ▊
```

Figure 10.5   Running `npm run build`

Webpack built two bundles (bundle.js and vendor.bundle .js) and two corresponding source map files (bundle.js.map and vendor.bundle.js.map), and it copied index.html into the dist output directory shown in fig ure 10.6.

The index.html file doesn't include any `<script>` tags for loading Angular. Everything the application needs is located in two bundles included in two `<script>` tags.

Figure 10.6   The content of the dist directory

Listing 10.10   basic-webpack-starter/index.html

```html
<!DOCTYPE html>
<html>
<head>
  <meta charset=UTF-8>
  <title>Basic Webpack Starter</title>
  <base href="/">
</head>
<body>
  <my-app>Loading...</my-app>
  <script src="vendor.bundle.js"></script>
  <script src="bundle.js"></script>
</body>
</html>
```

You can open the command window in the dist directory and run the familiar live-server from there to see this simple application running. We took the screenshot in figure 10.7 after the application stopped at the breakpoint in main.ts to illustrate source maps in action. Even though the browser executes code from JavaScript bundles, you can still debug the code of the specific TypeScript module thanks to generated source maps.

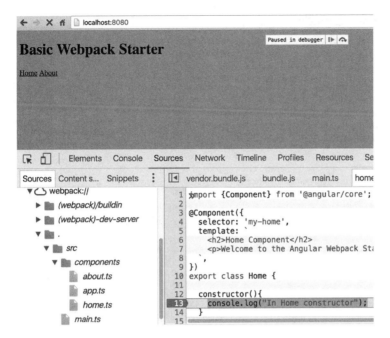

Figure 10.7   Placing a breakpoint in the TypeScript module

10.2.2   npm start

If instead of npm run build you run the npm start command, the dist directory won't be created, and webpack-dev-server will do the build (including source map generation) and serve the application from memory. Just open your browser to localhost://8080, and your app will be served. The application weighs 2.7 MB, but you'll do a lot better by the end of this chapter.

The basic Webpack project presented in this section is good for demo purposes. But real-world applications require more advanced work with Webpack, which we'll discuss in the next section.

10.3   Creating development and production configurations

In this section, we'll show you two versions of Webpack configuration files (one for development and one for production) that you can use as a starting point in your real-world Angular projects. All the code shown in this section is located in the angular2-webpack-starter directory. The application is the same as in the previous section and consists of two components: Home and About.

This project has more npm scripts in package.json and includes two configuration files: webpack.config.js for the development build and webpack.prod.config.js for production.

10.3.1 Development configuration

Let's start with the development configuration file, webpack.config.js, which gets some minor additions compared to the file in the previous section. You add one new plugin, DefinePlugin, that allows you to create variables that are visible from your application code and can be used by Webpack during the build.

> **Listing 10.11   angular2-webpack-starter/webpack.config.js**

```
const path                = require('path');
const CommonsChunkPlugin = require('webpack/lib/optimize/
    CommonsChunkPlugin');
const CopyWebpackPlugin   = require('copy-webpack-plugin');
const DefinePlugin        = require('webpack/lib/DefinePlugin');

const ENV  = process.env.NODE_ENV = 'development';
const HOST = process.env.HOST || 'localhost';
const PORT = process.env.PORT || 8080;

const metadata = {
  env : ENV,
  host: HOST,
  port: PORT
};

module.exports = {
  devServer: {
    contentBase: 'src',
    historyApiFallback: true,
    host: metadata.host,
    port: metadata.port
  },
  devtool: 'source-map',
  entry: {
    'main'  : './src/main.ts',
    'vendor': './src/vendor.ts'
  },
  module: {
    loaders: [
      {test: /\.css$/,  loader: 'raw', exclude: /node_modules/},
      {test: /\.css$/,  loader: 'style!css?-minimize', exclude: /src/},
      {test: /\.html$/, loader: 'raw'},
      {test: /\.ts$/,   loader: 'ts'}
    ],
    noParse: [path.join(__dirname, 'node_modules', 'angular2', 'bundles')]
  },
  output: {
    path    : './dist',
    filename: 'bundle.js'
  },
  plugins: [
    new CommonsChunkPlugin({name: 'vendor', filename: 'vendor.bundle.js',
```

Loads the
DefinePlugin
that allows
you to define
variables

Node.js uses a NODE_ENV
environment variable, which
you can set on your server:
for example, export
NODE_ENV=production
on Linux.

The dev server will start on the specified host and
port. The metadata constant is visible from
index.html as well, so you can define the baseURL
property there if your application isn't deployed
in the root directory of your web server.

The raw-loader doesn't transform the files
but inlines them as strings in the templates.
You use it for CSS and HTML files.

```
    ➡ minChunks: Infinity}),
  new CopyWebpackPlugin([{from: './src/index.html', to: 'index.html'}]),
  new DefinePlugin({'webpack': {'ENV': JSON.stringify(metadata.env)}})   ◄──┐
],                                                                          │
  resolve: { extensions: ['.ts', '.js']}
};
```

Defines the ENV variable to be used in the application code

The NODE_ENV variable is used by Node.js. To access the value of NODE_ENV from JavaScript, you use a special process.env.NODE_ENV variable. In listing 10.11, you set the value of the ENV constant to the value of the NODE_ENV environment variable if defined, or to development if not. The use of the constants HOST and PORT is similar, and the metadata object will store all these values.

  The ENV variable is used in main.ts to invoke the Angular function if (webpack .ENV === 'production') enableProdMode();. When production mode is enabled, Angular's change-detection module doesn't perform an additional pass to ensure that the UI isn't modified in the lifecycle hooks of the components.

> **NOTE** Even if you don't set the Node environment variable in the command window, it has a default value of development, set in the webpack.config.js file.

10.3.2 *Production configuration*

Now let's take a look at the webpack.prod.config.js production configuration file, which uses additional plugins: CompressionPlugin, DedupePlugin, OccurrenceOrderPlugin, and UglifyJsPlugin.

Listing 10.12 angular2-webpack-starter/webpack.prod.config.js

```
const path = require('path');

const CommonsChunkPlugin    = require('webpack/lib/optimize/
➡ CommonsChunkPlugin');
const CompressionPlugin     = require('compression-webpack-plugin');
const CopyWebpackPlugin     = require('copy-webpack-plugin');
const DedupePlugin          = require('webpack/lib/optimize/DedupePlugin');
const DefinePlugin          = require('webpack/lib/DefinePlugin');
const OccurrenceOrderPlugin = require('webpack/lib/optimize/
➡ OccurrenceOrderPlugin');
const UglifyJsPlugin        = require('webpack/lib/optimize/UglifyJsPlugin');

const ENV = process.env.NODE_ENV = 'production';   ◄──┐
const metadata = {env: ENV};

module.exports = {
  devtool: 'source-map',
  entry: {
    'main'  : './src/main.ts',
    'vendor': './src/vendor.ts'
```

Sets the value of the ENV constant to the value of the NODE_ENV environment variable if defined, or to "production" if not

```
  },
  module: {                          The html-loader turns the HTML file into a string
    loaders: [                       replacing the corresponding require() call.
      {test: /\.css$/,  loader: 'to-string!css', exclude: /node_modules/},
      {test: /\.css$/,  loader: 'style!css', exclude: /src/},
      {test: /\.html$/,  loader: 'html?caseSensitive=true'},
      {test: /\.ts$/,    loader: 'ts'}
    ],
    noParse: [path.join(__dirname, 'node_modules', 'angular2', 'bundles')]
  },
  output: {
    path     : './dist',             CompressionPlugin uses the gzip utility to
    filename: 'bundle.js'            prepare compressed versions of assets
  },                                 that match this regular expression.
  plugins: [
    new CommonsChunkPlugin({name: 'vendor', filename: 'vendor.bundle.js',
      minChunks: Infinity}),
    new CompressionPlugin({regExp: /\.css$|\.html$|\.js$|\.map$/}),
    new CopyWebpackPlugin([{from: './src/index.html', to: 'index.html'}]),
    new DedupePlugin(),
    new DefinePlugin({'webpack': {'ENV': JSON.stringify(metadata.env)}}),
    new OccurrenceOrderPlugin(true),
    new UglifyJsPlugin({                   DedupePlugin searches for equal
      compress: {screw_ie8 : true},        or similar files and deduplicates
      mangle: {screw_ie8 : true}           them in the output.
      }
    })
  ],                                   For optimization reasons, Webpack
  resolve: { extensions: ['.ts', '.js'] }   replaces the names of the modules with
};                                       numeric IDs, and OccurrenceOrderPlugin
                                         gives the shortest IDs to the most
UglifyJsPlugin minifies the JavaScript and uses the   frequently used modules.
mangler tool to rename local variables into single letters.
```

You'll start the build process using the npm script commands included in the package.json file, which has more commands than those we discussed in section 10.2. Note that the build command explicitly specifies the webpack.prod.config.js file with the production configuration, and the start command will use the development configuration from webpack.config.js, which is a default name used by the Webpack development server.

Listing 10.13 angular2-webpack-starter/package.json

Removes all the content from the dist directory. You use an npm package, rimraf, which is the equivalent of the rm -rf Linux command but works on all platforms.

npm automatically runs the prebuild command (if present) right before the npm run build command; this is the right time to clean the dist directory and run tests.

```
"scripts": {
  "clean": "rimraf dist",
  "prebuild": "npm run clean && npm run test",
  "build": "webpack --config webpack.prod.config.js --progress --profile
    --colors",
```

The npm run build command runs the Webpack build with the specified command-line options and configuration file. In this case, you use the file webpack.prod.config.js.

**The npm start command
performs the build in memory
and serves the application
using webpack-dev-server.**

**The preserve command runs before
serve and creates the build.**

```
"start": "webpack-dev-server --inline --progress --port 8080",
"preserve:dist": "npm run build",
"serve:dist": "static dist -H '{\"Cache-Control\": \"no-cache,
    must-revalidate\"}' -z",
"test": "karma start karma.conf.js"
"prebuild:aot": "npm run clean",
    "build:aot": "ngc -p tsconfig.aot.json && webpack --config
        webpack.prod.config.aot.js --progress --profile --colors",
    "preserve:dist:aot": "npm run build:aot",
    "serve:dist:aot": "static dist -H '{\"Cache-Control\": \"no-cache,
        must-revalidate\"}' -z"
}
```

**The serve:dist command serves the
bundled app using the static web server.**

**This is a command for
running tests with Karma.**

Typically, after running `npm install`, you'll use the following two commands (you won't set the `NODE_ENV` environment variable in the command line):

- `npm start`—Starts the Webpack development server in development mode, and serves a non-optimized application. If you open the Developer Tools in the browser, you'll see that the application started in development mode because the variable `ENV` has the value `development`, as set in webpack.config.js.

- `npm run serve:dist`—Runs `npm run build` to create optimized bundles in the dist directory, and starts a static web server and serves the optimized version of the application. If you open the Developer Tools in the browser, you won't see a message saying that the application started in development mode, because it runs in production mode; the `ENV` variable has the value `production`, as set in webpack.prod.config.js.

- `npm run serve:dist:aot`—Invokes the Angular ngc compiler for ahead-of-time (AoT) compilation before building the bundles. This removes the need to include ngc in the application code and further optimizes the bundle size.

TIP We keep development and production scripts in separate files, even though it's possible to reuse the same file by selectively applying certain sections of the configuration based on the value of the environment variable. Some people define two files and reuse the development configuration in the production one (for example, `var devWebpackConfig = require('./webpack.config.js';))`. In our experience, this hurts the readability of the configuration script, so we keep complete build configurations in the separate files.

NOTE The example webpack.config.js and webpack.prod.config.js have less than 60 lines each. If you were to use Gulp to prepare a similar build configuration, it would include a couple of hundred lines of code.

10.3.3 *A custom type-definition file*

You need to add a custom type-definition file to the app to prevent tsc compiler errors. There are two reasons you may get compilation errors in the app:

- Webpack will load and transform all of your CSS and HTML files. During the transformation, Webpack will replace all occurrences like the following:

```
styles: ['home.css'],
template: require('./home.html')
```

with the transformed content:

```
styles: [require('./home.css')],
template: require('./home.html')
```

This is Webpack's own `require()` function, not the one from Node.js. If you'll be running the tsc compiler, the preceding code will result in compilation errors because it doesn't recognize `require()` with such a signature.

- The app uses the ENV constant defined in the Webpack configuration files:

```
if (webpack.ENV === 'production') {
  enableProdMode();
}
```

To make sure the compiler won't complain about this variable, create a custom typings.d.ts type definitions file with the following content.

Listing 10.14   angular2-webpack-starter/typings.d.ts

```
declare function require(path: string);

declare const webpack: {
  ENV: string
};
```

Type definitions that start with the `declare` keyword don't have a direct link to the actual implementations of the variables (such as the `require()` function and the ENV constant), and it's your responsibility to update the preceding file if the code changes (for example, if you decide to rename ENV as ENVIRONMENT).

Figure 10.8 shows a screenshot taken after we ran the command `npm run serve:dist` and opened the app in the browser. Note that this version of the application made just three requests to the server, and the total size of the application is 180 KB. This application is a little smaller than the auction, but you can still compare the number of the server requests and the size shown in figure 10.1 to see the difference and appreciate the job done by Webpack.

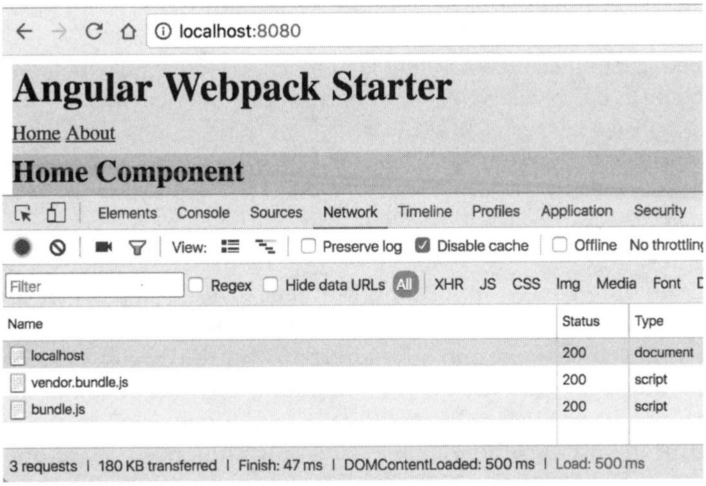

Figure 10.8 After running `npm run serve:dist`

Now let's see how ahead-of-time compilation will affect the size of the app. Run the command `npm run serve:dist:aot`. The app size is only 100 KB! This is pretty impressive, isn't it?

NOTE   At the time of this writing (Angular 2.1.0), AoT compilation produces footprints smaller than JIT only for small applications.

Establishing continuity

If you're a project manager, you need to make sure the main processes of your project are automated. The biggest mistake a project manager can make is to allow John Smith, an expert developer, to manually build and deploy applications on request. John is a human being, and he can get sick, take a vacation, or even quit one day. Automating the build and deployment processes serves as a guarantee of continuity for the business of software development. The following processes have to be established during the early stages of your project:

- *Continuous integration (CI)*—This is an established process that runs build scripts multiple times a day, such as after each code merge in the source code repository. The build scripts include unit tests, minification, and bundling. You need to install and configure a CI server to guarantee that the master branch of the application code is always in a working condition, and you'll never hear the question, "Who broke the build?"
- *Continuous delivery (CD)*—This is a process that prepares your application for deployment. CD is about offering your users additional features and bug fixes.
- *Continuous deployment*—This is the process of deploying the new version of an application that was prepared during the CD phase. Continuous deployment allows you to get frequent feedback from your users, ensuring that your team is working on something that users really need.

Front-end developers often work in collaboration with a team that works on the server side of the application. That team may already have CI and CD processes in place, and you'll need to learn how to integrate your build with whatever tools are used for the server side.

(continued)

If you still believe that manual deployment isn't a crime, read about what happened to Knight Capital Group, which went bankrupt in 45 minutes because of a human error during deployment. In 2014, Doug Seven wrote an article, "Knightmare: A DevOps Cautionary Tale," describing this incident (http://mng.bz/1kDr). The bottom line is that the build and deployment process should be automated and repeatable, and it can't depend on any single technician.

TIP If you're building a large application with megabytes of JavaScript code, you may want to split your application code into multiple modules (entry points) and turn each of them into a bundle. Say your web application has a user-profile module that's not used very often. Removing the code that implements the user profile will lower the initial size of the home page of your app, and the code for the user profile will be loaded only when needed. A popular Instagram web application defines more than a dozen entry points.

10.4   What's Angular CLI?

Initially the entry barrier into the world of Angular development was pretty high because of the need to learn and manually configure multiple tools. Even to get started with a simple application, you needed to know and use the TypeScript language, the TypeScript compiler, ES6 modules, SystemJS, npm, and a development web server. To work on a real-world project, you also needed to learn how to test and bundle your app.

To jump-start the development process, the Angular team created a tool called Angular CLI (https://github.com/angular/angular-cli), which is a command-line tool that covers all the stages of the Angular application lifecycle, from scaffolding and generating an initial app to generating boilerplate for your components, modules, services, and so on. The generated code also includes preconfigured files for unit tests and bundling with Webpack.

You can install Angular CLI globally by using following command:

```
npm install -g angular-cli
```

Angular CLI and Webpack

Angular CLI is powered by Webpack. Internally, the CLI-generated project includes Webpack configuration files similar to the ones discussed in this chapter.

Even though Angular CLI uses Webpack internally, it doesn't allow you to modify the Webpack configuration, which may prevent you from implementing specific build requirements (such as a custom bundling strategy) using CLI. In that case, you can configure your project manually (without CLI) using the knowledge gained in this chapter.

10.4.1 *Starting a new project with Angular CLI*

After CLI is installed, the executable binary ng becomes available on your PATH. You'll use the ng command to invoke Angular CLI commands.

To create an Angular application, use the new command:

```
ng new basic-cli
```

CLI will generate a new directory called basic-cli, which will include all the files required for a simple app. To run this app, enter the command ng serve, and open your browser at http://localhost:4200. You'll see a page that renders the message "app works!" . CLI automatically installs all the required dependencies and creates a local git repository in the folder. Figure 10.9 shows the generated project structure.

Let's take a quick look at the main project files and directories:

Figure 10.9 CLI project structure

- *e2e*—The directory for end-to-end tests.
- *src/app*—The main directory for the application code. For routes and child components, you usually create subdirectories here, but the CLI doesn't mandate this.
- *src/assets*—Everything in this folder will be copied as is in the dist directory during the build process.
- *src/environments*—Here you specify environment-specific settings. You can create an arbitrary number of custom environments, such as QA, staging, and production.
- *angular-cli.json*—The main Angular CLI configuration file. Here you can customize the locations for files and directories that CLI relies on, such as global CSS files and assets.

10.4.2 *CLI commands*

CLI provides a few commands you can use to manage an Angular application. Table 10.1 lists the most commonly used commands that come in handy while developing and preparing a production version of an application.

Typically, you'll run the ng build command with the options -prod --aot to build an optimized version of your app. Without these options, the size of the generated bundle of a basic generated app is about 2.5 MB. Creating bundles using ng build -prod reduces the bundle size to 800 KB and also generates the gzipped version of the bundle (190 KB).

Table 10.1   Frequently used CLI commands

Command	Description
ng serve	Builds the bundles in memory and starts the included webpack-dev-server, which will run and rebuild the bundles each time you make changes in your app code.
ng generate	Generates various artifacts for your project. You can also use a shorter version of this command: ng g. To list all the available options, invoke ng help generate. Examples: ■ ng g c <component-name>—Generates four files for the component: a TypeScript file for the source code, a TypeScript file for the component unit tests, an HTML file for the template, and the CSS file for styling the component's view. If you want to keep CSS and templates inline in the generated component, run this command with options: for example, ng g c product --inline-styles --inline-template. If you don't want to generate the spec file, use the option --spec=false. ■ ng g s <service-name>—Generates two TypeScript files: one for the source code and another one for the unit tests.
ng test	Runs unit tests using the Karma test runner.
ng build	Produces JavaScript bundles with the transpiled application code and all the dependencies inlined. Saves the bundles in the dist directory.

To optimize the bundle for production deployment, turn on ahead-of-time compilation by running ng build --prod --aot. Now the size of the bundle is about 450 KB, and its gzipped version is as small as 100 KB. Figure 10.10 shows the content of the dist directory of the basic-cli app after running this command.

> **NOTE**   To see this 100 KB bundle loaded in the browser, you need to use a web server that supports serving prebuilt gzipped files. For example, you can use the static node server that you used in section 10.3.2.

This concludes our brief overview of Angular CLI, which eliminates the need to manually create multiple configuration files and produces highly optimized production builds. You can find a description of all the Angular CLI commands at https://cli.angular.io/reference.pdf.

0.688d48f52a362bd543fc.bundle.map	Today, 10:05 PM	3 KB	Document
favicon.ico	Today, 10:05 PM	5 KB	Windows icon image
index.html	Today, 10:05 PM	517 bytes	HTML document
inline.d41d8cd98f00b204e980.bundle.map	Today, 10:05 PM	13 KB	Document
inline.js	Today, 10:05 PM	1 KB	JavaScript
main.1ba1f6138d72e2f7118a.bundle.js	Today, 10:05 PM	445 KB	JavaScript
main.1ba1f6138d72e2f7118a.bundle.js.gz	Today, 10:05 PM	100 KB	gzip compressed archive
main.1ba1f6138d72e2f7118a.bundle.map	Today, 10:05 PM	3.3 MB	Document
styles.defd4e11283d3aa66903.bundle.js	Today, 10:05 PM	4 KB	JavaScript
styles.defd4e11283d3aa66903.bundle.map	Today, 10:05 PM	30 KB	Document

Figure 10.10   The dist directory after production build

You may ask, "Why did we have to learn the internals of Webpack if Angular CLI will configure Webpack for us?" We wanted you to know how things work under the hood in case you decide to manually create and fine-tune your builds without Angular CLI. Also, in the future Angular CLI may allow you to change the autogenerated config files of Webpack, and it's good to know how to do this.

> **TIP** To speed up installing dependencies of Angular CLI projects, use the Yarn package manager instead of npm. See https://yarnpkg.com for details.

10.5 Hands-on: deploying the online auction with Webpack

In this exercise, you won't be developing any new application code. The goal is to use Webpack to build and deploy an optimized version of the online auction. You'll also integrate the Karma test runner into the build process.

For this chapter, we refactored the auction project from chapter 8, which used the same package.json file between the client and server portions of the application. Now the client and server will be separate applications with their own package.json files. Keeping the client and the server code separate simplifies build automation.

Angular and security

Angular has built-in protection against common web application vulnerabilities and attacks. In particular, to prevent cross-site scripting attacks, it blocks malicious code from entering the DOM. With images, an attacker can replace the image with malicious code in the `src` attribute of an `<img>` tag.

The auction application uses images from the http://placehold.it website, which will be blocked during bundling unless you specifically write that you trust this site. This chapter's auction adds code stating that you trust the images from http://placehold.it and they don't need to be blocked.

That's why you add the code to prevent image-sanitizing in the auction components that use images coming from a third-party server. For example, a constructor for `Pro-ductItemComponent` looks like this:

```
constructor(private sanitizer: DomSanitizer) {
  this.imgHtml = sanitizer.bypassSecurityTrustHtml(`
    <img src="http://placehold.it/320x150">`);
}
```

You can find more details about Angular security in the Angular documentation at http://mng.bz/pk57.

The package.json file from the client directory has the npm scripts required to build the production bundle as well as run webpack-dev-server in development mode. The server directory has its own package.json file with npm scripts to start the auction's Node server—no bundling is needed there. Technically, you have two independent applications with their own dependencies configured separately. You'll start this hands-on project using the source code located in the auction directory from chapter 10.

10.5.1 Starting the Node server

The server's package.json file looks like this.

```
{
  "name": "ng2-webpack-starter",
  "description": "Angular 2 Webpack starter project suitable for a production
  grade application",
  "homepage": "https://www.manning.com/books/angular-2-development-with-
  typescript",
  "private": true,
  "scripts": {
    "tsc": "tsc",
    "startServer": "node build/auction.js",
    "dev": "nodemon build/auction.js"
  },
  "dependencies": {
    "express": "^4.13.3",
    "ws": "^1.0.1"
  },
  "devDependencies": {
    "@types/compression": "0.0.29",
    "@types/es6-shim": "0.0.27-alpha",
    "@types/express": "^4.0.28-alpha",
    "@types/ws": "0.0.26-alpha",
    "compression": "^1.6.1",
    "nodemon": "^1.8.1",
    "typescript": "^2.0.0"
  }
}
```

Note that you define the `tsc` script here to ensure that the local version of Type-Script 2.0 will be used even if you have an older version of the compiler installed globally. In the command line, change to the server directory and run `npm install` to get all the required dependencies for the server's portion of the application.

To use the local compiler, run the command `npm run tsc`, which will transpile the server's code and create auction.js and model.js (and their source maps) in the build directory, as configured in tsconfig.json. This is the code for the auction's server.

Start the server by running the command `npm run startServer`. It'll print the message "Listening on 127.0.0.1:8000" on the console.

10.5.2 Starting the auction client

You can start the auction client in either development or production mode using different npm script commands. The npm scripts section of the client's package.json has the following commands:

```
"scripts": {
  "clean": "rimraf dist",
  "prebuild": "npm run clean && npm run test",
  "build": "webpack --config webpack.prod.config.js --progress --profile",
  "startWebpackDevServer": "webpack-dev-server --inline --progress --
    port 8080",
  "test": "karma start karma.conf.js",
  "predeploy": "npm run build && rimraf ../server/build/public && mkdirp
  ➥ ../server/build/public",
  "deploy": "copyup dist/* ../server/build/public"
}
```

Most of the commands should look familiar to you, because you used them in web-pack.prod.config.js in listing 10.12. You add a new `deploy` command, which uses the `copyup` command to copy files from the client's dist directory to the server's build/public directory. Here you use the `copyup` command from the copyfiles npm package (https://www.npmjs.com/package/copyfiles). You use this package for cross-platform compatibility when it comes to copying files. You also add the `test` command to run tests with Karma (see section 10.5.3).

Because there's a `predeploy` command, it'll run automatically each time you run `npm run deploy`. In turn, `predeploy` will run the `build` command, which will automatically run `prebuild`. The latter will run `clean` and `test`, and only after all these commands succeed will the `build` command do the build. Finally, the `copyup` command will copy the bundles from the dist directory into the server/build/public directory.

Before starting the client portion of the auction, you need to open a separate command window, change to the client directory, and run the command `npm install`. Then start the auction app in development mode by running `npm run startWebpack-DevServer`. webpack-dev-server will bundle your Angular app and begin listening for the browser's requests on port 8080. Enter `http://localhost:8080` in your browser, and you'll see the familiar UI of the auction app.

> **NOTE** The development build is done in memory, and the auction application is available on port 8080, which is the port configured in the webpack .config.js file.

Open the Network tab in Chrome Developer Tools. You'll see the application load the freshly built bundles—and the size of the application is pretty large.

Check Webpack's log on the console, and you'll see which files went to which bundle (or *chunk*). In this case, you built two chunks: bundle.js and vendor.js. Figure 10.11 shows a small fragment of the Webpack log, but you can see the size of each file. The bundled application (bundle.js) weighs 285 KB, whereas the vendor code (vendor.bundle.js) is 3.81 MB.

```
Version: webpack 2.1.0-beta.21
Time: 25082ms
                                       Asset      Size  Chunks           Chunk Names
    f4769f9bdb7466be65088239c12046d1.eot    20.1 kB          [emitted]
    fa2772327f55d8198301fdb8bcfc8158.woff   23.4 kB          [emitted]
   448c34a56d699c29117adc64c43affeb.woff2     18 kB          [emitted]
    e18bbf611f2a2e43afc071aa2f4e1512.ttf    45.4 kB          [emitted]
    89889688147bd7575d6327160d64e760.svg     109 kB          [emitted]
                                   bundle.js    285 kB    0  [emitted]  main
                            vendor.bundle.js   3.81 MB    1  [emitted]  vendor
                               bundle.js.map    275 kB    0  [emitted]  main
                        vendor.bundle.js.map   4.05 MB    1  [emitted]  vendor
                                  index.html  315 bytes     [emitted]
```

Figure 10.11   Console output fragment

At the top, you'll see some font files that weren't bundled, because in the web-pack.config.js file you specified the `limit` parameters to avoid inlining large fonts into the bundle:

```
{test: /\.woff$/,  loader: "url?limit=10000&minetype=application/font-woff"},
{test: /\.woff2$/, loader: "url?limit=10000&minetype=application/font-woff"},
{test: /\.ttf$/,   loader: "url?limit=10000&minetype=application/
➥ octet-stream"},
{test: /\.svg$/,   loader: "url?limit=10000&minetype=image/svg+xml"},
{test: /\.eot$/,   loader: "file"}
```

The last line instructs the file-loader to copy fonts with a .eot extension into the build directory. If you scroll the console output, you'll see that all the application code went to chunk {0}, and vendor-related code went to chunk {1}.

> **NOTE**   In development mode, you didn't deploy the Angular app under the Node server. The Node server ran on port 8000, and the auction client was served on port 8080 and communicated with the Node server using the HTTP and WebSocket protocols. You'll deploy the Angular app under the Node server next.

Now, stop the webpack-dev-server (not the Node server) by pressing Ctrl-C in the command window from which you started the client. Start the *production build* by running the command `npm run deploy`. This command will prepare the optimized build and copy its files into the ../server/build/public directory, which is where all the static content of the Node server belongs.

There's no need to restart the Node server, because you only deployed the static code there. But to see the production version of the auction, you need to use port 8000, where the Node server runs.

Open your browser to the URL http://localhost:8000. You'll see the auction application served by the Node server. Open the Chrome Developer Tools panel in the Network tab, and refresh the application. You'll see that the size of the optimized

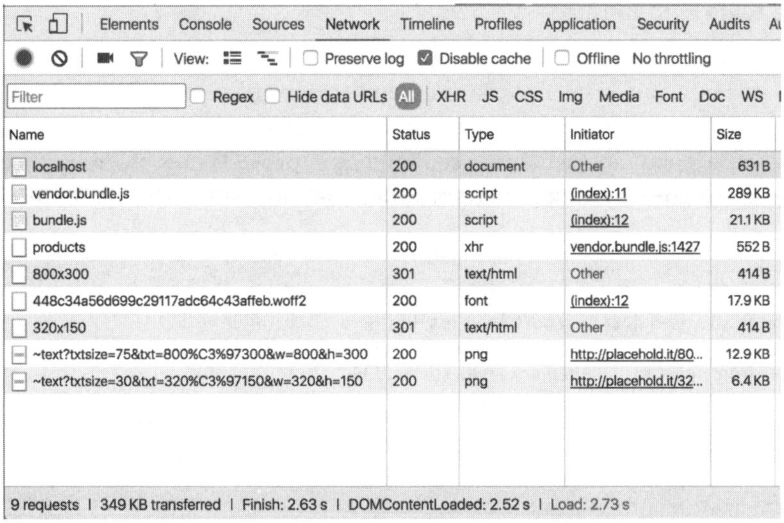
Elements Console Sources Network Timeline Profiles Application Security Audits
View: Preserve log Disable cache Offline No throttling
Filter Regex Hide data URLs All XHR JS CSS Img Media Font Doc WS
Name Status Type Initiator Size
localhost 200 document Other 631 B
vendor.bundle.js 200 script (index):11 289 KB
bundle.js 200 script (index):12 21.1 KB
products 200 xhr vendor.bundle.js:1427 552 B
800x300 301 text/html Other 414 B
448c34a56d699c29117adc64c43affeb.woff2 200 font (index):12 17.9 KB
320x150 301 text/html Other 414 B
~text?txtsize=75&txt=800%C3%97300&w=800&h=300 200 png http://placehold.it/80... 12.9 KB
~text?txtsize=30&txt=320%C3%97150&w=320&h=150 200 png http://placehold.it/32... 6.4 KB
9 requests | 349 KB transferred | Finish: 2.63 s | DOMContentLoaded: 2.52 s | Load: 2.73 s

Figure 10.12 What's loaded in the prod version of the auction

application is drastically smaller. Figure 10.12 shows that the total size of the application is 349 KB (compared with 5.5 MB in the unbundled version shown earlier in figure 10.1).

The browser made nine requests to the server to load index.html, two bundles, and the gray images that represent products. You can also see the request for data about products that the client made using Angular's `Http` request. The line that ends with `.woff2` is the font loaded by Twitter's Bootstrap framework.

url-loader works like file-loader, but it can inline files smaller than the specified limit into the CSS where they're defined. You specified 10,000 bytes as a limit for the files with names ending with .woff, .woff2, .ttf, and .svg. One larger file (17.9 KB) wasn't inlined.

Each font is represented in multiple formats, such as .eot, .woff, .woff2, .ttf, and .svg, and there are several non-exclusive options for dealing with fonts:

- Inline all of them into the bundle, and let the browser choose which one it wants to use.
- Inline the font format supported by the oldest browser you want your app to support. This means newer browsers will download files two to three times larger than they need to.
- Inline none of them, and let the browser choose and download the one it supports best.

The strategy here was to inline only the selected fonts that meet certain criteria and to copy the others into the build folder, which can be considered a combination of the first and last options.

10.5.3 Running tests with Karma

In chapter 9, you developed three specs for unit testing `ApplicationComponent`, `StarsComponent`, and `ProductService`. You'll reuse the same specs here, but you'll run them with Karma as a part of the building process.

Because the client and server are separate npm projects now, the Karma configuration files karma.conf.js and karma-test-runner.js are located in the client directory.

Listing 10.16   auction/client/karma.conf.js

In chapter 9, you used dots to report progress, but here you use the more descriptive mocha reporter that prints messages from specs rather than dots (see figure 10.13).

```
module.exports = function (config) {
  config.set({
    browsers     : ['Chrome', 'Firefox'],
    frameworks   : ['jasmine'],
    reporters    : ['mocha'],              ⟵    Specifies when the script
    singleRun    : true,                        to run Karma tests should
    preprocessors: {'./karma-test-runner.js': ['webpack']},   ⟵   be preprocessed by the
    files        : [{pattern: './karma-test-runner.js', watched: false}],  ⟵   karma-webpack plugin
    webpack      : require('./webpack.test.config.js'),
    webpackServer: {noInfo: true}          ⟵
  });
};
```

Specifies when the script to run Karma tests should be preprocessed by the karma-webpack plugin

Loads the test specs included in the karma-test-runner.js file

Specifies the Webpack config file that Karma should use

Turns off Webpack logging so its messages won't clutter Karma's output

---

The karma.conf.js file is a lot shorter than the one from chapter 9, because you don't need to configure files for SystemJS anymore—Webpack is the loader now, and the files are already configured in webpack.test.config.js. Following is the karma-test-runner.js script for running Karma.

Listing 10.17   auction/client/karma-test-runner.js

```
Error.stackTraceLimit = Infinity;

require('reflect-metadata/Reflect.js');
require('zone.js/dist/zone.js');
require('zone.js/dist/long-stack-trace-zone.js');
require('zone.js/dist/proxy.js');
require('zone.js/dist/sync-test.js');
require('zone.js/dist/jasmine-patch.js');
require('zone.js/dist/async-test.js');
require('zone.js/dist/fake-async-test.js');

var testing = require('@angular/core/testing');
var browser = require('@angular/platform-browser-dynamic/testing');
```

```
testing.TestBed.initTestEnvironment(
    browser.BrowserDynamicTestingModule,
    browser.platformBrowserDynamicTesting());

Object.assign(global, testing);


var testContext = require.context('./src', true, /\.spec\.ts/);

function requireAll(requireContext) {
  return requireContext.keys().map(requireContext);
}

var modules = requireAll(testContext);
```

The webpack.test.config.js file is shown next. It's simplified for testing because you don't need to create bundles during testing. The Webpack dev server isn't needed because Karma acts as a server.

```
const path        = require('path');
const DefinePlugin = require('webpack/lib/DefinePlugin');

const ENV  = process.env.NODE_ENV = 'development';
const HOST = process.env.HOST || 'localhost';
const PORT = process.env.PORT || 8080;

const metadata = {
  env : ENV,
  host: HOST,
  port: PORT
};

module.exports = {
  debug: true,
  devtool: 'source-map',
  module: {
    loaders: [
      {test: /\.css$/,  loader: 'raw', exclude: /node_modules/},
      {test: /\.css$/,  loader: 'style!css?-minimize', exclude: /src/},
      {test: /\.html$/, loader: 'raw'},
      {test: /\.ts$/,   loaders: [
        {loader: 'ts', query: {compilerOptions: {noEmit: false}}},
        {loader: 'angular2-template'}
      ]}
    ]
  },
  plugins: [
    new DefinePlugin({'webpack': {'ENV': JSON.stringify(metadata.env)}})
  ],
  resolve: { extensions: ['.ts', '.js']}
  }
};
```

The client/package.json file has the following Karma-related content.

Listing 10.19   auction/client/package.json

```
"scripts": {
...
"test": "karma start karma.conf.js"
}
...
"devDependencies": {
...
    "karma": "^1.2.0",
  "karma-chrome-launcher": "^2.0.0",
  "karma-firefox-launcher": "^1.0.0",
  "karma-jasmine": "^1.0.2",
  "karma-mocha-reporter": "^2.1.0",
  "karma-webpack": "^1.8.0",
}
```

To run the tests manually, run the npm test command in the command window from the client directory. You'll see output like that shown in figure 10.13.

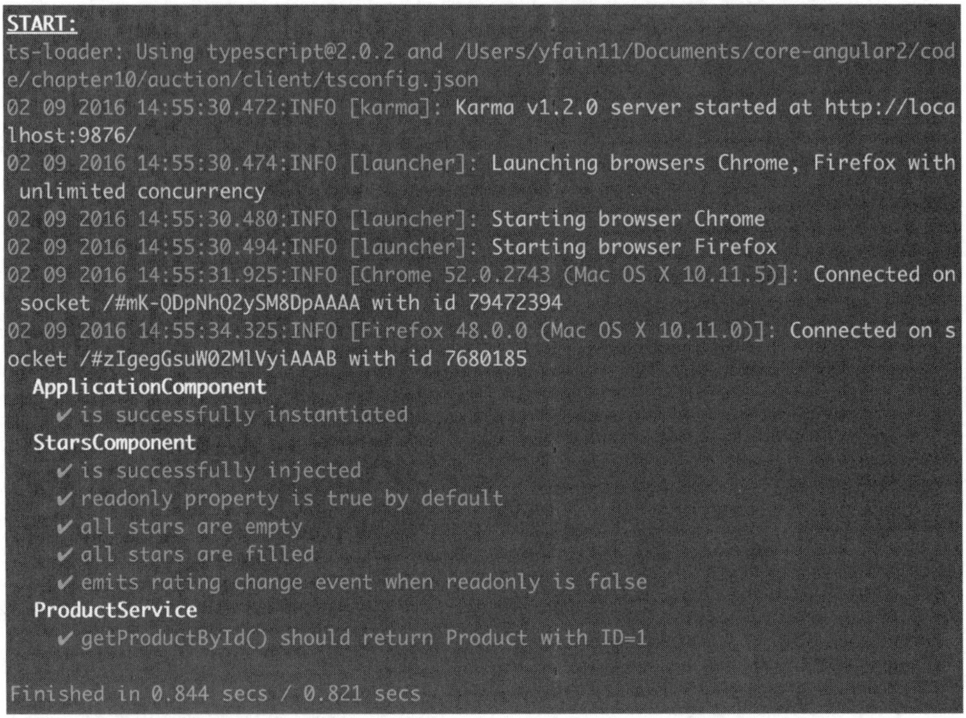

```
START:
ts-loader: Using typescript@2.0.2 and /Users/yfain11/Documents/core-angular2/cod
e/chapter10/auction/client/tsconfig.json
02 09 2016 14:55:30.472:INFO [karma]: Karma v1.2.0 server started at http://loca
lhost:9876/
02 09 2016 14:55:30.474:INFO [launcher]: Launching browsers Chrome, Firefox with
 unlimited concurrency
02 09 2016 14:55:30.480:INFO [launcher]: Starting browser Chrome
02 09 2016 14:55:30.494:INFO [launcher]: Starting browser Firefox
02 09 2016 14:55:31.925:INFO [Chrome 52.0.2743 (Mac OS X 10.11.5)]: Connected on
 socket /#mK-QDpNhQ2ySM8DpAAAA with id 79472394
02 09 2016 14:55:34.325:INFO [Firefox 48.0.0 (Mac OS X 10.11.0)]: Connected on s
ocket /#zIgegGsuW02MlVyiAAAB with id 7680185
  ApplicationComponent
    ✔ is successfully instantiated
  StarsComponent
    ✔ is successfully injected
    ✔ readonly property is true by default
    ✔ all stars are empty
    ✔ all stars are filled
    ✔ emits rating change event when readonly is false
  ProductService
    ✔ getProductById() should return Product with ID=1

Finished in 0.844 secs / 0.821 secs
```

Figure 10.13   Running Karma

To integrate the Karma run into the build process, you can modify the npm `prebuild` command to look like this:

```
"prebuild": "npm run clean && npm run test"
"build": "webpack ...",
```

Now, if you run the command `npm run build`, it'll run `prebuild`, which will clean the output directory, run the tests, and then do the build. If any of the tests fail, the `build` command won't run.

You're done with the final hands-on project for this book. If this was a real-world application, you'd continue fine-tuning the build configuration, cherry-picking the files you want to include or exclude from the build. Webpack is a sophisticated tool, and it offers endless possibilities for optimizing the bundles. The Angular team is working on an optimization of the Angular code using the ahead-of-time compilation, and we wouldn't be surprised if the Angular framework will add only 50 KB to your application's code.

> **NOTE** The source code that comes with this chapter includes a directory called extras that contains another implementation of the auction in which the Angular portion has been generated with Angular CLI. Check the `scripts` section in angular-cli.json to see how to add third-party libraries to an Angular CLI project.

10.6 Summary

This chapter wasn't about writing code. The goal was to optimize and bundle code for deployment. The JavaScript community has a few popular tools for build automation and bundling of web applications; our choice is the combination of Webpack and npm scripts.

Webpack is an intelligent and sophisticated tool, but we presented a small combination of loaders and plugins that work for us. If you're looking for a more complete Webpack configuration, try angular2-webpack-starter (http://mng.bz/fS4T).

These are the main takeaways from this chapter:

- The process of preparing deployment bundles and running builds should be automated in the early phases of development.
- To minimize the number of requests the browser makes to load your application, combine the code into a small number of bundles for deployment.
- Avoid packaging the same code into more than one bundle. Keep third-party frameworks in a separate bundle so other bundles of your application can share them.
- Always generate source maps, because they allow you to debug the source code in TypeScript. Source maps don't increase the size of the application code and are generated only if your browser has the Developer Tools open, so using source maps even for production builds is encouraged.

- To run build and deployment tasks, use npm scripts, because they're simple to write and you already have npm installed. If you're working on preparing a build for a large and complex project, and you feel the need for a scripting language to describe various build scenarios, introduce Gulp into your project workflow.
- To quickly start your development in Angular and TypeScript, generate your first projects with Angular CLI.

appendix A
An overview
of ECMAScript 6

ECMAScript is a standard for client-side scripting languages. The first edition of the ECMAScript specification was released in 1997, and the sixth edition was finalized in 2015. The seventh edition is already in the works. The ECMAScript standard is implemented in several languages, and the most popular implementation is JavaScript. In this appendix, we'll look at the JavaScript implementation of ECMAScript 6 (ES6), also known as ECMAScript 2015.

At the time of writing, not all web browsers fully support the ES6 specification; you can visit the ECMAScript compatibility site at http://mng.bz/ao59 to see the current state of ES6 support. The good news is that you can and should develop in ES6 today and use a transpiler like Traceur (https://github.com/google/traceur-compiler) or Babel (https://babeljs.io) to turn the ES6 code into an ES5 version supported by all web browsers.

> **NOTE** If you'd like to test your ES6 code in upcoming versions of popular web browsers, download the latest nightly build of Firefox at https://nightly.mozilla.org or use the remote version of Internet Explorer at https://remote.modern.ie. You can also get the Canary build of Chrome at http://mng.bz/9rub. You may need to enable experimental JavaScript features by visiting the URL chrome://flags (for Chrome) or about://flags (for IE).

We assume you're familiar with the ES5 syntax and APIs, and we'll cover only selected new features introduced in ES6. If your JavaScript skills are a little rusty, read the online appendix from *Enterprise Web Development* by Yakov Fain et al. (O'Reilly, 2014), which is available on GitHub at http://mng.bz/ElII. The specification for ES7 (a.k.a.

ES 2016) was released in 2016. It's a small release. The ECMAScript 2017 language specification is published at https://tc39.github.io/ecma262.

In this appendix, we'll often show code snippets in ES5 and their ES6 equivalents. But ES6 doesn't deprecate any old syntax, so you'll be able to safely run legacy ES5 or ES3 code in future web browsers or standalone JavaScript engines.

A.1   How to run the code samples

The code samples for this appendix come in the form of simple HTML files that include scripts in ES6, so you can run and debug them in your browser's developer tools if your browser fully supports ES6. What if it doesn't? There are several options:

- Use the ES6 Fiddle website (www.es6fiddle.net), which allows you to copy and paste a fragment of ES6 code into the field on the left, click Play, and see the console output on the right, as shown in figure A.1.

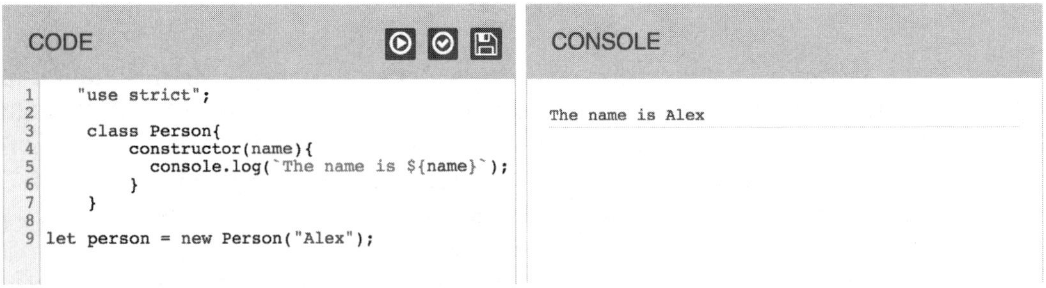

CODE	CONSOLE
1 "use strict";	
2	The name is Alex
3 class Person{	
4 constructor(name){	
5 console.log(`The name is ${name}`);	
6 }	
7 }	
8	
9 let person = new Person("Alex");	

Figure A.1   Using ES6 Fiddle

- Use the Traceur or Babel transpiler to convert your code from ES6 to ES5. Interactive tools that allow you to quickly run code fragments are called Read-Eval-Print-Loop (REPLs). You can use a REPL from Traceur (http://mng.bz/bI91) or Babel (http://babeljs.io/repl). Figure A.2 shows Babel's REPL. At left you can see the code written in ES6; the right side shows the generated ES5 equivalent. The console output produced by the code sample (if any) is shown at lower right.

A.2   Template literals

ES6 introduces a new syntax for working with string literals, which can contain embedded expressions. This feature is known as *string interpolation*.

In ES5, you'd use concatenation to create a string that contains string literals mixed in with the values of variables:

```
var customerName = "John Smith";
console.log("Hello" + customerName);
```

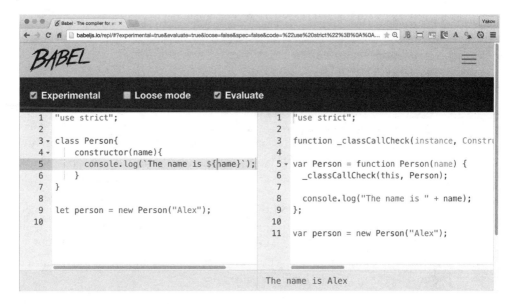

Figure A.2 Using the Babel REPL

In ES6, template literals are surrounded with back-tick symbols. You can embed expressions inside the literal by placing them between curly braces prefixed with a dollar sign. In the next code snippet, the value of the variable `customerName` is embedded in the string literal:

```
var customerName = "John Smith";
console.log(`Hello ${customerName}`);

function getCustomer(){
  return "Allan Lou";
}
console.log(`Hello ${getCustomer()}`);
```

The output of this code is

```
Hello John Smith
Hello Allan Lou
```

This example embeds the value of the `customerName` variable into the template literal and then embeds the value returned by the `getCustomer()` function. You can use any valid JavaScript expression between the curly braces.

A.2.1 Multiline strings

Strings can span multiple lines in your code. Using back-ticks, you can write multiline strings without needing to concatenate them or use the backslash character:

```
var message = `Please enter a password that
               has at least 8 characters and
               includes a capital letter`;
```

```
console.log(message);
```

The resulting string treats all spaces as part of the string, so the output looks like this:

```
Please enter a password that
               has at least 8 characters and
               includes a capital letter
```

A.2.2 *Tagged template strings*

If a template string is preceded by a function name, the string is evaluated first and then passed to the function for further processing. The string parts of a template are given as an array, and all the expressions that were evaluated in the template are passed as separate arguments. The syntax looks a little unusual, because you don't use parentheses as in regular function calls:

```
mytag`Hello ${name}`;
```

Let's see how it works by printing an amount with a currency sign that depends on the region variable. If the value of the region is 1, you keep the amount unchanged and prepend it with a dollar sign. If the value of region is 2, you need to convert the amount, applying 0.9 as an exchange rate, and prepend it with a euro sign. The template string looks like this:

```
`You've earned ${region} ${amount}!`
```

Let's call the tag function currencyAdjustment. The tagged template string looks like this:

```
currencyAdjustment`You've earned ${region} ${amount}!`
```

The currencyAdjustment function takes three arguments: the first represents all string parts from the template string, the second gets the region, and the third is for the amount. You can add any number of arguments after the first one. The complete example is shown in the following listing.

Listing A.1 Printing a currency amount

```
function currencyAdjustment(stringParts, region, amount) {
    console.log( stringParts);
    console.log( region );
    console.log( amount );

  var sign;
  if (region==1){
    sign="$"
```

```
    } else{
      sign='\u20AC';                          <———— Euro sign
      amount=0.9*amount;        <———┐
                                     Converts to Euros using
                                     0.9 as the exchange rate
    }
    return `${stringParts[0]}${sign}${amount}${stringParts[2]}`;
}

var amount = 100;
var region = 2;                   <———— Europe: 2, USA: I

var message = currencyAdjustment`You've earned ${region} ${amount}!`
console.log(message);
```

The currencyAdjustment function gets a string with embedded region and amount and parses the template, separating the string parts from these values (blank spaces are also considered string parts). Let's print these values first for illustration. Then this function will check the region, apply the conversion, and return a new string template. Running listing A.1 produces the following output:

```
["You've earned "," ","!"]
2
100
You've earned €90!
```

For more details on tagged templates, refer to the "Template Literals" chapter in *Exploring ES6* by Axel Rauschmayer, available at http://exploringjs.com.

A.3 *Optional parameters and default values*

In ES6, you can specify default values for function parameters (arguments) that will be used if no value is provided during function invocation. Say you're writing a function to calculate tax that takes two arguments: the annual income and the state where the person lives. If the state value isn't provided, you want to use Florida.

In ES5, you'd need to start the function body by checking whether the state value was provided, and otherwise use Florida:

```
function calcTaxES5(income, state){

    state = state || "Florida";

    console.log("ES5. Calculating tax for the resident of " + state +
                              " with the income " + income);
}

calcTaxES5(50000);
```

Here's what this code prints:

```
"ES5. Calculating tax for the resident of Florida with the income 50000"
```

In ES6, you can specify the default value right in the function signature:

```
function calcTaxES6(income, state = "Florida") {

  console.log("ES6. Calculating tax for the resident of " + state +
                              " with the income " + income);
}

calcTaxES6(50000);
```

The output looks similar:

```
"ES6. Calculating tax for the resident of Florida with the income 50000"
```

Rather than provide a hardcoded value for an optional parameter, you can even invoke a function that returns one:

```
function calcTaxES6(income, state = getDefaultState()) {
  console.log("ES6. Calculating tax for the resident of " + state +
  ➡ " with the income " + income);
}

function getDefaultState(){
  return "Florida";
}
```

Just keep in mind that the `getDefaultState()` function will be invoked each time you invoke `calcTaxES6()`, which may have performance consequences. This new syntax for optional parameters allows you to write less code and makes the code easier to understand.

A.4   Scope of variables

The scoping mechanism in ES5 is rather confusing. Regardless of where you declare a variable with the keyword `var`, the declaration is moved to the top of the scope. This is called *hoisting*. The use of the `this` keyword also isn't as straightforward as in languages like Java or C#.

ES6 eliminates this hoisting confusion (discussed in the next section) by introducing the keyword `let`, and the `this` confusion is cured by using arrow functions. Let's look closer at the hoisting and `this` problems.

A.4.1   Variable hoisting

In JavaScript, all variable declarations are moved to the top, and there's no block scope. Look at the following simple example that declares the variable `i` inside the for loop but uses it outside as well:

```
function foo(){

  for(var i=0;i<10;i++){
```

```
    }

  console.log("i=" + i);
}

foo();
```

Running this code will print i=10. The variable i is still available outside the loop, even though it seems as though it was meant to be used only inside. JavaScript automatically hoists the variable declaration to the top.

In this example, hoisting doesn't cause any harm, because there's only one variable named i. If two variables with the same name are declared inside and outside the function, however, this may result in confusing behavior. Consider listing A.2, which declares the variable customer on the global scope. A bit later, we'll introduce another customer variable in the local scope, but for now it's commented out.

Listing A.2　Hoisting a variable declaration

```
<!DOCTYPE html>
<html>
<head>
    <title>hoisting.html</title>
</head>
<body>

<script>
    "use strict";

    var customer = "Joe";

    (function (){
        console.log("The name of the customer inside the function is "   +
        ➥ customer);

        /*  if (2 > 1) {
              var customer = "Mary";
           }*/

    })();

    console.log("The name of the customer outside the function is "   +
    ➥ customer);
</script>

</body>
</html>
```

Open this file in the Chrome browser, and look at the console output in Chrome Developer Tools. As expected, the global variable customer is visible inside and outside the function, as shown in figure A.3.

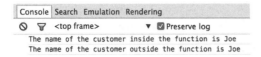

Figure A.3 Variable declaration is hoisted.

Uncomment the `if` statement that declares and initializes the `customer` variable inside the curly braces. Now you have two variables with the same name—one on the global scope and another on the function scope. Refresh the page in the web browser. The console output is different—the function's `customer` variable has the value `unde-fined`, as shown in figure A.4.

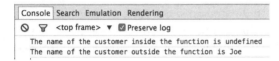

Figure A.4 Variable initialization isn't hoisted.

The reason for this behavior is that in ES5, variable declarations are hoisted to the top of the scope, but variable initializations aren't. So the declaration of the second unini-tialized `customer` variable was hoisted to the top of the function, and `console.log()` printed the value defined inside the function, which shadows the value of the global variable `customer`.

Function declarations are hoisted too, so you can invoke a function before it's declared:

```
doSomething();

function doSomething(){
    console.log("I'm doing something");
}
```

On the other hand, function expressions are considered variable initializations, so they aren't hoisted. The following code snippet will produce `undefined` for the `doSomething` variable:

```
doSomething();

var doSomething = function(){
    console.log("I'm doing something");
}
```

Let's see what ES6 changes in terms of scoping.

A.4.2 *Block scoping with let and const*

Declaring variables with the ES6 keyword `let` instead of `var` allows variables to have block scoping. Here's an example.

Listing A.3 Variables with block scoping

```
<!DOCTYPE html>
<html>
<head>
    <title>let.html</title>
</head>
<body>

<script>
    "use strict";

    let customer = "Joe";

    (function (){
        console.log("The name of the customer inside the function is " +
        ➥ customer);

        if (2 > 1) {
         let customer = "Mary";
         console.log("The name of the customer inside the block is " +
         ➥ customer);
        }

    })();

    for (let i=0; i<5; i++){
        console.log("i=" + i);
    }

    console.log("i=" + i);   //
      prints Uncaught ReferenceError: i is not defined

</script>

</body>
</html>
```

Now the two customer variables have different scopes and values, as shown in figure A.5.

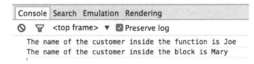

Figure A.5 Block scoping with `let`

If you declare a variable with `let` in a loop, it'll be available only inside the loop:

```
for (let i=0; i<5; i++){
  console.log("i=" + i);
}

console.log("i=" + i);   // ReferenceError: i is not defined
```

Testing the let keyword in the Traceur REPL

To get an idea what the transpiled code looks like, visit Traceur's Transcoding Demo web page (http://mng.bz/bl91), which allows you to enter ES6 syntax and convert (transcode) it into ES5 in interactive mode. Paste the code from listing A.3 into the text box at left, and you'll see its ES5 version on the right, as shown here.

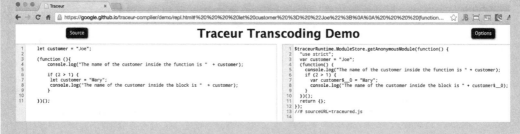

Transpiling ES6 to ES5 with the Traceur REPL

As you can see, Traceur introduces a separate `customer$_0` variable to distinguish it from the `customer` variable. Open the web console in your browser while working with the Traceur REPL, and you'll see the results of your code execution immediately.

To put it simply, if you're developing a new application, don't use `var`. Use `let` instead. The `let` keyword allows you to assign and reassign a value to a variable as many times as you want.

If you want to declare a variable that can't change its value after it's assigned, declare it with the `const` keyword. Constants also support block scope.

> **NOTE** The only difference between `let` and `const` is that the latter won't allow the assigned value to be changed. The best practice is to use `const` in your programs; if you see that this value needs to change, replace `const` with `let`.

A.4.3 *Block scope for functions*

If you declare a function inside a block (within curly braces), it won't be visible from outside the block. The following code will throw an error saying "doSomething is not defined":

```
{
  function doSomething(){
    console.log("In doSomething");
  }
}

doSomething();
```

In ES5, the doSomething() declaration would be hoisted, and it would print "In doSomething". Declaring a function inside a block wasn't recommended in ES5 (see "ES5 Implementation Best Practice" at http://mng.bz/Bvym), because doing so may produce inconsistent results across browsers, which may parse this syntax differently.

A.5 Arrow function expressions, this, and that

ES6 introduced arrow function expressions, which provide a shorter notation for anonymous functions and add lexical scope for the this variable. In some other programming languages (such as C# and Java), a similar syntax is called *lambda expressions.*

The syntax of arrow function expressions consists of arguments, the fat arrow sign (=>), and the function body. If the function body is just one expression, you don't even need curly braces. If a single-expression function returns a value, there's no need to write the return statement—the result is returned implicitly:

```
let sum = (arg1, arg2) => arg1 + arg2;
```

The body of a multiline arrow function expression should be enclosed in curly braces and use the explicit return statement:

```
(arg1, arg2) => {
  // do something
  return someResult;
}
```

If an arrow function doesn't have any arguments, use empty parentheses:

```
() => {
  // do something
  return someResult;
}
```

If the function has just one argument, no parentheses are required:

```
arg1 => {
  // do something
}
```

The following code snippet passes arrow function expressions as arguments to the array's reduce() method to calculate a sum, and to filter() to print the even numbers:

```
var myArray = [1,2,3,4,5];
console.log( "The sum of myArray elements is " +
            myArray.reduce((a,b) => a+b));  // prints 15
console.log( "The even numbers in myArray are " +
            myArray.filter( value => value % 2 == 0)); // prints 2 4
```

Now that you're familiar with the syntax of arrow functions, let's see how they stream-line working with the this object.

In ES5, figuring out which object is referred to by the this keyword isn't always a simple task. Search online for "JavaScript this and that," and you'll find multiple posts where people complain about this pointing to the "wrong" object. The this refer-ence can have different values depending on how the function is invoked and on whether strict mode was used (see the documentation for "Strict Mode" on the Mozilla Developer Network at http://mng.bz/VNVL). We'll illustrate the problem first, and then we'll show you the solution offered by ES6.

Consider the code in the thisAndThat.html file, which invokes the getQuote() function every second. The getQuote() function prints random generated prices for the stock symbol provided to the StockQuoteGenerator() constructor function.

Listing A.4   thisAndThat.html

```html
<!DOCTYPE html>
<html>
<head>
    <title>thisAndThat.html</title>
</head>
<body>

<script>

    function StockQuoteGenerator(symbol){

        // this.symbol = symbol;    // is undefined inside getQuote()

        var that = this;
        that.symbol = symbol;

        setInterval(function getQuote(){
            console.log("The price quote for " + that.symbol
                    + " is " + Math.random());
        }, 1000);
    }

    var stockQuoteGenerator = new StockQuoteGenerator("IBM");

</script>

</body>
</html>
```

The line that's commented out illustrates the wrong ways of using this when a value is needed in a function that seemingly has the same this reference but doesn't. If you hadn't saved the value of the this variable in that, the value of this.symbol would be undefined in the getQuote() function invoked in setInterval() or as a callback. In getQuote(), this points at the global object, which is not the same as this defined by the StockQuoteGenerator() constructor function.

The other possible solution for ensuring that a function runs in a particular `this` object is to use the JavaScript `call()`, `apply()`, or `bind()` function.

NOTE If you're not familiar with the `this` problem in JavaScript, see Richard Bovell's article "Understand JavaScript's 'this' with Clarity and Master It" (http://mng.bz/ZQfz).

The fatArrow.html file illustrates the arrow function solution that eliminates the need to store `this` in that as you did in thisAndThat.html.

Listing A.5 fatArrow.html

```
<!DOCTYPE html>
<html>
<head>
    <title>fatArrow.html</title>
</head>
<body>

<script>

  "use strict";

  function StockQuoteGenerator(symbol){

      this.symbol = symbol;

      setInterval(() => {
              console.log("The price quote for " + this.symbol
                    + " is " + Math.random());
              }, 1000);
  }

  var stockQuoteGenerator = new StockQuoteGenerator("IBM");

</script>

</body>
</html>
```

The arrow function that's given as an argument to `setInterval()` uses the `this` value of the enclosing context, so it will recognize IBM as the value of `this.symbol`.

A.5.1 Rest and spread operators

In ES5, writing a function with a variable number of parameters requires using a special `arguments` object. This object is *similar* to an array, and it contains values corresponding to the arguments passed to a function. The implicit `arguments` variable can be treated as a local variable in any function.

ES6 has rest and spread operators, and both are represented by three dots (…). The rest operator is used to pass a variable number of arguments to a function, and it has to be the last one in the arguments list. If the name of the function argument starts with the three dots, the function will get the rest of the arguments in an array.

For example, you can pass multiple customers to a function using a single variable name with a rest operator:

```
function processCustomers(...customers){
  // implementation of the function goes here
}
```

In this function, you can handle the customers data the same way you'd handle any array. Imagine that you need to write a function to calculate taxes that must be invoked with the first argument, income, followed by any number of arguments representing the names of the customers. Listing A.6 shows how you can process a variable number of arguments using first the old and then the new syntax. The calcTaxES5() function uses the object named arguments, and the calcTaxES6() function uses the ES6 rest operator.

Listing A.6   rest.html

```
<!DOCTYPE html>
<html>
<head>
    <title>rest.html</title>
</head>
<body>

<script>

  "use strict";

// ES5 and arguments object
  function calcTaxES5(){

      console.log("ES5. Calculating tax for customers with the income ",
                        arguments[0]);

      var customers = [].slice.call(arguments, 1);

      customers.forEach(function (customer) {
          console.log("Processing ", customer);
      });
  }

  calcTaxES5(50000, "Smith", "Johnson", "McDonald");
  calcTaxES5(750000, "Olson", "Clinton");

// ES6 and rest operator
  function calcTaxES6(income, ...customers) {
      console.log("ES6. Calculating tax for customers with the income ",
          ➥ income);
```

income is the first element.

Extracts an array starting from the second element

```
        customers.forEach(function (customer) {
            console.log("Processing ", customer);
        });
    }

    calcTaxES6(50000, "Smith", "Johnson", "McDonald");
    calcTaxES6(750000, "Olson", "Clinton");

</script>

</body>
</html>
```

Both functions, calcTaxES5() and calcTaxES6(), produce the same results:

```
ES5. Calculating tax for customers with the income 50000
Processing Smith
Processing Johnson
Processing McDonald
ES5. Calculating tax for customers with the income 750000
Processing Olson
Processing Clinton
ES6. Calculating tax for customers with the income 50000
Processing Smith
Processing Johnson
Processing McDonald
ES6. Calculating tax for customers with the income 750000
Processing Olson
Processing Clinton
```

There's a difference in handling customers, though. Because the arguments object isn't a real array, you have to create an array in the ES5 version by using the slice() and call() methods to extract the names of the customers starting from the second element in arguments. The ES6 version doesn't require you to use these tricks, because the rest operator gives you a regular array of customers. Using the rest arguments makes the code simpler and more readable.

If the rest operator can turn a variable number of parameters into an array, the spread operator can do the opposite: turn an array into a list of arguments. Say you need to write a function that will calculate tax for three customers with a given income. This time, the number of arguments is fixed, but the customers are located in an array. You can use the spread operator, the three dots (...), to turn the array into a list of separate arguments.

Listing A.7 spread.html

```
<!DOCTYPE html>
<html>
<head>
    <title>spread.html</title>
</head>
<body>
```

```
<script>

  "use strict";

  function calcTaxSpread( customer1, customer2, customer3, income) {
      console.log("ES6. Calculating tax for customers with the income ",
      ➥ income);

      console.log("Processing ", customer1, customer2, customer3);
  }

  var customers = ["Smith", "Johnson", "McDonald"];

  calcTaxSpread(...customers, 50000);          ⟵——— Spread operator

</script>

</body>
</html>
```

In this example, instead of extracting the values from the `customers` array and then
providing these values as function arguments, you use an array with the spread operator, as if you're saying to the function, "You need three arguments, but I'm giving you
an array. Spread it out." Note that as opposed to the rest operator, the spread operator
doesn't have to be the last one in the argument list.

A.5.2 *Generators*

When a browser executes a regular JavaScript function, it runs without interrupting its
own flow to the end. But the execution of a *generator function* can be paused and
resumed multiple times. A generator function can yield control to the calling script,
which runs on the same thread. As soon as the code in a generator function reaches
the keyword `yield`, it gets suspended, and the calling script can resume the function's
execution by calling `next()` on the generator.

    To turn a regular function into a generator, you need to place an asterisk between
the keyword `function` and the function name. Here's an example:

```
function* doSomething(){

  console.log("Started processing");

  yield;

  console.log("Resumed processing");
}
```

When you invoke this function, it doesn't immediately execute the function code but
returns a special `Generator` object, which serves as an iterator. The following line
won't print anything:

```
var iterator = doSomething();
```

To start executing the body of the function, you need to call the next() method on the generator:

```
iterator.next();
```

After this line, the doSomething() function will print "Started processing" and will be suspended because of the yield operator. Calling next() again will print "Resumed processing".

Generator functions are useful when you need to write a function that produces a stream of data. Imagine that you need a function to retrieve and produce stock prices for a specified symbol (IBM, MSFT, and so on). If a stock price falls below a specified value (the limit price) you want to purchase this stock.

The following generator function, getStockPrice(), emulates this scenario. For simplicity, it doesn't retrieve prices from the stock exchange, but instead generates random numbers using Math.random().

Listing A.8   getStockPrice()

```
function* getStockPrice(symbol){

  while(true){
    yield Math.random()*100;

    console.log(`resuming for ${symbol}`);
  }
}
```

If there's a value after yield, it's returned to the caller, but the function isn't completed yet. Even though getStockPrice() has an infinite loop, it will yield (return) the price only if the script that invoked getStockPrice() calls next() on this generator, as follows.

Listing A.9   Invoking getStockPrice()

Creates the Generator object but doesn't execute the body of getStockPrice() that will provide a stream of prices for IBM

```
let priceGenerator = getStockPrice("IBM");  ⊲
```

Sets the limit price to 15 and the initial price to $100

```
const limitPrice = 15;
let price = 100;
```

Requests stock prices until they fall below $15

```
while ( price > limitPrice){

    price = priceGenerator.next().value;
    console.log (`The generator returned ${price}`);
}

console.log(`buying at ${price} !!!`);
```

Requests the next price, and prints it to the console

If the price falls below $15, the loop is over, and the program prints a message about buying the stock and its price.

Running listing A.9 will print something similar to the following on the browser's console:

```
The generator returned 61.63144460879266
resuming for IBM
The generator returned 96.60782956052572
resuming for IBM
The generator returned 31.163037824444473
resuming for IBM
The generator returned 18.416578718461096
resuming for IBM
The generator returned 55.80756475683302
resuming for IBM
The generator returned 14.203652134165168
buying at 14.203652134165168 !!!
```

Note the order of the messages. When you call the next() method on priceGenerator, the execution of the suspended getStockPrice() method resumes at the line below yield, which prints "resuming for IBM". Even though the control flow went outside the function and then came back, getStockPrice() remembers that the value of symbol was "IBM". When the yield operator returns control to the outside script, it creates a snapshot of the stack so it can remember all the values of the local variables. When execution of the generator function is resumed, these values haven't been lost.

With generators, you can separate the implementation of certain operations (such as getting a price quote) and the consumption of the data produced by these operations. The consumer of the data lazily evaluates the results and decides whether requesting more data is necessary.

A.5.3   *Destructuring*

Creating instances of objects means constructing them in memory. *Destructuring* means taking objects apart. In ES5, you could deconstruct any object or a collection by writing a function to do it. ES6 introduces the destructuring assignment syntax that allows you to extract data from an object's properties or an array in a simple expression by specifying a *matching pattern*.

A destructuring expression consists of a matching pattern, the equal sign, and the object or array that you want to pull apart. It's easier to explain by example, which we'll do next.

DESTRUCTURING OBJECTS

Let's say that a getStock() function returns a Stock object that has the attributes symbol and price. In ES5, if you wanted to assign the values of these attributes to separate variables, you'd need to create a variable to store the Stock object first, and then write two statements assigning the object attributes to corresponding variables:

```
var stock = getStock();
var symbol = stock.symbol;
var price = stock.price;
```

In ES6, you just need to write a matching pattern on the left and assign the `Stock` object to it:

```
let {symbol, price} = getStock();
```

It's a little unusual to see curly braces on the left of the equal sign, but this is part of the syntax of a matching expression. When you see curly braces on the left, think of them as a block of code and not the object literal.

The following script demonstrates getting the `Stock` object from the `getStock()` function and destructuring it into two variables.

Listing A.10 Destructuring an object

```
function getStock(){

    return {
        symbol: "IBM",
        price: 100.00
    };
}

let {symbol, price} = getStock();

console.log(`The price of ${symbol} is ${price}`);
```

Running this script will print the following:

```
The price of IBM is 100
```

In other words, you bind a set of data (object attributes, in this case) to a set of variables (symbol and price) in one assignment expression. Even if the `Stock` object had more than two attributes, this destructuring expression would still work, because symbol and price would match the pattern. The matching expression lists only the variables for the object attributes you're interested in.

Listing A.10 works because the names of the variables are the same as the names of the `Stock` attributes. Let's change symbol to sym:

```
let {sym, price} = getStock();
```

Now the output will change because JavaScript doesn't know that the object's symbol attribute should be assigned to the sym variable:

```
The price of undefined is 100
```

This is an example of a wrong matching pattern. If you really want to map the variable named sym to the symbol attribute, introduce an alias name for symbol:

```
let {symbol: sym, price} = getStock();
```

If you provide more variables on the left than the number of attributes the object has, the extra variables will get the value undefined. If you add a stockExchange variable on the left, it will be initialized with undefined, because there's no such attribute in the object returned by getStock():

```
let {sym, price, stockExchange} = getStock();
console.log(`The price of ${symbol} is ${price} ${stockExchange}`);
```

If you apply the preceding destructuring assignment to the same Stock object, the console output will look like this:

```
The price of IBM is 100 undefined
```

If you want the stockExchange variable to have a default value, such as "NASDAQ", you can rewrite the destructuring expression like this:

```
let {sym, price, stockExchange="NASDAQ"} = getStock();
```

You can also destructure nested objects. Listing A.11 creates a nested object that represents the Microsoft stock and passes it to the printStockInfo() function, which pulls the stock symbol and name of the stock exchange from this object.

Listing A.11   Destructuring a nested object

```
let msft = {symbol: "MSFT",
    lastPrice: 50.00,
    exchange: {
        name: "NASDAQ",
        tradingHours: "9:30am-4pm"
    }
};

function printStockInfo(stock){
    let {symbol, exchange:{name}} = stock;
    console.log(`The ${symbol} stock is traded at ${name}`);
}

printStockInfo(msft);
```

Running this script will print the following:

```
The MSFT stock is traded at NASDAQ
```

DESTRUCTURING ARRAYS

Array destructuring works much like object destructuring, but instead of curly brackets, you use square ones. Whereas when destructuring objects you need to specify variables that match attributes, with arrays you specify variables that match indexes. The following code extracts the values of two array elements into two variables:

```
let [name1, name2] = ["Smith", "Clinton"];
console.log(`name1 = ${name1}, name2 = ${name2}`);
```

The output looks like this:

```
name1 = Smith, name2 = Clinton
```

If you just want to extract the second element of this array, the matching pattern looks like this:

```
let [, name2] = ["Smith", "Clinton"];
```

If a function returns an array, the destructuring syntax turns it into a function with a multiple-value return, as shown in the getCustomers() function:

```
function getCustomers(){
    return ["Smith", , , "Gonzales"];
}

let [firstCustomer,,,lastCustomer] = getCustomers();
console.log(`The first customer is ${firstCustomer} and the last one is
➥ ${lastCustomer}`);
```

Now let's combine array destructuring with rest parameters. Let's say you have an array of multiple customers, but you want to process only the first two. The following code snippet shows how to do it:

```
let customers = ["Smith", "Clinton", "Lou", "Gonzales"];

let [firstCust, secondCust, ...otherCust] = customers;

console.log(`The first customer is ${firstCust} and the second one is
➥ ${secondCust}`);
console.log(`Other customers are ${otherCust}`);
```

Here's the console output produced by this code:

```
The first customer is Smith and the second one is Clinton
Other customers are Lou,Gonzales
```

On a similar note, you can pass the matching pattern with a rest parameter to a function:

```
var customers = ["Smith", "Clinton", "Lou", "Gonzales"];

function processFirstTwoCustomers([firstCust, secondCust, ...otherCust]) {

    console.log(`The first customer is ${firstCust} and the second one is
    ➥ ${secondCust}`);
    console.log(`Other customers are ${otherCust}`);

}

processFirstTwoCustomers(customers);
```

The output is the same:

```
The first customer is Smith and the second one is Clinton
Other customers are Lou,Gonzales
```

To summarize, the benefit of destructuring is that you can write less code when you need to initialize some variables with data that's located in object properties or arrays.

A.6   *Iterating with forEach(), for-in, and for-of*

Looping through a collection of objects can be done using different JavaScript keywords and APIs. In this section, we'll show you how to use the new `for-of` loop. We'll compare it with `for-in` loops and the `forEach()` function.

A.6.1   *Using the forEach() method*

Consider the following code, which iterates through an array of four numbers. This array also has an additional `description` property, which is ignored by `forEach()`:

```
var numbersArray = [1, 2, 3, 4];
numbersArray.description = "four numbers";

numbersArray.forEach((n) => console.log(n));
```

The output of the script looks like this:

```
1
2
3
4
```

The `forEach()` method takes a function as an argument and properly prints four numbers from the array, ignoring the `description` property. Another limitation of `forEach()` is that it doesn't allow you to break the loop prematurely. You'd need to use the `every()` method instead of `forEach()` or come up with some other hack to do that. Let's see how the `for-in` loop can help.

A.6.2   *Using the for-in loop*

The `for-in` loop iterates over the *property names* of objects and data collections. In JavaScript, any object is a collection of key-value pairs, where a key is a property name and a value is the property value. The array has five properties: four for the numbers and `description`. Let's iterate through the properties of this array:

```
var numbersArray = [1, 2, 3, 4];
numbersArray.description = "four numbers";

for (let n in numbersArray) {
  console.log(n);
}
```

The output of the preceding code looks like this:

```
0
1
2
3
description
```

Running this code through a debugger shows that each of these properties is a
`string`. To see the actual values of the properties, you should print the array elements
using the `numbersArray[n]` notation:

```
var numbersArray = [1, 2, 3, 4];
numbersArray.description = "four numbers";

for (let n in numbersArray) {
   console.log(numbersArray[n]);
}
```

Now the output looks like this:

```
1
2
3
4
four numbers
```

As you can see, the `for-in` loop iterated through all the properties, not only the data,
which may not be what you need. Let's try the new `for-of` syntax.

A.6.3 *Using for-of*

ES6 introduced the `for-of` loop, which allows you to iterate over data regardless of
what other properties the data collection has. You can break out of this loop if need
be by using the `break` keyword:

```
var numbersArray = [1, 2, 3, 4];
numbersArray.description = "four numbers";

console.log("Running for of for the entire array");
for (let n of numbersArray) {
   console.log(n);
}

console.log("Running for of with a break");
for (let n of numbersArray) {
   if (n >2) break;

   console.log(n);
}
```

This script produces the following output:

```
Running for of for the entire array
1
2
3
4
Running for of with a break
1
2
```

The `for-of` loop works with any iterable object, including `Array`, `Map`, `Set`, and others. Strings are iterable as well. The following code prints the content of the string "John", one character at a time:

```
for (let char of "John") {
  console.log(char);
}
```

A.7   Classes and inheritance

Both ES3 and ES5 support object-oriented programming and inheritance. But with ES6 classes, the code is easier to read and write.

In ES5, objects can be created either from scratch or by inheriting from other objects. By default, all JavaScript objects are inherited from `Object`. This object inheritance is implemented via a special property called `prototype`, which points at this object's ancestor. This is called *prototypal inheritance*. For example, to create an `NJTax` object that inherits from the object `Tax`, you can write something like this:

```
function Tax() {
  // The code of the tax object goes here
}

function NJTax() {
  // The code of New Jersey tax object goes here
}

NJTax.prototype = new Tax();          ◁── Inherits NJTax
                                            from Tax
var njTax = new NJTax();
```

ES6 introduced the keywords `class` and `extends` to bring the syntax in line with other object-oriented languages such as Java and C#. The ES6 equivalent of the preceding code is shown next:

```
class Tax {
  // The code of the tax class goes here
}
```

```
class NJTax extends Tax {
  // The code of New Jersey tax object goes here
}

var njTax = new NJTax();
```

The `Tax` class is an ancestor or *superclass*, and `NJTax` is a descendant or *subclass*. You can also say that the `NJTax` class has the "is a" relation with the class `Tax`. In other words, `NJTax` is a `Tax`. You can implement additional functionality in `NJTax`, but `NJTax` still "is a" or "is a kind of" `Tax`. Similarly, if you create an `Employee` class that inherits from `Person`, you can say that `Employee` is a `Person`.

You can create one or more instances of the objects, like this:

First instance of the Tax object
```
var tax1 = new Tax();
var tax2 = new Tax();
```
Second instance of the Tax object

> **NOTE** Class declarations aren't hoisted. You need to declare the class first and then work with it.

Each of these objects will have properties and methods that exist in the `Tax` class, but they will have different *state*; for example, the first instance could be created for a customer with an annual income of $50,000 and the second for a customer who earned $75,000. Each instance would share the same copy of the methods declared in the `Tax` class, so there's no duplication of code.

In ES5, you can also avoid code duplication by declaring methods not inside the objects, but on their prototypes:

```
function Tax() {
  // The code of the tax object goes here
}

Tax.prototype = {
  calcTax: function() {
    // code to calculate tax goes here
  }
}
```

JavaScript remains the language with prototypal inheritance, but ES6 allows you to write more elegant code:

```
class Tax(){

  calcTax(){
    // code to calculate tax goes here
  }
}
```

> **Class member variables aren't supported**
>
> The ES6 syntax doesn't allow you to declare class member variables as in Java, C#, or TypeScript. The following syntax is *not* supported:
>
> ```
> class Tax {
>   var income;
> }
> ```

A.7.1   *Constructors*

During instantiation, classes execute the code placed in special methods called *constructors*. In languages such as Java and C#, the name of the constructor must be the same as the name of the class; but in ES6, you specify the class's constructor by using the `constructor` keyword:

```
class Tax{

  constructor (income){
    this.income = income;
  }
}

var myTax = new Tax(50000);
```

A constructor is a special method that's executed only once: when the object is created. If you're familiar with the syntax of Java or C#, the preceding code still may look a little unusual: it doesn't declare a separate class-level `income` variable, but creates it dynamically on the `this` object, initializing `this.income` with the values of the constructor's argument. The `this` variable points at the instance of the current object.

The next example shows how you can create an instance of an `NJTax` subclass, providing the income of 50,000 to its constructor:

```
class Tax{
    constructor(income){
        this.income = income;
    }
}

class NJTax extends Tax{
    // The code of New Jersey tax object goes here
}

var njTax = new NJTax(50000);

console.log(`The income in njTax instance is ${njTax.income}`);
```

The output of this code snippet is as follows:

```
The income in njTax instance is 50000
```

Because the NJTax subclass doesn't define its own constructor, the one from the Tax superclass is automatically invoked during the instantiation of NJTax. This wouldn't be the case if a subclass defined its own constructor. You'll see such an example in section A.7.4.

Note that you can access the value of income from outside of the class via the njTax reference variable. Can you hide income so it's not visible from outside the object? We'll discuss this in section A.9.

A.7.2 Static variables

If you need a class property that's shared by multiple instances of the object, you need to create it outside of the class declaration. In the following example, the counter variable is shared by both instances of the object A:

```
class A{
 }

A.counter = 0;

var a1 = new A();
A.counter++;
console.log(A.counter);

var a2 = new A();
A.counter++;
console.log(A.counter);
```

The code produces this output:

```
1
2
```

A.7.3 Getters, setters, and method definitions

The syntax for the object's getter and setter methods isn't new in ES6, but let's review it before going on to the new syntax for defining methods. Setters and getters bind functions to object properties. Consider the declaration and the use of the object literal Tax:

```
var Tax = {
  taxableIncome:0,
  get income() {return this.taxableIncome;},
  set income(value){ this.taxableIncome=value}
};

Tax.income=50000;
console.log("Income: " + Tax.income); // prints Income: 50000
```

Note that you assign and retrieve the value of income using dot notation, as if it were a declared property of the Tax object.

In ES5, you'd need to use the `function` keyword, such as `calculateTax = func-tion(){...}`. ES6 allows you to skip the `function` keyword in any method definition:

```
var Tax = {
    taxableIncome:0,
    get income() {return this.taxableIncome;},
    set income(value){ this.taxableIncome=value},
    calculateTax(){ return this.taxableIncome*0.13}
};

Tax.income=50000;
console.log(`For the income ${Tax.income} your tax is ${Tax.calculateTax()}`);
```

The output of this code comes next:

```
For the income 50000 your tax is 6500
```

Getters and setters offer a convenient syntax for working with properties. For example, if you decide to add some validation code to the `income` getter, the scripts using the `Tax.income` notation won't need to be changed. The bad part is that ES6 doesn't support private variables in classes, so nothing stops programmers from accessing the variable used in a getter or setter (such as `taxableIncome`) directly. We'll talk about hiding (encapsulating) variables in section A.9.

A.7.4   *The super keyword and the super function*

The `super()` function allows a subclass (descendant) to invoke a constructor from a superclass (ancestor). The `super` keyword is used to call a method defined in a superclass. Listing A.12 illustrates both `super()` and `super`. The Tax class has a `calculateFederalTax()` method, and its `NJTax` subclass adds the `calculateStateTax()` method. Both of these classes have their own versions of the `calcMinTax()` method.

Listing A.12   super() and super

```
"use strict";

class Tax{
    constructor(income) {
        this.income = income;
    }

    calculateFederalTax(){
        console.log(`Calculating federal tax for income ${this.income}`);
    }

    calcMinTax(){
        console.log("In Tax. Calculating min tax");
        return 123;
    }
}
```

```
class NJTax extends Tax{
    constructor(income, stateTaxPercent){
        super(income);
        this.stateTaxPercent=stateTaxPercent;
    }

    calculateStateTax(){
        console.log(`Calculating state tax for income ${this.income}`);
    }

     calcMinTax(){
        super.calcMinTax();
        console.log("In NJTax. Adjusting min tax");
    }
}

var theTax = new NJTax(50000, 6);

theTax.calculateFederalTax();
theTax.calculateStateTax();

theTax.calcMinTax();
```

Running this code produces the following output:

```
Calculating federal tax for income 50000
Calculating state tax for income 50000
In Tax. Calculating min tax
In NJTax. Adjusting min tax
```

The NJTax class has its own explicitly defined constructor with two arguments, income and stateTaxPercent, which you provide while instantiating NJTax. To make sure the constructor of Tax is invoked (it sets the income attribute on the object), you explicitly call it from the subclass's constructor: super("50000");. Without this line, listing A.12 would report an error; and even if it didn't, the code in Tax wouldn't see the value of income.

If you need to invoke the constructor of a superclass, it has to be done in the subclass's constructor by calling the function super(). The other way of invoking code in superclasses is by using the super keyword. Both Tax and NJTax have a calcMinTax() method. The one in the Tax superclass calculates the base minimum amount according to federal tax laws, whereas the subclass's version of this method uses the base value and adjusts it. Both methods have the same signature, so you have a case for *method overriding*.

By calling super.calcMinTax(), you ensure that the base federal tax is taken into account for calculating state tax. If you didn't call super.calcMinTax(), the method-overriding would kick in, and the subclass's version of the calcMinTax() method would apply. Method overriding is often used to replace the functionality of the method in the superclass without changing its code.

> **A warning about classes and inheritance**
>
> ES6 classes are just syntactic sugar that increases code readability. Under the hood, JavaScript still uses prototypal inheritance, which allows you to replace the ancestor dynamically at runtime, whereas a class can have only one ancestor. Try to avoid creating deep inheritance hierarchies, because they reduce the flexibility of your code and complicate refactoring if it's needed.
>
> Although using the `super` keyword or `super()` function lets you invoke code in the ancestor, you should try to avoid using them, because they introduce tight coupling between the descendant and ancestor objects. The less the descendant knows about its ancestor, the better. If the ancestor of the object changes, the new one may not have the method you're trying to invoke with `super()`.

A.8   *Asynchronous processing with promises*

To arrange asynchronous processing in previous implementations of ECMAScript, you had to use *callbacks*, which are functions that are given as arguments to another function for invocation. Callbacks can be called synchronously or asynchronously.

In section A.6, you passed a callback to the `forEach()` function for synchronous invocation. In making AJAX requests to the server, you pass a callback function to be invoked asynchronously, when the result arrives from the server.

A.8.1   *A callback hell*

Let's consider an example of getting data about some ordered products from the server. It starts with an asynchronous call to the server to get the information about the customers, and then for each customer you'll need to make another call to get the orders. For each order, you need to get products. The final call will get the products' details.

In asynchronous processing, you don't know when each of these operations will complete, so you need to write callback functions that are invoked when the previous one is complete. Let's use the `setTimeout()` function to emulate delays, as if each operation requires one second to complete.

Listing A.13   Nested callback functions

```
function getProductDetails() {

    setTimeout(function () {
        console.log('Getting customers');
        setTimeout(function () {
            console.log('Getting orders');
            setTimeout(function () {
                console.log('Getting products');
                setTimeout(function () {
                    console.log('Getting product details')
                }, 1000);
```

```
      }, 1000);
    }, 1000);
  }, 1000);
};

getProductDetails();
```

Running this code will print the following messages with one-second delays:

```
Getting customers
Getting orders
Getting products
Getting product details
```

The level of nesting in listing A.13 already makes it difficult to read. Now imagine if you were to add application logic and error processing to it. Writing code this way is often referred to as *callback hell* or a *triangle of doom* (the empty spaces in the code take the shape of a triangle).

A.8.2 *ES6 promises*

ES6 introduced *promises*, which allow you to eliminate this nesting and make the code more readable, while maintaining the same functionality as with callbacks. The `Promise` object waits and listens for the result of an asynchronous operation and lets you know if it succeeded or failed so you can proceed with the next steps accordingly. The `Promise` object represents the future result of an operation, and it can be in one of these states:

- *Fulfilled*—The operation successfully completed.
- *Rejected*—The operation failed and returned an error.
- *Pending*—The operation is in progress, neither fulfilled nor rejected.

You instantiate a `Promise` object by providing two functions to its constructor: the function to call if the operation is fulfilled, and the function to call if the operation is rejected. Consider a script with a `getCustomers()` function.

Listing A.14 Using a promise

```
function getCustomers(){

  return new Promise(
    function (resolve, reject){

      console.log("Getting customers");
        // Emulate an async server call here
      setTimeout(function(){
        var success = true;
        if (success){
          resolve( "John Smith");          ⟵——— Got the customer
        }else{
```

```
        reject("Can't get customers");
      }
    },1000);

  }
 );
}

let promise = getCustomers()
  .then((cust) => console.log(cust))
  .catch((err) => console.log(err));
console.log("Invoked getCustomers. Waiting for results");
```

The `getCustomers()` function returns a `Promise` object, which is instantiated with a function that has `resolve` and `reject` as the constructor's arguments. In the code, you invoke `resolve()` if you receive the customer information. For simplicity, `set-Timeout()` emulates an asynchronous call that lasts 1 second. You also hardcode the success flag to be true. In a real-world scenario, you could make a request with the `XMLHttpRequest` object and invoke `resolve()` if the result was successfully retrieved or `reject()` if an error occurred.

At the bottom of listing A.14, you attach `then()` and `catch()` methods to the `Promise()` instance. Only one of these two will be invoked. When you call `resolve("John Smith")` from inside the function, it results in the invocation of the `then()` that received "John Smith" as its argument. If you changed the value of `success` to `false`, the `catch()` method would be called with the argument "Can't get customers".

Running listing A.14 prints the following messages on the console:

```
Getting customers
Invoked getCustomers. Waiting for results
John Smith
```

Note that the message "Invoked getCustomers. Waiting for results" is printed before "John Smith". This proves that the `getCustomers()` function worked asynchronously.

Each promise represents one asynchronous operation, and you can chain them to guarantee a particular order of execution. Let's add a `getOrders()` function that can find the orders for a specific customer, and chain it with `getCustomers()`.

Listing A.15   Chaining promises

```
'use strict';

function getCustomers(){

  let promise = new Promise(
    function (resolve, reject){

      console.log("Getting customers");
        // Emulate an async server call here
      setTimeout(function(){
```

```
        let success = true;
        if (success){
          resolve( "John Smith");          ⟵—— Got the customer
        }else{
          reject("Can't get customers");
        }
      },1000);

    }
  );
  return promise;
}

function getOrders(customer){

  let promise =  new Promise(
     function (resolve, reject){

        // Emulate an async server call here
      setTimeout(function(){
        let success = true;
        if (success){
          resolve( `Found the order 123 for ${customer}`);    ⟵—— Got the order
        }else{
          reject("Can't get orders");
        }
      },1000);

    }
  );
  return promise;
}

getCustomers()
.then((cust) => {console.log(cust);return cust;})
  .then((cust) => getOrders(cust))
  .then((order) => console.log(order))
  .catch((err) => console.error(err));
console.log("Chained getCustomers and getOrders. Waiting for results");
```

This code not only declares and chains two functions, but also demonstrates how you can print intermediate results on the console. The output of listing A.15 follows (note that the customer returned from getCustomers() was properly passed to getOrders()):

```
Getting customers
Chained getCustomers and getOrders. Waiting for results
John Smith
Found the order 123 for John Smith
```

You can chain multiple function calls using then() and have just one error-handling script for all chained invocations. If an error occurs, it will be propagated through the entire chain of thens until it finds an error handler. No thens will be invoked after the error.

Changing the value of the success variable to false will result in listing A.15 printing the message "Can't get customers", and the getOrders() method won't be called. If you remove these console prints, the code that retrieves customers and orders looks clean and is easy to understand:

```
getCustomers()
  .then((cust) => getOrders(cust))
  .catch((err) => console.error(err));
```

Adding more thens doesn't make this code less readable (compare it with the triangle of doom from listing A.13).

A.8.3   *Resolving several promises at once*

Another case to consider is asynchronous functions that don't depend on each other. Say you need to invoke two functions in no particular order, but you need to perform some action only *after* both of them are complete. Promise has an all() method that takes an iterable collection of promises and executes (resolves) all of them. Because the all() method returns a Promise object, you can add then() or catch() (or both) to the result.

Let's see what happens if you use all() with the getCustomers() and getOrders() functions:

```
Promise.all([getCustomers(), getOrders()])
.then((order) => console.log(order));
```

This code produces the following output:

```
Getting customers
Getting orders for undefined
["John Smith","Order 123"]
```

Note the "Getting orders for undefined" message. This happens because you haven't resolved the promises in an orderly fashion, so getOrders() hasn't received the customer as its argument. Certainly, using Promise.all() isn't a good idea in this scenario, but there are situations when it makes perfect sense. Imagine a web portal that needs to make several asynchronous calls to get the weather, stock market news, and traffic information. If you want to display the portal page when all of these calls have completed, Promise.all() is what you need:

```
Promise.all([getWeather(), getStockMarketNews(), getTraffic()])
.then(renderGUI);
```

Compared to callbacks, promises make your code more linear and easier to read, and they represent multiple states of an application. On the negative side, promises can't be canceled. Imagine an impatient user who clicks a button several times to get some data from the server. Each click creates a promise and initiates an HTTP request. There's no way to keep only the last request and cancel the uncompleted ones. The next step in the evolution of a `Promise` object is an `Observable` object, which may be introduced in future ECMAScript specifications; in chapter 5, we explain how to use it today.

> **NOTE** The new Fetch API for getting resources over the network may soon become a replacement for the `XMLHttpRequest` object. The Fetch API is based on promises—see the Mozilla Developer Network documentation for the API for details (http://mng.bz/mbMe).

A.9 Modules

In any programming language, splitting code into modules helps organize the application into logical and possibly reusable units. Modularized applications allow programming tasks to be split between software developers more efficiently. Developers get to decide which API should be exposed by the module for external use and which should be used internally.

ES5 doesn't have language constructs for creating modules, so we have to resort to one of these options:

- Manually implement a module design pattern as an immediately initialized function (see Todd Motto's article "Mastering the Module Pattern" at https://toddmotto.com/mastering-the-module-pattern/).
- Use third-party implementations of the AMD (http://mng.bz/JKVc) or CommonJS (http://mng.bz/7Lld) standard.

CommonJS was created for modularizing JavaScript applications that run outside the web browser (such as those written in Node.js and deployed under Google's V8 engine). AMD is primarily used for applications that run in a web browser.

In any decent-sized web application, you should minimize the amount of JavaScript code loaded to the client. Imagine a typical online store. Do you need to load the code for processing payments when users open the application's home page? What if they never click the Place Order button? It would be nice to modularize the application so the code is loaded on an as-needed basis. RequireJS is probably the most popular third-party library that implements the AMD standard; it lets you define dependencies between modules and load them into the browser on demand.

Starting with ES6, modules have become part of the language, which means developers will stop using third-party libraries to implement various standards. Even though web browsers don't support ES6 modules natively, there are polyfills that let you start using JavaScript modules today. We use the polyfill called SystemJS in this book.

A.9.1 Imports and exports

Typically, a module is just a file with JavaScript code that implements certain functionality and provides a public API so other JavaScript programs can use it. There's no special keyword to declare that the code in a particular file is a module. But in the script, you can use the keywords `import` and `export`, which turn the script into an ES6 module.

The `import` keyword allows one script to declare that it needs to use variables or functions defined in another script file. Similarly, the `export` keyword lets you declare variables, functions, or classes that the module should expose to other scripts. In other words, by using the `export` keyword, you can make selected APIs available to other modules. The module's functions, variables, and classes that aren't explicitly exported remain encapsulated in the module.

> **NOTE** The main difference between a module and a regular JavaScript file is that when you add a file to a page with a `<script>` tag, it become part of a global context, whereas the declarations in modules are local and never become part of the global namespace. Even exported members are available only to those modules that import them.

ES6 offers two types of `export` usage: named and default. With named exports, you can use the `export` keyword in front of multiple members of the module (such as classes, functions, and variables). The code in the following file (tax.js) exports the variable `taxCode` and the function `calcTaxes()`, but the `doSomethingElse()` function remains hidden to external scripts:

```
export var taxCode;

export function calcTaxes() { // the code goes here }

function doSomethingElse() { // the code goes here}
```

When a script imports named exported module members, their names must be placed in curly braces. The main.js file illustrates this:

```
import {taxCode, calcTaxes} from 'tax';

if (taxCode === 1) { // do something }

calcTaxes();
```

Here, `tax` refers to the filename of the module, minus the file extension.

One of the exported module members can be marked as `default`, which means this is an anonymous export, and another module can give it any name in its `import` statement. The my_module.js file that exports a function may look like this:

```
export default function() { // do something }          ◁——— No semicolon

export var taxCode;
```

The main.js file imports both named and default exports while assigning the name `coolFunction` to the default one:

```
import coolFunction, {taxCode} from 'my_module';

coolFunction();
```

Note that you don't use curly braces around `coolFunction` but you do around `tax-Code`. The script that imports a class, variable, or function that was exported with the `default` keyword can give them new names without using any special keywords:

```
import aVeryCoolFunction, {taxCode} from 'my_module';

aVeryCoolFunction();
```

But to give an alias name to a named export, you need to write something like this:

```
import coolFunction, {taxCode as taxCode2016} from 'my_module';
```

The `import` statements don't result in copying the exported code. Imports serve as references. The script that imports modules or members can't modify them, and if the values in the imported modules change, the new values are immediately reflected in all places where they were imported.

A.9.2 *Loading modules dynamically with the ES6 module loader*

The early drafts of the ES6 specification defined a dynamic module loader named `System`, but it didn't make it into the final version of the spec. In the future, the `System` object will be natively implemented by browsers as a promise-based loader that can be used as follows:

```
System.import('someModule')
    .then (function(module){
        module.doSomething();
      })
    .catch (function(error){
        // handle error here
      })
      ;
```

Because no browsers implement the `System` object yet, we use polyfills. One of the `System` polyfills is the ES6 Module Loader, and another is SystemJS.

> **NOTE** Although es6-module-loader.js is a polyfill for the `System` object that loads *only* ES6 modules, the universal SystemJS loader supports not only ES6 modules, but AMD and CommonJS modules as well. We use SystemJS throughout this book (except chapter 10, which uses a loader from Webpack), starting in chapter 3. With SystemJS, you can dynamically download JavaScript code along with CSS and HTML files.

The polyfill for the ES6 Module Loader is available on GitHub at http://mng.bz/MD8w. You can download and unzip this loader, copy the es6-module-loader.js file to your project directory, and include it in your HTML file before your application scripts:

```
<script src="es6-module-loader.js"></script>
<script src="my_app.js"></script>
```

To make sure your ES6 script works in all browsers, you'll need to transpile it to ES5. This can be done either up front as a part of your build process or on the fly in a browser. We'll show you the latter scenario using the Traceur compiler.

You'll need to include the transpiler, the module loader, and your script(s) in the HTML file. You can either download the Traceur script to your local directory or provide a direct link to it, like this:

```
<script src="https://google.github.io/traceur-compiler/bin/traceur.js">
</script>
<script src="es6-module-loader.js"></script>
<script src="my-es6-app.js"></script>
```

Let's consider a simple application for an online store that has shipping and billing modules loaded on demand. The application consists of one HTML file and two modules. The HTML file has one button labeled Load the Shipping Module. When the user clicks this button, the application should load and use the shipping module, which in turn depends on the billing module. The shipping module is as follows.

Listing A.16   shipping.js

```
import {processPayment} from 'billing';

export function ship() {
    processPayment();
    console.log("Shipping products...");
}

function calculateShippingCost(){
    console.log("Calculating shipping cost");
}
```

The ship() function can be invoked by external scripts, and calculateShipping-Cost() is private. The shipping module starts with the import statement so it can invoke the processPayment() function from the billing module that's shown next.

Listing A.17   billing.js

```
function validateBillingInfo() {
    console.log("Validating billing info...");
}

export function processPayment(){
    console.log("processing payment...");
}
```

The billing module also has a public processPayment() function and a private one called validateBillingInfo().

The HTML file includes one button with a click event handler that loads the shipping module using `System.import()` from es6-module-loader.

Listing A.18   moduleLoader.html

```html
<!DOCTYPE html>
<html>
<head>
    <title>modules.html</title>
    <script src="https://google.github.io/traceur-compiler/bin/traceur.js">
    </script>
    <script src="es6-module-loader.js"></script>
</head>
<body>

  <button id="shippingBtn">Load the Shipping Module</button>

<script type="module">

let btn = document.querySelector('#shippingBtn');
btn.addEventListener('click', () => {

    System.import('shipping')
        .then(function(module) {
            console.log("Shipping module Loaded. ", module);

            module.ship();

            module.calculateShippingCost();          <─── Throws an error
        })
        .catch(function(err){
            console.log("In error handler", err);
        });
});

</script>

</body>
</html>
```

`System.import()` returns an ES6 `Promise` object; when the module is loaded, the function specified in `then()` is executed. In case of an error, control goes to the `catch()` function.

In the `then()`, you print the message to the console and invoke the `ship()` function from the shipping module, which invokes `processPayment()` from billing. After that, you try to invoke the module's `calculateShippingCost()` function, which results in an error because this function wasn't exported and remains private.

TIP If you use Traceur and have an inline script in the HTML file, use `type="module"` to make sure Traceur transpiles it to ES5. Without it, this script won't work in browsers that don't support the `let` keyword and arrow functions.

To run this example on your computer, you'll need to have node.js with npm installed. Then download and install es6-module loader in any directory by running the following npm command:

```
npm install es6-module-loader
```

After that, create an application folder, and copy the es6-module-loader.js file there (this is a minimized version of the loader that was downloaded by npm). The sample application has three additional files, shown in listings A.16–A.18. For simplicity, keep all these files in the same folder.

> **NOTE**   To see this code in action, you need to serve it using a web server. You can install a basic HTTP server like live-server as explained in section 2.1.4.

We ran moduleLoader.html in Google Chrome and opened Chrome Developer Tools. Figure A.6 shows what the Chrome browser looks like after clicking the Load the Shipping Module button.

Look at the XHR tab in the middle of the window. The HTML page loads shipping.js and billing.js only after the user clicks the button. These files are small (440 and 387 bytes, including HTTP response objects), and making an additional network call to get them seems like overkill. But if the application consists of 10 modules of 500 KB each, modularization with lazy loading makes sense.

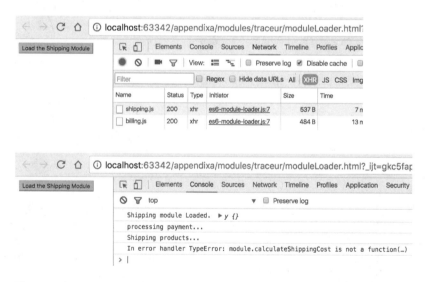

Figure A.6   Using es6-module-loader

At the bottom of the figure, on the Console tab, you can see the message from the script in `moduleLoader` indicating that the shipping module was loaded. Then it calls the function from `ship()` from the shipping module and generates an error trying to call the `calculateShippingCost()` function, as expected.

NOTE The goal of this appendix was to get you familiar with the ES6 syntax. For in-depth coverage, read the book *Exploring ES6* by Axel Rauschmayer (http://exploringjs.com/es6/). Eric Douglas maintains a compilation of various ES6 learning resources on GitHub at http://mng.bz/cZfX.

appendix B
TypeScript as a language
for Angular applications

You may be wondering, why not just develop in JavaScript? Why do we need to use other programming languages if JavaScript is already a language? You wouldn't find articles about languages for developing Java or C# applications, would you?

The reason is that developing in JavaScript isn't overly productive. Say a function expects a string value as an argument, but the developer mistakenly invokes it by passing a numeric value. With JavaScript, this error can be caught only at runtime. Java or C# compilers won't even compile code that has mismatching types, but JavaScript is forgiving because it's a dynamically typed language.

Although JavaScript engines do a good job of guessing the types of variables by their values, development tools have a limited ability to help you without knowing the types. In mid- and large-size applications, this JavaScript shortcoming lowers the productivity of software developers.

On larger projects, good IDE context-sensitive help and support for refactoring are important. Renaming all occurrences of a variable or function name in statically typed languages is done by IDEs in a split second, even in projects that have thousands of lines of code; but this isn't the case in JavaScript, which doesn't support types. IDEs can help with refactoring much better when the types of the variables are known.

To be more productive, you may consider developing in a statically typed language and then convert the code to JavaScript for deployment. Currently there are dozens of languages that compile to JavaScript (see the list of languages that compile to JS on GitHub at http://mng.bz/vjzi). The most popular are TypeScript (www.typescriptlang.org), CoffeeScript (http://coffeescript.org), and Dart (www.dartlang.org).

> **Why not use the Dart language?**
> We spent quite a bit of time working with Dart, and we like the language, but it has some drawbacks:
>
> - Interoperability with third-party JavaScript libraries isn't that great.
> - Development in Dart can be done only in a specialized version of the Chrome browser (Dartium) that comes with the Dart VM. No other web browsers have it.
> - The generated JavaScript isn't easily readable by a human.
> - The community of Dart developers is rather small.

The Angular framework is written in TypeScript, and in this appendix we'll cover its syntax. All the code samples in this book are written in TypeScript. We'll also show you how to turn TypeScript code into its JavaScript version so it can be executed by any web browser or a standalone JavaScript engine.

B.1 Why write Angular apps in TypeScript?

You can write applications in ES6 (and even in ES5), but we use TypeScript as a substantially more productive way for writing JavaScript. Here's why:

- TypeScript supports types. This allows the TypeScript compiler to help you find and fix lots of errors during development before even running the app.
- Great IDE support is one of TypeScript's main advantages. If you make a mistake in a function or a variable name, it's displayed in red. If you pass the wrong number of parameters (or wrong types) to a function, the wrong ones show in red. IDEs also offer great context-sensitive help. TypeScript code can be refactored by IDEs, whereas JavaScript has to be refactored manually. If you need to explore a new library, just install its type-definitions file, and the IDE will prompt you with available APIs so you don't need to read its documentation elsewhere.
- Angular is bundled with type definitions files, so IDEs perform type checking while using the Angular API and offer context-sensitive help right out of the box.
- TypeScript follows the ECMAScript 6 and 7 specifications and adds to them types, interfaces, decorators, class member variables (fields), generics, and the keywords `public` and `private`. Future releases of TypeScript will support the missing ES6 features and implement the features of ES7 (see the TypeScript "Roadmap" on GitHub at http://mng.bz/Ri29).
- TypeScript interfaces allow you to declare custom types that will be used in your application. Interfaces help prevent compile-time errors caused by using objects of the wrong types in your application.
- The generated JavaScript code is easy to read, and it looks like hand-written code.
- Most of the code samples in the Angular documentation, articles, and blogs are given in TypeScript (see https://angular.io/docs).

B.2   *The role of transpilers*

Web browsers don't understand any language but JavaScript. If the source code is written in TypeScript, it has to be *transpiled* into JavaScript before you can run it in the browser's or a standalone JavaScript engine.

Transpiling means converting the source code of a program in one language into source code in another language. Many developers prefer to use the word *compiling*, so phrases like "TypeScript compiler" and "compile TypeScript into JavaScript" are also valid.

Figure B.1 shows a screenshot with TypeScript code on the left and its equivalent in an ES5 version of JavaScript generated by the TypeScript transpiler. In TypeScript, we declared a variable `foo` of type `string`, but the transpiled version doesn't have the type information. In TypeScript, we declared a class `Bar`, which was transpiled in a class-like pattern in the ES5 syntax. If we had specified ES6 as a target for transpiling, the generated JavaScript code would look different.

Figure B.1   Transpiling TypeScript into ES5

A combination of Angular with statically typed TypeScript simplifies the development of medium and large web applications. Good tooling and the static type analyzer substantially decrease the number of runtime errors and will shorten the time to market. When complete, your Angular application will have lots of JavaScript code; and although developing in TypeScript will require you to write more code, you'll reap the benefits by saving time on testing and refactoring and minimizing the number of runtime errors.

B.3   *Getting started with TypeScript*

Microsoft has open-sourced TypeScript, and it hosts the TypeScript repository on GitHub at http://mng.bz/Ri29. You can install the TypeScript compiler using npm or download it from www.typescriptlang.org. The TypeScript site also has a web-hosted TypeScript compiler (a playground), where you can enter TypeScript code and compile it to JavaScript interactively, as shown in figure B.2.

In the TypeScript playground, you enter TypeScript code on the left, and its JavaScript version is displayed on the right. Click the Run button to execute the transpiled code (open the browser's Developer Tools to see the console output produced by your code, if any).

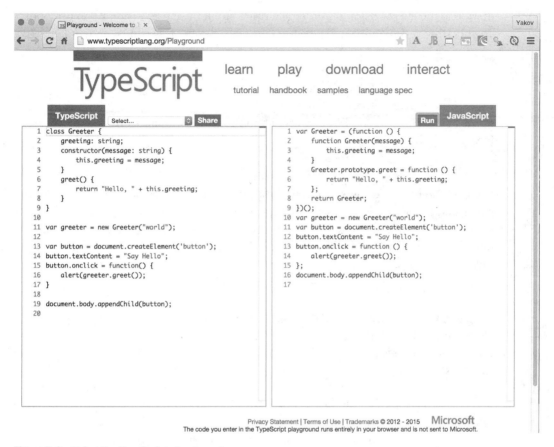

Figure B.2 Using the TypeScript playground

Interactive tools will suffice for learning the language's syntax, but for real-world development you'll need to use the right tooling to be productive. You may decide to use an IDE or a text editor, but having the TypeScript compiler installed locally is a must for development.

B.3.1 *Installing and using the TypeScript compiler*

The TypeScript compiler is itself written in TypeScript. You'll use Node.js's npm package manager to install the compiler. If you don't have Node, download and install it from http://nodejs.org. Node.js comes with npm, which you'll use to install not only the TypeScript compiler, but also many other development tools throughout the book.

To install the TypeScript compiler globally, run the following npm command in the command or terminal window:

```
npm install -g typescript
```

The -g option installs the TypeScript compiler globally on your computer, so it's available from the command prompt for all of your projects. To develop Angular 2 applications, download the latest version of the TypeScript compiler (we use version 2.0 in this book). To check the version of your TypeScript compiler, run the following command:

```
tsc --version
```

Code written in TypeScript has to be transpiled into JavaScript so web browsers can execute it. TypeScript code is saved in files with the .ts extension. Say you wrote a script and saved it in the file main.ts. The following command will transpile main.ts into main.js.

```
tsc main.ts
```

You can also generate source map files that map the source code in TypeScript to the generated JavaScript. With source maps, you can place breakpoints in your TypeScript code while running it in the browser, even though it executes JavaScript. To compile main.ts into main.js while also generating the main.map source map file, you run the following command:

```
tsc --sourcemap main.ts
```

Figure B.3 shows a screenshot we took while debugging in Chrome Developer Tools. Note the breakpoint at line 15. You can find your TypeScript file in the Sources tab of the Developer Tools panel, place a breakpoint in the code, and watch the values of the variables on the right.

During compilation, TypeScript's compiler removes all TypeScript types, interfaces, and keywords from the generated code to produce valid JavaScript. By providing compiler options, you can generate JavaScript compliant with ES3, ES5, or ES6 syntax. Currently ES3 is the default. Here's how to transpile the code to ES5-compatible syntax:

```
tsc --t ES5 main.ts
```

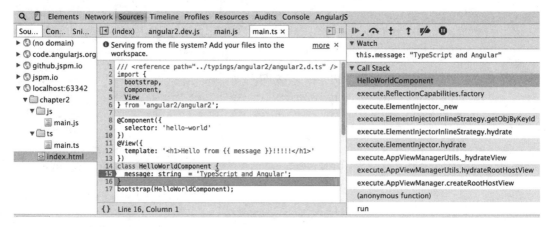

Figure B.3   Debugging TypeScript in Chrome Developer Tools

> ### Transpiling TypeScript in a web browser
>
> During development, we use tsc installed locally, but transpiling can also be done either on the server during deployment or on the fly when the web browser loads your application. In this book, we use the SystemJS library, which internally uses tsc to transpile and dynamically load app modules.
>
> Keep in mind that transpiling on the fly in the browser may introduce delays in displaying your app's content on the user's device. If you use SystemJS to load and transpile your code in the browser, source maps will be generated by default.

If you want to compile your code in memory without generating output .js files, run tsc with the `--noEmit` option. We often use this option in development mode because we just need to have executable JavaScript code in the browser's memory.

You can start your TypeScript compiler in watch mode by providing the `-w` option. In this mode, whenever you modify and save your code, it's automatically transpiled into the corresponding JavaScript files. To compile and watch all .ts files, run the following command:

```
tsc -w *.ts
```

The compiler will compile all the TypeScript files, print error messages (if any) on the console, and continue watching the files for changes. As soon as a file changes, tsc will immediately recompile it.

> **NOTE** Typically, we don't use the IDE to compile TypeScript. We use either SystemJS with its in-browser compiler or a bundler (Webpack) that uses a special TypeScript loader for compilation. We use the TypeScript code analyzer provided by the IDEs to highlight errors, and the browser to debug TypeScript.

The TypeScript compiler allows you to preconfigure the process of compilation (specifying the source and destination directories, source map generation, and so on). The presence of the tsconfig.json configuration file in the project directory means you can enter `tsc` on the command line, and the compiler will read all the options from tsconfig.json. A sample tsconfig.json file is shown here.

Listing B.1 tsconfig.json

```json
{
    "compilerOptions": {
        "target": "es5",
        "module": "commonjs",
        "emitDecoratorMetadata": true,
        "experimentalDecorators": true,
        "rootDir": ".",
        "outDir": "./js"
    }
}
```

This config file instructs tsc to transpile the code into ES5 syntax. The generated JavaScript files will be located in the js directory. The tsconfig.json file may include the `files` section that lists the files that have to be compiled by TypeScript. Listing B.1 doesn't include this list because you use the `rootDir` option to request the compilation of all files starting from the root directory of the project.

If you want to exclude some of your project's files from compilation, add the `exclude` property to tsconfig.json. This is how you can exclude the entire content of the node_modules directory:

```
"exclude": [
    "node_modules"
  ]
```

You can read more about configuring the compilation process and the TypeScript compiler's options at in the TypeScript documentation (http://mng.bz/rf14).

> **NOTE** Most of the Angular examples in this book use *annotations* (a.k.a. *decorators*) with classes or class members (such as @Component and @Input). Annotations are a way to add metadata to the annotated classes or their members. See the "What's metadata?" sidebar in section 2.1.1 for more details.

B.4   *TypeScript as a superset of JavaScript*

TypeScript fully supports ES5 and most of the ES6 syntax. Just change the name extension of a file with JavaScript code from .js to .ts, and it'll become valid TypeScript code. The only two exceptions we've seen so far are handling optional function parameters and assigning a value to an object literal.

In JavaScript, even if a function is declared with two parameters, you can invoke it by providing only one, whereas in TypeScript you need to append a question mark to the parameter name to make it optional. In JavaScript, you can initialize a variable with an empty object literal and immediately attach a property using dot notation, whereas in TypeScript you'd need to use square brackets.

But these differences are minor. What's more important is that because it's a superset of JavaScript, TypeScript adds a number of useful features to JavaScript. We'll review them next.

> **TIP** If you're in the middle of converting a JavaScript project to TypeScript, you can use the tsc compiler's `--allowJs` option. The TypeScript compiler will check the input .js files for syntax errors and emit valid output based on the `--target` and `--module` options of tsc. The output can be combined with other .ts files as well. Source maps are still generated for .js files, just as with .ts files.

B.5   *Optional types*

You can declare variables and provide types for all or some of them. The following two lines are valid TypeScript syntax:

```
var name1 = 'John Smith';

var name2: string = 'John Smith';
```

If you use types, TypeScript's transpiler can detect mismatched types during development, and IDEs will offer code completion and refactoring support. This will increase your productivity on any decent-sized project. Even if you don't use types in declarations, TypeScript will guess the type based on the assigned value and will still do type checking afterward. This is called *type inference*.

The following fragment of TypeScript code shows that you can't assign a numeric value to a name1 variable that was meant to be a string, even though it was initially declared without a type (JavaScript syntax). After initializing this variable with a string value, the inferred typing won't let you assign the numeric value to name1. The same rule applies to the variable name2, which is declared with an explicit type:

```
var name1 = 'John Smith';
name1 = 123;
```

Assigning a value of a different type to a variable is valid in JavaScript but invalid in TypeScript because of the inferred type.

```
var name2: string = 'John Smith';
name2 = 123;
```

Assigning a value of a different type to a variable is valid in JavaScript but invalid in TypeScript because of the explicitly declared type.

In TypeScript, you can declare typed variables, function parameters, and return values. There are four keywords for declaring basic types: number, boolean, string, and void. The latter indicates the absence of a return value in a function declaration. A variable can have a value of type null or undefined, similar to JavaScript.

Here are some examples of variables declared with explicit types:

```
var salary: number;
var name: string = "Alex";
var isValid: boolean;
var customerName: string = null;
```

All of these types are subtypes of the any type. If you don't specify a type while declaring a variable or a function argument, TypeScript's compiler will assume that it has the type any, which will allow you to assign any value to this variable or function argument. You may as well explicitly declare a variable, specifying any as its type. In this case, inferred typing isn't applied. Both of these declarations are valid:

```
var name2: any = 'John Smith';
name2 = 123;
```

If variables are declared with explicit types, the compiler will check their values to ensure that they match the declarations. TypeScript includes other types that are used in interactions with the web browser, such as HTMLElement and Document.

If you define a class or an interface, it can be used as a custom type in variable declarations. We'll introduce classes and interfaces later, but first let's get familiar with TypeScript functions, which are the most-used constructs in JavaScript.

B.5.1 Functions

TypeScript functions (and function expressions) are similar to JavaScript functions, but you can explicitly declare parameter types and return values. Let's write a JavaScript function that calculates tax. It'll have three parameters and will calculate tax based on the state, income, and number of dependents. For each dependent, the person is entitled to a $500 or $300 tax deduction, depending on the state the person lives in.

Listing B.2 Calculating tax in JavaScript

```javascript
function calcTax(state, income, dependents) {
    if (state == 'NY') {
        return income * 0.06 - dependents * 500;
    } else if (state == 'NJ') {
        return income * 0.05 - dependents * 300;
    }
}
```

Say a person with an income of $50,000 lives in the state of New Jersey and has two dependents. Let's invoke `calcTax()`:

```javascript
var tax = calcTax('NJ', 50000, 2);
```

The `tax` variable gets the value of 1,900, which is correct. Even though `calcTax()` doesn't declare any types for the function parameters, you can guess them based on the parameter names.

Now let's invoke it the wrong way, passing a `string` value for a number of dependents:

```javascript
var tax = calcTax('NJ', 50000, 'two');
```

You won't know there's a problem until you invoke this function. The `tax` variable will have a `NaN` value (not a number). A bug sneaked in just because you didn't have a chance to explicitly specify the types of the parameters. Let's rewrite this function in TypeScript, declaring types for parameters and the return value.

Listing B.3 Calculating tax in TypeScript

```typescript
function calcTax(state: string, income: number, dependents: number): number{

    if (state == 'NY'){
        return income*0.06 - dependents*500;
    } else if (state=='NJ'){
        return income*0.05 - dependents*300;
    }
}
```

Now there's no way to make the same mistake and pass a string value for the number of dependents:

```
var tax: number = calcTax('NJ', 50000, 'two');
```

The TypeScript compiler will display an error saying, "Argument of type 'string' is not assignable to parameter of type 'number'." Moreover, the return value of the function is declared as number, which stops you from making another mistake and assigning the result of the tax calculations to a non-numeric variable:

```
var tax: string = calcTax('NJ', 50000, 'two');
```

The compiler will catch this, producing the error "The type 'number' is not assignable to type 'string': var tax: string." This kind of type-checking during compilation can save you a lot of time on any project.

B.5.2 *Default parameters*

While declaring a function, you can specify default parameter values. The only limitation is that parameters with default values can't be followed by required parameters. In listing B.3, to provide NY as a default value for the state parameter, you *can't* declare it as follows:

```
function calcTax(state: string = 'NY', income: number, dependents: number):
➡ number{
    // the code goes here
}
```

You need to change the order of the parameters to ensure that there are no required parameters after the default one:

```
function calcTax(income: number, dependents: number, state: string = 'NY'):
➡ number{
    // the code goes here
}
```

There's no need to change even one line of code in the body of calcTax(). You now have the freedom to invoke it with either two or three parameters:

```
var tax: number = calcTax(50000, 2);
// or
var tax: number = calcTax(50000, 2, 'NY');
```

The results of both invocations will be the same.

B.5.3 *Optional parameters*

In TypeScript, you can easily mark function parameters as optional by appending a question mark to the parameter name. The only restriction is that optional parameters must come last in the function declaration. When you write code for functions with optional parameters, you need to provide application logic that handles the cases when the optional parameters aren't provided.

Let's modify the tax-calculation function: if no dependents are specified, it won't apply any deduction to the calculated tax.

Listing B.4   Calculating tax in TypeScript, modified

```
function calcTax(income: number, state: string = 'NY', dependents?: number):
    number{

    var deduction: number;

    if (dependents) {                    ◁───── Handles the optional value in dependents
        deduction = dependents*500;
    }else {
      deduction = 0;
    }

    if (state == 'NY'){
        return income*0.06 - deduction;
    } else if (state=='NJ'){
        return income*0.05  - deduction;
    }
}

var tax: number = calcTax(50000, 'NJ', 3);
console.log("Your tax is " + tax);

var tax: number = calcTax(50000);
console.log("Your tax is " + tax);
```

Note the question mark in `dependents?: number`. Now the function checks whether the value for `dependents` was provided. If it wasn't, you assign 0 to the `deduction` variable; otherwise, you deduct 500 for each dependent.

Running listing B.4 will produce the following output:

```
Your tax is 1000
Your tax is 3000
```

B.5.4   *Arrow-function expressions*

TypeScript supports simplified syntax for using anonymous functions in expressions. There's no need to use the `function` keyword, and the fat-arrow symbol (`=>`) is used to separate function parameters from the body. TypeScript supports the ES6 syntax for arrow functions (appendix A has more details on arrow functions). In some other programming languages, arrow functions are known as *lambda expressions*.

Let's look at the simplest example of an arrow function with a single-line body:

```
var getName = () => 'John Smith';
console.log(getName());
```

The empty parentheses denote that the preceding arrow function has no parameters. A single-line arrow expression doesn't need curly braces or an explicit return statement, and the preceding code fragment will print "John Smith" on the console. If you try that code in TypeScript's playground, it'll convert it to the following ES5 code:

```
var getName = function () { return 'John Smith'; };
console.log(getName());
```

If the body of your arrow function consists of multiple lines, you'll have to enclose it in curly braces and use the return statement. The following code snippet converts a hardcoded string value to uppercase and prints "PETER LUGER" on the console:

```
var getNameUpper = () => {
    var name = 'Peter Luger'.toUpperCase();
    return name;
}
console.log(getNameUpper());
```

In addition to providing a shorter syntax, arrow-function expressions remove the infamous confusion with the this keyword. In JavaScript, if you use the this keyword in a function, it may not point at the object where the function is being invoked. That can result in runtime bugs and require additional time for debugging. Let's look at an example.

Listing B.5 has two functions: StockQuoteGeneratorArrow() and StockQuote-GeneratorAnonymous(). Each second, both of these functions invoke Math.random() to generate a random price for the stock symbol provided as a parameter. Internally, StockQuoteGeneratorArrow() uses the arrow-function syntax, providing the argument for setInterval(), whereas StockQuoteGeneratorAnonymous() uses the anonymous function.

Listing B.5 Using an arrow-function expression

Assigns the stock
symbol to this.symbol

```
function StockQuoteGeneratorArrow(symbol: string){

    this.symbol = symbol;

    setInterval(() => {
        console.log("StockQuoteGeneratorArrow. The price quote for " +
        this.symbol
            + " is " + Math.random());
    }, 1000);

}

var stockQuoteGeneratorArrow = new StockQuoteGeneratorArrow("IBM");

function StockQuoteGeneratorAnonymous(symbol: string){
```

Uses the arrow function
as the argument of
setInterval() to invoke
it every second (1,000
milliseconds)

**Assigns the stock symbol
to this.symbol**

```
this.symbol = symbol;                    ◄──┘

                                              Uses the anonymous function as
                                              the argument of setInterval()

    setInterval(function () {        ◄──┘
        console.log("   StockQuoteGeneratorAnonymous.The price quote for " +
        ➥ this.symbol
            + " is " + Math.random());
    }, 1000);
}
```

```
var stockQuoteGeneratorAnonymous = new StockQuoteGeneratorAnonymous("IBM");
```

In both cases, you assign the stock symbol ("IBM") to the symbol variable on the this object. But with the arrow function, the reference to the instance of the StockQuote-GeneratorArrow() constructor function is automatically saved in a separate variable; when you refer to this.symbol from the arrow function, it properly finds it and uses "IBM" in the console output.

But when the anonymous function is invoked in the browser, this points at the global Window object, which doesn't have the symbol property. Running this code in the web browser will print something like this every second:

```
StockQuoteGeneratorArrow. The price quote for IBM is 0.2998261866159737
StockQuoteGeneratorAnonymous.The price quote for undefined is
➥ 0.9333276399411261
```

As you see, when you use the arrow function, it recognizes IBM as the stock symbol, but it's undefined in the anonymous function.

> **NOTE** TypeScript replaces the this in the arrow function expression with a reference to the outer scope's this by passing in the reference. This is why the code in the arrow in StockQuoteGeneratorArrow() properly sees this.symbol from the outer scope.

Our next topic is TypeScript classes, but let's take a brief pause and summarize what we've covered so far:

- Typescript code is compiled into JavaScript using the tsc compiler.
- TypeScript allows you to declare the types of variables, function parameters, and return values.
- Functions can have parameters with default values and optional parameters.
- Arrow-function expressions offer a shorter syntax for declaring anonymous functions.
- Arrow-function expressions eliminate the uncertainty in using the this object reference.

Function overloading

JavaScript doesn't support function overloading, so having several functions with the same name but different lists of arguments isn't possible. The TypeScript creators introduced function overloading, but because the code has to be transpiled into a single JavaScript function, the syntax for overloading isn't elegant.

You can declare several signatures of a function with one and only one body, where you need to check the number and types of the arguments and execute the appropriate portion of the code:

```
function attr(name: string): string;
function attr(name: string, value: string): void;
function attr(map: any): void;
function attr(nameOrMap: any, value?: string): any {
  if (nameOrMap && typeof nameOrMap === "string") {
      // handle string case
  } else {
      // handle map case
  }

  // handle value here
}
```

B.6   *Classes*

If you have Java or C# experience, you'll be familiar with the concepts of classes and inheritance in their classical form. In those languages, the definition of a class is loaded in memory as a separate entity (like a blueprint) and is shared by all instances of this class. If a class is inherited from another one, the object is instantiated using the combined blueprint of both classes.

TypeScript is a superset of JavaScript, which only supports *prototypal inheritance*, where you can create an inheritance hierarchy by attaching one object to the *prototype* property of another. In this case, an inheritance (or rather, a linkage) of *objects* is created dynamically.

In TypeScript, the `class` keyword is syntactic sugar to simplify coding. In the end, your classes will be transpiled into JavaScript objects with prototypal inheritance. In JavaScript, you can declare a constructor function and instantiate it with the new keyword. In TypeScript, you can also declare a class and instantiate it with the new operator.

A class can include a constructor, fields (a.k.a. properties), and methods. Properties and methods declared are often referred as *class members*. We'll illustrate the syntax of TypeScript classes by showing you a series of code samples and comparing them with the equivalent ES5 syntax.

Let's create a simple `Person` class that contains four properties to store the first and last name, age, and Social Security number (a unique identifier assigned to every legal resident of the United States). At left in figure B.4 you can see the TypeScript

```
1  class Person {                              1  var Person = (function () {
2      firstName: string;                      2      function Person() {
3      lastName: string;                       3      }
4      age: number;                            4      return Person;
5      ssn: string;                            5  })();
6  }                                           6  var p = new Person();
7                                              7  p.firstName = "John";
8  var p = new Person();                       8  p.lastName = "Smith";
9                                              9  p.age = 29;
10 p.firstName = "John";                       10 p.ssn = "123-90-4567";
11 p.lastName = "Smith";                       11
12 p.age = 29;
13 p.ssn = "123-90-4567";
```

Figure B.4   Transpiling a TypeScript class into a JavaScript closure

code that declares and instantiates the Person class; on the right is a JavaScript closure
generated by the tsc compiler. By creating a closure for the Person function, the
TypeScript compiler enables the mechanism for exposing and hiding the elements of
the Person object.

TypeScript also supports class constructors that allow you to initialize object variables while instantiating the object. A class constructor is invoked only once during
object creation. The left side of figure B.5 shows the next version of the Person class,
which uses the constructor keyword that initializes the fields of the class with the values given to the constructor. The generated ES5 version is shown on the right.

Some JavaScript developers may see little value in using classes, because they can
easily program the same functionality using constructor functions and closures. But
people who are just starting with JavaScript will find the syntax of classes easier to read
and write, compared to constructor functions and closures.

```
1  class Person {                                       1  var Person = (function () {
2      firstName: string;                               2      function Person(firstName, lastName, age, ssn) {
3      lastName: string;                                3          this.firstName = firstName;
4      age: number;                                     4          this.lastName;
5      ssn: string;                                     5          this.age = age;
6                                                       6          this.ssn = ssn;
7      constructor(firstName:string, lastName: string,  7      }
8          age: number, ssn: string) {                  8      return Person;
9                                                       9  })();
10         this.firstName = firstName;                  10 var p = new Person("John", "Smith", 29, "123-90-4567");
11         this.lastName;                               11
12         this.age = age;
13         this.ssn = ssn;
14     }
15 }
16
17 var p = new Person("John", "Smith", 29, "123-90-4567");
```

Figure B.5   Transpiling a TypeScript class with `constructor`

B.6.1 Access modifiers

JavaScript doesn't have a way to declare a variable or a method as *private* (hidden from external code). To hide a property (or a method) in an object, you need to create a closure that neither attaches this property to the `this` variable nor returns it in the closure's `return` statement.

TypeScript provides `public`, `protected`, and `private` keywords to help you control access to the object's members during the development phase. By default, all class members have `public` access, and they're visible from outside the class. If a member is declared with the `protected` modifier, it's visible in the class and its subclasses. Class members declared as `private` are visible only in the class.

Let's use the `private` keyword to hide the value of the `ssn` property so it can't be directly accessed from outside of the `Person` object. We'll show you two versions of declaring a class with properties that use access modifiers. The longer version of the class looks like this.

Listing B.6 Using a private property

```
class Person {
    public firstName: string;
    public lastName: string;
    public age: number;
    private _ssn: string;

    constructor(firstName:string, lastName: string, age: number, ssn: string) {
        this.firstName = firstName;
        this.lastName = lastName;
        this.age = age;
        this._ssn = ssn;
    }
}

var p = new Person("John", "Smith", 29, "123-90-4567");
console.log("Last name: " + p.lastName + " SSN: " + p._ssn);
```

Note that the name of the private variable starts with an underscore: _ssn. This is just a naming convention for private properties.

The last line of listing B.6 attempts to access the _ssn private property from outside, so the TypeScript code analyzer will give you a compilation error: "Property 'ssn' is private and is only accessible in class 'Person'". But unless you use the `--noEmitOn-Error` compiler option, the erroneous code will still transpile into JavaScript:

```
var Person = (function () {
    function Person(firstName, lastName, age, _ssn) {
        this.firstName = firstName;
        this.lastName = lastName;
        this.age = age;
        this._ssn = _ssn;
    }
```

```
    return Person;
})();

var p = new Person("John", "Smith", 29, "123-90-4567");
console.log("Last name: " + p.lastName + " SSN: " + p._ssn);
```

The keyword `private` only makes it private in the TypeScript code. IDEs won't show private members in the context-sensitive help when you try to access properties of an object from outside, but the production JavaScript code will treat all properties and methods of the class as public anyway.

TypeScript allows you to provide access modifiers with the constructor's arguments, as shown in the following short version of the `Person` class.

Listing B.7 Using access modifiers

```
class Person {

    constructor(public firstName: string,
        public lastName: string, public age: number,  private _ssn: string) {
    }
}

var p = new Person("John", "Smith", 29, "123-90-4567");
```

When you use a constructor with access modifiers, the TypeScript compiler takes it as an instruction to create and retain the class properties matching the constructor's arguments. You don't need to explicitly declare and initialize them. Both the short and long versions of the `Person` class generate the same JavaScript.

B.6.2 Methods

When a function is declared in a class, it's called a *method*. In JavaScript, you need to declare methods on the prototype of an object; but with a class you declare a method by specifying a name followed by parentheses and curly braces, as you would in other object-oriented languages.

The next code snippet shows how you can declare and use a `MyClass` class with a `doSomething()` method that has one argument and no return value.

Listing B.8 Creating a method

```
class MyClass{

    doSomething(howManyTimes: number): void{
        // do something here
    }
}

var mc = new MyClass();
mc.doSomething(5);
```

Static and instance members

The code of listing B.8, as well as the class shown in figure B.4, creates an instance of the class first and then accesses its members using a reference variable that points at this instance:

```
mc.doSomething(5);
```

If a class property or method were declared with the keyword `static`, its values would be shared between all instances of the class, and you wouldn't need to create an instance to access static members. Instead of using a reference variable (such as `mc`), you'd use the name of the class:

```
class MyClass{

    static doSomething(howManyTimes: number): void{
        // do something here
    }
}

MyClass.doSometing(5);
```

If you instantiate a class and need to invoke a class method from within another method declared in the same class, you must use the `this` keyword (for example, `this.doSomething(5)`). In other programming languages, using `this` in the class code is optional, but the TypeScript compiler will complain that it can't find the method if `this` isn't explicitly used.

Let's add public setter and getter methods to the `Person` class to set and get the value of _ssn.

Listing B.9 Adding a setter and a getter

```
class Person {
    constructor(public firstName: string,
        public lastName: string, public age: number,  private _ssn?: string) {
    }

    get ssn(): string{                  ⟵──── Getter method
        return this._ssn;
    }

    set ssn(value: string){             ⟵──── Setter method
        this._ssn = value;
    }
}

var p = new Person("John", "Smith", 29);
p.ssn = "456-70-1234";

console.log("Last name: " + p.lastName + " SSN: " + p.ssn);
```

In this version, makes the last argument of the constructor optional (_ssn?)

Assigns the value to _ssn after creating the instance of the Person object using the ssn setter

In lisitng B.9, the getter and setter don't contain any application logic; but in real-world applications, these methods would perform validation. For example, the code in the getter and setter may check whether the caller is authorized to get or set the value of _ssn.

NOTE Getters and setters are supported in JavaScript as well, starting with the ES5 specification.

Note that in the methods, you use the `this` keyword to access the property of the object. It's mandatory in TypeScript.

B.6.3 Inheritance

JavaScript supports prototypal *object-based* inheritance, where one object can use another object as a prototype. TypeScript has the keyword `extends` for inheritance of classes, like ES6 and other object-oriented languages. But during transpiling to JavaScript, the generated code uses the syntax of the prototypal inheritance.

Figure B.6 shows how to create an `Employee` class (line 9) that extends the class `Person` (shown in a screenshot from the TypeScript playground). On the right, you can see the transpiled JavaScript version, which uses prototypal inheritance. The TypeScript version of the code is more concise and easier to read.

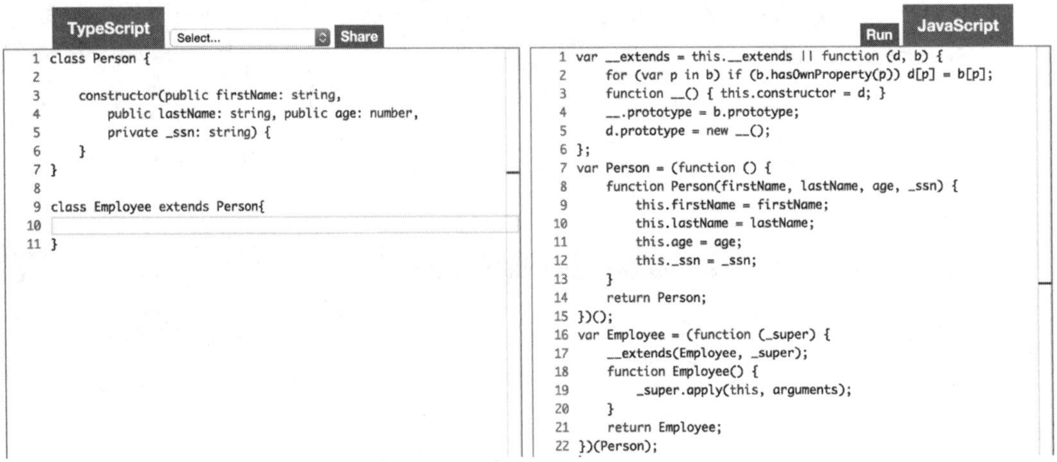

```
TypeScript      Select...      Share
1  class Person {
2
3     constructor(public firstName: string,
4        public lastName: string, public age: number,
5        private _ssn: string) {
6     }
7  }
8
9  class Employee extends Person{
10
11 }
```

```
Run      JavaScript
1  var __extends = this.__extends || function (d, b) {
2      for (var p in b) if (b.hasOwnProperty(p)) d[p] = b[p];
3      function __() { this.constructor = d; }
4      __.prototype = b.prototype;
5      d.prototype = new __();
6  };
7  var Person = (function () {
8      function Person(firstName, lastName, age, _ssn) {
9          this.firstName = firstName;
10         this.lastName = lastName;
11         this.age = age;
12         this._ssn = _ssn;
13     }
14     return Person;
15 })();
16 var Employee = (function (_super) {
17     __extends(Employee, _super);
18     function Employee() {
19         _super.apply(this, arguments);
20     }
21     return Employee;
22 })(Person);
```

Figure B.6 Class inheritance in TypeScript

Let's add a constructor and a `department` property to the `Employee` class.

Listing B.10 Using inheritance

```
class Employee extends Person{
    department: string;              ⟵——  Declares a property department
```

```
constructor(firstName: string, lastName: string,
        age: number, _ssn: string, department: string){

    super(firstName, lastName, age, _ssn);

    this.department = department;
}
```

Creates a constructor that has an additional department argument

A subclass that declares a constructor must invoke the constructor of the superclass.

If you invoke a method declared in a superclass on the object of the subclass type, you can use the name of this method as if it were declared in the subclass. But sometimes you want to specifically call the method of the superclass, and this is when you should use the super keyword.

The super keyword can be used two ways. In the constructor of a derived class, you invoke it as a method. You can also use the super keyword to specifically call a method of the superclass. It's typically used with method overriding. For example, if both a superclass and its descendant have a doSomething() method, the descendant can reuse the functionality programmed in the superclass and add other functionality as well:

```
doSomething(){
    super.doSomething();

    // Add more functionality here
}
```

You can read more about the super keyword in section A.7.4. We're halfway through this appendix, so let's take a breather and review what you've learned so far:

- Even though you can write Angular applications using JavaScript's ES5 or ES6 syntax, using TypeScript has benefits during the development stage of your project.

- TypeScript allows you to declare the types of the primitive variables as well as to develop custom types. Transpilers erase the information about types, so your applications can be deployed in any browser that supports the syntax of ECMAScript 3, 5, or 6.

- The TypeScript compiler turns .ts files into their .js counterparts. You can start the compiler in watch mode so this transformation will be initiated on any change in any .ts file.

- TypeScript classes make the code more declarative. The concept of classes and inheritance is well known to developers who use other object-oriented languages.

- Access modifiers help control access to class members during development, but they aren't as strict as they are in languages such as Java and C#.

We'll continue introducing more TypeScript syntax constructs starting in the next section; but if you're eager to see how TypeScript and Angular work together, feel free to jump to section B.9.

B.7   *Generics*

TypeScript supports parameterized types, also known as *generics*, which can be used in a variety of scenarios. For example, you can create a function that can take values of any type, but during its invocation in a particular context you can explicitly specify a concrete type.

Take another example: an array can hold objects of any type, but you can specify which particular object types (for example, instances of `Person`) are allowed in an array. If you (or someone else) were to try to add an object of a different type, the TypeScript compiler would generate an error.

The following code snippet declares a `Person` class, creates two instances of it, and stores them in the `workers` array declared with the generic type. Generic types are denoted by placing them in the angle brackets (for example, `<Person>`).

Listing B.11   Using a generic type

```
class Person {
    name: string;
}

class Employee extends Person{
    department: number;
}

class Animal {
    breed: string;
}

var workers: Array<Person> = [];

workers[0] = new Person();
workers[1] = new Employee();
workers[2] = new Animal();   // compile-time error
```

In this code snippet, you declare the `Person`, `Employee`, and `Animal` classes and a `workers` array with the generic type `<Person>`. By doing this, you announce your plans to store only instances of the class `Person` or its descendants. An attempt to store an instance of an `Animal` in the same array will result in a compile-time error.

If you work in an organization that allows animal workers (such as police dogs), you can change the declaration of `workers` as follows:

```
var workers: Array<any> = [];
```

> **NOTE** You'll see another example of using generics in section B.8. There you'll declare a `workers` array of the interface type.

Can you use generic types with any object or a function? No. The creator of the object or function has to allow this feature. If you open TypeScript's type definition file (lib.d.ts) on GitHub at http://mng.bz/I3V7 and search for "interface Array," you'll see the declaration of the Array, as shown in figure B.7. (Type definition files are explained in section B.10.)

The <T> in line 1008 means TypeScript allows you to declare a type parameter with Array and the compiler will check for the specific type provided in your program. Listing B.11 specifies this generic <T> parameter as <Person>. But because generics aren't supported in ES6, you won't see them in the code generated by the transpiler. It's just an additional safety net for developers at compile time.

You can see another T in line 1022 in figure B.7. When generic types are specified with function arguments, no angle brackets are needed. But there's no actual T type in TypeScript. The T here means the push method lets you push objects of a specific type into an array, as in the following example:

```
workers.push(new Person());
```

In this section, we've illustrated just one use case for working with generic types with an array that already supports generics. You can create your own classes or functions

```
1004   ///////////////////////////////
1005   /// ECMAScript Array API (specially handled by compiler)
1006   ///////////////////////////////
1007
1008   interface Array<T> {
1009       /**
1010         * Gets or sets the length of the array. This is a number one higher than the h
1011         */
1012       length: number;
1013       /**
1014         * Returns a string representation of an array.
1015         */
1016       toString(): string;
1017       toLocaleString(): string;
1018       /**
1019         * Appends new elements to an array, and returns the new length of the array.
1020         * @param items New elements of the Array.
1021         */
1022       push(...items: T[]): number;
1023       /**
1024         * Removes the last element from an array and returns it.
1025         */
1026       pop(): T;
1027       /**
1028         * Combines two or more arrays.
1029         * @param items Additional items to add to the end of array1.
1030         */
```

Figure B.7   The fragment of lib.d.ts describing the Array API that support generics as well. If somewhere in the code you try to invoke the function saySomething() and provide a wrong argument type, the TypeScript compiler will give you an error:

```
function saySomething<T>(data: T){

}

saySomething<string>("Hello");

saySomething<string>(123);
```

Replaces T with a string

Produces a compiler error because 123 isn't a string

The generated JavaScript won't include any generic information, and the preceding code snippet will be transpiled into the following code:

```
function saySomething(data) {
}
saySomething("Hello");
saySomething(123);
```

If you'd like to learn about generics in depth, refer to the "Generics" section in the TypeScript Handbook (http://mng.bz/447K).

B.8   Interfaces

JavaScript doesn't support the concept of interfaces, which in other object-oriented languages are used to introduce a *code contract* that an API has to abide by. An example of a contact can be class X declaring that it implements interface Y. If class X won't include an implementation of the methods declared in interface Y, it's considered a violation of the contract and won't compile.

TypeScript includes the keywords interface and implements to support interfaces, but interfaces aren't transpiled into JavaScript code. They just help you avoid using the wrong types during development.

In TypeScript, there are two patterns for using interfaces:

- Declare an interface that defines a custom type containing a number of properties. Then declare a method that has an argument of such a type. The compiler will check when this method is invoked that the object given as an argument includes all the properties declared in the interface.
- Declare an interface that includes abstract (non-implemented) methods. When a class declares that it implements this interface, the class must provide an implementation for all the abstract methods.

Let's consider these two patterns by example.

B.8.1   Declaring custom types with interfaces

When you use JavaScript frameworks, you may run into an API that requires some sort of configuration object as a function parameter. To figure out which properties must be provided in this configuration object, you need to either open the documentation for the API or read the source code of the framework. In TypeScript, you can declare an interface that includes all the properties, and their types, that must be present in a configuration object.

Let's see how this can be done in the Person class, which contains a constructor with four arguments: firstName, lastName, age, and ssn. This time, you'll declare an IPerson interface that contains the four members, and you'll modify the constructor of the Person class to use an object of this custom type as an argument.

Listing B.12   Declaring an interface

```
interface IPerson {

    firstName: string;
    lastName: string;
    age: number;
    ssn?: string;
}
```
⟵ Declares an IPerson interface with ssn as an optional member (note the question mark)

```
class Person {

    constructor(public config: IPerson) {
    }
}
```
⟵ The class Person has a constructor with one argument of type IPerson.

```
var aPerson: IPerson = {
    firstName: "John",
    lastName: "Smith",
    age: 29
}
```
⟵ Creates an aPerson object literal with members compatible with IPerson

```
var p = new Person(aPerson);
console.log("Last name: " + p.config.lastName );
```
⟵ Instantiates the Person object, providing an object of type IPerson as an argument

TypeScript has a structural type system, which means if two different types include the same members, the types are considered compatible. Having the same members means the members have the same names and types. In listing B.12, even if you didn't specify the type of the aPerson variable, it still would be considered compatible with IPerson and could be used as a constructor argument while instantiating the Person object.

If you change the name or type of one of the members of IPerson, the TypeScript compiler will report an error. On the other hand, if you try to instantiate a Person that contains an object with all the required members of IPerson and some other members, it won't raise a red flag. You could use the following object as a constructor argument for a Person:

```
var anEmployee: IPerson = {
    firstName: "John",
    lastName: "Smith",
```

```
    age: 29,
    department: "HR"
}
```

The `department` member wasn't defined in the `IPerson` interface, but as long as the object has all other members listed in the interface, the contract terms are fulfilled.

The `IPerson` interface didn't define any methods, but TypeScript interfaces can include method signatures without implementations.

B.8.2   *Using the implements keyword*

The `implements` keyword can be used with a class declaration to announce that the class will implement a particular interface. Say you have an `IPayable` interface that's declared as follows:

```
interface IPayable{
    increase_cap:number;

    increasePay(percent: number): boolean
}
```

Now the `Employee` class can declare that it implements `IPayable`:

```
class Employee implements IPayable{

    // The implementation goes here
}
```

Before going into implementation details, let's answer this question: "Why not just write all required code in the class rather than separating a portion of the code into an interface?" Let's say you need to write an application that lets you increase salaries for the employees of your organization. You can create an `Employee` class (that extends `Person`) and include the `increaseSalary()` method there. Then the business analysts may ask you to add the ability to increase pay to contractors who work for your firm. But contractors are represented by their company names and IDs; they have no notion of salary and are paid on an hourly basis.

You can create another class, `Contractor` (not inherited from `Person`), that includes some properties and an `increaseHourlyRate()` method. Now you have two different APIs: one for increasing the salary of employees, and another for increasing the pay for contractors. A better solution is to create a common `IPayable` interface and have `Employee` and `Contractor` classes provide *different implementations* of `IPayable` for these classes, as illustrated next.

Listing B.13   Using multiple interface implementations

```
interface IPayable{

    increasePay(percent: number): boolean
}
```
> The IPayable interface includes the signature of the increasePay() method that will be implemented by the Employee and Contractor classes.

```
class Person {                                          ◄──┐  The Person class serves as a
    // properties are omitted for brevity                  │  base class for Employee.

    constructor() {              The Employee class inherits from Person
    }                            and implements the IPayable interface. A
}                                class can implement multiple interfaces.

class Employee extends Person implements IPayable{  ◄──    The Employee class
                                                           implements the
    increasePay(percent: number): boolean{  ◄──            increasePay() method. The
                                                           salary of an employee can
        console.log("Increasing salary by " + percent)     be increased by any
        return true;                                       amount, so the method just
    }                                                      prints the message on the
                                                           console and returns true
}                                                          (allowing the increase).

class Contractor implements IPayable{
    increaseCap:number = 20;

    increasePay(percent: number): boolean{      ◄──────────┐
        if (percent < this.increaseCap) {
            console.log("Increasing hourly rate by " + percent)
            return true;
        } else {
            console.log("Sorry, the increase cap for contractors is",
             ➦ this.increaseCap);
            return false;               The implementation of increasePay() in the
        }                               Contractor class is different. Invoking
    }                                   increasePay() with an argument that's
}                                       more than 20 results in the "Sorry"
                                        message and a return value of false.

var workers: Array<IPayable> = [];
workers[0] = new Employee();
workers[1] = new Contractor();

workers.forEach(worker => worker.increasePay(30));  ◄──
```

The Contractor class includes a property that places a cap of 20% on pay increases.

Declaring the array with the <IPayable> generic lets you place any objects of the IPayable type there (but see the following annotation).

Now you can invoke the increasePay() method on any object in the workers array. Note that you don't use parentheses with the arrow-function expression that has a single worker argument.

Running listing B.13 produces the following output on the browser's console:

```
Increasing salary by 30
Sorry, the increase cap for contractors is 20
```

Why declare classes with the implements keyword?

Listing B.13 illustrates the structural subtyping of TypeScript. If you remove `implements Payable` from the declaration of either `Employee` or `Contractor`, the code will still work, and the compiler won't complain about lines that add these objects to the `workers` array. The compiler is smart enough to see that even if the class doesn't explicitly declare `implements IPayable`, it implements `increasePay()` properly.

> **(continued)**
> But if you remove `implements IPayable` and try to change the signature of the in-crease`Pay()` method from any of the classes, you won't be able to place such an object into the `workers` array, because that object would no longer be of the `IPayable` type. Also, without the `implements` keyword, IDE support (such as for refactoring) will be broken.

B.8.3   Using callable interfaces

TypeScript has an interesting feature known as a *callable interface* that contains a *bare* function signature (a signature without a function name). The following example shows a bare function signature that takes one parameter of type `number` and returns a `boolean`:

```
(percent: number): boolean;
```

The bare function signature indicates that the instance of the interface is callable. In listing B.14, we'll show you a different version of declaring `IPayable`, which contains a bare function signature. For brevity, we've removed the inheritance in this example. You'll declare separate functions that implement rules for pay increase for employees and contractors. These functions will be passed as arguments and invoked by the constructor of the `Person` class.

Listing B.14   Callable interface with a bare function

```
interface IPayable {                                ◁─┐ Callable interface that includes
    (percent: number): boolean;                        │ a bare function signature
}

class Person {                                         ┌─ The constructor of the Person class
    constructor(private validator: IPayable) {  ◁─┤ takes an implementation of the callable
    }                                                  └─ interface IPayable as an argument.

    increasePay(percent: number): boolean {     ◁─┐ The increasePay() method invokes the
        return this.validator(percent);            │ bare function on the passed
    }                                              │ implementation of IPayable, supplying
}                                                  └─ the pay increase value for validation.

var forEmployees: IPayable = (percent) => {           ┌─ The rules for salary
    console.log("Increasing salary by ", percent);  ◁─┤ increases for employees are
    return true;                                      │ implemented using the
};                                                    └─ arrow-function expression.

var forContractors: IPayable = (percent) => {   ◁─┐ The rules for pay increases for
    var increaseCap: number = 20;                  │ contractors are implemented using
                                                   └─ the arrow-function expression.
    if (percent < increaseCap) {
        console.log("Increasing hourly rate by", percent);
        return true;
```

```
        } else {
            console.log("Sorry, the increase cap for contractors is ",
            ➥ increaseCap);
            return false;
        }
}

var workers: Array<Person> = [];

workers[0] = new Person(forEmployees);
workers[1] = new Person(forContractors);

workers.forEach(worker => worker.increasePay(30));
```

Instantiates two Person objects, passing different rules for pay increases

Invokes increasePay() on each instance, validating the 30% pay increase

Running listing B.14 will generate the following output on the browser's console:

```
Increasing salary by 30
Sorry, the increase cap for contractors is 20
```

Interfaces support inheritance with the `extends` keyword. If a class implements interface A that's extended from interface B, the class must implement all members from A and B.

Treating classes as interfaces

In TypeScript, you can think of any class as an interface. If you declare `class A {}` and `class B {}`, it's perfectly legal to write `class A implements B {}`. You can see an example of this syntax in section 4.4.

TypeScript interfaces don't generate any output when transpiled to JavaScript, and if you place just an interface declaration into a separate file (such as ipayable.ts) and compile it with tsc, it will generate an empty ipayable.js file. If you load the code that imports the interface from a file (such as from ipayable.js) using System-JS, you'll get an error because you can't import an empty file. You need to let SystemJS know that it has to treat `IPayable` as a module and register it in the global System registry. This can be done while configuring SystemJS by using the `meta` annotation, as shown here:

```
System.config({
  transpiler: 'typescript',
  typescriptOptions: {emitDecoratorMetadata: true},
  packages: {app: {defaultExtension: 'ts'}},
  meta: {
    'app/ipayable.ts': {
      format: 'es6'
    }
  }
}
```

In addition to providing a way to create custom types and minimize the number of type-related errors, the mechanism of interfaces greatly simplifies the implementation of the Dependency Injection design pattern explained in chapter 4.

This concludes our brief introduction to interfaces. You can find more details in the "Interfaces" section of the TypeScript Handbook (http://mng.bz/spm7).

> **NOTE** The TypeDoc utility is a convenient tool for generating program documentation based on the comments in your TypeScript code. You can get it at www.npmjs.com/package/typedoc.

We're almost done with this TypeScript syntax overview. It's time to bring TypeScript and Angular together.

B.9   Adding class metadata with annotations

There are different definitions of the term *metadata*. The popular definition is that metadata is data about data. We think of metadata as data that describes code. TypeScript decorators provide a way to add metadata to your code. In particular, to turn a TypeScript class into an Angular component, you can *annotate* it with metadata. Annotations start with an @ sign.

To turn a TypeScript class into an Angular UI component, you need to decorate it with the @Component annotation. Angular will internally parse your annotations and generate code that adds the requested behavior to the TypeScript class:

```
@Component({
  // Include here the selector (the name) to identify
  // the component in the HTML document.

  // Provide the template property with the
  // HTML fragment to render the component.
  // Component styling also goes here.
})
class HelloWorldComponent {
  // The code implementing the component's
  // application logic goes here.
}
```

When you use annotations, there should be an annotation processor that can parse the annotation content and turn it into code that the runtime (the browser's JavaScript engine) understands. In the context of this book, Angular's compiler ngc performs the duties of the annotation processor.

To use the annotations supported by Angular, you need to import their implementation in your application code. For example, you need to import the @Component annotation from the Angular module:

```
import { Component } from 'angular2/core';
```

Although the implementation of these annotations is done in Angular, you may want a standardized mechanism for creating your own annotations. This is what TypeScript *decorators* are for. Think of it this way: Angular offers you its annotations that let you decorate your code, but TypeScript allows you to create your own annotations with the support of decorators.

B.10 Type-definition files

For several years, a large repository of TypeScript definition files called *Definitely Typed* was the only source of TypeScript type definitions for the new ECMAScript API and for hundreds of popular frameworks and libraries written in JavaScript. The purpose of these files is to let the TypeScript compiler know the types expected by the APIs of these libraries. Although the http://definitelytyped.org repository still exists, npmjs.org became a new repository for type-definition files, and we use it in all the code samples in this book.

The suffix of any definition filename is *d.ts*, and you can find the definition files in Angular modules in the subfolders of the node_modules/@angular folder after running npm install as explained in chapter 2. All required *.d.ts files are bundled with Angular npm packages, and there's no need to install them separately. The presence of the definition files in your project will allow the TypeScript compiler to ensure that your code uses the correct types while invoking the Angular API.

For example, Angular applications are launched by invoking the bootstrapModule() method, giving it the root module for your application as an argument. The application_ref.d.ts file includes the following definition for this function:

```
bootstrapModule<M>(moduleType: ConcreteType<M>,
compilerOptions?: CompilerOptions | CompilerOptions[]):
Promise<NgModuleRef<M>>;
```

By reading this definition, you (and the tsc compiler) know that this function can be invoked with one mandatory parameter of type ConcreteType and an optional array of compiler options. If the application_ref.d.ts file wasn't a part of your project, TypeScript's compiler would let you invoke the bootstrapModule function with a wrong parameter type, or without any parameters at all, which would result in a runtime error. But application_ref.d.ts is present, so TypeScript would generate a compile-time error reading "Supplied parameters do not match any signature of call target." Type-definition files also allow IDEs to show context-sensitive help when you're writing code that invokes Angular functions or assigns values to objects' properties.

B.10.1 Installing type-definition files

To install TypeScript type-definition files for a library or framework written in JavaScript, developers have used type-definition managers: tsd and Typings. The former was deprecated because it only let us get *.d.ts files from definitelytyped.org. Prior to the release of TypeScript 2.0, we used Typings (https://github.com/typings/typings), which allowed us to bring in type definitions from an arbitrary repository.

With the release of TypeScript 2.0, there's no need to use type-definition managers for npm-based projects. Now the npmjs.org npm repository includes a @types organization that stores type definitions for the popular JavaScript libraries. All libraries from definitelytyped.org are published there.

Let's say you need to install a type-definitios file for jQuery. Running the following command will install the type definitions in the node_modules/@types directory and save this dependency in the package.json file of your project:

```
npm install @types/jquery --save-dev
```

In this book, you'll install type definitions using similar commands in many sample projects. For example, ES6 has introduced the `find()` method for arrays, but if your TypeScript project is configured to use ES5 as a target for compilation, your IDE will highlight the `find()` method in red because ES5 doesn't support it. Installing the type-definition file for es6-shim will get rid of the redness in your IDE:

```
npm i @types/es6-shim --save-dev
```

What if tsc can't find the type-definition file?

At the time of writing (TypeScript 2.0), there's a chance tsc won't find type-definition files located in the node_modules/@types directory. If you run into this issue, add the required files to the `types` section of tsconfig.json. Here's an example:

```
"compilerOptions": {
  ...
  "types":["es6-shim", "jasmine"],
}
```

Module resolution and the reference tag

Unless you use CommonJS modules, you'll need to explicitly add a reference to your TypeScript code, pointing at the required type definitions, like this:

```
/// <reference types="typings/jquery.d.ts" />
```

You use CommonJS modules as a tsc option, and each project includes the following option in the tsconfig.json file:

```
"module": "commonjs"
```

When tsc sees an `import` statement referring to a module, it automatically tries to find the <module-name>d.ts file in the node_modules directory. If that's not found, it goes up one level and repeats the process. You can read more about this in the "Typings for npm Modules" section in the TypeScript Handbook (http://mng.bz/ih4z). In upcoming releases of tsc, the same strategy will be implemented for AMD module resolution.

Angular includes all required definition files, and you don't need to use a type-definition manager unless your application uses other third-party JavaScript libraries. In this case, you need to install their definition files manually to get context-sensitive help in your IDE.

Angular uses the ES6 syntax in its d.ts files, and for most modules you can use the following import syntax: `import {Component} from 'angular2/core';`. The definition of the `Component` class will be found. You'll be importing all other Angular modules and components.

CONTROLLING CODE STYLE WITH TSLINT

TSLint is a tool you can use to ensure that your programs are written according to specified rules and coding styles. You can configure TSLint to check that the TypeScript code in your project is properly aligned and indented, that the names of all interfaces start with a capital *I*, that class names use CamelCase notation, and so on.

You can install TSLint globally using the following command:

```
npm install tslint -g
```

To install the TSLint node module in your project directory, run the following command:

```
npm install tslint
```

The rules you want to apply to your code are specified in a tslint.json configuration file. A sample rules file comes with TSLint. The file's name is sample.tslint.json, and it's located in the docs directory. You can turn specific rules on or off as needed.

For details on using TSLint, visit www.npmjs.com/package/tslint. Your IDE may support linting with TSLint out of the box.

> **IDEs**
>
> We want to make the content of this book IDE-agnostic, and we don't include instructions specific to any IDE. But several IDEs support TypeScript. The most popular are WebStorm, Visual Studio Code, Sublime Text, and Atom. All of these IDEs and editors work under Windows, Mac OS, and Linux. If you develop your TypeScript/Angular applications on a Windows computer, you can use Visual Studio 2015.

B.11 An overview of the TypeScript/Angular development process

The process of developing and deploying TypeScript/Angular applications consists of multiple steps, which should be automated as much as possible. There are multiple ways to do that. The following is a sample list of steps that could be performed to create an Angular application:

1. Create a directory for your project.
2. Create a package.json file that lists all of your application dependencies, such as Angular packages, Jasmine testing frameworks, and so on.

3 Install all the packages and libraries listed in package.json using the command npm install.

4 Write the application code.

5 Load your application into the browser with the help of the SystemJS loader, which not only loads, but also transpiles TypeScript into JavaScript in the browser.

6 Minimize and bundle your code and resources with the help of Webpack and its plugins.

7 Copy all the files into the distribution directory using the npm scripts.

Chapter 2 explains how to start a new Angular project and work with the npm package manager and the SystemJS module loader.

> **NOTE** Angular-CLI is a command-line utility that can scaffold your project, generate components and services, and prepare builds. We introduce Angular CLI in chapter 10.

> **NOTE** We haven't mentioned the subject of error handling in this appendix, but because TypeScript is a superset of JavaScript, error handling is done the same way as in JavaScript. You can read about different types of errors in the JavaScript Reference article on the Error constructor, on the Mozilla Developer Network (http://mng.bz/FwfO).

index

MORE TITLES FROM MANNING

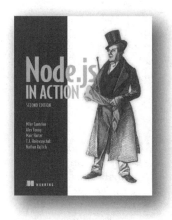

Node.js in Action, Second Edition
by Mike Cantelon, Alex Young, Marc Harter,
  T.J. Holowaychuk, and Nathan Rajlich

ISBN: 9781617292576
450 pages
$49.99
February 2017

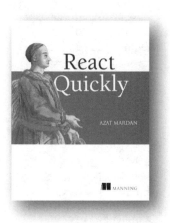

React Quickly
by Azat Mardan

ISBN: 9781617293344
400 pages
$44.99
March 2017

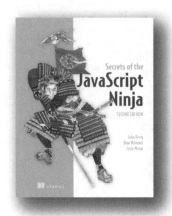

*Secrets of the JavaScript Ninja,
Second Edition*
by John Resig, Bear Bibeault, and Josip Maras

ISBN: 9781617292859
464 pages
$44.99
August 2016

For ordering information go to www.manning.com